To Carol
From
Mom + Dad

With all our love and
God's Blessings

Happy Mothers Day
May 8, 1988

COMPLETE GUIDE TO
HARDY PERENNIALS

COMPLETE GUIDE TO
HARDY PERENNIALS

By

FRANCES PERRY

187 PLANTS ILLUSTRATED IN COLOUR
72 IN BLACK AND WHITE

CHARLES T. BRANFORD COMPANY
BOSTON 59, MASSACHUSETTS
1958

CONTENTS

PLATES IN COLOUR

Plates 1–32 are from paintings: 1, 2, 5, 6, 8, 10–13, 16–18, 20, 23–28 *and* 30–32 *by Pamela Freeman;* 4, 7, 9, 14, 21 *and* 22 *by Dorothy Fitchew;* 3, 15, 19 *and* 29 *by Paul Jones*

Plates 33–40 are from colour photographs by John Hinde, reproduced from ' *The Border in Colour* ' *by T. C. Mansfield (Collins, 1944)*

The drawings on pages 54 and 61 are by Pamela Freeman

PLATES IN BLACK AND WHITE

The Black and White Plates are from paintings by Dorothy Fitchew

8

PREFACE

ALTHOUGH entirely artificial in its concept, a good herbaceous border is frequently the best loved and most beautiful of all garden features—and this, in spite of the fact that it represents an instance in which Man presumes to improve on Nature.

Bringing plants of similar growth habits together serves to show the wide range of material to be found in one group of plants. It also extends the flowering season in the border, shows a rich diversity of shapes and shades, and provides a pattern of colour for many months in the year. Routine labour tasks are also reduced—for how much easier it is to carry out the seasonal tasks of mulching, spraying and staking with a group of plants than on individual specimens scattered around the garden.

In preparing this book, it has been a constant source of grief to realise how many fine border plants have become scarce or almost non-existent. New varieties of delphiniums, iris, lupins and the like are constantly coming along, but where are the old garden favourites our parents knew and grew? Probably only in old gardens or tucked away in Botanic Institutions. I am accordingly well aware that some of the plants mentioned in the following pages will not easily be come by. But in order to make the book comprehensive they should not be omitted, and one can only hope that public demand may stimulate growers to find again and propagate some of these treasures of the past. They were too good to lose.

The system of nomenclature provoked some thought. We hope the work will appeal to both amateur and professional growers; but, after talking to people, I found that whilst many gardeners like "ordinary names," the pet names of their childhood, others accepted only the scientific terms and required these too to be up to date.

Wherever possible, therefore, I have tried to give both, and for many of the common names I am indebted to the American Joint Committee on Horticultural and Nomenclature's *Standardized Plant Names*. The R.H.S. Dictionary of Gardening has been the guide for the rest.

Invariably in a book of this description the author is indebted to others. The illustrations, which add so much to the work, have been executed by Mrs. Pamela Freeman, Miss Dorothy Fitchew and the Australian artist, Paul Jones. I am grateful to all three. Mr. R. Trevelyan and Miss L. Lonsdale-Cooper of the firm of Wm. Collins have advised on presentation problems; my husband prepared the border plans; I would thank also my colleague, Lewis Ibbotson, for the notes on electrical heating and soil warming.

I have loved hardy perennials all my life and feel they are among the most satisfactory plants to grow. I hope that some of the pleasure I have felt in preparing these pages may find an echo in the hearts of others, and that these too will derive interest and happiness in the years to come in the cultivation of their herbaceous borders.

FRANCES PERRY

Enfield, 1957

CHAPTER I

INTRODUCTION:
THE HISTORY OF HERBACEOUS BORDERS

A LOVE of plants and gardens seems to be inherent in most people. In the rush and bustle of modern life, their ever changing pattern spells peace and sanity, whatever the conditions of life and the world around.

Because of the ease with which they may be raised and managed, herbaceous plants have long been popular in the gardens of the world. Requiring less room than trees and with no annually recurring sowing problems, they give a rich and rapid return for labour and outlay. And this in effect is what we are looking for to-day. There are those who sigh for the old days when frames and greenhouses bulged with bedding plants, ready for planting out when the spring frosts were done. But present-day economic circumstances limit the amount of labour that can be hired, and the cost of purchasing plants upon any but a modest scale is quite prohibitive. The average gardener now has to undertake most of the work himself and must plan accordingly.

DEFINITION

A perennial is a plant which lasts for an indefinite number of years, but certainly more than two. Sometimes its term of life is short, particularly if climatic conditions do not suit—as in the colder parts of Britain and America, and then it must be renewed fairly frequently. On the other hand there are plants such as Peonies and Burning Bush (Dictamnus) which can remain undisturbed in the same spot for half a century, and still flower freely year after year. From this it follows that trees and shrubs too are perennials, but their difference lies in the fact that they are not herbaceous.

Herbaceous perennials die to the ground every year, which means in effect that they have annual stems and perennial rootstocks. This characteristic naturally distinguishes them from shrubs, but it so happens that there are a few border-line cases which retain their foliage during the winter but are not woody like shrubs. The garden Pink is a well-known example. It keeps its foliage during the winter, and on account of a semi-woody nature is termed suffruticose. Red Hot Pokers (Kniphofia) and *Iris barbata* also retain some leaves, these being soft and pliable to the touch. As new foliage grows in spring the old leaves gradually wither away.

Bulbous plants have herbaceous top growth, but the rootstocks are peculiar in that they are made up of leaf modifications, which are swollen and distended in order to store food. Corms on the other hand are stems —solid, and bulging with food into bulb-like structures. Because of a peculiar state of dormancy which they assume, bulbous plants can be transported great distances without harm, a characteristic which has given them a place apart in the garden. Both bulbs and corms, however, are commonly used for extending the range of flowering material in the herbaceous border.

ADVANTAGE OF GROUPING

It is obviously sound gardening policy to group plants needing similar care and treatment. To replant, stake and put down for winter a collection of plants is certainly quicker and easier than dealing with a dozen individuals in a dozen different places. In its purest sense the herbaceous border is made up on these lines. It is strictly confined to hardy herbaceous perennials and bars shrubs, annuals and tender bedding subjects entirely.

There are times, however, when this method is not always successful. Thus disappointments may follow if sufficient attention has not been paid to siting, or in adequately preparing the ground, or even when the wrong plants have been grown for a particular soil. A common example is the mixed border on the fringe of a shrubbery. The variety of pockets and spaces afforded before its sheltering belt is inviting. The site seems warm and protected and we tend to overlook the competition for food and even light, in which the taller shrubs will have immeasurable advantage.

At its best the herbaceous border is a remarkably beautiful feature, but it relies for its success on skilled planning and maintenance. Nowhere in the garden will the perennials show to better advantage than grouped in bold masses amongst others of their kind. Although somewhat artificial —for Nature does not keep herbaceous perennials in a group apart, and the subjects themselves hail from all parts of the world—a successful border never fails to evoke admiration. It speaks highly for the cultural skill and artistic tastes of the gardener, for one must realise at the outset that a good border *does not happen*. It is planned and reflects the personal taste of the designer as surely as a painting or an arrangement of flowers.

HERBACEOUS PLANTS IN THE GARDEN

Nevertheless there are other places besides the border for herbaceous perennials, for there is a very rich supply of hardy plants. Their number and variety is almost without limit and many show a tenacity of life which has ensured survival under the most trying conditions.

A simple border has been the expression of flower gardening during all time, and so it is hardly surprising to find that there are perennials for almost all positions and soils. Whether we garden on chalk or gravel, in clay or loam, in sun or shade, in arid ground or bog, there are plants to suit our peculiar conditions.

FLOWER BORDERS IN GRASS

Grass is the perfect foil for the colour and brightness of flowers, and small beds set in turf can be very pleasing. In Britain, however, and to a lesser degree in America, we are apt to fill such plots with bedding material—a task which involves the propagation of plants under glass, planting out at the busiest time of the year, and later, either winter storage away from frosts, or death and destruction to the whole of the crop.

In Sweden things are managed differently. During a visit paid just after the war I was struck by the ingenious manner in which certain perennials were grown and presented. They were in small beds—some only about two feet across—set in apparent informality about the lawns. Frequently one species of plant only was growing in the bed, but sometimes there were groups of varying shades and heights. Usually fairly permanent plants, such as Red Hot Pokers, Peonies, Lilies and Plantain Lilies were selected for such treatment. While many might not care for individual plots made up in this manner, it does seem that the sacrifice of so many borders to plants which perish every year robs our gardens of finer and more worthwhile subjects.

One great advantage of a border in grass is that it can be seen from all sides. Various aspects of the plants are presented and more latitude in grouping and heights is allowed.

The only place where failure might be expected is in the vicinity of trees—particularly evergreens. These are often so thickly planted that their hungry roots leach the soil of food and moisture, whilst the heavy curtain of leaves keeps the ground beneath heavy, dank and lifeless. When the trees are hard cut back, however, and the ground enriched with leaf or similar organic material, what delightful places are made for the woodland perennials! Here Hellebores, Solomon's Seal, white-flowered Trilliums, Hostas and Asters—to mention but a few—will find a situation to their liking.

FLOWER BORDERS NEAR THE HOUSE

In many situations near the house, opportunities will occur for the planting of hardy perennials. Here the very opposite conditions from those of the shrubbery will prevail. The walls will not feed from the borders and they afford protection from the winds of spring and storms of winter. Here our choicest and most colourful plants may find a home.

Tall Delphiniums, ever-flowering Erigerons, the Chimney Bellflower (*Campanula pyramidalis*) and a host of others.

If the beds run lengthwise from the house, into a light or open background, keep the paler colours near at hand and the stronger ones away in the distance. But, if the walls of the house are light in colour and the border flanks evergreens or a dark hedge, stronger contrasts will be obtained from reversing the technique.

In any case pay particular attention to the walls. Red flowers will be lost before red brickwork, and white against a light distemper. In the latter instance try bright oranges, scarlets and the more vivid shades of blue. Grey stone blocks make the perfect background for all shades of blue and purple, and light pastel shades are a safe choice before brick.

MIXED BORDERS

While the purist will shy from all thought of mixing plants in the herbaceous border, and refuse to consider any but true herbaceous perennials, more and more people are turning to-day to mixed planting schemes. The reason is not hard to find.

The use of shrubs and bulbs extends the season of interest considerably; the former are very long lived and if carefully chosen need little attention from one year's end to another. Thoroughly prepared in the first instance, such borders remain for years without deep digging in the usual sense.

In the pockets formed between two or three background shrubs attractive flower groupings may be made, and when these become old and exhausted it is possible to lift and replant without major upheavals in the border. All of this is economical of labour—the biggest issue in gardening to-day. As the years pass I believe we shall see more and more of these mixed-type borders, and the large herbaceous border in its truest sense will only be seen in the country's show gardens and various large parks.

RESERVE BORDERS

Flowers for cutting are always wanted for the house, but nothing maddens the average gardener more than to see his precious border plants cut about for this purpose. Denuding them of even a few blooms defeats the designer's plans, and is disheartening (to say the least of it) to those who should be reaping the results of their labours.

By far the best plan—both from the house and garden point of view—is to put down a few reserve beds specially for cut-flower purposes. These need not be large, and can be tucked away in some odd corner, possibly in the vegetable plot or between fruit trees. Such beds should be well manured and prepared in the first instance and not made more than three feet in width. This allows for easy gathering of the blooms without unnecessarily disturbing the soil.

The plants selected for reserve borders should either be long-flowering, as Chrysanthemum, Aster, Alstroemeria and Iris, or else produce blooms intermittently over a long period like Gaillardia, Coreopsis, Erigeron and Scabious.

A further use for such beds would be as nursery grounds for surplus plants. From time to time losses occur in the main border and these can be made good with spares brought over from the reserve borders.

BACKGROUND OF THE HERBACEOUS BORDER

The history of the herbaceous border as a separate feature is not a long one. Old gardening books make no specific mention of it, although a general reference to borders is not uncommon.

In Ancient Persia the love of flowers must have induced these people to grow them in beds, for we read that they " bordered their walks with tufts of flowers ". But, most evidence of flower borders in the past comes from chronicles of medieval times and the physic gardens of the monasteries. A writer of these times says of a garden near Lake Constance, that " the herbaria or physic garden is smaller, with a border of plants all round the wall, and four beds on either side of the central wall." Although no reference was made to herbaceous plants as such, it seems fairly certain that this type of perennial would be employed in a garden of this nature.

Spenser in 1590 remarks, after watching the aerial activities of a bird, " He doth flie from bed to bed, from one to other border ", whilst Pepys the diarist, whom one suspects of having slight interest in gardening, asserts that " the best way is to make gardens plain, as we have in England better walks of gravel and greens . . . than anyone . . . and as for flowers, they are best seen in a small plot by themselves; besides, their borders spoil the walks of another garden."

Phillip Miller's *Dictionary of Gardening* which appeared in 1724 comments on what can only be a true herbaceous border. " Gardeners are making borders along the sidewalks for their choicest flowers ", and " where flowers are desired, there may be borders continued round the extent of the lawn, immediately before the plantation of shrubs, which if properly planted with hardy flowers to succeed each other will afford a more pleasing prospect."

In 1827 Loudon gives lists of border flowers under the titles " Perennials, bulbs, biennials and annuals—hardy and half-hardy ", and then in 1890 the phrase is coined. George Nicolson, eminent curator of the Royal Botanic Gardens, Kew, gives this advice for planting out— " the best results are obtained when the border is mainly made up of hardy herbaceous perennials."

And so we have the suggestion and the germ takes root. But Nicolson only started an idea and most credit for the rapid spread of this type of gardening should go to two great plantsmen of the 19th century, Miss Gertrude Jekyll and William Robinson. It was they, with their common-sense approach to gardening, inspired writings and love of Nature in its most unfettered sense, who really preached a love of good plants and fine gardening. " Select only good plants," says Robinson, " throw away weedy kinds, there is no scarcity of the best;" and, of borders, " there is no arrangement of flowers more graceful, varied, or capable of giving more delight, and none so easily adapted to almost every kind of garden." In *The English Flower Garden* he also remarks, " The true way to make gardens yield a return of beauty for the labour and skill given them is the permanent one . . . let the beds be planted as permanently and as well as possible, so that there will remain little to do for years."

In America at about the same time the pendulum was swinging in another direction. In the 1880's nearly every well-to-do household maintained its flower garden, and in these gardens herbaceous plants were well represented. A wide range appears to have been known and grown, and there was great interest in the exchanging and acquiring of new species. Even the smaller gardens could boast their dozen or more species, and it seems likely that this happy state of affairs would have gone on but for one fact. Tender bedding plants came into favour. Magnificent displays of these at the Philadelphia Centennial Exhibition seem to have attracted public fancy, for the cultivation of hardy plants at the turn of the century largely lapsed in favour of mass bedding schemes and ' tender ' plants for summer effect.

Since that time, however, the pendulum has swung back and Americans to-day are very ' perennial ' conscious. The work they have done for Hemerocallis and Iris particularly has had repercussions throughout the entire world—the varieties they have introduced grace gardens everywhere, and their scientific study of the plants themselves has given greater understanding of their cultural requirements and troubles. Happily most of the plants they raise seem to thrive in British gardens, and conversely those from Great Britain and Europe have ' taken ' to America. Flowers have become our best ambassadors, bearing out the truth of the old Chinese proverb—Habits and customs differ, but all peoples have the love of flowers in common.

Plate 1: 1. HIMALAYAN BLUE POPPY, *Meconopsis betonicifolia*. 2. VIRGINIAN COWSLIP, *Mertensia virginica*. 3. PASQUE FLOWER, *Pulsatilla vulgaris*. 4. COWSLIP LUNGWORT, *Pulmonaria angustifolia*. 5. SIBERIAN BUGLOSS, *Brunnera macrophylla*. 6. GENEVA BUGLE, *Ajuga genevensis*

Plate 2: 1. ARMENIAN CRANESBILL, *Geranium psilostemon.* 2. SHOOTING STAR, *Dodecatheon meadia.* 3. FRINGED BLEEDING HEART, *Dicentra eximia.* 4. PIG SQUEAK, *Bergenia cordifolia.* 5. CORAL BELLS, *Heuchera sanguinea*

CHAPTER II

PREPARING THE BORDER

THE NUMBER and variety of hardy herbaceous perennials makes it possible to select suitable plants for almost any position. Whether the soil is heavy or light, swamp-like or arid, on a high elevation or low, and irrespective of whether the situation is exposed, sheltered or shaded, there are good plants which will flourish there if only skill is exercised in selecting and planting them.

Many will thrive under diverse conditions. Hemerocallis for example is an excellent plant for a warm sunny border, but it is equally at home in a moist shady one near trees. Indeed, some of the best plants I ever saw grew perfectly happily with their feet *lapped all the time by water*. There are others with equally broad tastes, but the gardener must know them for no two plants are necessarily alike, and one cannot afford to be dogmatic over any point in Nature.

In spite of the fact that there are plants for all soils and situations, the great majority—and those which flower most freely—like plenty of sun and a rich loam soil. In order to make the border really colourful and truly representative of the many genera which include herbaceous perennials, these factors should be remembered.

Whenever possible, choose a site which is exposed to full sunlight for most of the day. It may with advantage be sheltered on the north and east by shrubs or trees, for these break the force of strong winds and in spring provide dividends with early flowers. Walls, buildings, fences or hedges serve the same purpose, providing excellent, sunny borders in front of them. Twin borders either side of a walk, or one running through a lawn on the west side of a building are other suggestions.

BACKGROUNDS

The question of backgrounds has to be considered here for if the protective windbreak runs close to the border, its effect may be either adverse or advantageous. A hedge for example feeds from the beds, leaching the soil in its neighbourhood of valuable plant food. Privet and Yew are notorious offenders in this respect. On the other hand, they furnish a living green background, which shows off the bright colours of the flowers to advantage.

Hedges bring other problems: those of maintenance. They must be clipped and trimmed periodically, occasionally fed and at times sprayed because they harbour noxious pests. And so, if Yew or similar living material is used, always leave a pathway between it and the back-row plants of the border. The farther these are away from the hedge the better they will thrive. The convenience of the path will also be worth the sacrifice of space, particularly when it becomes necessary to get to the back to stake and tend the plants, or the hedge requires cutting. The width need not be more than 2 ft., but the feature should be remembered and taken into account when planning the layout and dimensions of the border.

Walls and fences protect plants but do not rob them of food. They provide the means for supporting choice climbers and wall shrubs, and walls particularly, tone to a mellow shade which is very pleasing. But they can at times harbour pests and should be sprayed from time to time with winter wash or D.D.T. Their construction moreover is very expensive, and unless one is fortunate enough to find a wall already standing in the garden, few can go to the expense of building.

Very narrow borders under walls also at times present other problems. Sudden squalls of wind gusts may snap branches or topple the back of the border giants, particularly if these are not staked. A corner plant of vigorous habit, an evergreen shrub or even the provision of a small piece of fencing or a wattle hurdle will break the force of the wind and safeguard the border occupants.

BORDER WIDTHS

Having settled on the site for the border, be extremely generous over the width. Five to six feet must be looked upon as an absolute minimum, with a spread to twelve or even fifteen feet if conditions allow. Do not skimp at this juncture if you wish for good results. A narrow bed cannot be effectively patterned. It has no depth, and remains a narrow bed in the most constrained sense—suitable only for a twin row of spring or summer bedding plants.

To plan a border well one needs to follow through with the pattern and colours. As an analogy to this consider a stair carpet and a wide hall runner. The stair carpet only has room for an edging and very small pattern, but the width of the hall runner gives just that little extra and offers considerably more scope for design. And in the garden the same principle holds good.

EDGINGS

Towards the path side of the border the limit of area must be defined in some way. If the path is grass the straight cut turf edge is usually all that is needed. When the bed borders the lawn the same point applies. Gravel or brick paths sometimes have their edges defined with plants or soil should be worked when too moist to crumble, as its clay content will soon become hard and lumpy and completely impervious to plant roots.

The majority of gardens are usually reasonably drained, but in low-lying localities or on some clay soils there is a risk of water standing after storms or in winter. Such conditions are not good for plants. They cannot grow if waterlogged at the roots, and those that are not too well established may be lost if the condition continues. Some system of drainage, about 2½ feet down, must be arranged in this instance.

Referring to the third point in ground preparation we have to remember that the preliminary digging, before planting, is probably the only thorough one the border will get for years. Even if part of it is broken up and replanted, certain individuals will be left, so that at no time will the same opportunities occur for cleaning, manuring and cultivating. With this point in mind give plenty of organic material in the initial preparation. Put this between the first and second spit or spread it through the top twelve inches. There is no need to make the subsoil as fertile as the top, as most plants feed from surface roots, and in any case salts are constantly being washed down.

It is not wise to add artificial fertilisers at this stage. Many plants will not be helped and unlike bulky organic manures they cannot improve the physical condition of the soil. Lime, too, should be applied with caution. Some plants of the border may be calcifuges and allergic to its presence, many prefer a slightly acid soil, and lime seekers are easily accommodated by individual attention.

It is true that plants require calcium for food, but it is almost invariably present in the soil in sufficient quantities for this purpose. Its other uses are to assist in the breakdown of complex chemicals into the simple elements essential to plants; it is a soil sweetener and a valuable aid to flocculation (see page 23) when dealing with heavy clays.

In the herbaceous border the use of lime will be governed by the acidity or otherwise of the ground, and also by the types of plants to be grown. A quick estimate of the lime content may be obtained by taking some fresh soil, breaking it up finely, placing it in a jam jar and wetting the top with a few drops of dilute hydrochloric acid. Soils with less than one per cent show no bubbling after this treatment and need liming. Those with 1–4 per cent effervesce weakly and for a short time and will need lime in all areas except those devoted specifically to calcifuges or lime haters. When the effervescence is strong sufficient lime is already present and no more need be added. A B.D.H. soil tester gives more accurate results.

Hydrated lime is best for use in the herbaceous border and has the quickest action. It is perfectly safe round plants and may be applied at rates up to 1 lb. per square yard. Chalk or ground limestone are slower in action but perfectly safe even at rates up to 2 lb. per square yard.

AFTER PLANTING

Although *well-rotted* stable dung is generally considered to be the most satisfactory manure—both for feeding and physically improving the soil, the increasing cost, added to the difficulties in obtaining supplies, makes this impracticable for many gardeners. Fortunately there are a number of good substitutes, all of which fulfil the physical requirements, i.e. retain moisture in a dry soil and open up the soil particles (and so improve drainage) in clays. Although some contain more plant foods than others, all by reason of their absorbent nature are able to hold and retain mineral and organic salts from fertilisers and other sources. Well-rotted garden compost is the best of these but other good substitutes are peat, spent hops, leaf-mould, rotted grass cuttings, bark fibre and shoddy.

For the fourth point it will be found that a light open soil at the surface prevents caking after rain or watering. Maintain an open texture by cultivation, hoeing, etc., and in clay soils add gritty material such as sand or crushed brick. For the rest study the natural characteristics of your particular soil. Get to know its peculiar problems and constituents and help it to a high degree of fertility by correct cultivation and manuring. The aim of all gardeners is the textbook ' fertile loam ', a soil which is not found naturally but comes as the result of good husbandry. In practice it represents a judicious mixture of clay, sand and humus, and according to the degree of preponderance of the first or second ingredient is termed a ' clay loam ' or a ' sandy loam'. Such soils permit of all manures being fully utilised and most plants grow in them to perfection.

CLAY SOILS

If we could sift a pound of dry soil through a series of increasingly fine sieves, we should be left with a fine dusty substance, made up of the soil's smallest particles—clay. It is a highly valuable residue however, being retentive of water and plant foods and also a repository of food in its own right. Thus, potash and other substances are found in clay, although these are only slowly released as the result of cultivation. But fine particles pack down more tightly than coarse ones and from the gardener's point of view too much clay constitutes a nuisance because it results in a closeness of constitution, bad aeration, excessive retention of water and difficulty in cultivation. This in turn makes for bad drainage, waterlogging and a cold and sometimes sour soil, and plant roots do not easily develop an intensive root system.

The cold solidity of clay soil is not only brought about by the closeness of its particles, but induced by a certain peculiar property it possesses. Each minute particle is surrounded by a spongy substance known as a colloid, which like a sponge is very absorbent. Under wet conditions these colloids absorb water and swell, making a sticky jelly, but, when the weather is dry they lose moisture and shrink, forming the well-known cracks one associates with clay soil.

The stickiness of clay is accordingly linked with this property and the fineness of its particles. If we work such soils when wet the colloids swell and the particles are packed so closely together that they virtually form a solid block and water cannot get through. Much the same thing happens when a potter kneads a clay cup. Keeping his material constantly moist, he kneads and pummels the clay, fashioning the shape as he goes. Closer and closer the particles are packed, the colloids swell, and the vessel holds water. Baking retains the shape and destroys the colloids, but by then the particles are so closely kneaded that the vessel can still hold water. When we work clay in a wet state we emulate the potter and can temporarily spoil the texture of the soil.

However, clay possesses another property, that of flocculation. This means that the particles can at times clot together or coagulate. The effect of this is to create better soil groupings, so that air spaces automatically form and thus give better drainage and aeration. Various chemicals possess the power of inducing flocculation, but the most important one from the gardener's point of view is lime. When lime is applied to the soil it becomes converted into carbonate of lime, and some of this will continually be going into solution as bicarbonate of lime, a salt which possesses great flocculating powers.

Flocculation is frequently brought about in another manner. When a soil is of good texture its finest particles remain in a state of temporary coagulation or flocculation, behaving in fact as though the soil, as a whole, was built up of large fragments. By digging the ground in autumn and leaving it rough, exposing the clods to the weather so that they alternately freeze and thaw, get soaked and dry and undergo various alternations of temperature, they experience a certain amount of spontaneous flocculation, and if caught in the right degree of partial dryness, easily crumble. It is for this reason we should dig clay in the autumn, leaving it rough all winter and, choosing the first fine day in spring, when the soil does not stick to the feet, bring it down with a fork or rake to a fine tilth.

In general therefore the preparation of a heavy or clay soil should be based on autumn digging, leaving the ground alone when wet, incorporating bulky organic manures to maintain soil fertility and improve its physical condition, and, in some instances, spreading lime. Lime, however, must never be applied *at the same time* as manure as it causes the latter to rot away too quickly. Rather give manure in the autumn and apply the lime as a spring dressing.

In very wet soils the incorporation of sand, brick rubble and very old weathered ashes will also help drainage and make cultivation easier.

SANDY SOILS

Sandy soils are the antithesis of clay. The particles are large and completely indestructible. They are practically pure silica and almost devoid of plant food. When sand is present in any quantity the soil is found to be light to work, as it is easily drained and well aerated and therefore warms up well early in the year. When we have too much sand, however, it causes excessive drainage and a ' hungriness ' results. Everything is leached through the soil very rapidly and little plant food or moisture is retained. A proportion of 60 per cent in any soil makes it practically unworkable, and reclamation becomes a slow and tedious process.

Light soils are also apt to become weedy and there is a general shortage of potash, lime and soluble mineral constituents.

In preparing such ground for border planting the first aim must be directed towards increasing its water retaining capacity. The application of bulky organic manures must be generous, for such material binds the soil together, and acts like a sponge in retaining both water and soluble salts. When lime is needed, marl or chalk is better than the powdered types, as their breakdown is less rapid.

Potash is an element associated with the health and well-being of the plant and in great demand at all stages of its growth. Since the sandy soils are normally deficient in potash it must be applied extraneously either in a general manure such as animal dung, or as a mixed fertiliser like National Growmore, or alone as sulphate of potash.

CALCAREOUS SOILS

Calcareous soils are those which overlie a chalk or limestone formation, and their fertility to a great extent depends on the depth of this layer. Where this is shallow the ground will be poor and hungry and it may be difficult to cultivate good plants.

Additional complications can be caused by chlorosis, a yellowing of the leaves, due to the inability of the plants to assimilate iron (associated with nitrogen in the green colouring matter of the leaves), because of the preventive action of calcium.

Chalk soils are warm and well drained, but, due to that very fact, quickly lose their organic matter. This must be kept up by all possible means—dung, compost, green manures, leaves, etc., while in later years, an occasional spring mulch will work wonders in retaining soil fertility and moisture. Since potash is naturally lacking, this must be supplied. Kainit is the best form in this particular instance. Chalk soils are usually rich in phosphate, but if not bonemeal or superphosphate have the most lasting effect.

PEAT SOILS

Peat soils in the purest sense are not good foundations for the herbaceous border. Being compounded of excessive quantities of organic substances—mostly plant remains—and usually subject to waterlogging, in peat soils the nitrifying bacteria, which break down humus, are few or absent. The material is unable to rot naturally and becomes acid, with a notable deficiency of soluble mineral constituents, such as salts of lime and potash. Remedial measures consist of drainage, lightening the material with sand and sweetening it with lime. The aim is to get much more air into the organic material, making it warmer and providing oxygen for the bacteria. The latter are among the gardener's best friends, being mobile microscopic organisms which have the power to fix atmospheric nitrogen and also break down humus. To do this they need a satisfactory temperature, not too hot or too cold, oxygen, calcium carbonate, humus material (in this case supplied by the peat) and sufficient moisture. Lack of these essentials prevents the functioning of nitrifying bacteria, air is cut off from the soil, and vegetable material tends to accumulate, becoming peat in course of time.

Drainage and the provision of sand or similar gritty substances therefore help aeration, whilst lime serves to neutralise the prevailing acidity and encourages nitrification. This makes healthier growing conditions for plants and renders available for their use some of the vast quantities of nitrogen which have accumulated through the years.

PATH MAKING

In order to be able to enjoy herbaceous borders one must be afforded the means to get near them. For this reason paths are important, and should be studied not only from the point of view of transport, but in relationship to the flower beds and surroundings. In many cases the gardener may prefer to make them first.

When considering the medium to be used thought should be given to the degree of wear it is likely to undergo. Grass looks best from an aesthetic point of view but is definitely less durable than gravel, while, for kitchen garden beds concrete is likely to prove the most serviceable for constant wheelbarrow traffic.

Whichever material is employed, the gardener should see to it that all his paths are durable enough to keep the feet reasonably dry at any season, that they are wide enough to use in comfort, and that they fit in with and conform to the general design.

The width should never be less than necessary to accommodate a wheelbarrow comfortably. This will be somewhere in the region of 4 feet and anything between this and 6 feet is a good width for the ordinary garden. It should also be remembered that perfectly straight paths are normally made wider than curved ones, and that *too* great a width, or the choice of unsuitable material can completely spoil the balance and detract from the charm of the border.

GRASS PATHS

Grass paths are undoubtedly the most attractive ones for use in conjunction with flower borders. The soft green colour forms a perfect setting for the bright-hued blooms of the plants beyond. But grass paths take a lot of upkeep. They must be regularly mown in summer, the edges demand constant attention, whilst weeding, feeding, rolling and other cultural activities will be necessary from time to time. They are not built for barrow traffic, and in order to preserve their lush freshness the gardener will find it necessary to protect the grass with old sacks when working nearby.

When preparing grass paths first take out a spit of soil over the whole length. Now lay 4–5 in. of sifted ash or clinker above the subsoil. This will prevent water lying under the turf in winter weather, or after storms and will also discourage worms. Five to six inches of good screened loam should then be placed over the clinkers, and the whole trodden, raked and rolled. Grass seed may now be sown, using a hard-wearing mixture, or turf can be laid on top of the loam.

If heavy traffic is expected in the vicinity of the border and yet grass paths are definitely desired, stepping-stones introduced into the turf will take a lot of the wear. Irregular shaped pieces of York paving stone are excellent for the purpose although symmetrical paving stones may be used if a more formal effect is desired. In either case set the stones *just below* the level of the turf, so that the knives of the mowing machine ride clear when cutting.

GRAVEL PATHS

It would be difficult to find a path medium better than gravel for hard work and general use. The colour of walks is important, and yellow gravel is of a pleasing shade which contrasts happily with all flowers and greenery. It drains readily and packs down firmly, and is easily repaired since the material is widely stocked and distributed.

In order to facilitate drainage, gravel paths should always be made with a camber. In wet climates it may be necessary to use pipe drains as well at the sides, but where the rainfall is not excessive, all the water that sinks from the paths to the adjoining soil will be of benefit to the plants.

As in the case of the grass path, begin by laying a good foundation. At least a spit of the original soil should be removed, and the area exposed covered with 6 inches of hard core. All sorts of material may be used for this purpose, stones, flints, brickbats, clinkers, burnt clay—in short any hard substance which contains nothing pernicious to plant life. Leave this material a little higher in the centre than at the side to form a camber. Now lay 2–3 inches of finely screened gravel and sand, and roll and bind the whole together, maintaining the camber. The height of the latter should be in the region of 3 inches for a 6 feet wide path. This will allow water to run to the sides and quickly drain away.

Paths are sometimes objectionable from the surface being too loose, because the gravel does not possess good binding qualities. Or, although it binds firmly in dry weather, it becomes tacky and sticks to the feet after rain. This is usually due to the presence of a proportion of loam mixed with the gravel, and can be remedied by sifting the latter and at the same time washing away the offending material with a hose.

Gravel paths will need to be kept weed free, and usually one or two applications of sodium chlorate each year take care of this problem. Raking and loosening the top periodically and rolling in a little more gravel and sand keeps the surface clear, so that properly made and with little attention, the path stands up to hard wear for many years.

OTHER TYPES OF PATHS

Apart from grass and gravel perhaps the favourite material for path making to-day is paving stone. This is rarely put down in complete sections, but broken up into irregular pieces and then fitted together in haphazard patterning. Attractive effects are thus obtained and the resultant paths are particularly suitable for walks near buildings or where there is likely to be constant traffic. Sometimes the pieces are joined together with a thin cement mixture—a provision which effectively prevents weeds, but at other times soil only is packed between the pieces; or again, some sections may be concreted, with pockets left here and there for plants.

The chief mistake of amateurs who undertake this work comes from not paying sufficient attention to foundation, with the result that the levels become uneven and corners of stone stick up to trip the unwary.

Begin by excavating the soil in the usual way and then lay a substantial layer (4–5 in.) of hardcore. Leave this as level and firm as possible and then spread a thin layer of concrete over the top, leaving the surface rough. This makes a firm bed for the pieces of paving which can then be laid in place and held with a four-to-one sand and cement mixture. Cobbles worked between the paving pieces look most attractive or the whole can be covered with paving stone.

When plants are to be used as inserts between the pieces the concrete foundation must be omitted. In this case the soil foundation must be built up, with screened ashes placed below the stones and extra soil worked in where the plants are to be.

Brick paths mellow to a very pleasant shade and have an old world appearance, particularly charming in an old garden. Economic considerations will probably decide whether this material is to be used, but sometimes old building foundations or walls may be profitably gleaned over.

They can be laid to various patterns with the joints left open and packed with sand or else cemented together. Avoid bricks which chip too easily, also very smooth ones which turn slippery in wet weather.

It is also possible to make attractive flower garden paths using a combination of two or more materials. Grass, paving pieces, tiles, gravel, bricks and cobbles can be interspersed one with the other or used separately. The guiding principles to the employment of any material must be suitability and sound workmanship. Paths should remain for years without the need for reconstruction, they should exist for a purpose, be of a width that is practical, and conform to and fit in at all times with the house, beds and surrounding garden.

CHAPTER III

PLANNING AND PLANTING THE BORDER

WITHOUT doubt, the best period for the actual constructional work of border making is in autumn. Even the heaviest soil is comparatively manageable at this time, the ground is still warm and friable, and other garden tasks appear less urgent as the growing season wanes.

From September onwards is also a good time for cleaning a site, for burning weeds and rubbish, and for digging and manuring the soil. This can then be left rough, to weather during the winter months and so break down into a friable tilth by spring.

And if autumn is a time for doing, then winter is the period for planning, for plan one must if the border is to be worthy of the work it involves. The arrangement of flowers in a mixed border requires a knowledge not only of the plants themselves, but of their requirements as to position and space. As Gertrude Jekyll once said—" it is here that we can show the true summer flowers at their best "; but it is here, more than anywhere else, that the " art of many sacrifices " must be put into practice.

Except when plants are chosen for purely seasonal effect, the aim of most gardeners will be to make the period of flowering and colour as long as possible. The theory of the ever-blooming border is of course pure fallacy, for anyone with horticultural knowledge and experience realises that the whole idea is completely impracticable. The Delphinium, Lupin, and Michaelmas Daisy which will continue to produce blooms from early summer to late autumn have not yet been evolved, and until they are there must be periods of withering and flowerless foliage. Nevertheless if full colour cannot be obtained all the time, it is still possible to produce peak periods interspersed with more frugal ones, and by this means interest is sustained and held for months on end.

Haphazard planting therefore should never be countenanced. Every plant in the border must be considered on merit and sited, and by far the best method of doing this is to start by drawing out a plan to scale on a large sheet of paper. Now arrange various colonies of plants by means of pencil lines, drawing these out so that one dovetails into the others like the pieces of a jig-saw puzzle. Into the spaces made the groups of plants can be fitted, after due consideration has been given to their height, colour, season and various other traits. Like the jig-saw, the pieces of pattern fall into place, excepting that this can be more exciting than any puzzle for you stand or fall by the result.

It seems to me that a border made in this way cannot fail to give more pleasure than one copied slavishly from a book or catalogue, for it is the gardener's own conception of beauty and ideas that are portrayed, and his or her tastes will be manifested in a very personal and charming manner. However, for general guidance to the beginner, some specimen plans are given in Chapter VII, p. 271.

Once the scale plan of the border has been committed to paper, and rough placements made for the various plant groupings, the real work of filling in the names can go forward. This method has many advantages. It enables the designer to consider the border as a whole, giving it balance and stability, and allows him opportunity for changing his mind countless times before the actual planting begins. Quite a number of points must be considered before deciding on the identity of the units, and since all of them are important we should study them one by one.

HEIGHT

When the border presents a frontal view only (as when it lies before a wall or fence) one naturally aims at grouping the tallest subjects towards the back. In mixed borders particularly the aim is to have plenty of flowers, and by adopting some form of graduation one achieves not only an unbroken front of colour but each series of blooms helps to hide the stalks of those behind.

This is not to imply that each group of blossom should reach down uniformly in a series of steps. Such regimentation would not only look unnatural but become boring after a while. Here and there a light feathery subject such as Thalictrum, Sidalcea or Campanula can be brought slightly forward, to break the pattern and provide interest from its seeming isolation.

With two-sided borders the position is somewhat different. Here there will be views not only from the front and back, but sometimes from the sides as well. The tallest plants will be given a central position, with the lowest growing specimens right in the foreground, practically as edging subjects. A border with two faces is much harder to plan than a one-view type, and knowledge of the heights of all plants to be used is very important.

GROWTH SPAN

To a certain extent this point should be considered in conjunction with height, for so often the tall-growing perennial is also the rampageous one. It is frequently a problem for amateurs to estimate the quantity of plants needed to fill a border and members of the same family do not necessarily behave in the same way. The plants must all be given sufficient space to allow for full development, and inasmuch as herbaceous borders do not reach maturity until the second year after planting (particularly if spring set) there will be unavoidable gaps and bare patches during the first season. As a general rule, it may be reckoned that those plants with underground creeping rootstocks, e.g. Michaelmas Daisies, Heleniums, Sunflowers, Bergamot, etc., will spread most rapidly and require more room or periodic dividing than compact subjects like Catananche, Pyrethrum and Scabious.

Here, too, I would emphasise the value of generous planting. Rarely does a single plant make an effective display, and groupings of 3, 5, 7 or even 11—may be necessary for fine effects. It should always be remembered that bold splashes of colour are the aim. Go for a coup in a bold way and then have done with it. Don't spoil its effect by constant repetition down the border. If you achieve a fine clump of red Phlox and want Phlox again, try a mauve or pink variety in the next group.

Single specimens can only be tolerated in exceptional circumstances. An old established Peony may make a plant which is large enough to stand alone, or sometimes a solitary Yucca or Acanthus can be used in a key position. But, as a general rule groups of plants are to be preferred, and these groups should be made up of plants in odd numbers. This always seems to give a better effect than when even numbers are used. Since the amateur is unlikely to have any sure knowledge of the ultimate growth development of all the perennials he needs, resort must be made to nurserymen's catalogues or the experience of friends. Some idea of planting distances may serve as a guide to those undertaking the task for the first time, and so specific subjects have had this information concluded in the alphabetical lists in Chapter VI.

COLOUR

With colour we come to one of the most important features of the border, yet one which is not always fully exploited. There are people who affirm that colours in Nature never clash, and in Nature's art as opposed to Man's, such a statement is probably true. In the former instance the disposition of plants is completely natural, there is more green to serve as foil and background and one finds only natives of the same environment as plant associates. In the herbaceous border this is not generally true, and I have yet to be convinced that a scarlet Poppy looks well cheek by jowl with an orange Alstroemeria or mauve Liatris. Anyone who has visited Chelsea Flower Show on a really hot day, and looked at the Tulip displays and similar bright-hued flowers, knows the relief to the eyes of grass and trees when they step outside the tents. The truth is we can have *too* much colour, even in flowers, and the clever designer is the one who employs brilliance subtlely, mixing the pastel shades with the primary hues and exploiting the characteristic features and beauties of each. There is no reason at all why scarlet and orange flowers should not be near neighbours, provided that a paler subject or silver foliaged plant is set between. Apart from muting too strident colours this will spread the interest and create softer and much more pleasing effects.

When considering colour one should not lose sight of foliage. The many shades of green assumed by leaves are as varied as the flower colours themselves and can be strikingly beautiful as background to individual subjects.

Some gardeners like to make borders in which one colour predominates and then the various leaf shades are particularly useful. As example of this one might consider the famous herbaceous borders of the late Sir Philip Sassoon at Trent Park. Here the theme was orange and yellow and apart from the many flowers in those shades, full use was made of the gold striped *Iris pallida aurea fol. var.*, bronzy red Peony leaves, gold leaved Creeping Jenny (*Lysimachia nummularia*) and various Plantain Lilies. Shrubs are often incorporated in colour borders, and at Trent one found Brooms, *Rosa xanthina* and golden Philadelphus mixed with the true herbaceous perennials.

When soft tones are preferred a blue and grey border affords much pleasure. In such a scheme silver foliaged plants like Echinops, *Iris pallida argentea fol. var.*, Catmint, Gypsophila, *Stachys lanata* and Lavender will form strong backgrounds, whilst Delphiniums, *Salvia x superba*, Michaelmas Daisies, blue Lupins, Scabious and Flax provide colour and spread the interest throughout the season.

Colour harmony then is one of the most important principles in the flower garden, and as knowledge advances so will the desire for making interesting plant associations. Some studies are worth planting for the sheer beauty of their groupings alone, such as the caerulean blue *Linum narbonense* associated with soft yellow Lupins and ruby red Heuchera, or pale pink Hollyhocks behind a feathery cloud of double Gypsophila and flanked in turn with the rich blue stars of *Aster yunnanensis* 'Napsbury.'

Or, consider Peony 'Sarah Bernhardt', a bewitching shade of pink, before Delphinium 'Jack Tar'—the bluest of all Delphiniums—and one or two Madonna Lilies; and, at summer's end *Lobelia fulgens* near any silver foliaged plant like *Stachys lanata* or *Senecio cineraria*. Even though the latter is not always hardy it is worth stretching a point and wintering a few plants in frames, if only for the beauty of this plant association in early autumn.

It is placements like these, that give character to the border and lift it above the level of ordinariness to become something distinctive and beautiful.

SEASON

It was at one time the fashion for those with large gardens to devote certain areas to seasonal borders. In June there might be an Iris or a Peony border, one devoted to Asters in September, or perhaps an early

Plate 3: 1. Virginian Pokeweed, *Phytolacca americana* A. (*flower*); B. (*fruit*). 2. Scarlet Avens, *Geum chiloense* 'Mrs. Bradshaw'. 3. Bleeding Heart, *Dicentra spectabilis* 4. Lupin, *Lupinus*

Plate 4: 1. MERRY BELLS, *Uvularia grandiflora.* 2. LEOPARD'S BANE, *Doronicum plantagineum* 'Harpur Crewe'. 3. PHEASANT'S EYE, *Adonis amurensis.* 4. BARRENWORT, *Epimedium pinnatum.* 5. BITTER VETCH, *Orobus aurantiacus*

Plate 5: 1. Lemon Peony, *Paeonia mlokosewitschi.* 2. Leon's Peony, *Paeonia leoni.* 3. Common Red Peony, *Paeonia officinalis rubra plena.* 4. Russo's Peony, *Paeonia russi.* 5. Fringed Peony, *Paeonia tenuifolia*

Plate 6: 1. GARLAND LARKSPUR, *Delphinium belladonna.* 2. SPIDERWORT, *Tradescantia virginiana* 'Blue Stone'. 3. FLEABANE, *Erigeron hybridus* 'Merstham Glory'. 4. BOUQUET LARKSPUR, *Delphinium grandiflorum.* 5. CORSICAN BORAGE, *Borago laxiflora*

or late summer or even an autumn border given entirely to plants flowering at these times. By these means very colourful effects could be obtained.

But changing economic circumstances make this a thing of the past and to-day borders devoted solely to one genus are likely to be found only in public parks or botanic gardens. Most of us must be content with one all-purpose border, but we do seek to make this as bright as we can for as long a period as possible. Of course, if personal circumstances entail residence away from home for certain specific periods in a year, allowances should be made and the border planned accordingly.

As a general rule, however, the gardener will include in his mixed border a few very early and a few very late subjects, with the bulk of the plants arranged so that the late-flowering kinds like Asters, Rubellum Chrysanthemums and *Phlox decussata* are planted to form a foreground to earlier blooming perennials such as Lupins, Peonies, Poppies and Geums. As the blossoms of the latter fade their dingier moments are masked with the developing herbage of their later flowering neighbours.

Another means of extending seasonal effects comes from using shrubs and bulbous subjects. This practice is becoming increasingly common to-day. Winter blooming shrubs such as *Viburnum fragrans* and *Prunus subhirtella autumnalis*, or wall types like *Garrya elliptica*, *Chimonanthus fragrans* and Forsythia are employed as background subjects, giving the beauty of their flowers in spring and a rich canopy of foliage for the rest of the season. Groups of early flowering, scarlet Fosteriana Tulips or clumps of sweetly scented Narcissus extend the interest early in the year right to the front of the border, while at the other end of the season, Gladioli and Dahlias are increasingly employed. The former in particular are exceptionally useful, especially when used in association with *Iris barbata*. Iris have a short season but the foliage remains tidy and since it is of similar structure to that of Gladioli does not look out of place when the latter comes to flower.

Other devices of a similar nature will occur at times to those who study the weak spots in their herbaceous border. It is easy enough to arrange colour for short periods, but the real proof of the plantsman's skill lies in his ability to obtain the maximum displays from the minimum area.

FRAGRANCE

It sometimes seems that fragrance is the forgotten sense; we are prone to produce Roses without scent and odourless Sweet Peas, and we have been singularly successful in taking the sweet smell entirely from Cyclamen. And yet, fragrance is one of the garden's most precious attributes, lending an added charm to any plants so blessed. As Robinson said, " a man who makes a garden should have a heart for plants that have the gift of sweetness as well as beauty of form or colour". And although the number of fragrant herbaceous perennials is not extensive, yet sufficient exist to merit consideration.

INDIVIDUAL IDIOSYNCRASIES

The last point takes into account individual peculiarities as they relate to specific plants. There are, for example, perennials like *Iris barbata* and Scabious which like lime, but *I. sibirica* and Lithosperum are better without it. *Lobelia fulgens*, Monarda and Phlox resent dryness at the roots and benefit from an annual mulch and the incorporation of a little peat round the roots at planting time.

On a heavy soil Gaillardias, Catmint and Catananche are not always happy. We can help them to establishment by working several handfuls of sand round their roots.

Again, whilst some plants want full sun and do not give of their best when this is withheld, yet there are others which fare best when partially shaded.

Certain subjects ' die ' badly, that is to say the foliage collapses after flowering to an unsightly brownness. As the plants are perennial it is necessary (in order to safeguard next year's flowers), to let the process go on naturally, but one cannot deny that the interim period is ugly. Poppies, Monkshood and Anchusa are particularly prone to this dying down process, but their failing glories can be easily hidden by planting a late flowerer like Gypsophila or Chrysanthemum immediately in front of them. Never give untidy plants a front row position, but rather set them firmly midway in the border.

Other traits and peculiarities will present themselves to the gardener as time goes on—certain plants want staking, others mulching or protecting in winter. Get to know them and *note everything on your plan*. It will save untold labour later on and the record serves as a constant reminder of the plants themselves and the conditions they need.

PLANNING FOR SPECIAL EFFECTS

When planning borders for some special effect, such as fragrance, permanency, seasonal effects, colour tones, etc., first study the list of plants suitable for such positions in Chapter VII, p. 254, and then draw a scale plan of the proposed site. Calling to mind what you know of these plants and augmenting this with further information from books or catalogues, fill in the gaps in the planting scheme in the usual manner. Colour, season, growth span and height will all have to be considered together with the special feature for which the border is designed.

In this way a permanent border will be made up of plants which present practically no cultural problems for years on end. In the average border many perennials have to be lifted and divided about every third year, otherwise the flowers become sparse or poor or the plants themselves outgrow their allotted space. There are, however, a few subjects such as

Peonies and Oriental Poppies which increase slowly and do best when left alone. These form the basis of the permanent border and are a boon to the busy man.

In the town garden a special selection of plants is necessary. As a general rule those with shiny or smooth foliage do better in the polluted or smoky atmosphere of a town than woolly leaved plants. The hairs on the foliage of the latter seem to trap soot particles and build up a poisonous residue which ultimately kills the plants. Many seaside perennials, however, seem to thrive in towns, notably Pinks and Lavender (Lavendula)

PLANTING AND AFTERCARE

The planting of herbaceous perennials is best undertaken during the dormant season; preferably in early autumn (late September to mid-November) or from late February onwards in spring. In the first instance the ground is still warm from summer's sun, and the newly planted roots continue to grow and settle in before the worst of the weather arrives. In cold, wet soils it is not wise to plant any but the toughest perennials during the winter months. I have known choice Delphiniums lost simply because they had insufficient time to become established before the onset of frosts, snow and winter rains.

From experience, too, I would say that it is also courting disaster to move hairy leaved plants in late autumn. They seem more prone to attack by bacterial disease and such pests as slugs and millipedes when at a disadvantage from poor root anchorage than when firmly established later on. I have always had fewer failures after spring planting Catananches, Gaillardias and *Aster amellus* than from moving them in autumn.

At the same time it must be admitted that a plant really settled in and established in *early* autumn, has almost a season's start on spring transplanted stock. The important thing is this early establishment and the right choice of plants, for, while many perennials take happily to autumn planting, there are a number which should always be passed over until spring. At this time of year the sap is rising and the roots settle in quickly and easily without any check to growth. The point is applicable to all soils, but particularly in heavy ones. Amongst a number of perennials best transplanted in spring are Gaillardias, *Aster amellus* (but not the *novae-angliae* or *novi-belgii* types), Scabious, Catananches and Chrysanthemums, but in the alphabetical list, Chapter 6, I have included a note where this point applies.

At the same time it should be mentioned that many nurserymen to-day send out herbaceous roots ex-pots. Provided that these are received before the roots are too advanced and in such a tangled state that the ' soil-ball ' needs to be broken, such plants can be set in the ground even during the summer. They must, however, be adequately watered both during and immediately subsequent to the settling in process.

PLANTING TECHNIQUES

Before planting an entirely new border it will be necessary to visit the site and rake down the soil to a fine tilth. Plants must never be set amongst huge clods of earth, or they suffer from drought later in the season.

Faced with the whole empty expanse the border will probably seem bare and vast, and those not too good at estimating distances would be well advised to sort out the planting areas first. The best way to manage this is to take a complete set of labels for the plants, and put them as nearly as possible in the positions in the border they occupy on the plan. If you are still uncertain about the area allotted to each kind of plant, outline the groupings with sand, in the same design as the plan. With this completed you are now ready for work and know at a glance where each plant should be sited.

When it comes to planting the knowledge already obtained of the plant (particularly as it relates to individual idiosyncrasies), will prove invaluable. Each can be afforded their requisite needs—be it shade, lime, moisture at the roots or sun.

Plant firmly, but exercise discretion over individuals. If a certain perennial resents dryness don't set it on sloping ground, but arrange for the roots to be planted in plenty of moisture retentive material (like peat or leaf mould), and leave it planted in a shallow, saucer-like depression. This will ensure that rains and dews wash down to its feeding roots instead of running away into the open ground. Later, the work of the hoe and other factors will level the depression, but by then the plant should be established enough to fend for itself.

A bucket of sand or shingle is invaluable when dealing with plants needing well-drained soil, particularly on clays. Sprinkle this liberally round the roots when planting, and if necessary spread a thin mulch beneath the collar. This will prevent the lower leaves resting on wet sticky soil, a common cause of disease infection or foliage injury. Some doubtfully hardy plants may be grown on raised flower beds. These beds are made 9 in. or 1 ft. above path level and the plants are set in position with a good deal of sand round the roots. The raised ground allows moisture to drain away, thus giving the plants comparative root drainage in winter.

Quality of top growth depends to some extent on quality of root growth, so that by careful planting the latter not only become more quickly and strongly active, but a better plant results. The right way to plant perennials is to spread the roots equally about each plant, with the tips pointed downwards and then firm the soil up to and around the old planting mark.

Immediately after planting give the roots a good watering (unless the soil is in very moist condition), and the next day run the hoe over the border to remove footmarks and planting traces. Hard caked soil should never be left in the vicinity of perennials. Should the ground by any chance be particularly dry at planting time give it a good watering with a hose the *day before*. This prevents a sticky texture during the operation itself, and makes planting easier.

AFTERCARE

(*a*) *Weeding*. The first season after planting the chief task of the gardener will lie in keeping the area free from weeds. In an established border the plants should be so arranged that they present an almost solid mass of foliage. To see soil in any quantity between the plants is not only un-natural but spoils the appearance aesthetically. But in a first-year border this point is unavoidable. The plants have to be widely spaced to allow for future development, and the ground between is bound to become weedy. Keep these weeds down, by hoeing, if possible before they attain any size. Large individuals may have to be taken out by hand. It will help both the border and the weed problem the first season, if a few annuals or bedding plants are introduced amongst the perennials.

In later seasons weeds are unlikely to give much trouble after June. By then the mass of herbage will be tall and strong enough to cope with any rivalry, and only a few persistent perennials like Bellbine and Gout-weed will survive such smothering top growth.

(*b*) *Staking*. To prevent the border from becoming bedraggled through certain plants sprawling untidily after wind or rain, some form of support must be provided for the taller and weaker-stemmed occupants. It is unfortunate that such measures are necessary, but man's attainments in raising new plants—often with larger or a greater number of flowers—are frequently obtained only at a price. Rarely do the true species need staking, but so many garden varieties have achieved size and substance at the cost of stamina and must receive support.

The task is not one that can be lightly undertaken. There is no operation in the cultivation of herbaceous plants which requires greater knowledge and discretion. Nothing looks more unnatural than a bent, straggly plant tied up lumpily to a single stake, and nothing looks worse than a stray support, much larger than need be, placed where a slender one would do. See p. 61.

The general rule is never to stake unless absolutely necessary, but then support early, and so effectively that such aids are not seen when the border is at the height of its glory.

For Delphiniums, Hollyhocks, Eremuri and similar plants which carry their inflorescences on single spikes, use stout bamboo canes, painted green to render them inconspicuous. These should be placed in position when the stems are about a foot high to avoid damaging the roots, and each spike will need its own cane. Tie in the shoots regularly as they grow, using green twist or raffia. When the spikes reach their full length the canes should reach to just below the inflorescence and be completely invisible.

Apart from these very tall or top-heavy perennials few others will need individual supports. Those of a sprawling nature and bushy growth, like Coreopsis, Erigeron, Helenium and Michaelmas Daisy, can be most efficiently supported with pea-sticks. These may be of varying lengths according to the plants concerned, but with the maximum height of each *just below* the level of the flower heads.

Be sure to attend to this type of staking well before it is needed. If they are placed in position in early April the shoots will grow round and through the sticks, which form a very secure but completely invisible support. It is absolutely essential that the young shoots should be secured whilst they *are still erect*, since the partial dislocation that takes place during their falling down after a storm is almost sure to be completed during any attempt to pull them erect and tie them in afterwards.

Large meshed wire netting is sometimes used for supporting slender stemmed species like Dianthus or Phlox. This is cut approximately to the size of the clump and supported on canes 6 to 9 in. up from the ground. As the stems grow they penetrate the netting and so receive complete support. By dipping the material in green paint beforehand it becomes practically invisible.

(c) *Manuring and Mulching.* Whilst every care should be taken to ensure the enrichment of the land when preparing the border, it is obvious that any manures then applied cannot have an indefinite effect. Land poor in humus material becomes dry during the summer months and then one is faced with the problem of watering. Growing plants need a great deal of moisture, but if one waters thoughtlessly more harm is done than good. Plants under drought conditions develop high suction powers due to material changes in the cell's contents. After watering, this pulling power is reduced because the solution in these cells is weakened by dilution. If we water our plants sketchily and then leave them, we shall have weakened their resistance to drought conditions, and as this water is transpired or evaporated they will be in even worse condition than before. Hence the old saying " once you start watering you must continue " has foundation in fact.

If watering cannot be sustained it is best to mulch the ground instead. The border must first be cleared of weeds, watered thoroughly, then hoed to loosen the soil and finally mulched all over with a liberal application of well-rotted dung or compost. If the whole border cannot be mulched, single out for attention those plants which experience has shown feel drought conditions most acutely. By mulching in this manner moisture is conserved and the manure provides a stimulant for healthy root action. The one disadvantage lies in the fact that the moisture provided by the mulch encourages woodlice, millipedes and slugs, but application of bran and metaldehyde, aldrin, Paris Green or Kamforite H (the last on the soil *just before* the mulch is applied), do much to eradicate or deter these pests.

But even in mulching one must be careful. No large amount of highly fermentable or unripe manure should be used. Also too much stimulant applied late in the season induces late, soft growth, making the plants prone to disease and in the northern states of America or the north of Scotland particularly, tending to make them less hardy. Apart from periodically mulching all or parts of the border—and leaf mould, peat, spent hops or bark fibre can be used for the purpose if manure is unobtainable—an occasional dressing with coarse bonemeal will be of value to the plants. About 4 oz. to the square yard makes a liberal dressing and it can be scattered over the ground and later hoed in.

(*d*) *Seasonal care and Wintering.* Apart from such routine tasks as weeding, watering, manuring and staking the gardener will be well advised to visit the border from time to time and remove the old flower heads. As well as looking depressingly untidy, spent blooms may go on to make seeds and this can have repercussions in several ways.

The leaves are the factories of the plant. They, and they alone can make food. And so, every time a plant makes a new leaf it is like opening another branch of a bank, for more capital comes back to the parent stock. But when a flower is produced this represents an expenditure of capital. It is the advertising campaign, having strong influence on the next generation but of no direct benefit to the present. And if flowers take capital to produce, or in other words food from the plant, seeds need even more.

With many perennials the matter is of small moment. So prolific is their growth that they can well afford to produce flowers, leaves *and* fruits. But there are others less robust, and the expenditure of too much capital in seed production (with modern varieties of Lupins for example) places undue strain on the plants. Russell Lupins are not long lived in any event, and if we allow them to expend their energies in making seed, their life is likely to be of still shorter duration.

Again, unwanted seedlings can be an embarrassment in a border. The offspring of named garden varieties are unlikely to come true and will probably be inferior to the plants from which they spring. In some instances it is possible for them to flower the first season, and this results in a heterogeneous miscellany of flowers which encroach on the territory of others and completely defeat the designer's original planting plan. By removing the spent blooms one prevents such possibilities, and also, many flowers so treated produce a second crop of blossom later in the season.

With the approach of autumn the border begins to assume a dejected appearance, finally achieving the effect of a forest of brown stalks, when the first frost has passed. Everything should now be made tidy for winter.

In the north of Britain and the colder and more exposed parts of America it would be well to leave the dead stems intact on the plants. These will take the worst of the weather and serve to protect the young shoots and roots beneath.

But, in milder districts this practice is not only unnecessary but at times unhygienic. Spores of disease may be retained in the dead herbage and the hollow stems of many provide refuge for various pests. In the southern districts of England, therefore, all dead material should be removed. Cut the stems fairly close to the ground and lightly fork between the plants. A few perennials will retain their foliage during winter, Iris and Kniphofia for example, and these should be passed over at this time. Later the bed can be revisited, and those with strap-shaped leaves like Kniphofia should have these drawn up together above the crown and fastened. This protects the heart of the plant from standing moisture, a common cause of winter death. Rain or snow seeps or melts in the crown and later freezes, thus fatally damaging the tissues of the plant. As an alternative, cover the crown with an inverted shard or piece of slate and then heap the whole with leaves or straw, sand or weathered ashes during the worst of the weather.

Eremuri will need a straw or leaf protection, particularly during the first season, and in more exposed parts it would be wise to cover Agapanthus, Alstroemerias, Ostrowskias, and other doubtfully hardy plants. See Chapter VI.

Make a practice of visiting the border periodically during the winter months to ensure that all is well. Tread back firmly any newly planted perennials which have lifted after frost. This is a common cause of winter losses.

About every third year it will be necessary to overhaul all or part of the border. Some plants will have grown so vigorously as to threaten the very existence of more delicate subjects, and others will need replanting in more fertile soil. The operation can take place in spring or autumn according to opportunity, and one section of the ground should be cleared at a time, heeling the plants until wanted in a spare piece of ground. Never disturb permanent perennials in this periodic overhaul, however, for subjects like Peonies, Dictamnus, Oriental Poppies, Madonna Lilies and Eryngium are best left undisturbed for years on end. After digging over and manuring the other parts of the ground, the heeled-in perennials can be returned. Naturally they will first be trimmed over and divided.

In spring any loose straw or other debris from winter's mulches should be dug in and the border again cleaned. Spring, autumn or winter manures or fertilisers will also be applied at the appropriate time.

As soon as the first spring growths appear the gardener must again be busy. Staking, weeding, tying and setting traps for soil pests will be his immediate concern, but he should also thin the growths round certain rampant growers. Infinitely better results will be gained by reducing the number of stems of Phlox, Delphiniums and Michaelmas Daisies for example, and this is an operation which should not be postponed.

Finally, and in all seasons, keep the intrusive types of the border under control. It only takes a season or two for invasive perennials like Heleniums, Michaelmas Daisies, and Golden Rod to overrun completely their own and their neighbour's territory, thus taking over a preponderant amount of space and spoiling or smothering more choice but less vigorous subjects.

CHAPTER IV

PESTS AND DISEASES

THE number of known pests and diseases which can attack garden plants are very considerable. More research has been expended upon food crops than garden plants, but, as with vegetables so with flowers, the strong healthy plant is the resistant one and no amount of feeding or preventive measures afterwards can make a weakling into a worthwhile border occupant.

Apart from specific troubles relating to a particular family or genus, there are general disorders which can affect all plants. Some of these are caused by pests, others by disease, while a not unimportant section is concerned with environment, which means that the cultivation is at fault rather than any outside agent.

Speaking generally, the causes of plant troubles are either (a) *hereditary* which means that there is inherent weakness in the plant, which may, therefore, be regarded as having an internal source of disease; (b) *environmental*, which occurs when plants are grown under wrong conditions, as in waterlogged soils or arid areas, or when the soil nutrients are unbalanced, deficient or excessive, and (c) *living organisms* and pests which cause parasitic and contageous infection.

INHERITED TROUBLES

Many garden plants which have developed constitutional changes, have had these traits deliberately exploited as worthwhile features. The absence or reduction of chlorophyll (the green colouring matter in foliage) has provided variegated leaves; fasciated or malformed flowers have been ' accepted '; as have top heavy or greatly enlarged inflorescences. Often these characteristics are attained at the expense of vigour and the varieties tend to degenerate, become self-sterile or fade out.

The so called ' reversion ' of plants is in general due to the spread of virus diseases. When victim of this the plants degenerate into poor uninteresting specimens. Although rarely transmitted through the seed, such diseases are readily carried through the living tissue in all types of vegetative propagation. Damage to the tissue caused by a knife or biting or sucking insect may also cause the infected sap to be carried to another plant.

ENVIRONMENT

In the main the chief sources of trouble in this section are as follows:

SHORTAGE OF WATER causes bud dropping, very common in dry seasons.

EXCESS OF WATER, indicated by yellowing leaves, sour-smelling roots and ultimately, in very bad cases, by death. Grey mould often develops on the lower shoots in the early stages.

LACK OF LIGHT gives elongated growth and straggling, drawn shoots with pale leaves. Seedlings damp off under such conditions.

EXCESS LIGHT destroys chlorophyll or the green parts of the leaf which make the plant's food. Some species can stand more light than others, and damage of this kind is only likely to occur with natural shade plants in very hot summers.

SPRAYS, FUNGICIDES, ETC., if wrongly used may cause scorching to the leaves or even defoliation.

NUTRITIONAL DISORDERS. A wide range of symptoms can follow excess or deficiency of general or trace elements. In the main these characteristics generally occur on highly manured crops or when the ground is continually cultivated. For this reason fruit and vegetables are the chief victims, but occasionally garden plants show signs of deficiency of magnesium. At such times the foliage assumes a purple tinting at the leaf margins. A dressing of commercial Epsom Salts (magnesium sulphate) at the rate of 2–4 oz. per square yard round the plants soon brings back the green colouring matter. Too much lime may turn the leaves pale or chlorotic, as it prevents the plant taking in other elements such as iron. This is most marked on chalk soils and is remedied with dressings of aluminium sulphate (3–6 oz. per square yard).

LIVING ORGANISMS

CATERPILLARS AND WEEVILS. These bite leaves or plant tissue and must be destroyed with a stomach poison such as derris, arsenate of lead or hellebore.

EELWORMS. A number of herbaceous plants are attacked by the stem and bulb eelworm, *Anguillulina dipsaci*. Phlox and Chrysanthemums are particularly susceptible, but eelworms have also been known to attack

Oenotheras, Primulas, and *Campanula persicifolia*. The worms themselves are microscopic, but their presence leads to infected plants
becoming stunted or distorted. Often whole branches, or at times
only the lower leaves of a plant, suddenly wither and die. They are
usually introduced to the garden in the first place through infected
plants, but as part of their life is spent either in the soil or in dried-up
underground portions of stems or herbaceous plants, the original
attack may be spread by careless disposal of old or infected roots, by
surface drainage water or even through tools or footwear.

Sometimes when one lifts an infected plant small worms will be
seen adhering to the roots. These are often mistaken for eelworms,
but they are nematodes and quite harmless. It should be stressed that
eelworms *cannot be seen* with the naked eye. Infected plants should be
burnt. There are methods of destroying the pests, but these are
matters for the specialist and only worthwhile in very exceptional
circumstances.

FUNGUS DISEASES. This is a collective name given to living organisms
(fungi or bacteria), responsible for disease in plants. Mostly they are
parasites living on or inside the host and drawing nourishment from
its tissues. Well-known examples are mildew which causes a white
powdery outgrowth on stems, leaves or even flowers and fruits; black
spot which manifests itself in the form of round black spots on the
leaves; and rust which shows rusty outgrowths or spots, chiefly on
the foliage.

Many of these troubles yield to various fungicides, particularly
those containing sulphur or copper. Direct control by sprays or dusts,
however, often have to be repeated several times, especially if rain
washes the material away. It should be remembered, too, that a
healthy plant is far more resistant to disease than a weak one, so that
every endeavour should be made to build up the vitality of the plant
by good cultivation, e.g. garden hygiene (burning of rubbish, diseased
plants, etc.), providing adequate light and air, weed control and wise
manuring.

The chief fungicides used by the gardener are:

Lime Sulphur. Purchased as a manufactured liquid, and used according
to the manufacturer's instructions mixed with water.

Bordeaux Mixture. Serviceable against rusts, and to protect growing
plants against fungi.

Copper sulphate	..	$4\frac{1}{2}$ oz.
Quicklime	.. ..	9 oz.
Water ..	.. ..	5 gal.

Dissolve the copper sulphate in most of the water and use the
rest for slaking the quicklime. Mix and stir well. Use at once.

Store in wooden or enamelled vessels. Bordeaux powder can also be bought all ready for mixing with water.

Burgundy Mixture. This is very similar to preceding but rather more powerful. It is prepared with washing soda instead of quicklime, viz:

4 oz. copper sulphate
5 oz. washing soda
$2\frac{1}{2}$ gal. of water

There are also several proprietary copper fungicidal sprays such as Coppesan, Bouisol and Soltosan.

Sulphur. Powdered Green Sulphur or Flowers of Sulphur applied dry, either through a dredge or tied in a muslin bag and shaken over the plants, is especially effective against mildews and moulds. It is, moreover, harmless to animals.

SOIL PESTS AND BITING INSECTS. Slugs, wireworms, millipedes. Attack with soil fumigants, aldrin, naphthalene, carbon bisulphide, or poison baits, metaldehyde, Paris Green or by trapping.

Lead Arsenate Wash.* Used to cover foliage of plants attacked by caterpillars, weevils, chafers and Sawfly larvae.

Lead arsenate paste .. $\frac{1}{2}$ lb.
or Lead arsenate powder $\frac{1}{4}$ lb.
Water ..   ..   ..   10 gal.

Mix one or other with the water and stir vigorously. Keep agitated all through spraying. Avoid touching food crops and be careful of plants in bloom or bees may be affected.

Metaldehyde. Used as a poison bait for slugs and snails.

Metaldehyde (*crushed*) $\frac{1}{2}$ oz.
Bran ..   ..   .. $1\frac{1}{2}$ lb.

Mix with bran to a crumbly mash and place in small heaps under slates or tins.

Poison Baits* for caterpillars, weevils, woodlice, leatherjackets, slugs, etc.

Paris Green ..   .. $\frac{1}{4}$ lb.
Bran ..   ..   ..   7 lb.
Water ..   ..   .. $\frac{1}{2}$ gal.

Mix the Paris Green with the bran, add sufficient water to moisten the whole. Spread about near plants.

Paris Green ..   ..   2 oz.
Dried Blood ..   ..   7 lb.

Spread near plants. It should be noted, however, that Paris

---

* Whilst all insecticides and fungicides should be kept out of the way of small children, those marked with an asterisk are dangerous to all forms of animal life if taken internally.

Green is exceedingly poisonous and must not be left within reach of dogs, cats, poultry or wild birds. Under the Pharmacy Act of 1933 the purchaser must sign the Poison's Book when buying Paris Green, nicotine and lead arsenate.

SUCKING INSECTS suck the sap, causing distortion. Aphis, capsid bugs and red spider. Control with a contact poison like nicotine, pyrethrum or derris.

*Nicotine Soap Wash.** For controlling thrips, capsid bugs, aphis, leaf hoppers and leaf miners.

Nicotine (95/96%)	$\frac{1}{2}$ to 1 fl. oz.
Potash soft soap	$\frac{3}{4}$ to 1 lb.
Water	10 gal.

Boil the soap in a little water, allow to cool, add the nicotine and stir well. Add the remaining water.

VIRUS DISEASES cause strange symptoms such as stunted growth, blindness (so that the plants do not flower), spotting on the foliage (without the powdery effect of fungus or rust), streaks of different colour up the stems or leaves, or yellow patches on the leaves. Destroy plants so affected as they cannot be cured.

DISEASES AND PESTS OF HARDY BORDER PLANTS

ACONITUM (*Monkshood*)

Mildew (*Erysiphe polygoni*). Forms a white floury covering which spoils the look of the plants and checks development. Control.—Burn tops and withered leaves in autumn. Dust with flowers of sulphur.

Smut (*Urocystis anemones*) causes dark swollen spots on leaves, which expose a sooty black powder when they are open. Control.—Root out and destroy.

ALTHAEA (Hollyhock)

Rust (*Puccinia malvacearum*). Attacks undersides of leaves chiefly, but sometimes stems and leaf-stalks as well. Orange yellow, round pustules which later become greyish brown; causes leaf withering, stunting and sometimes death. Control.—Very heavily infected plants should be burnt. Save seed only from healthy plants. Cut stems to ground level in autumn and burn top growth. Remove first leaves in spring and burn (to prevent re-infection) and during season dust with a copper fungicide such as Bordeaux.

ALYSSUM

Downy Mildew (*Peronospora galligena*). White, blister-like spots on under-

sides of leaves, which may also curl or become distorted. Control.
—Cut off diseased tops and spray with Bordeaux.

ANEMONE

Smut (*Urocystis anemones*). See ACONITUM, page 46.

Black Rot (*Sclerotinia tuberosa*). Occurs chiefly on the Wood Anemone
(*A. nemorosa*) and its varieties and slowly kills them. Hard black
bodies are found in the dead rhizomes. Control.—Dig out with
surrounding soil and burn.

Anemone Rust (*Puccinia fusca*). Attacks chiefly *A. nemorosa*, causing
chocolate-brown pustules on the undersides of the leaves, especially
towards the edges. Affected plants become taller than healthy
ones, with smaller leaves. Control.—Dig out and burn.

Cluster Cup Rust (*Puccinia pruni-spinosae*). Linked in its life history with
the Plum. Produces orange cups on leaf under surfaces. Attacked
plants seldom flower. Control.—Destroy.

AQUILEGIA (Columbine)

Leaf Spots. Two kinds attack foliage. Control.—Spray or dust with
a fungicide like flowers of sulphur.

Rust (*Puccinia agrostidis*). Linked with rust on *Agrostis* grasses on which
it overwinters. Orange cluster cups on leaf reverses, which cause
twisting or distortion. Control.—Destroy.

Mildew (*Ersiphe polygoni*). See page 46.

Leaf Miner (*Phytomyza aquilegiae*). Causes serpentine markings between
the leaf tissues. Foliage withers and dies. Control.—Spray with
nicotine or B.H.C. (a synthetic insecticide with similar action to
nicotine) on undersides of leaves May and June.

ARMERIA (Thrift)

Rust (*Uromyces armeriae*). Light brown pustules on leaves and flower
stalks. Control.—Spray with Burgundy Mixture.

ASTER (Michaelmas Daisy)

Mildew (*Erysiphe cichoracearum*). White floury covering to leaves, etc.
Control.—See ACONITUM, page 46.

Verticillium Wilt (*Verticillium vilmorinii*). Foliage withers because the
mycelium blocks the water conducting vessels. Control.—Burn
diseased plants.

CAMPANULA

Leaf Spot. White or brown spots on foliage. Control.—Spraying with
a proprietary fungicide or Bordeaux.

Rust (*Coleosporium campanulae*). Linked with the cluster cup fungus of

Pines. Reddish-yellow pustules on undersides of leaves. Control.—
Destroy.

Aphis. Spray with derris or nicotine.

CHRYSANTHEMUM

Rust (Puccinia chrysanthemi). Yellowish-green spots on the undersides
of the leaves. Less prevalent near big towns. Control.—Some
varieties are resistant. Burn infected leaves and rubbish, spray
with lime sulphur several times during the season.

Leaf Miner (Agromyza rufipes). Control.—Remove infected leaves and
burn. Spray frequently with a nicotine soap wash or B.H.C. (a
synthetic insecticide) directed to the undersides of the leaves in
May and June.

Eelworm. Attacks Asters, Pyrethrums, Rudbeckias, Phlox, Dahlias
and Chrysanthemums. Starts with dark patches on the leaves,
and eventually spreads so that they wither, turn dark brown
or black and hang down the stem. Flowers become blind or
deformed. Control.—Pull up and burn, examine other genera likely
to be affected. Cuttings can be taken from diseased plants if the
stools are immersed in a warm water bath at 110° F. for 20 min.,
but the amateur is best advised to destroy his stock.

Gall Midge. More prevalent in the United States than Britain. Causes
small, cone-shaped galls both sides of the leaves, stems and buds.
Flowers go blind or become misshapen, leaves twist and the stems
become distorted. Control.—Burn stools at once. This is a
notifiable pest in Britain. Spray frequently with a nicotine soap
wash as a preventative measure.

Capsid and Aphis. Control.—Prevent with frequent nicotine soap
sprays.

Mildew (Oidium chrysanthemi). More troublesome in greenhouses.
Control.—Dust with Flowers of Sulphur.

Blotch (Septoria leucanthemi). Attacks *C. maximum* varieties, causing
brown spots with dark edges on the leaves, which go on to make
holes. Control.—Pick off infected leaves and burn. Spray with
a fungicide such as Bordeaux.

CONVALLARIA (Lily of the Valley)

Leaf Spot (Dendrophoma convallariae). Spots first red, then brown and
eventually cover most of the leaf. Control.—Spray with a copper
fungicide.

Grey Mould (Botrytis paeoniae). Brown spots on leaves and stems,
followed by grey mould. Tissue completely disintegrates leaving
only veins and skin. Can also attack Peony. Control.—Grub up
and burn.

Plate 7: 1. PENSTEMON, *Penstemon hartwegii* 'Southgate Gem'. 2. PYRETHRUM, *Chrysanthemum coccineum* 'Evenglow'. 3. ORIENTAL POPPY, *Papaver orientale* 'Marcus'. 4. *P. orientale* 'Mrs. Perry'. 5. UTAH PENSTEMON, *Penstemon utahensis*

Plate 8: 1. Dusty Meadow Rue, *Thalictrum speciosissimum (glaucum).* 2. Fernleaf Yarrow, *Achillea filipendulina.* 3. Mullein, *Verbascum thapsiforme.* 4. Double Buttercup, *Ranunculus acris flore-pleno.* 5. Himalayan Cowslip, *Primula Florindae.* 6. Globe Flower, *Trollius Ledebourii*

Plate 9: Iris—1. YUNNAN, *forrestii*. 2. THE DOUGLAS, *douglasiana*. 3. SIBERIAN, *sibirica* 'Marcus'. 4. YELLOWBAND, *ochroleuca*. 5. *chrysographes* 'Margot Holmes'. 6. *barbata* 'Louvois'. 7. *barbata* 'St. Agnes'. 8. VARIEGATED SWEET, *pallida argentea*

Plate 10: 1. COLUMBINE MEADOW RUE, *Thalictrum aquilegiifolium.* 2. CHINESE MAY APPLE, *Podophyllum versipelle.* 3. NODDING SAGE, *Salvia nutans.* 4. WILLOW AMSONIA, *Amsonia tabernaemontana*

DELPHINIUM

Mildew (*Erysiphe polygoni*). Foliage becomes white and unsightly. Not very serious, appears more in autumn. Control.—Dust with Flowers of Sulphur.

Leaf Spot or Black Blotch (*Pseudomones delphinii*). Large black spots appear on the leaves, causing distortion. Control.—Burn diseased plants. Spray soil and replacements with Bordeaux in spring.

Delphinium Moth (*Polychrisia moneta*). Greenish caterpillar in May and June. Also attacks Aconitum. Control.—Hand pick, dust with nicotine. Cut stems down in autumn to prevent overwintering.

DIANTHUS (Carnation and Pink)

Bud Rot (*Fusarium poae*). Attacks the buds which rot, shrivel or swell up or give deformed flowers. Control.—Remove and burn buds.

Ring Spot (*Didymellina dianthi*). Round spots with a reddish margin on the leaves and stems. Sometimes they wither and flowers are poor. Control.—Spray with Bordeaux.

Split Calyxes. Due to fluctuations in temperature, too much nitrogen or wet positions. A leaf miner also attacks border Carnations and should be killed by hand, or deterred with B.H.C. dust.

EPIMEDIUM (Barrenwort)

A mosaic disease sometimes attacks this plant causing leaf spotting and stunted growth. Affected plants must be destroyed.

GAILLARDIA (Blanket Flower)

May be attacked by the downy mildew (*Bremia lactucae*) which attacks Lettuce. Control.—Spray with Bordeaux.

GEUM (Avens)

Downy Mildew (*Peronospora gei*). Spray with a copper fungicide like Bordeaux.

GYPSOPHILA (Chalk Plant)

Stem Rot (*Schlerotinia serica*). Rotting of the stems and leaves at ground level. Control.—Burn infected plants. The spores live for years so disinfection of the soil may be necessary in bad cases.

Rust (*Puccinia lychnidearum*). Causes light-brown pustules on leaves. Comparatively harmless.

HELIANTHUS (Sunflower)

Grey Mould (*Botrytis cinerea*). Can cause severe damage if plants are crowded and in damp weather. Plants are attacked at base, wilt and die. Control.—Beware of excess nitrogen. Rotate plants. Remove diseased material.

Mildew, rust and downy mildew also attack Helianthus at times. See page 46.

HELLEBORUS (Christmas Rose)

Leaf Spot (Coniothyrium hellebori). Large, irregular black or brown spots on foliage and sometimes stems and flowers. Very much worse in wet weather. Control.—Remove and burn diseased material. Spray with Bordeaux at monthly intervals throughout summer and early autumn.

Downy Mildew (Peronospora pulveracea). Spray or dust with Bordeaux or Green Sulphur.

IRIS

Leaf Spot (Didymellina macrospora). Attacks all kinds of Iris, also Hemerocallis. Small yellowish-brown spots appear on leaves, with a light margin. These later turn brown with a dark edge and become dotted with fungus. Control.—Remove diseased foliage. Spray with Bordeaux (4 parts), and soft soap (4 parts) to 50 parts water, at regular intervals.

Rust (Puccinia iridis). Of minor importance, controlled by removing infected leaves.

Bacterial Rot (Bacterium carotovorum). Soft wet rot of rhizomes and lower parts of leaves. Control.—Plant rhizomes in dry situation, very shallow. Cut away infected parts dipping knife in strong Permanganate of Potash. Dip cut areas for some minutes in corrosive sublimate solution. (1 part to 1,000 parts water.)

LOBELIA (Cardinal Flower)

Leaf Blotch (Septoria lobeliae). Chiefly on *L. syphilitica*, pale spots on leaves spreading inwards, older leaves killed. Control.—Pick off and burn infected leaves.

Lobelia fulgens can be affected by the virus of Cucumber mosaic. No cure.

LUPINUS (Lupin)

Flower Dropping. White varieties particularly often drop their flowers, but the cause is unexplained at present.

Brown Spot (Ceratophorum setosum). Small dark brown spots on leaves, stems, pods and seeds. Seedlings from latter usually die. Control. —Save seed only from healthy plants. Spray with fungicide. Grey moulds and mildews also attack Lupins.

Browning (Cucumis virus). Infected plants have brown stem streaks and dead brown spots on leaves. Flower spikes thin with great spaces between blooms. Leaves distorted. Control.—Incurable, burn.

PAEONIA (Peony)

Blotch (Septoria paeoniae). Attacks leaves causing yellowish brown blotches with sunken centres and purple edges. Later the centres of these blotches drop out. Control.—Spray with Bordeaux in spring.

Wilt (Botrytis paeoniae). Commonest disease of the Peony. A grey mould which later turns soft and brown appears at the base and causes the shoots to wither. Cold wet weather encourages its spread. Sometimes buds are attacked and turn brown. Control.— As soon as the shoots begin to droop they should be cut out at ground level. Spray at fortnightly intervals with Bordeaux. Transplanting into fresh soil is also beneficial after the roots are washed clean. In acid soils add lime and avoid dressing suspected plants with dung, or coverings of leaves in winter.

Peonies may also be affected with Cucumber mosaic and Tomato spotted wilt viruses. There are no cures for these.

PHLOX

Leaf Spot (Septoria spp.). Various fungi attack Phlox leaves causing them to dry up and die prematurely. Some varieties are more resistant than others, notably Mia Ruys and Europa. Control.— Grow resistant kinds and spray with a fungicidal spray or dust.

Mildew, eelworm (see page 48) and Leafy Gall which causes short abortive growth at or below soil level, also attack Phlox. There is no cure for the last named.

CHAPTER V

PROPAGATION

PLANT propagation is indeed a science; fascinating to watch, single minded in its objective, at times perplexing but always enthralling. It is also the most important part of gardening, for without increase plants cannot become widespread or even maintained beyond a certain limit of time.

The most common and the easiest method of raising plants is by means of seed. Many farm and vegetable crops are so treated, but any plants which give viable seed from which young plants can be raised reasonably true to type, or whose exact parental form is not important, may be reproduced in this way.

In order to understand the type of herbaceous perennial which will be so propagated, it is necessary for the gardener to have some knowledge of plant anatomy and structure. The seed as a unit is a tough little body, capable of withstanding extreme degrees of dryness, cold and heat. It contains, within a fairly strong exterior, an embryo plant together with sufficient food to nurture it until it produces roots and can fend for itself. Several factors are necessary for germination—moisture, air and warmth for the actual process, followed by light and food for the roots to maintain growth. It follows that if seed is kept reasonably dry it is unable to germinate, and can then be transported over great distances and kept for months or even years in a dormant state. But it must be remembered, too, that the period of time during which a seed retains its vitality differs considerably between species.

Weed seeds have been known to lie dormant in the ground for years and still germinate when conditions have been conducive to growth. On the other hand the seeds of some plants, and particularly certain species of Primula, are extremely averse to drying and deteriorate rapidly if not sown as soon as gathered. Considerable research has been effected in estimating the longevity of flower seeds, particularly in America, and as far as herbaceous perennials are concerned the following findings may be of interest to readers.

PERIOD FOR WHICH SOME SEEDS RETAIN THEIR VITALITY:

1–2 *years*   Delphinium, Phlox, Kniphofia.

2 *years*	Aquilegia, Echinops, Eupatorium, Iris barbata, Liatris, Lythrum, Stokesia.
1–3 *years*	Aster, Macleaya.
2–3 *years*	Achillea, Armeria, Digitalis, Eryngium, Gaillardia, Heliopsis, *Lobelia cardinalis*, Platycodon, Veronica.
2–5 *years*	Centaurea, Pentstemon.
3 *years*	Anthemis, Campanula, Heuchera, Scabiosa.
3–4 *years*	Agrostemma, Baptisia, Lychnis.
3–5 *years*	Chrysanthemum, Dianthus, Helenium, Hollyhock, Papaver, Rudbeckia.
4 *years*	Aconitum, Pyrethrum.
4–5 *years*	Physalis, *Salvia farinacea*.
5 *years*	Gypsophila, *Linum perenne*, Lupinus.

If one examines any simple flower it will be seen that apart from petals and sepals, the interior of the bloom contains two other types of organs. The greater number of these are stamens, each of which possesses a slender stalk-like filament which in turn supports one or more pollen sacs or anthers. These anthers produce pollen grains, which are the male reproductive bodies.

The other organ is usually situated in the centre of the flower and is known as the pistil. Most plants possess only one, although they can have more. Irises, for instance, have three. The pistil is made up of three parts, an *ovary* or enlarged base which contains the immature seeds (ovules), a *style* or stalk, and a *stigma* or tip which is receptive to pollen.

In order that a plant shall produce seed this stigma must be pollinated, which means that pollen from its own or a similar flower must be conveyed to it. When this occurs the pollen grain grows a tube (pollen tube), which penetrates right through the style until it finally enters the ovules or undeveloped seeds in the ovary. Once this occurs, the contents of the tube are emptied into the ovules, fusion takes places and fertilization is complete. The seeds then grow in the normal way. (See diagram, page 54.)

A species is a natural form, found wild in some part of the world, the offspring of which if self-pollinated, comes up like the parent. It is the type plant and reasonably constant in reproduction.

It follows that seeds provide an excellent method of raising plant species; and amongst hardy plants quite a number of perennials come into this category. *Macleaya cordata, Anemone hupehensis* and *Acanthus spinosus* are examples of such species which come true from seed.

As a general rule flowers can only be pollinated by members of their own or closely related species. Inter-generic crosses are rare. But when two species are mated genetical complications follow. Some of the resultant offspring will be like parent A, others like B, whilst a third batch will show characteristics of both. If these again are crossed with a third

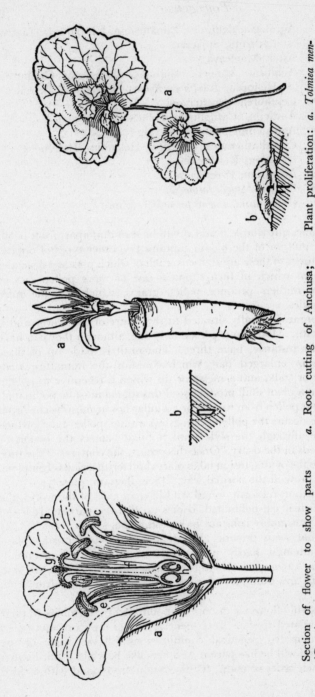

Section of flower to show parts (*Geranium pratense*): *a.* sepals; *b.* petals; *c.* anther; *d.* filament; *e.* stamens; *f.* style; *g.* stigma; *h.* ovaries.

Root cutting of Anchusa; *a.* Position of planting. *b.*

Plant proliferation: *a. Tolmiea menziesii; b.* Leaf cutting pegged into soil.

species, further complications ensue and there can be no guarantee regarding the appearance of the seedlings.

Crosses between species are known as hybrids and many of our finest garden flowers are hybrid or derived from mixed parental backgrounds. The distinguishing traits which make them outstanding—larger or freer flowers, colour breaks, doubling, improved habit, etc.—are rarely transmitted through seed, and so other means have to be sought when reproducing named varieties. Occasionally, however, through constant roguing, a trait runs reasonably true. In these cases seed sowing is practised again. As examples of this occurrence we may cite varietal forms of Brassica—Cauliflowers, Brussel Sprouts, Kale, Red Cabbage, etc., all of which are derived from a single species, but, through constant roguing, the gardener can sow seed of any of these crops with a confident expectation of a 100 per cent ' true to name ' result. Amongst hardy plants Geum ' Mrs. Bradshaw ' is constantly raised from seed, the large blooms and semi-doubling of the flowers which characterise this variety being transmitted to the seedlings.

Again, the offspring of some varieties of garden flowers are so good that, unless definite colour schemes are planned, the gardener may with confidence sow the seed. Practically all the resultant plants will be satisfactory, although colours may vary very considerably. A race of plants which gives reliable garden forms in this way is known as a strain; Russell Lupins and the Pacific Strain of Delphiniums are examples.

The other instance in which seed is used as a means of reproduction occurs when crosses have been deliberately made by the gardener. New varieties sometimes occur as sports or mutations without warning; that is, a plant or part of a plant suddenly develops characters different from the type variety or species. As example of this we may cite *Anemone* × *hybrida* var. ' Honorine Jobert.' This white-flowered variety appeared on a branch of a pink variety, probably of *A. hupehensis* in the garden of a Monsieur Jobert in Zurich about 1858. In order to perpetuate the sport it was propagated asexually, and is, of course, reproduced from cuttings to this day.

But sometimes the gardener attempts to raise new varieties to order, and to that end removes the stamens of a flower before the pollen is ripe and then covers the bloom with a muslin bag. This precaution is taken to prevent indiscriminate pollination by insects or wind. Later, when the stamens of the mutilated flower are ready, pollen is taken from another plant and transferred to the stigma. If fertilisation takes place (as it frequently does not) the resultant seedlings may or may not produce a worthwhile hybrid. Too often it is not the best but the worst traits which come out in the offspring.

Various perils will also face the seedlings in their growth to the flowering stage—insect pests, disease and weather hazards to mention a few. Some of the seedlings may flower the first year, but with other genera the hybridist will have to wait from four to six years to see the results of his work. After nursing the plants all this time it will be rare indeed if more than 2 per cent are worth saving, so that only the enthusiast will find the work involved really worthwhile. Even to-day with our advanced scientific knowledge, the law of chance still plays a big part in raising new plants, and most of the modern varieties which grace our gardens are derived by selection (from beds of seedlings) and not by deliberate crossing.

Sowing the Seed

Outdoors. Very many hardy herbaceous plants may be raised from seed sown directly into the open ground. Thorough preparation of the ground and good conditions for germination are, however, essential factors for success.

Make the seedbed in a sheltered part of the garden where it is under the eye, and can be weeded and watered as necessary. In the main the ground should be prepared as recommended for the various soil types in Chapter II, but before sowing the seeds, break down any hard lumps, remove large stones, and generally bring the soil by raking to a fine even tilth. Never work the ground when it sticks to the feet or more harm will be done than good.

Fine soil particles become particularly desirable when dealing with seedlings. When the seed germinates it uses the little food it contains to throw out roots, and these must quickly come into contact with moisture or die. The smaller the seed, the more tiny these roots will be and if they are unlucky enough to be sown in loose ground full of lumps, they may well find their way into an air pocket between several large particles. Here there will be neither food nor moisture and the unlucky seedling perishes almost as soon as it starts to live.

That is why it is so important to get the ground *firm* and to a *fine tilth.* Rolling or treading may be necessary if it seems too loose, and finally raking. The smaller the seed the finer the soil particles must be, so that while a hay rake may be used before sowing large seeds, the smaller tined garden rake must be brought into use for the finest ones.

Herbaceous perennials are best sown in drills, using a garden line to ensure straightness. Use a draw hoe to make these and keep them shallow; half an inch depth is ample for most seeds. If the ground is very dry it may be watered *after* the drill is drawn and just before sowing. Sow thinly and cover the seed by scuffling the soil gently with the foot, or by using a rake held upright.

Sometimes herbaceous plant seed is sown in cold frames, when it may be set in drills or sown broadcast. In the latter instance be sure to sow thinly and afterwards cover the seed with good soil sifted through a fine sieve.

Under glass. Although seed sowing out of doors can only be practised at certain seasons (usually between April and October), it is possible to extend this period when glass is available. Even very slight warmth hastens germination, and conditions generally are so much more within the gardener's control under glass that a higher degree of success may be anticipated.

The seed can be sown in pots, pans or boxes, but the first essential is to see that these are scrupulously clean. Damping-off disease (*botrytis*) is a formidable enemy and it is foolish to take precautions against it by using sterilised soil if the disease spores are retained in dirty receptacles.

Crock the latter after cleaning, placing broken flower-pot shards over the drainage holes of pots and pans, and along the central drainage slit in seed boxes. Next spread a layer of coarse roughage over the crocks (old leaves, peat or coconut fibre, etc.) and then fill to within an inch of the top with compost. The roughage acts as a buffer between crocks and soil and prevents fine particles of the latter drifting through and fouling the drainage.

Use the compost in a moderately moist state. A useful test for determining its condition is to squeeze a small quantity in the hand and then throw it into the air. The soil should bind to the palm when squeezed, but disintegrate when it touches the hand again on falling.

The compost itself is important. It must contain food (loam), moisture retentive material (peat) and some substance which will ensure good drainage (sand).

When considering these basic materials never be satisfied with anything but the best. The nature of the seed compost is highly important for it starts and feeds the plant in its early days.

Always use well-rotted turfy loam, material which has been watered from time to time and stacked turf side downwards for several months. Before going into the potting compost the loam must be partially sterilised to destroy weed seeds, harmful fungoid diseases like ' damping off ' and various undesirable soil organisms, including wireworm and eelworms. A small quantity can be sterilised at home by tying about a bushel of *dry* soil in a sack and suspending this above one or two gallons of water in a domestic copper. The water should then be quickly brought to the boil and kept going vigorously for about 35 minutes. At the end of this time the steam will have completely penetrated and soaked the soil, and it will be sufficiently sterilised. Spread it out to cool and dry, and it can then be mixed with the other ingredients.

The second essential in seed composts is the moisture retentive material, and either horticultural peat or leaf soil can be employed for the purpose. As a matter of principle the first substance is most generally used, for it is readily procurable and completely sterile. Leaf mould on the other hand varies considerably according to the type of tree which produced it and the manner in which it was prepared. Oak or beech give the best grade material, but one should avoid leaf soil from any damp, low-lying locality. This frequently contains eelworms, earthworms and sometimes spores of disease. Where doubt is felt always use peat, and the best kinds for horticultural use are the moss and sedge peats, sold as peat moss, granulated peat, peat mould, etc. On no account confuse these with peat moss litter, which is used in stables and quite unsuitable for seed and potting composts.

The third basic ingredient is sand, a material which is completely sterile, but useful because it keeps the soil open and friable. To this end it should be coarse but clean and free from any foreign or organic particles.

Provided that the above materials are up to standard a useful seed compost can be prepared at home, using these as a basis. Different gardeners have different ideas regarding proportions, but a mixture which the author has used for many years in raising herbaceous perennials is made up as follows:

> 1 part by bulk good sifted loam
> 1 ,, ,, ,, ,, leaf mould or peat
> 1 ,, ,, ,, ,, coarse sand

In recent years, however, the work of the John Innes Institution at Bayfordbury on seed and potting composts has received considerable publicity. The findings of this research station have been of the utmost value to gardeners, for it has given the world a standard recipe for seed and potting composts which can be used for almost all plants. Whilst many gardeners will prefer to mix their own materials, those without the requisite facilities can purchase the compost already prepared from most nurserymen and horticultural sundriesmen. The mixture contains all the essentials for balanced growth, in proportions decided as the result of many and varied experiments.

The ingredients are as follows:

> 2 parts by bulk medium loam
> 1 part ,, ,, leaf or peat
> 1 ,, ,, ,, coarse sand

To every bushel of the above mixture add:

> $1\frac{1}{2}$ oz. superphosphate
> $\frac{3}{4}$ oz. chalk or limestone

The latter materials were added because it was found that phosphate —so necessary to the plant in its early stages of development—was singularly lacking in many loams. Phosphorus gives increased resistance to disease and cold, promotes growth of leaf and root in the seedling stage and fruit development in a later period. The calcium is added in the form of chalk or limestone to render more effective the benefits received from the superphosphate. It also reduces soil acidity and makes available other plant nutrients in the soil.

After filling pots and pans with loam, press each one down evenly (paying particular attention to the edges) and leave the surface smooth and even. Now sow the seed thinly and cover this in turn with a light layer of silver sand or finely-sieved compost. A pot rammer or the base of a similar sized flower pot is useful for giving even pressure, and leaves a flat surface. After labelling, the pots must be watered but this should not be performed overhead except with very large seeds. The smaller ones, with their scanty covering of soil are easily dislodged with water, and best treated by the immersion method. Half-fill a bath with water and stand the receptacles in this so that the water level lies just below the rims of the pots. Leave them until the soil surface appears moist.

Now remove the pots to a frame or greenhouse and cover the top with a sheet of paper to prevent drying out. Directly the seeds germinate this paper must be removed or the seedlings will become pale and drawn and eventually topple over. As soon as they are large enough to handle prick them out into boxes, using John Innes Potting Compost No. 1,*and in due course, after hardening off they can be put outside in their permanent positions or a prepared nursery bed. The decision as to which course to take will be linked with the time anticipated before blooming. Geums and Lupins for instance usually flower the first season and can be set in the border with confidence, but others are very slow growing and need bringing along gently before being put in any permanent situation.

VEGETATIVE PROPAGATION

We have already noted that seed is not infallible as a means of plant propagation, especially where named varieties are concerned. The characteristics which make a garden plant good are rarely transmitted through the seed. Frequently such varieties are sterile and therefore produce no seed at all. Plants like this must be propagated vegetatively, that is to say, growing pieces of the original must be detached from the clump and rooted separately. By these means their individualities are preserved—doubling, variegation, colour breaks, etc.—for a part of the living plant is taken, and their survival is assured.

Division. When seed sowing fails division is not only the most obvious means of increase but perhaps the easiest. As the name implies it involves pulling the plants to pieces and dividing these up so that each unit possesses a shoot or shoots and some fibrous roots. Many perennials lend themselves readily to this means of propagation. They have fibrous rather

* *John Innes Potting Compost No. 1.*

7 parts by bulk loose medium loam
3 „ „ „ good peat
2 „ „ „ coarse silver sand
To each bushel of this mixture add:
1½ ozs. hoof and horn
1½ ozs. superphosphate
¾ oz. sulphate of potash
¾ oz. ground limestone or chalk.

than tuberous roots and make a good deal of top-shoot growth. It is easy to split the clump with a knife or handfork. Very obstinate roots sometimes have to be persuaded to break by levering them apart with two digging forks. These are thrust back to back in the middle of the clump, and then the fork handles are pulled firmly apart, a process which tears the clump in two.

As long as a division has a shoot and some roots it will grow. Asters, Helianthus, Phlox and Heleniums are typical examples of plants which can be divided, but it should be appreciated that when a large rootstock is split up, the newest growths will be towards the outside. The centre of the clump, having been cramped and starved for some time is less likely to produce good plants and should be discarded.

Fleshy rooted perennials like Delphiniums are best divided early in the year. They take less kindly to disturbance than fibrous plants, and with the spring resurgence soon settle down and make new roots. Any wounds inflicted on plants during transplanting should be cleaned up with a knife and dusted with charcoal as an antiseptic measure.

Although spring and autumn are generally reckoned good seasons for dividing perennials, I would hesitate to disturb Pyrethrums, *Aster amellus*, Chrysanthemums, Scabious, Catananche or Lupins in the latter period, particularly in heavy land. Too often they remain dormant all winter, insecurely anchored and a prey to pest and disease during the most trying months of the year. Far better to wait until spring and be sure of satisfactory results.

Iris barbata presents an individual problem. Moved in spring, the roots are broken and it fails to flower during the current season. But divided in autumn it barely settles before June arrives and then again it is not ready to flower. The fact is that this plant needs nearly a twelve-month to recover after division. For this reason the rhizomes should be lifted immediately *after* flowering (about July), cut up into segments— each with a fan of leaves and 4 to 5 in. of rhizome—and replanted. It soon settles in and flowers better than ever next season.

Soft Cuttings. This is the nurseryman's means of increase and the quickest way of obtaining a stock of plants in a short time. I can recollect being personally involved once with a new Chrysanthemum variety, which by means of soft cuttings, was increased to 10,000 plants at the end of a single season. Propagation with a vengeance, and certainly not possible by any other means.

As the name implies, a softwood cutting is a young soft piece of the current year's growth. Since these come through the ground early in the year, spring or early summer is naturally the best time for this operation. When numbers of a given plant are required the rootstock is lifted about February, boxed or potted, and brought into a warm greenhouse. A temperature round about 56° F., combined with moisture soon induces the stool to throw up shoots, and these are the parts needed for cuttings. If

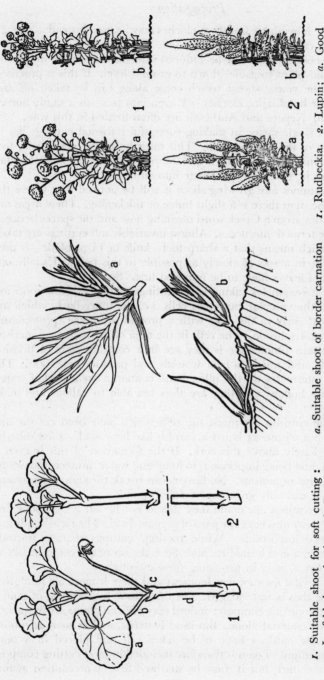

a. Suitable shoot for soft cutting :
a. Leaf blade or lamina; *b*. Petiole
or leaf stalk; *c*. Node; *d*. Internode.
2. The cutting made.

a. Suitable shoot of border carnation
for layering; *b*. Prepared shoot pegged
down, still attached to parent plant.

1. Rudbeckia. 2. Lupin; *a*. Good
and *b*. bad staking.

no greenhouse is available frames or cloches may be used instead, although naturally the cuttings take longer to come through.

But softwood cuttings can be induced later in the season simply by cutting the old plant (outside) down to ground level. If this is practised about July, the young shoots which come along can be taken off and inserted under handlights, cloches—or even jam jars—in a shady corner of the garden. Nepeta and Anthemis are often treated in this way.

The chief single factor in making successful softwood cuttings lies in the condition of the cutting itself. This must be young yet sturdy, free from disease and short jointed. When the young shoots are several inches long they can be taken off and made into cuttings.

If one examines any growing shoot it will be noticed that where the leaves join the stem there is a slight bulge or thickening. These areas are known as nodes, from a Greek word meaning nose and the spaces between the nodes are termed internodes. Almost invariably soft cuttings are taken at a node which means that a sharp tool—knife or razor-blade—is used to sever the stem across as closely as possible to this point. Usually one or two pairs of leaves have to be removed first. See p. 61.

There is a reason for taking such cuttings at nodes. New roots are formed from the vascular cambium cells, i.e. the inner bark, which are richly charged early in the year with a protein substance (protoplasm) and dilute sugar solution. The cells in the area of the nodes are meristematic at certain times, that is they are in a constant state of division and so ready and quick to heal wounds and produce new roots. The cells in the internodes on the other hand contain a great deal of water, often they are hollow, and they are thus less able to callous and make roots.

When the cuttings are made the cells which have been cut die and turn corky, but within 24 hours a varnish like fatty acid, called suberin, forms immediately above this cork. If the formation of this is even it makes a seal, and being impervious to fungi and water, protects the wound from destructive organisms. No fungus can break through a continuous cork layer—it can only grow superficially upon it.

After the cuttings are made they should not be left lying about, but put straight away into boxes or pans of prepared soil. The right conditions now are very important. While rooting, cuttings require warmth, moisture, oxygen and humidity, and the make up of the compost has an important part to play in providing these essentials.

Oxygen is vital for root development and there is more air in a gritty soil than one that is waterlogged. For this reason a good deal of sand is included in the cutting compost; indeed very difficult plants are frequently rooted in this material alone. But sand is sterile, and as soon as rooting takes place the cuttings have to be taken out and placed in a more nourishing medium. Loam is therefore included in most cutting composts right from the start, but it must be sterilised first as precaution against

' damping off' and other diseases. Since the unrooted cutting must never dry out, peat, which retains moisture, is also added. On this basis a good cutting compost for hardy herbaceous perennials can be made up as follows:

> 1 part by bulk sterilised and finely sifted loam
> 2 ,, ,, ,, horticultural peat
> 2 ,, ,, ,, coarse sand

Prepare the cutting pans in the same manner as for seed sowing; that is, clean and crock them, add roughage and fill to within an inch of the top with compost. Sprinkle a little fine sand over the latter and then firmly insert the cuttings, using a dibber or sharpened piece of wood. Make sure that the base of each cutting touches the soil and does not hang in a soil pocket, or rooting will not take place. Finally, the cuttings should be watered with a rose-headed can and placed in a propagating frame or under a bell jar.

The use of hormone preparations hastens the process of callousing and rooting and is, therefore, particularly useful with difficult cuttings. It has the effect of accelerating cell division, with a consequent speeding up of the whole process of rooting. But such materials are highly poisonous and must only be used strictly according to the maker's specification. Immoderate doses cause erratic growth, distortion and sometimes death to the cuttings. It is important, too, to see that the hormone preparation is fresh, as some kinds deteriorate with keeping.

While hormones may be useful for particular stubborn cuttings, they should not be looked upon as indispensable aids to rooting. The great majority of herbaceous plants need no such inducement and present few difficulties when taken and struck in the normal way.

The period needed for rooting differs with different plants, but is mostly between three and six weeks. These weeks, however, are vitally important and during the whole of the time the cuttings must not be allowed to flag or dry out.

Soft cuttings have leaves and so the natural function of passing off water vapour (transpiration) takes place all the time. But with no roots to send along fresh supplies the plant cannot keep pace with the wastage and has to be protected from excessive loss in this direction. It is for this reason that we keep softwood cuttings in a close atmosphere, as in a frame or under a bell jar. Water vapour is given off by the plant and from the soil, but in such a confined space the air soon becomes saturated and incapable of absorbing more. The cuttings, therefore, preserve their rigidity and rooting can go forward in a humid atmosphere.

Some precautions, however, must be taken against bright sunlight. The sun's rays shining through glass are very powerful and can soon dry out all plants they strike. The gardener must therefore cover his frames with sacks or paper whenever the sun is shining, but only then. If the covering is retained in dull weather the plants would soon become drawn and lose their green colour. Since the green leaves of a plant are associated with the making of food, this would be disastrous.

A stale atmosphere also must be avoided and so the frames are opened or cloches lifted once a day in order to change the air. The interior of the glass should be wiped at the same time to remove condensation.

Once the cuttings are rooted they will need no further shading, and the lights can be removed to maintain a more buoyant atmosphere. Gradually they can be hardened off and removed to an outside frame or nursery bed, according to weather conditions. Many will become established and flower during the first season, although most will not reach full maturity until the second or third year.

Sometimes soft cuttings are taken with a fragment of the old stem or root attached. These are known as ' heel ' cuttings.

Root Cuttings. Although a large proportion of herbaceous plants can be propagated from soft cuttings, there remain a few which do not make the type of short growth needed for the purpose. Sometimes these produce only basal leaves and flowers, or they may have hollow stems, or shoots which exude milky or mucilaginous sap. While the majority can be perpetuated from seed, this method will not do for the named garden varieties, which must be propagated vegetatively.

A number of these perennials, however, possess substantial rootstocks; fleshy appendages with active growth principles present in marked degree. This phenomenon is exploited by the propagator, who uses severed pieces of root to make new plants, thus unconsciously emulating the action of the gardener who by digging carelessly round Couch Grass and Bindweed, breaks the roots in a hundred pieces, each portion of which is capable of growing and making a new plant.

Although the professional grower is in the habit of making root cuttings in winter, this is merely a matter of convenience. It is simply a job which can be undertaken when the weather is too bad to work out of doors. The method can be employed almost any time during the whole twelve months, although the highest percentage of ' takes ' usually comes from spring or early summer cuttings.

Amongst a number of plants which can be propagated in this way are Oriental Poppies, Anchusa, Echinops, Acanthus, Japanese Anemones, Eryngiums, Catananche, Phlox and *Primula denticulata*.

When making root cuttings it is best to start by lifting the plant in its entirety. Clean the roots and then cut them up into small segments, making each one between one and three inches long, according to the type of plant used and the width of the material. These pieces when planted should be set the right way up, and in order to facilitate recognition when a considerable number have been prepared, the operator should make a nick in the base of each cutting. See p. 54.

Thick roots like Poppy can be inserted the correct way up in deep boxes of gritty soil. It is best to half-fill the latter, then place the cuttings

Plate 11: 1. TUBE CLEMATIS, *Clematis heracleifolia.* 2. ITALIAN BUGLOSS, *Anchusa azurea*
'Morning Glory'. 3. BLUE INDIGO, *Baptisia australis.* 4. CATMINT, *Nepeta mussinii.*
5. CHICORY, *Cichorium intybus*

Plate 12: 1. HEWITT'S MEADOW RUE, *Thalictrum dipterocarpum* 'Hewitt's Double'. 2. BLUE CARDINAL FLOWER, *Lobelia syphilitica*. 3. BLUE LETTUCE, *Lactuca bourgaei*. 4. LILAC CRANESBILL. *Geranium grandiflorum*. 5. SIBERIAN DRAGON'S HEAD, *Dracocephalum ruyschianum*. 6. FLAX, *Linum narbonense*

Plate 13: 1. ROSE CAMPION, *Lychnis Coronaria atrosanguinea*. 2. PURPLE LOOSESTRIFE, *Lythrum Salicaria* 'Robert'. 3. PURPLE TOADFLAX, *Linaria purpurea*. 4. CHINESE TRUMPET FLOWER, *Incarvillea Delavayi*

Plate 14: 1. Chamomile, *Anthemis tinctoria* 'Grallagh Gold'. 2. Butterfly Weed, *Asclepias tuberosa*. 3. Straw Foxglove, *Digitalis lutea*. 4. Caucasian Inula, *Inula orientalis*. 5. Jacob's Rod, *Asphodeline lutea*

(1–2 in. apart) perpendicularly—like a row of soldiers—and finally cover them right over with half an inch of sandy soil. The boxes can then be stood outside in a sheltered place or in a cold frame to sprout.

With very slender cuttings like Phlox or Anemone such a method would be very tedious, so in these cases the roots are cut into two-inch lengths and spread *horizontally* on the box of soil. They are then covered with sand.

A method of propagating Phlox which we have found very satisfactory consists of cutting the roots into two-inch lengths, and tying these in small bundles of 20 or 25. Each bundle is then inserted the right way up in a flower pot of soil, and immediately growths appear at the surface the soil is removed and each cutting potted separately. Once sprouting occurs the cuttings must not be left in the bundle or they will either become completely entwined with roots, or start to rot off in the centre. If cuttings are taken this way in mid-August a 100 per cent ' take ' can be anticipated.

One curious feature in connection with root cuttings is worth noting. Many plants raised from seed show a distinctive juvenile type of foliage when young, which changes later to the more usual leaf shape. Young Acanthus leaves for example are quite different from those of an older plant, being less cut and with rounded tips. If root cuttings are taken from a young and old plant simultaneously, the cuttings will take on the degree of maturity of the parent plant. Those from the young plant will have juvenile foliage and those from the old one mature leaves. Since the plants have to develop to a certain stage before flowering, this point is not without interest to the gardener.

Leaf Cuttings. Only a very few hardy perennials are propagated from leaf cuttings, although a number of greenhouse plants like Gloxinias, Saintpaulias, *Begonia rex* and Echeverias are so increased. In the shady flower border, however, one sometimes sees a North American near-saxifrage called *Tolmeia menziesii*. This has green and chocolate spikes of flowers, and rough, ivy-shaped foliage. In spring when the plant comes to bloom this foliage is normal, but as summer advances almost every leaf develops a new plant at the point where the leaf-stalk joins the blade. If these leaves are detached and pegged down into a pan or box of sandy soil, they soon throw out roots and set up an independent existence. *Tolmeia menziesii* may also be grown as a house plant, and when semi-starved produces young plants on every leaf, a circumstance which has earned it the name of Pick-a-back Plant in America. See p. 54.

Layering. The soft herbaceous growth of most border perennials is obviously unsuitable for layering, for a woody type of stem is essential to this operation. In border plans, however, Pinks and border Carnations are an essential for those who seek fragrance and long-flowering qualities in the front row. Carnations are not herbaceous in the true sense of the word, but neither are they woody; instead they show some characteristics of both and accordingly are termed suffruticose. And border Carnations are usually increased by layering. See p. 61.

The operation generally takes place about July when the gardener packs a little fresh gritty soil round his stock plants. The young, non-flowering shoots are the ones to layer, and they are prepared by stripping two pairs of leaves from each stem to expose the joints or nodes. Using a sharp knife, the operator then makes a cut—which starts upwards and then runs horizontally for about half an inch through the middle of one of the joints. Thus the stem is half-severed, and the cut end is then pressed into the new soil so that it remains open under the surface. Layering pins, pieces of bent twig or even hairpins may be used to hold the layer firm, and finally soil is pressed back over the buried portion.

In dry weather it may be necessary to keep the layers watered, but as a rule they produce roots (at the cut area) in 5 or 6 weeks. In early autumn they can be separated from the parent plant and put out in their permanent positions.

Grafting. Grafting is the operation of inserting one part of a plant into another, and so making it grow on foreign roots. As a horticultural process it is one of the oldest of garden crafts.

Amongst hardy plants grafting is confined to subjects which normally are difficult to strike or are weak growing on their own roots, or the practice is adopted to enable certain varieties to thrive in adverse climates or in uncongenial soil.

To succeed with herbaceous grafting it is necessary to have close moist conditions prevailing, so that evaporation slows down. A propagating frame in a greenhouse is ideal but the temperature must be kept lower than is usual with cuttings. The usual methods employed are side or cleft grafts. In the first instance the scion (young shoot) is taken several inches long and trimmed to a wedge at the cut end. A cut is then made in the stem of the stock, downward pointing close to ground level, and the scion inserted in this and tied in position. The top of the stock is not removed and the new shoot stands up beside its stem. It is then kept in the propagating frame to unite, when the top stock growth (above the scion) is cut away.

Herbaceous Peonies are frequently grafted when stocks of new varieties are wanted in a hurry. An eye of the desired kind is inserted into the tuber of some strong-growing variety, such as *P. officinalis*, from which all its own eyes have been removed. Usually the scion is trimmed to a V shape and the stock cut like a wedge. The two parts then fit into each other, and after being plunged for a time in soil so that the graft is covered, they readily unite. As the operation is usually performed about August, the grafts must be kept moist and shaded until the union is complete. When this occurs ventilation is given gradually but the plants are left in the frame throughout the winter, and transplanted the following spring.

Grafting is also employed to a great extent commercially when raising double forms of *Gypsophila paniculata*. Seedlings of the single form are grown in frames or boxes and used when two years old. About February roots of the double kinds which are to provide the scions, are brought into a greenhouse and planted in light soil to induce growth. When the shoots are two inches long they are taken off and made to a wedge shape at the base. The stocks meanwhile are cut down to within an inch of the ground and prepared for the scions by being opened down the middle with a sharp knife. The cut should be about an inch long. The wedge-shaped scion is then inserted and tied in position. In England these grafts are often made on a bench, the plants being potted separately after tying. On the Continent, however, and especially in Holland, I have seen them grafted at ground level in cold frames. No tying was effected in this instance, but an inch layer of screened ashes was lightly spread amongst the plants, completely covering the points of union and probably acting is a deterrent to slugs and woodlice.

Proliferation. By this is meant an unusual method of vegetative propagation, which produces young plantlets on parts of the plant other than the root. *Tolmeia menziesii* with its plant-bearing leaves is an example of proliferation, but other subjects may even carry such growths on the flowers or the stems.

Usually the individuals which adopt such measures of increase are shy flowering or their seed is abortive. When the blooms fade one sometimes finds bright green foliage leaves clustered on the old branches of the inflorescence. These increase in little tufty bunches, so that before long they have the appearance of young plantlets with swollen bases and clumps of small leaves. Left to themselves they eventually fall to the ground, but if the gardener separates them artificially they soon root in a box of soil and become good plants.

Amongst the few herbaceous perennials which have this strange characteristic are Dentaria, which carries bulbies-like buds in the leaf axils; *Dicentra eximia*, which carries plantlets on the abortive flower heads; *Cardamine pratensis*, in which young plants may appear at the base of each leaflet, and Hemerocallis and Lupins, some varieties of which occasionally carry shoots, capable of being rooted, in the axils of the stem leaves.

GLASS AS AN AID TO PROPAGATION

As already implied, the use of glass, whether in the form of a frame, belljar, cloche or greenhouse, is a great aid to the successful propagation of plants. Controlled temperature and atmospheric humidity create even-growing conditions, the most important single factor to success.

Warmth at the critical growing period is vitally important, so it follows that those with heated frames or greenhouses score immeasureably over others using cold frames or cloches. By employing heat the gardener is able to extend the period of propagation and is not dependent on weather conditions outside.

There are, of course, various ways of heating glasshouses, with boilers fed by coke, anthracite, oil, gas or electricity. With a larger house boilers connected to water pipes and fired with coke or anthracite are probably the most economical. Pipes 4 in. in diameter are usually accommodated under the benching at the side of the house. These should rise gently from the boiler to an expansion tank at the highest point and return at a similar angle to the boiler. The propagating benches are built over these, often with a glass frame top to conserve the heat and humidity.

A greenhouse approximately 8 ft. wide will be served by a single 4-inch flow, but wider houses should have this increased to two, or even three sides of the house if over 12 ft. across. The return pipes will be in duplicate in each case.

Hot-water boilers can also be built for gas or oil heating. Although usually more expensive to run, they are more reliable and easier to manage than small coke boilers.

Small houses can also be heated direct by oil lamps without water pipes. Only high-grade paraffin should be used for these lamps, which must be kept scrupulously clean. Although specially designed so as to emit no oil fumes, they can become objectionable if allowed to get in dirty condition. Generally speaking, such heaters are most suitable for occasional use, to keep out frost from otherwise cold or slightly heated houses.

To-day, however, electricity is being used increasingly both for glasshouse heating and soil warming. It is clean, reliable and time saving, all of which are important factors in the life of the average gardener.

ELECTRICAL HEATING FOR PLANT PROPAGATION

' Bottom heat ' is a term frequently used by the gardener in connection with the germination of seeds or the rooting of cuttings, it being well known that soil temperature is just as important as air temperature in both these operations. In the past this bottom heat has been provided either by placing the seed boxes in a propagating case standing over the hot-water pipes or over a hot bed of fermenting manure inside a frame.

To-day manure hot beds are rarely seen. Manure is sometimes difficult to obtain at the right time; it is expensive, and in any case making a hot bed is laborious, messy and time consuming. Placing a propagating case over hot-water pipes is still often practised but frequently this means running the rest of the greenhouse at a higher temperature than is necessary, with consequent increase in fuel consumption.

With the advent of electrical soil warming, not only can the normally heated greenhouse be run more efficiently, but early propagation can be carried out both in the ' cold ' greenhouse and the cold frame. Once the equipment is installed the method of use is simple, clean and time saving. It is also efficient and economical if carried out correctly.

Equipment. Soil warming can be accomplished by two types of equipment which employ a transformer operated from mains voltage. This transformer should be one which is designed especially for horticultural work and made by a reliable manufacturer. It is the most expensive item of the outfit but it should last a lifetime. Galvanised iron wires are used to warm the soil at a voltage of 6 to 10 volts for small installations. These wires are robust and not easily damaged by cultivating tools. Even if the current has been left switched on and the wires are damaged or severed there is no possibility of danger to the gardener. The low voltage transformer method is suitable only for A.C. supplies.

The second type is a mains voltage cable which consists of a heating wire covered with an insulating and protective sheathing. This cable can be connected to either A.C. or D.C. electricity mains. Although cheaper in the first instance it is easier to damage this cable with a spade or fork than the galvanised wire and if this happens the damaged cable must be replaced. As there is a possibility of shock to the gardener if the cable is damaged when the current is on it should be a maxim never to leave the current switched on when working near the cable.

The Electricity Supply. If electricity is not already available in the greenhouse, a competent electrician should be employed to install the supply from the dwelling house. At the same time it is well worth while insisting on a switch in the dwelling house. Convenience is one of the chief advantages of electrical power, and to have to visit the greenhouse every time the current needs switching on or off is not making the best use of electricity. It is also an advantage to have a second switch in the greenhouse so that the current can be switched on or off on the spot. A golden rule to adopt is ' Switch off if handling material on the soil-warmed bench'. The electrician will install a special water-tight power point in the greenhouse so that all that is now left to be done is to lay the cable and plug in.

Laying the Cable. The bottom of the bench should first be covered with corrugated asbestos sheets, tiles or roofing felt. Nine-inch wide boards should be erected round the area to be used to hold in the materials of the bed, and form a foundation on which glass can be placed when the bed is in use. A 2-inch layer of sand is now placed on the bench and on this the warming wire is distributed evenly, taking care not to have any sharp right-angle bends. The cable must not come into contact with itself or overlap at any point, and the distance between one part of the cable and next part parallel to it should be about 6 inches. The diagram on page 70 shows a good method of laying the wire.

If galvanised wire is used it will be necessary to peg it down at intervals as it is very springy material and difficult to keep in place. Suitable pegs can be made from other pieces of galvanised wire bent to the shape of a

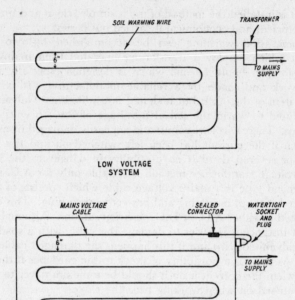

Electrical heating for plant propagation: laying the cable.

hairpin. If corrugated iron sheets are used on the bottom of the bench it is advisable to staple the wire to wooden battens to ensure that the wire will not come into contact with the sheeting. On no account cut pieces of the warming cable for this purpose. It is made to the correct length according to its resistance. This electrical resistance has been measured for the particular wire and therefore it is unwise to purchase any ordinary galvanised wire, even though it looks the same.

Having laid the cable, then cover it with a further 2 inches of sand. On this layer the seed boxes or pans will stand. Ashes should not be used in place of sand or they will quickly cause corrosion of the wires and impede the transfer of heat.

In order to minimise heat losses any space in between pots or boxes or any area of sand not covered by a pan or a box should be covered with a layer of moist peat 3–4 inches thick. It is important not to have a layer of peat underneath the boxes or pans as this will insulate the latter from the heat below.

Working the System. The temperature required underneath the boxes may vary from 55° F.–65° F. according to the time of year and the type of plant and propagation being carried out. Having decided the temperature needed there are three main methods of controlling it.

1. The Dosage Method. This means switching on for a certain period so that each square foot of bench receives a minimum of 40 watts in 24 hours. Thus if the cable gives a loading of 5 watts per square foot the current would be on for 8 hours. The ' on ' period is usually at night since this is usually the coldest part of the 24 hours and it is also the ' off peak ' period as far as electricity consumption is concerned.

2. The Inspection Method. This is more accurate since a thermometer is inserted into the bed, below a box or pot, so that the actual temperature can be checked and controlled as necessary.

3. Thermostatic Control. For propagation work thermostatic control is the most reliable and least time consuming, but it does mean the extra cost of a thermostat. The latter should be of the rod type, and lie horizontally in the top layer of sand, at right angles to the wires and just under the boxes or pans. The current switch is always in the ' on ' position and the thermostat, which has been previously set to the desired temperature, will switch current on or off according to the temperature of the bed.

The Propagating Frame. The preparation of this follows exactly the same lines as the propagating bench in the greenhouse. The minimum loading is 5 watts per square foot and in very cold weather the running may be continuous. Much will depend on external temperatures, but thermostatic control does save a lot of money during changeable weather, when the gardener may be away from home all day. During frosty nights it is advisable to place straw mats or sacks over the frame lights, and thick walled frames will obviously conserve the heat better than flimsy structures and make for more economical running costs. Added protection can be obtained by attaching a mains voltage cable on porcelain insulators to the walls inside the frame for the purpose of heating the air.

Running Costs. Electricity can be very expensive if used in unreasonable ways. For propagation work on a small scale the expense is by no means prohibitive. For example, an area 3 ft. by 4 ft. on the greenhouse bench could be prepared and would hold a dozen seed boxes. Using 5 watts per square foot the size of cable used would be equivalent to a 60-watt household lamp. A unit of electricity is used when 1,000 watts has been the loading for one hour. As the days become warmer during April and early May less current would be needed and the cost would be considerably reduced. Normally a cold greenhouse or a cold frame with soil warming would be used for propagating from March onwards, but if space heating is also available then propagation may start in January.

1. The high voltage cable is *not* recommended when there is a possibility of damage by cultivating tools. It is, however, suitable

for soil warming in benches and frames, and space heating frames and enclosed benches.

2. Choose a cable which gives a loading of 5–6 watts per square foot of bench.

3. Purchase reliable equipment specially made for the job.

4. The electrical installation should be carried out by a competent electrician.

CHAPTER VI

ALPHABETICAL LIST OF HARDY
HERBACEOUS PLANTS

ACANTHUS (*Acanthaceae*): Bear's Breeches. From *akanthos* (Gk.) 'thorn'. A favourite plant with the Greeks and Romans who used it for decorative purposes. The leaf and scroll (which acts as a stalk) form the principal adornment of the Corinthian capital.

Acanthus are stately perennials with fine foliage, mostly native to Southern Europe. In key positions, in narrow borders (where the foliage may be appreciated) or in individual beds they make superb specimens. Warm, well-drained soil suits them best, but they are adaptable and will grow almost anywhere and in sun or shade, although they flower best in the former. Once planted, they are difficult to eradicate because each broken part of the root is capable of growing. See also page 65. They are all hardy in a warm, well-drained position. Propagation by root cuttings, division in spring or seed. The following species are the best in cultivation.

A. caroli-alexandri. Greece. Flowers in a dense spike, white-suffused rose. Leaves few, 3–4 in. broad. Front of the border.
1–1½ ft. July. 2 ft. sq.

A. longifolius. Dalmatia. Purple flowers set in spiny red bracts and arranged on spikes 1 ft. long. Leaves basal, 2–3 ft. not spiny.
2–3 ft. June. 3 ft. sq.

A. mollis. Italy. The most commonly planted species. Leaves heart-shaped, many-lobed, 2 ft. long, 1 ft. wide, not spiny. The flower spikes are slightly downy, and carry loosely arranged white or rose flowers. Var. *latifolius* is a larger leaved, bigger and more robust form. Var. *niger* (Spain, Portugal), has leaves shining green, unarmed with spines, and purplish-white flowers.
3–4 ft. Summer. 4 ft. sq.

A. perringii. Asia Minor. Leaves grey green, 6 in. long, deeply toothed and spiny. Flowers handsome, rosy red with spiny bracts. Front of the border.
1–1½ ft. June–Aug. 1½ ft. sq.

A. spinosus. (*Plate 22, p. 97.*) South Europe. A strikingly handsome plant. Leaves shining dark green, deeply and irregularly cut, each division terminating in a spine. Flowers noble, white and purple with green shiny bracts on impressive spikes. They last weeks in water.
4 ft. July–Aug. 4 ft. sq.

A. spinosus var. *spinosissimus*. South Europe. Leaves dark green with glistening, whitish spines. Flowers rose, individually without stems, on a spike with acute, recurved bracts. *3–4 ft. Autumn. 4 ft. sq.*

ACHILLEA (*Compositae*): Milfoil; Yarrow. Named for the Greek hero Achilles, who was supposed to have used it medicinally.

A variable family which contains plants varying from high alpine species an inch or two tall, to 4 and 5 ft. border giants. The latter present few cultural problems. They are sun lovers and flourish in almost any soil which is not sour or badly drained. Although they like lime they thrive happily under acid conditions.

Propagation is usually effected by division of the roots in spring or after flowering, and in the species, from seed also. This should be sown as soon as possible after ripening, as, like many composites, it rapidly loses its vitality.

Plant the border varieties in early spring or autumn, and as the growth is strong and exhaustive, it pays to lift, divide and replant clumps every third year. Cut the shoots hard back in autumn.

A. clavenae. E. Alps. There is some confusion between this species and *A. argentea*. Most writers refer them both to *clavenae* as synonymous, but I have seen two distinct plants in cultivation under these names. *A. argentea* is a rock plant with silvery foliage and small white flowers in May, whilst *A. clavenae* is taller and looser growing, with larger white flowers and has jagged leaves and stems liberally felted with silky, silvery hairs. *9 in. May–June. 1 ft. sq.*

A. clypeolata. Of uncertain origin. A good front to middle border plant, forming mats of finely cut, hairy foliage. Flowers bright yellow, in dense, flat heads. *2½–3 ft. July–Sept. 2 ft. sq.*

A. decolorans (syn. *A. serrata*). Switzerland. A low-growing species with erect, branching stems, narrow-toothed leaves and sprays of small, yellowish-white flowers. Var. ' W. B. Child ' is an improvement on the type, with good pure white flowers which are useful for cutting; *flore-pleno* is double. *2½ ft. May–Aug. 2 ft. sq.*

A. filipendulina (syn. *A. eupatorium*): Fernleaf Yarrow (*plate 8, p. 48*): Caucasus. A handsome species, with large, flat plate-like heads of bright yellow flowers, and pinnately lobed, strongly aromatic foliage. Useful for late summer work in mid-border positions this species and its varieties can also be employed with effect at the edge of shrubberies, on the banks of streams or for roadside planting.

Among the best of the varieties are ' Parker's Var.' and ' Gold Plate '. Both have finer flower heads than the type. There is also a recently introduced hybrid between *A. filipendulina* and *A. clypeolata* known as ' Coronation Gold '. This grows 2½ ft. high and has mustard coloured flower heads. The inflorescence of this and other species can be dried for winter decoration. They should be gathered just before

reaching maturity and hung upside down in an airy shed. If the
flowers are arranged so that they reach into a cardboard box and are
then dusted with powdered alum, the latter preserves their bright
colour.

Other varieties of recent introduction are ' Canary Bird ', with
bright gold flower heads on erect 1½–2 ft. stems, flowering June–July;
' Flowers of Sulphur ', soft golden yellow, good for cutting, 2½ ft.
June–Aug., and ' Sungold ', rich yellow, 1½ ft. June–Aug.

5 ft.   July–Aug.   3 ft. sq.

A. grandiflora. Caucasus. A very old species useful for wild corners or poor
soil where little else will grow. It has creamy white flowers and smooth,
linear leaves.   *2–3 ft.   June–July.   1½ ft. sq.*

A. lingulata. Hungary. Stiff stemmed, resembling *A. ptarmica* but hairy.
Flowers white, numerous. Var. *buglossis* is grown in preference to the
type.   *1½ ft.   Summer.   2 ft. sq.*

A. millefolium. Yarrow; Milfoil. Europe including Britain. A common
wayside plant which has been employed medicinally. Several old
names denote its former uses—Nose-bleed, Soldier's Wound-Wort,
Knyghten Milfoil and Old Man's Pepper (the young leaves were once
used in salads). Varietal forms only will be grown in the border and
these in a front-row position. The leaves are cut into innumerable
parts and the flowers borne on flat plates or corymbs. Good varieties
are ' Cerise Queen ' which has rose-cerise flowers in July, 2 ft.;
' Crimson Beauty ', similar, but deeper in colour which does not fade;
' Fire King ' which is deeper still and probably the best of this section;
var. *rosea*, pink and var. *rubra*, deep pink.   *2 ft.   July–Aug.   2 ft. sq.*

A. ptarmica. Sneezewort. *(Plate I, p. 192.)* Europe including Britain. A
pretty, summer flowering perennial with erect, rather large corymbs
of white ' daisy ' flowers, and shining, tapering, finely serrated leaves.
All parts of the plant have a pungent flavour. When dried it excites
sneezing and has been used in Scotland as a substitute for snuff.
Several good garden forms with double flowers have been derived from
this species, notably ' The Pearl ', Perry's White ' and ' Snowball '.
All are popular for cut flower and wreath work and thrive satisfactorily
planted in clumps in full sun and well-drained soil.

1½ ft.   June–Aug.   2 ft. sq.

A. sibirica (syn. *A. mongolica*). N. temperate Asia. A species akin to but
in my opinion finer than *A. ptarmica*. This type makes a good garden
plant and is in flower for weeks. The addition of a few shrubby
pea-sticks keeps it a better shape.   *14–15 in.   June–Aug.   2 ft. sq.*

A. ' *taygetea* ' Hort. Derived from *A. millefolium* crossed with *A* ' *clypeolata* '
Hort. Silvery pinnate leaves and pale yellow flowers (2–4 in. across)
on 18-inch stems. A splendid subject for hot, dry, sunny places.
Good for cutting.   *1½ ft.   June–Sept.   3 ft. sq.*

ACONITUM (*Ranunculaceae*): Monkshood; Wolf's Bane. Name of uncertain origin but possibly from *akon* (Gk.), ' dart '. The plants have a sinister reputation as poisonous subjects, and fatal incidents have occurred following their mistaken identification for horse-radish. For this reason care should be exercised in planting Aconitums where children play. The plants, however, are extremely noble in growth and provide useful subjects for the border or wild garden. The blues of some varieties are very fine and contrast charmingly with pink or scarlet Phlox, whilst *A. carmichaelii* grows well in association with late-flowering Heleniums and *Achillea filipendulina*.

Aconitums prefer a rich cool soil, and are well suited to the middle or back of the border. They will grow in shade but make better specimens in sunshine, provided the soil does not dry out. It can be kept moist by annual mulches of leaf-mould or rotted compost. In very exposed districts a covering of leaves in autumn will make the plants winter hardy. Aconitums are subjects to leave alone if they seem happily situated, for they sometimes take time to settle down after disturbance. Propagation is by division in spring or autumn, or seed can be sown outside in April.

A. anglicum. Britain. Simple flower spikes, lilac blue, soft foliage.
2 ft. May and June. 2 ft. sq.

A. anthora: Pyrenees Monkshood. C. Europe. Upright leafy stem and pale yellow, helmet-like flowers. The root is substantial with bulb-like, elongated tubers. Var. *atrovirens* (Pyrenees), has dark green leaves and flowers of a deeper yellow. *2 ft. July–Sept. 2 ft. sq.*

A. cammarum. A name covering several species but the true Hungarian plant which is usually denoted, has loose spikes of purplish flowers.
4 ft. July–Sept. 2 ft. sq.

A. carmichaelii (syn. *A. fischeri*). Central China. Azure Monkshood. One of the best garden sorts. A sturdy, erect form with dark green, coarsely-toothed leaves and deep purple-blue flowers, in a terminal head, the pale-blue helmets having the top petals arched into a small beak.
2–3 ft. July–Aug. 2 ft. sq.

A. carmichaelii var. *wilsonii*. China. One of E. H. Wilson, the famous plant collector's greatest ' finds '. A vigorous perennial well suited to a back row position or the wild garden. Flowers blue or violet, slightly hairy, with large helmets. Branching habit with many side shoots 18 in. or so in length. ' Barker's Var.' (*Plate 26, p. 112*) is a much improved form, raised by the veteran plantsman Barker of Ipswich, who is also associated with the well-known *Aubrietia* ' Barker's Variety '. *Up to 6 ft. Sept.–Oct. 3 ft. sq.*

A. lycoctonum: Wolf's Bane. A very variable species, with yellow or whitish flowers. *3–6 ft. June–Sept. 2 ft. sq.*

A. napellus: Monkshood. Europe, Asia. A very poisonous plant, especially in the roots. It is, however, the best-known species and one used in medicine. Erect stems with deeply-cut and divided leaves, and broad helmeted blue or purplish flowers. There are a number of forms including *album* white, *bicolor* blue and white, ' Newry Blue ' very deep blue, and ' Spark's Variety ' very large, deep violet-blue, of branching habit. *3–4 ft. June–July. 2 ft. sq.*

A. pyramidale. S. Europe. A fine flowered monkshood of the *napellus* group. The branched inflorescence carries many rich violet flowers, whilst the deeply-cut leaves are also very attractive. The white form *album* is also a good garden plant. *3–4 ft. June–July. 2 ft. sq.*

A. volubile. An attractive species of unusual habit, which twines or climbs like a hop. For this reason it must be provided with peasticks or similar aids as soon as the shoots come through the ground in spring. Flowers violet with a gaping or open base, inflorescence drooping, leaves 5–7 divided.
12–16 ft. Aug.–Oct. Plant about 3 in a triangle 14 in. apart.

ACTAEA (*Ranunculaceae*): Baneberry; Cohosh. Generic name from *akte* (Gk) ' elder ' the leaves being somewhat similar. The common name derives from the fact that the berries are poisonous.

Actaeas have two attributes, showy spikes of small white flowers in spring, and clusters of berries in autumn. Natural denizens of the woodland, they do well in shady situations, providing the soil is leafy or otherwise rich in humus material. Propagate by division in spring or from seed, sown in the autumn, or spring after gathering. Old seed gives bad germination.

A. alba: White Baneberry. E.N. America. Very deeply cut leaves, flowers white and fringed, with green stalks which later turn red; berries white, often purplish at the end. In Pennsylvania it is known as ' rattlesnake-master ' from the use of its roots.
1–1½ ft. May–June. 1 ft. sq.

A. rubra: Red Baneberry. N. America. Perhaps the best of the genus. Flowers somewhat larger than in other species, berries scarlet. These are poisonous, and so too are the fleshy rhizomes and slender roots.
15–20 in. May–June. 1 ft. sq.

A. spicata: Cohosh; Herb Christopher. Europe, including Britain; Japan. Berries, shining black. These are poisonous but when mingled with alum make a good black dye. Leaflets ovate, less cut and toothed than others. *1–1½ ft. Summer. 1 ft. sq.*

ACTINOMERIS (*Compositae*): North American Sunflower. From *aktin* (Gk), ' ray ', *meris* ' part ', from the irregular shaped ray florets. Hardy herbaceous perennials of the sunflower type, but with smaller flowers of irregular shape. Cultivation as for Helianthus, sun or partial shade. Suitable for back of the border, shrubbery or wild garden. Propagation by division or seed sown outside April–May.

A. helianthoides. N. America. Flowers yellow, 2 in. across on bunching stems. *3–4 ft. July–Sept. 2½ ft. sq.*

A. squarrosa. Eastern N. America. Numerous loose sprays of small (2-inch) yellow flowers. Taller and coarser than *A. helianthoides.*
4–8 ft. July–Sept. 2–3 ft. sq.

ADENOPHORA (*Campanulaceae*): Ladybell; Gerand Bellflower. From *aden* (Gk) ' gland ', *phoreo* ' to bear '; referring to the nectary gland which circles the base of the style.

Hardy perennials of the Campanula family, mostly from Siberia, Japan and China and generally with blue flowers. The thick fleshy roots are impatient of disturbance and should be passed over when renovating the border. A damp subsoil suits them best, and whilst they prefer a warm, sunny spot, they will also grow in a partially shaded position. Propagation by seed sown immediately after gathering or in spring under glass. Division is not advisable as losses often follow.

A. bulleyana. China. Downy stemmed with pale-blue, funnel-shaped, nodding flowers on short stalks. These are freely produced in loose racemes. Lower leaves sword shaped and toothed, others oval oblong. This is probably the best of the genus. *4 ft. July–Aug. 2½ ft. sq.*

A. coronopifolia. Dahurica. A large-flowered species, violet-blue, with toothed, heart-shaped basal leaves, and stalkless upper ones.
1–2 ft. June. 2 ft. sq.

A. denticulata. Dahurica. Has toothed foliage and many small blue flowers borne in loose sprays. *1½ ft. July. 1½ ft. sq.*

A. lamarkii. E. Europe. Has smooth, oval, much toothed leaves and blue, funnel-shaped flowers. *1–2 ft. June. 1½ ft. sq.*

A. latifolia. Dahurica. Bears its slender pointed leaves in whorls. The flowers are blue. *1½ ft. July. 1½ ft. sq.*

A. lilifolia. Common Ladybell. Cent. Europe to Siberia. Lower leaves rounded or heart-shaped, tooth and stalked. Upper leaves without stalks, toothed and oval lanceolate. Flowers blue, fragrant and in loose upright sprays. *1½ ft. Aug. 2 ft. sq.*

A. polymorpha. Russia. Has pale-blue flowers and whorls of leaves. Var. *stricta* is more upright in habit. *2–3 ft. Aug. 2 ft. sq.*

A. potaninii. Bush Ladybell. China. Toothed, pointed, oval leaves, somewhat shrubby at the base, flowers light blue, each over an inch across, borne on large loose sprays.　　　　*2 ft.　July–Aug.　2 ft. sq.*

A. stylosa. E. Europe. An early-flowering species with blue flowers and smooth, oval leaves.　　　　　　　　　　　*1 ft.　May.　1 ft. sq.*

A. verticillata. Whorled Bellflower. Siberia, China, Korea. Leaves in whorls of 4, small pale-blue flowers on wiry stems.

2–3 ft.　June–July.　1½ ft. sq.

ADONIS (*Ranunculaceae*): Pheasant's Eye. Name connected with the Greek god Adonis, whose blood was reputed to have stained the petals of one species.

All the species are hardy and grow freely in any good garden soil. The types listed flower in spring, when they are useful for the front of the border or in the rock garden. Propagation by spring division or from seed sown immediately after gathering. Germination is slow.

A. amurensis. (*Plate 4, p. 32.*) Japan; Manchuria. This and its double form *plena* are two beautiful plants with large, golden, buttercup-like flowers nearly 2 in. across. The foliage is most attractive, being soft and very finely cut and divided—like Fennel or a dainty fern. Full sun or partial shade, but grow them in clumps and at a little distance from hungry plants of other genera. Pieces of slate thrust sideways into the soil surrounding them, protects them somewhat from such robbery.

The type has a number of Japanese varieties (white, rose and red striped) of which var. *naderkaki* is occasionally listed. This has large double flowers, yellow with a conspicuous green centre.

8–18 in.　Feb.–April.　1 ft. sq.

A. vernalis. Spring Adonis. Europe. Has large, single, yellow flowers with oblong somewhat toothed petals. There is a white form.

9–12 in.　April–May.　1 ft. sq.

AGAPANTHUS (*Liliaceae*): African Lily. From *agapas* (Gk) ' love ', *anthos* ' flower '.

Beautiful plants from South Africa which are often afforded conservatory treatment, or else grown in tubs which are placed outside for the summer months. With a little care however, several of the species can be grown and wintered outdoors. We have left *africanus*, *orientalis* (*umbellatus*) and its white form *albus* in our heavy Middlesex clay for the past three winters. In autumn, after the leaves have rotted, we cover the crowns with glass (such as an old light or several panes) and then heap this over with straw. The glass is raised about a foot so that air circulates underneath.

The beauty of Agapanthus lies in their magnificent umbels of flowers which are in most cases bright blue. These remain long in character and are particularly handsome in association with the long, smooth, strap-shaped leaves.

Grow the plants in rich soil and give them the warmest, sunniest possible position. Division in spring affords a ready means of increase.

A. africanus. African Lily. (*Plate 25, p. 112.*) Cape Peninsula. Flowers deep violet-blue, about 30 in an umbel. Var. *atro-caeruleus*, dark violet.   *18–20 in.   Summer.   2 ft. sq.*

A. campanulatus (syn. *umbellatus mooreanus*): S. Africa. Sky blue.
                                     1½ ft.   July–Sept.   2 ft. sq.

A. orientalis: S. & E. parts of S. Africa. The most commonly grown and a very variable species. There are varieties with larger blooms *maximus*; white flowers *albus* and *maximus albus*; *flore pleno* double; *variegatus* variegated foliage, *leichtlinii* a deep hyacinthine blue. The group is long-flowering, and a well-grown plant may produce 5 or 6 spikes each carrying over a 100 flowers in a season.
                                    1½–2 ft.   Summer.   2–3 ft. sq.

AGASTACHE (*Labiatae*): Mexican Bergamot. From *aga* (Gk) 'much' and *stachys* 'spike of wheat', alluding to the appearance of the flower spikes.

A small genus of perennials, only one of which is important in the border. This is *A. mexicana* (*Plate 24, p. 112*), originally introduced from Mexico by Dr. E. K. Balls in 1938 as *Brittonastrum mexicanum*. In appearance it more nearly resembles a slender Bergamot (*Monarda didyma*) being aromatic like that plant, and with rosy crimson, sage-like flowers. The leaves are somewhat nettle-like. It can be grown in any garden soil, but may need winter protection in all but the most favoured parts of the country. Propagation by seed, or division in spring.   *20–24 in.   July.   2 ft. sq.*

AJUGA (*Labiatae*): Bugle. Name said to be corrupted from Abiga, an allied plant.

Hardy, easily grown, carpeting plants, the perennials particularly suited to the damper parts of the garden. They do especially well on the heavier soils. Propagation by division.

A. genevensis. Geneva Bugle. (*Plate 1, p. 16.*) Europe. The most commonly grown species, with oblong, coarsely toothed, deep green leaves and spikes of sage-like flowers. These may be blue, rose or white. Var. *brockbankii* is a dwarf form with deep blue flowers. This species needs sun to produce its blooms.
                                    6–12 in.   June–July.   6 in. sq.

A. pyramidalis. Europe including Britain. A striking plant with oval-stalked basal leaves and stalkless stem ones, together with dense spikes of bright Gentian blue flowers.   *9 in.   April–June.   1 ft. sq.*

Plate 15: Campanula—1. WHITE PEACH-LEAVED BELLFLOWER, *persicifolia alba*. 2. COVENTRY BELLS, *trachelium*. 3. PEACHED-LEAVED BELLFLOWER, *persicifolia*. 4. *poscharskyana*. 5. DANESBLOOD, *glomerata*

Plate 16: 1. YELLOW WAXBELLS, *Kirengeshoma palmata.* 2. YELLOW HARDHEAD, *Centaurea macrocephala.* 3. CONEFLOWER, *Rudbeckia laciniata* 'Golden Glow'. 4. DOUBLE WELSH POPPY, *Meconopsis cambrica flore pleno.* 5. SUNDROPS, *Oenothera fruticosa major*

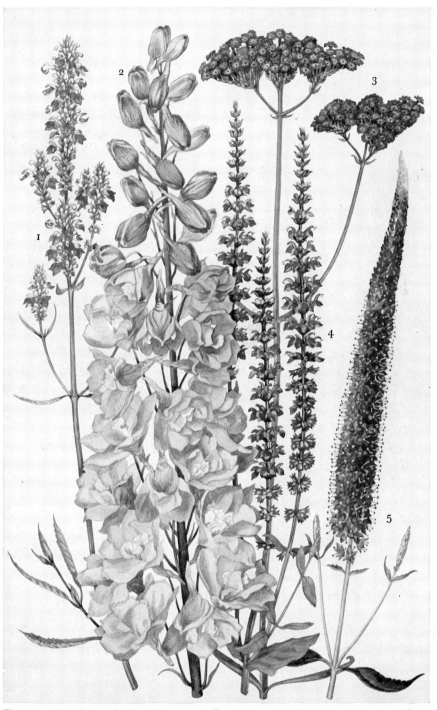

Plate 17: Bog Sage, *Salvia uliginosa.* 2. Bee Larkspur, *Delphinium elatum* seedling.
3. Verbena, *Verbena bonariensis.* 4. Sage, *Salvia × superba.* 5. Spiked Speedwell, *Veronica spicata* 'Romiley Purple'

Plate 18: 1. HIMALAYAN WHORLFLOWER, *Morina longifolia*. 2. FEATHERED BRONZE-LEAF, *Rodgersia pinnata elegans*. 3. PINK BURNING BUSH, *Dictamnus albus purpureus*. 4. BERGAMOT, *Monarda didyma* ' Cambridge Scarlet '

A. reptans. Common Bugle. Europe including Britain. Used more as a foliage plant than for its blue flowers, particularly varieties *variegata*, the leaves edged and splashed with creamy yellow (best grown in poor soil), and ' Rainbow ', foliage marbled with dark red, purple and yellow; *atropurpurea* and *multicolor* are also good foliage forms. All these kinds are useful for carpeting the soil in shady places and make admirable ground cover for lilies. *6–12 in. June–July. 1 ft. sq.*

ALSTROEMERIA (*Amaryllidaceae*): Peruvian Lily. Named after Baron Alstroemer, 18th century Swedish botanist and friend of Linnaeus.

This genus is composed of a number of highly coloured perennials, all native to South America. Many are perfectly hardy, at least in the west and southern half of the country, and in the more equable parts of America. The plant is nevertheless often given the reputation of being temperamental, and certainly it thrives for some and fails with others. Very often, however, such disappointments can be traced to incorrect planting in the first instance.

The rootstock is composed of thickened fibres, and unless these are well covered with soil the plants are not hardy. Underground growth starts very early in the year so that autumn or early spring is the best time for transplanting. Any hot dry situation suits them and because of transplanting difficulties it is advisable always to start with pot-grown plants. They must, however, be protected from frost for the first year, and the following represents a more or less fool-proof method which we have followed successfully for many years.

Excavate the soil at least 2 ft. deep and break the subsoil with a fork. Return 7 or 8 in. of sandy soil and brick rubble and plant the rootstocks in this. Barely cover the latter and leave. This means that a trench 15 or 16 in. deep lies above the crowns, and in case of frost the plants beneath should be protected with boards or twigs and straw. When growth commences in spring and the young shoots appear, add a little more soil, and continue in this manner—in the same way that you would fill a celery trench—until the hole is filled and the soil at normal ground level. In after years the *ligtu* and *aurantiaca* hybrids should prove perfectly hardy.

To be really effective Alstroemerias should be planted in bold groups, although care must be exercised in selecting neighbours which will not suffer by comparison with their vivid colours. Blue flowers like *Salvia superba*, Catananche, Scabious and Erigeron make good associates, also white flowers, but anything pink or red should be avoided. The blooms of Alstroemerias last well when cut, especially when only a little water is placed in the vase. If the latter is filled the stems soften and the spikes soon collapse. Always give the plants full sun and propagate by division or from seed.

A. aurantiaca. Chile. The best known and hardiest species, with long, smooth, leafy stems which terminate in striking umbels of orange flowers. These are frequently spotted with chocolate. Many fine forms have been derived from this species including *lutea*, yellow; ' Dover Orange ' and ' Moerheim Orange ', both improved forms of the type.   *3 ft.   June–Sept.   2 ft. sq.*

A. brasiliensis. Cent. Brazil. Needs the shelter of a warm wall if it is to winter out of doors. Flowers reddish yellow, spotted chocolate.
                                        3–4 ft.   July–Aug.   2 ft. sq.

A. chilensis. Chilean Alstroemeria. Chile. A very variable species with pink flowers which differ greatly in depth and intensity—from pale pink to bright red. Give a sheltered position and protect with litter, etc., during the worst of the weather.   *2 ft.   July.   1½ ft. sq.*

A. haemantha. Chile. Similar conditions to *A. chilensis.* Flowers bright red and yellow externally, and purple spotted inside. Many blooms on an umbel. There is a white form *albida*. *3 ft.   June–July.   2 ft. sq.*

A. ligtu (Plate 20, p. 96.). Chile. Perhaps the most beautiful hardy species. In 1933 Mr. Harold Comber introduced *A. ligtu* var. *angustifolia*, with pale pink flowers, from the Argentine Andes. After this plant received an Award of Merit from the Royal Horticultural Society, bulb growers crossed it with *A. haemantha* and produced the exciting and variously coloured *ligtu* hybrids so prized by gardeners to-day. These can be pink, orange, flame, yellow or rose and show a marked variation in habit and height. All are good for cutting. They do particularly well if grown in raised beds (see p. 36).
                                    1½–4 ft.   June–July.   2 ft. sq.

A. pelegrina. Chile. Less hardy than the others and only suitable outdoors in very mild districts. Flowers lilac, with yellow bases and purple blotches.   *1–2 ft.   June–Aug.   1 ft. sq.*

A. pulchella (syn. *A. psittacina*): Parrot Lily. N. Brazil. Unusual colouration, for the deep-red flowers are tipped with bright green.
                                        3 ft.   June–Sept.   2 ft. sq.

A. violacea. Chile. A species only hardy in very favoured situations, but characterised by the unusual colour of the flowers which are bright lilac. It has been crossed with *A. aurantiaca* and produced a variety known as ' Walter Fleming ' which is taller than the type (3 ft.) and has golden flowers flushed with rose outside but with maroon flecks inside.   *1–2 ft.   July.   1½ ft. sq.*

ALTHAEA *(Malvaceae)*: Hollyhock. From *altheo* (Gk.), ' to cure ', alluding to the plant's healing nature. The common Marsh Mallow (*A. officinalis*) contains a quantity of mucilage, particularly in the roots. These, when dried, may be peeled, and the thickened juices treated with sugar to make cough lozenges.

Hollyhocks (*Plate 20, p. 96*), (*A. rosea*), are the most important members of the genus and especially popular with those who love old-fashioned plants. Although perennial, they are best treated as biennials, raised from seed, planted outside in early May and moved again that autumn to their flowering quarters for the second year. When planting, ensure that the roots go straight down into the soil, with the crown about 2 inches below soil level. This encourages the roots to go after good anchorage and prevents rocking and wind disturbance later.

Double varieties of Hollyhocks come fairly true from seed but single varieties show considerable variation. If it is desired to perpetuate a special colour or variety, the plant should be lifted in spring and planted in sand in a frame to encourage the production of suckers. These are easily removed and rooted in sandy compost.

Hollyhocks grow in most reasonably fertile soils and are useful back of the border subjects. They look well associated with ' cottage ' plants—Lilies, Rosemary, blue Flax and also with the Plume Poppy (*Macleaya*), *Salvia* × *superba* and Michaelmas Daisies. Staking is necessary in windy situations.

Apart from the true *A. rosea* with rounded leaves, Antwerp Hollyhocks (*A. ficifolia*), with 5 or 7 angled, fig-like leaves are also grown. Both species come in many colours, from white, yellow and pink to deep red, and also parti-colours. Chaters Hybrids are a good strain of *A. rosea*. There are both single and double varieties, the best of the latter being ' Palling Belle ' pale pink, and ' Queen of Sheba ' primrose. *8 ft. July–Sept. 3 ft. sq.*

A. cannabina. S. France. A sturdy perennial with rose-pink flowers and divided leaves, which are coarsely toothed. Var. *narbonensis* is red.
6 ft. June. 3 ft. sq.

ALYSSUM (*Cruciferae*): Madwort. From *a* (Gk.) ' not ' *lyssa* ' madness'; it is reputed to cure hydrophobia.

Most Alyssums are rock garden plants or annuals, but the perennial species are somewhat woody and persist in winter. *A. saxatile* and its varieties are invaluable for the front of the border in early spring. They bloom before most other plants and the rich gold flowers are particularly welcome after winter's cold. They grow readily in ordinary well-drained soil, and should be given a sunny situation. Propagation by seed, or cuttings taken in early summer and rooted under a cloche in a shady spot.

The type plant has bright gold flowers and silver downy foliage, but excellent forms are *citrinum* (' Silver Queen '), lemon yellow; ' Dudley Neville ', sulphur; *plenum*, full gold double; ' Tom Thumb ' a dwarf form, and *variegatum*, leaves variegated in yellow and green.
6–12 in. May and June. 1½ ft. sq.

AMSONIA (*Apocynaceae*). Named after Dr. Charles Amson, an 18th century scientific traveller in America.

North American perennials, only valuable as garden plants when well grown. They must have deep soil and partial shade. Quantities of pale blue, small tubular flowers are borne on terminal heads, and the leaves are smooth and willow shaped. Propagation by division, seeds or cuttings taken in summer.

A. angustifolia: Feather Amsonia. Flowers periwinkle blue.

1–3 ft. Summer. 1 ft. sq.

A. tabernaemontana: Willow Amsonia. (*Plate 10, p. 49.*) Flowers pale blue and slightly hairy outside.   *1½–2½ ft. Summer. 1 ft. sq.*

ANAPHALIS (*Compositae*): Pearl Everlasting. Old Greek name for a similar plant.

Grey foliaged plants with crowded heads of ' everlasting ' flowers which are usually white and round. They are useful in dividing brightly coloured neighbours and are not unattractive in their own right. Well-drained soil is essential, in fact they will even grow at the edge of a gravel path. Propagation by division or cuttings in spring.

A. margaritacea. N. America, N.E. Asia. Flower heads very numerous, pearly white.   *1–2 ft. August. 1 ft. sq.*

A. triplinervis. Himalayas. Willow-like, densely hairy, white woolly leaves, flowers white.   *1½ ft. August. 1 ft. sq.*

A. yedoensis. Himalaya. A recent introduction with strong upright stems carrying compact heads of white semi-everlasting flowers. Good for cutting.   *1½ ft. July–Sept. 1 ft. sq.*

ANCHUSA (*Boraginaceae*): Bugloss. From *anchousa* (Gk) ' skin paint ', from the use of the roots in dyeing.

Coarse growing perennials with handsome bright blue flowers on rough, hairy stems. Some of the varieties of *A. azurea* when well grown rival the Delphinium for colour and spectacular effect. Grown in a mixed border they become particularly useful in early summer, and associate happily with Pyrethrums, Heuchera and golden Anthemis. Best results come from raising fresh stock annually; the old roots should be lifted after flowering and cut up into segments for root cuttings (see p. 64). Later the young plants can be put back in the border during the autumn tidying. Root cuttings can also be taken about February, but the former method gives better plants.

Anchusas need to be grown in well-drained soil, and ash or sand should be incorporated with the soil at planting time by those gardening on heavy clay. A sunny position is also advisable, and the plants look best in a mid-border position. Most of the species are attractive to bees.

A. azurea (syn. *A. italica*): Italian Bugloss. This is the commonest species and has large blue or blue-purple flowers. The varieties from this should, however, be grown in preference to the type, particularly 'Opal', pale blue; 'Pride of Dover', mid-blue; 'Morning Glory' (*Plate 11, p. 64*), dark blue with a spreading habit, 'Dropmore', deep blue; and 'Royal Blue', very large, deep Gentian blue.

3–5 ft.   Summer.   3 ft. sq.

A. caespitosa. Crete. A beautiful plant with narrow, rough leaves and sprays of intense blue flowers. Given a well-drained but rich soil and half-shaded situation the spikes may reach 12–15 in. The crowns should be protected against damp in winter.

1 ft.   July–August.   1 ft. sq.

A. sempervirens. Evergreen Bugloss. Europe including Britain. A stout bristly plant, with rich deep-green leaves and large deep blue, forget-me-not like flowers. It is useful for woodland planting.

1–2 ft.   May and June.   2 ft sq.

ANEMONE (*Ranunculaceae*): Windflower. From *anemos* (Gk), 'wind', because the flowers are easily swayed by wind.

A large family of generally hardy perennials, the majority of which are more suited to the rock garden, but a few make good border subjects. The species are valuable for various reasons. Some bloom very early in the season, others at the tail end, whilst several—including the well-known Japanese Anemones (*A. hupehensis*)—will thrive in extremely shady parts of the garden. Most of the border Anemones grow in ordinary garden soil, particularly if this is enriched occasionally with vegetable material (leafmould and peat). Generally speaking they are plants to leave alone when happily situated. Propagation varies and is given under each species.

A. canadensis. Meadow Anemone. N. America. Has several white starry blossoms, on a stem in May, with successional bloom intermittently all summer. It likes shade. Seed.   *1–2 ft.   May.   1½ ft. sq.*

A. caroliniana. E. United States. A shade loving species with tuberous rootstock and slender stems carrying solitary purple or whitish flowers. Seed.   *9 in.   May.   1 ft. sq.*

A. dichotoma. Meadow Anemone (*Plate III, p. 208*). E. United States. A shade-loving Anemone with several pure white flowers on a branching stem, and deeply cut leaves. Propagation by division.

1–2 ft.   May.   1 ft. sq.

A. hupehensis. Japanese Anemone. China. There is good reason to believe that this is the original wild form from which garden varieties of the so-called Japanese Anemone have been derived. Prior to its introduction from Hupeh (c. 1908), all varieties of Japanese Anemones in gardens had been obtained from the plants sent home by Fortune in 1844. The true species is pink and has five sepals, but most of the garden forms bear many more and vary in colour. Var. *elegans* (*Plate XIV, p. 241*) is an improved form. Propagation by root cuttings.

The best of the garden varieties, *A.* × *hybrida*, which are usually catalogued under the name *A. japonica* are:

Alice, semi-double, fuchsia pink.

Charmeuse, pink, double.

Herzblut, very bright deep red, semi-double, flowers small.

Honorine Jobert, a fine white form which arose as a sport from a red-flowered variety in the garden of a French banker, M. Jobert, in 1858.

Kriemhilde, semi-double, pale pink.

Lorelei, soft rose-pink.

Louise Uhink, large, white, semi-double.

Margarete, semi-double, large pink.

Max Vogel, semi-double, rosy-pink, *2 ft.*

Montrose, soft rose.

Prince Henry, purplish-pink.

Profusion, semi-double, red, rather dwarf, *2 ft.*

Queen Charlotte, deep pink.

September Charm, very large pink flowers.

Whirlwind (*Plate XIV, p. 241*), semi-double white.

$3\frac{1}{2}$ *ft. Sept. and Oct. 2 ft. sq.*

A. × *lesseri*. A fine variety of garden origin derived from *A. sylvestris* × *A. multifida*. Has rich orchid purple flowers early in the year. Grow in light shade. Root cuttings. $1\frac{1}{2}$–*2 ft. May–June. 2 ft. sq.*

A. narcissiflora. N. America, Europe. A beautiful plant for light shade with handsome, Buttercup-like basal leaves and white, cream or sometimes purplish flowers *1–2* in. across. Seed. *1–2 ft. May. 1 ft. sq.*

A. rivularis. N. India, Ceylon. Flowers white with a blue reverse. Requires light shade and a moist soil. Propagated from seed.

1–2 ft. April. 1 ft. sq.

A. sylvestris. Snowdrop Windflower. (*Plate I, p. 192.*) Dainty, snow white drooping flowers with bright gold stamens; fragrant. Leafy soil and light shade. Seed heads woolly. Propagated from seed.

6–18 in. April. 1 ft. sq.

A. virginiana. N. America. A pretty species for moist soil and light shade, with pale purplish flowers. Seed. *2 ft. May. 1 ft. sq.*

A. vitifolia (syn. *A. tomentosa*): Vine-leaved Windflower. (*Plate 30, p. 129.*) Upper Nepal. Will grow in considerable shade. Flowers white, leaves large and heart-shaped, white woolly on the undersides and stems. Propagated by root cuttings. Var. ' Albadura ' is pinkish-white.

2 ft. July. 2 ft. sq.

A. vitifolia var. *robustissima*. A more vigorous variety with pink flowers which may rightly belong to *hupehensis*. Propagation from root cuttings.

3 ft. Aug.–Oct. 2 ft. sq.

ANEMONOPSIS (*Ranunculaceae*). Greek name meaning ' like anemone '. One species, needing light, leafy soil. Propagated by seed or division in spring.

A. macrophylla. Japan. Loose racemes of flowers, purple without and lilac inside; leaves large and coarsely toothed.

2–3 ft. July. 2 ft. sq.

ANTHEMIS (*Compositae*): Chamomile. From *anthos* (Gk) ' flower ', an allusion to its free-flowering habit.

Handsome perennials with elegantly cut foliage and quantities of daisy flowers which are mostly white or yellow. Chamomile (*A. nobilis*) belongs to this family, a plant much esteemed for its tonic properties, but most of the other species have traces of the same pungent scent we associate with the true Chamomile.

The kinds listed will grow in practically any soil, provided it is well drained. They also like sun. The blooms are long lasting both on the plant and cut, but when first gathered they should be plunged to the necks in water for four or five hours before arranging. Normally the plants bloom from early summer until August, but continuity is easily assured by having two clumps. Allow one to flower at the normal time, but, as the other comes to bud, cut the flower stems off with shears. The roots then set to work to make new flowers and these will bloom just as those in the first group start to die. Increase by division, cuttings or seed.

A. cupaniana. Italy. Cushion-forming habit, the silvery-grey fern-like foliage attractive even when the plant has ceased to flower. Flower heads large, white, good for cutting. The plant is apt to sprawl and must sometimes be staked. *1 ft. June–Sept. 2 ft. sq.*

A. montana (syn. *A. macedonica*): White Chamomile. (*Plate II, p. 193.*) Syria.

A. nobilis var. *plena*. White single flowers used for Chamomile lawns, can be employed at the front of the border. Double white flowers.

3 in. July–Sept. 6 in. sq.

A. sancti-johannis. Bulgaria. A first-class plant which surprisingly has only been known to gardens in recent years. Dr. Turrill of Kew noted it during the First World War in Bulgaria, and after the cessation of hostilities went back and collected plants. It is a subject which must have a well-drained soil and full sun, and has a tendency at times to flower itself to death. Seedlings, however, come more or less true if the plant is isolated from other Anthemis. There is a larger-flowered, darker coloured form known as 'Merstham Variety'. The type is bright orange, with blooms $1\frac{1}{2}$ to 2 in. across.

$1\frac{1}{2}$ ft.   Summer.   2 ft. sq.

A. tinctoria. Ox-Eye Chamomile. Europe, including Britain. A fine plant with large, single, golden-yellow flowers in July and August. These are gathered by the French for the fine yellow dye they yield. Foliage much cut, downy beneath.

For garden purposes any of the following varieties will be grown in preference to the type:

Beauty of Grallagh, deep golden-yellow, *$2\frac{1}{2}$–3 ft.*

E. C. Buxton, lemon-yellow, *$2\frac{1}{2}$ ft.*

Golden Dawn, golden-yellow, full double, *2 ft.*

Grallagh Gold (*Plate 14, p. 65*), golden-yellow, flowers nearly 3 in. across, *$2\frac{1}{2}$ ft.*

Loddon, rich deep Buttercup-yellow, *3 ft.* Sometimes dies out after one or two seasons.

Moonlight, pale yellow, *$2\frac{1}{2}$ ft.*

Perry's Var., golden-yellow, *$2\frac{1}{2}$ ft.*

Thora Perry, grey foliage, deep gold flowers, *2 ft.*

All these varieties are excellent for cutting and need to be planted 2 ft. apart. Seed will not reproduce true, but division is an effective means of increase in spring or autumn. Do not plant them in too rich a soil, and remember they want full sun.

ANTHERICUM (*Liliaceae*) : From *antherikos* (Gk) 'wheat stalk ', alluding to the appearance of the flower spike.

Liliaceous plants with non-bulbous roots, suitable for the front of the border. Grow in a rich but light soil, and when in exposed positions protect them from the north-east. For best effects plant in groups of four or more, in places where they may remain undisturbed for years. A mulch of well-rotted manure in spring helps the flowers. Propagation by division or seed sown as soon as gathered.

A. liliago. St. Bernard's Lily. S. Europe. Narrow, grassy, channelled leaves and handsome spikes of white, lily-like flowers. Var. *major* is a larger counterpart of the type.   *$1\frac{1}{2}$ ft.   May and June. $1\frac{1}{2}$ ft. sq.*

A. ramosum. W. & S. Europe. Resembles a smaller-flowered form of *A. liliago.*   *2 ft.   June–July. $1\frac{1}{2}$ ft. sq.*

ANTIRRHINUM (*Scrophulariaceae*): Snapdragon. From *anti* (Gk) ' like ', ' *rhin* ' snout, from the shape of the flowers.

A large family of ornamental plants, the majority grown as annuals. They like well-drained soil and a little lime. The following species are useful to the gardener in special circumstances. Propagation by seed.

A. asarina. S. France. Scrambling habit, white flowers with a yellow

throat, and sticky rounded leaves. Will grow in practically bone-dry
positions. Only hardy when comparatively dry in winter.

3 in. June–Sept. 1 ft. sq.

A. glutinosum. Spain. Not too hardy. Very similar conditions to *A.
asarina.* Flowers yellowish-white, with lip striped red. Var. *roseum,*
pale pink. *3 in. July. 1 ft. sq.*

AQUILEGIA (*Ranunculaceae*): Columbine. From *aquila* (L) eagle, the
nectaries of the flower having a supposed resemblance to the eagle's
claw.

Old garden favourites, happy under ordinary border conditions
provided that the soil does not dry out in summer or become water-
logged in winter. For best effects give them partial shade, such as the
dappled light near the fringe of trees, and let the seed drop round the
parents, so forming wide colonies. In the border they will stand full
sun, but the blooms pass more quickly.

Aquilegias associate well with Lupins, bearded Irises and Daylilies, and generally speaking, should be given a front to mid-border
position.

Some of the flowers have short nectary tubes or spurs at the back
of the blooms, but in others these can be as long as or nearly as long
as the flower itself. Propagation by seed sown in spring, or the named
sorts must be divided.

A. alpina. Switzerland. Low growing, for the front of the border with
nodding deep blue, or blue and white flowers. The variety 'Hensole
Harebell' is a particularly fine hybrid from this plant and *A. vulgaris,*
with deep-blue flowers. *1 ft. May–June. 1 ft. sq.*

A. caerulea. Rocky Mountains. The State flower of Colorado, this species
has soft lavender blue and creamy-white flowers, with long slender
spurs. Var. *ochroleuca* is white or cream. 'Celestial Blue', blue and
white, 2½ ft. *1–2 ft. April–July. 1 ft. sq.*

A. canadensis. American Columbine. Nova Scotia. Flowers several on a
stem, lemon yellow with yellow and red tinged sepals.

1–2 ft. May–June. 1 ft. sq.

A. chrysantha. Golden Columbine. New Mexico. Free-flowering, each
bloom 2–3 in. across, pale yellow, tinged pink with deep gold petals.

3–4 ft. May–Aug. 1½ ft. sq.

A. clematiflora hybrida. A strain with no spurs, and of various shades of
pink and blue. *2–4 ft. May–July. 1½ ft. sq.*

A. flabellata. Japan. A beautiful species with nodding white flowers,
tinged violet-rose. There is a pure white variety called 'Munstead
White', or sometimes *nivea* or *nana alba*, which when in flower, is
reminiscent of a flight of tiny white birds. *6–10 in. May–July. 9 in. sq.*

A. formosa: Sitka Columbine. Western N. America. Resembling *A. canadensis* but larger. Flowers yellow or brick-red and yellow, spurs long. Many of the long-spurred strains of the garden are in part derived from this species. *2 ft. May–Aug. 1 ft. sq.*

A. fragrans. Himalayas. Flowers white or pale purple, fragrant and downy. Needs a sheltered position. *1½ ft. May–July. 1 ft. sq.*

A. × *hybrida*: Most of the perennial garden forms have a very mixed background and parentage. Several good strains have been evolved, which although the colours may vary, can be relied upon to throw good flowers. All flower between May and June. They should be given an area of approximately 1 ft. sq. In this group may be included:

Crimson star, large crimson sepals and spurs and white petals; very sturdy and free-flowering, *1½ ft.*

Mrs. Scott-Elliott Hybrids, long-spurred, colours crimson, purple, blue and pink, *3 ft.*

Pearson's Sky Blue, light blue, *3 ft.*

Rose Queen, soft rose and white, *3 ft.*

Snow Queen, pure white, *1½ ft.*

A. longissima. Texas. Flowers pale yellow with very long spurs (4 in. or more). Attractive, deeply cut leaves.

2 ft. July–Oct. 1½ ft. sq.

A. vulgaris. Granny's Bonnet. Europe, including Britain. Well-known plant with short spurs and variously coloured blooms. The species has produced many garden forms, including doubles. Indifferent seedlings should be rogued and only the better forms kept.

2 ft. May–June. 1½ ft. sq.

ARMERIA (*Plumbaginaceae*): Thrift. From *Flos Armeria*, an old name for one of the Sweet William Pinks.

Hardy evergreen plants, with round heads of flowers and grassy leaves. Mostly suited to the rock garden with the exception of those listed below. Thrifts will thrive in any soil which is well drained and exposed to the sun. They are propagated by division or seed sown as soon as ripe.

A. maritima, Thrift. Sea Pink. Europe incl. Britain. Useful edging or front of the border plant with rich green grassy foliage which persists in winter and rose, pink or white rounded flower-heads. Var. *alba*, white, var. *laucheana*, deep rose, var. *variegata* golden-yellow leaves.

½–1 ft. June–July. 1 ft. sq.

A. plantaginea. Cent. and S. Europe. Of tufted habit with long strap-like leaves and large, round, dense heads of pink flowers. Var. ' Bee's Ruby ' is bright ruby red. *1½ ft. June–July. 1 ft. sq.*

A. pseudoarmeria (syn. *A. cephalotes*): Giant Thrift. S. Europe. Larger

forms known as *A. gigantea (Plate 20, p. 96.)* Colours various, from pale pink to brick red. Stout stems, good for cutting, the variety *formosa* being particularly fine. Foliage grass-like, hugging the ground.
1½ ft. Summer. 1 ft. sq.

ARNEBIA (*Boraginaceae*). Old Arabic name.
A. echioides. Prophet Flower. Mediterranean Region, Armenia. An interesting front of the border perennial, with rough narrow leaves and spikes of tubular flowers which are bright primrose yellow on opening with a black spot at the base of each petal. This disappears as the flower ages. Propagated by seed or heel cuttings in autumn. Well-drained soil and sun. *9–12 in. May. 9 in. sq.*

ARTEMISIA (*Compositae*): From *Artemis* (Diana), Goddess of the Chase.
A group of plants, many of them shrubby, which are chiefly noted for their attractive, and often aromatic foliage. Several are useful for border work, particularly when used as a foil or background for brightly coloured subjects. Soil requirements vary; *A. lactiflora* will thrive in very moist and shaded situations, but others come from arid regions and need light, well-drained soil and sun. Propagation of the border kinds by division in spring.

A. gnaphalodes. N. America. Leaves small but densely white with down on both sides. Flowers insignificant, greenish white.
2–4 ft. Sept. 2 ft. sq.

A. lactiflora: White Mugwort. (*Plate XV, p. 256.*) China, India. Makes a large plant with Chrysanthemum-like foliage and creamy-white plumes of flowers in late summer. A good border plant and valuable for floral work. *4–5 ft. Autumn. 3 ft. sq.*

A. ludoviciana. N. America. Entire leaves completely covered with white down and large panicles of tiny brown and white flowers.
2–4 ft. Autumn. 2 ft. sq.

A. nutans. Sicily. A shrubby plant grown for its silvery-grey foliage, which is useful for associating with Lobelias, Chrysanthemums or Phlox. Winter indoors or protect against excessive damp. Var. ' Silver Queen ' is an improved form. *2½ ft. Flowers should be removed. 2 ft. sq.*

A. purshiana: Cudweed Wormwood. Western N. America. A very downy plant with long narrow leaves, heavily felted on both sides and slender spikes of whitish flowers. *2–3 ft. Sept. 1½ ft. sq.*

A. scoparia. Oriental Wormwood. Orient. Has small whitish flowers crowded closely on slender stems and silvery divided leaves.
3–5 ft. Sept. 2 ft. sq.

A. stelleriana: Dusty Miller. N. America. Perhaps the best species for

border use, the finely cut, grey, mealy foliage reaching a height of
2 ft. Particularly fine in association with scarlet *Lobelia fulgens* or blue
Aster frikarti. It has become naturalised in parts of Britain.

2–3 ft.   Late summer.   2 ft. sq.

ARUNCUS (*Rosaceae*): Goat's Beard.
A small genus of moisture-loving perennials which need a deep,
rich soil and some shade. Propagation by seed or division.

A. sylvester (syn. *Spiraea aruncus*.) (*Plate XII, p. 240*.) Siberia. A handsome
plant with fine, pinnate foliage and impressive plumes of creamy-
white flowers. The whole plant is very Spiraea-like, but being non-
shrubby is relegated to a distinct genus. Var. ' *kneiffii* ' has finely cut
foliage.   *4 ft.   June.   3 ft. sq.*

ASCLEPIAS (*Asclepiadaceae*): Milkweed or Silkweed. From *Aesculapius*,
Graeco-Roman God of Medicine.
Handsome border plants, thriving in most soils providing these do
not dry out. Very vigorous; care should be taken to prevent excessive
spreading. Some species are suitable only for the wild garden.
Propagated by seed or division.

A. hallii. Western N. America. A stout species, whorls of tough oval
oblong leaves and umbels of dull pink flowers.   *2–4 ft. Aug. 2 ft. sq.*

A. incarnata. Swamp Milkweed. N. America. A striking plant with
umbels of flesh-coloured flowers and lance-like leaves. The whole plant
is very smooth and has a somewhat fleshy appearance. There is a
white form, *alba* (*Plate XV, p. 256*). Both like a moist soil.

2–4 ft.   July–Aug.   2 ft. sq.

A. purpurascens. Eastern N. America. A sturdy plant with erect stems
clothed with oval, pointed leaves, downy beneath and umbels of
reddish-purple flowers.   *2–4 ft.   July.   2 ft. sq.*

A. speciosa. N. America. Has fragrant lilac-purple flowers on greyish
downy stems.   *2–3 ft.   June–Aug.   2 ft. sq.*

A. syriaca. Silkweed. Eastern N. America. A fragrant species with
purple flowers.   *3–5 ft.   July.   3 ft. sq.*

A. tuberosa. Butterfly Weed. (*Plate 14, p. 65*.) Eastern N. America.
Requires a sandy soil and sun; produces umbels of bright orange
coloured flowers, which cut well and last in water. The stems are
downy and clothed with small oblong leaves, arranged alternately up
to the flower heads.   *1½ ft.   July–Aug.   2 ft. sq.*

ASPHODELINE (*Liliaceae*). From *a* (Gk) ' not ', *spallo* ' surpass ',
that is, not exceeded in beauty.

A genus of lily-like plants with spikes of funnel-shaped flowers and grassy leaves. The fleshy roots will grow in practically any soil and should be propagated by division. Plant them in spring or autumn.

A. imperialis. Cappadocia. A back of the border subject with long straight stems carrying large reddish-white flowers. The leaves grow in a large rosette, some of them on the flower stems.

6–8 ft. July. 3 ft. sq.

A. lutea. Jacob's Rod, King's Spear. (*Plate 14, p. 65.*) Mediterranean Region. Flowers bell-shaped, soft yellow, starry-looking on the spikes, and fragrant. Var. *flore pleno* is similar, with double flowers.

3–4 ft. June–July. 2 ft. sq.

A. taurica. Asia Minor. Straight erect stems covered with white flowers, striped down the petals with green. 1–2 ft. June. 1 ft. sq.

ASPHODELUS (*Liliaceae*): Asphodel. Name derivation similar to Asphodeline.

Fleshy rooted plants with similar habit to Asphodeline. They are hardy and attractive. A deep sandy loam suits them best although they will grow in most soils. Propagation by division in spring.

A. albus. (*Plate II, p. 193.*) S. Europe. Has smooth grassy leaves, with a triangular shaped or keeled midrib, and naked flower stems covered with clusters of white, bell-shaped flowers. 2 ft. May. 1½ ft. sq.

A. cerasiferus. S. Europe. A more robust and branching species. Leaves sword-shaped, keeled as in *albus* but larger. The flowers are large, white, but sometimes brownish at the base. Many blooms are carried on each stem which makes the plant quite spectacular when in flower.

4–5 ft. Early Summer. 2 ft. sq.

A. microcarpus (syn. *A. ramosus*). S. Europe, N. Africa. Flat, leathery, strap-like leaves, rather thick and with a prominently pointed tip. Funnel-shaped flowers, pure white with a purplish stripe down the middle of each segment. The flower spikes branch freely and make an impressive display. 3 ft. April–May. 1½ ft. sq.

ASTER (*Compositae*): Michaelmas Daisy. From *aster* (Gk) 'star', from the appearance of the flowers.

A large and beautiful genus of wide distribution, one at least (Sea Starwort, *A. tripolium*) native to Great Britain. But the group is in the main peculiarly a North American one, the woods and fields of that country producing a great variety of species and forms. The first record of the Michaelmas Daisy in this country appears in 1633, when it was introduced by John Tradescant, a keen botanist, who with his father gave many new flowers to English gardens. The elder Tradescant was gardener to King Charles I, and in his lifetime collected one of the finest natural history museums ever known in this country. It is still in existence and now housed in the Ashmolean Museum at Oxford. *Aster tradescantii*, the first Michaelmas Daisy, commemorates the name of these useful botanists.

Michaelmas Daisies do well in either town or country, and are particularly useful for late summer and autumn work in the border. Many of the main groups, viz. *novae-angliae*, *novi-belgii* and *amellus*, have received attention from plant breeders, so that to-day it is possible to have varieties from 6 in. to 5 ft. tall, in a wide range of colours. The late Ernest Ballard probably did more for this genus than any other grower, and most of the best garden forms are of his raising.

Asters are not particular as to soil, but do need constant supplies of moisture during the growing season. They have fibrous rootstocks, which (with the exception of *A. amellus* and a few others) move well in autumn or spring; *A. amellus* should only be transplanted in spring. But, the roots are mat-like and invasive so need dividing about every third year; a practice which also provides a continuity of new stock. They grow best in full sun and can be given a front, back or mid-border position according to variety.

Perennial Asters associate well with *Chrysanthemum rubellum*, the latter providing the deep reds and yellows lacking in the former genus; but they also contrast happily with Red Hot Pokers, White Mugwort (*Artemisia lactiflora*) and Golden Rod. For best effects plant each variety in groups of 3, 5 or 7 (according to the size of the border) with 18 in. between the plants. Staking will be necessary with the taller varieties, and also certain of the newer, large-flowered types such as ' Peace '. Propagation by division or soft cuttings in spring.

A. acris. S. Europe. An attractive front to middle border species with erect, bushy habit, tiny, bright-green leaves and clustered heads of irregular light-violet flowers. These pale ray florets enclose a golden centre. The whole plant has powerful acrid properties and when bruised smells strongly of carrot.   *2 ft. August. 1½ ft. sq.*

A. acris var. ' Mrs. Berkeley '. Distinct and interesting with white flowers.
                                            1 ft. August. 1 ft. sq.

A. acris var. *nanus*. A dwarf form of the type, useful for edging purposes. The flowers are lavender-mauve.   *1 ft. August. 1 ft. sq.*

A. amellus. Italian Starwort. Europe and Western Asia. The earliest known member of the genus, and widely distributed in the wild state on limestone formations in Southern Europe. This fact should be recognised in the garden, and lime applied on heavy or sour soils.

In the garden *A. amellus* and its varieties are strikingly effective because of the large flowers (often 2½ in. across), the broad bright florets and prominent gold centres. Staking is not necessary as a rule, but the plants must not be transplanted in autumn.

The following named varieties are all worth growing:

Advance, deep violet-blue, similar to 'King George' but about two weeks later. *2 ft. Sept. 2 ft. sq.*

Bessie Chapman, rich violet-blue. *2½ ft. Aug.–Oct. 2 ft. sq.*

Heinrich Seibert, pinkish-violet, very large. *2 ft. Aug. 2 ft. sq.*

King George (*Plate 29, p. 128*), one of the oldest, having been introduced before the First World War. Deep violet-blue flowers. *1½ ft. July–Sept. 1½ ft. sq.*

Lady Hindlip, deep rose-pink, perhaps the best in this shade. *2½ ft. Aug.–Oct. 2 ft. sq.*

Mauve Beauty, large single mauve. *2 ft. Sept.–Oct. 2 ft. sq.*

Moerheim Gem, bright deep blue. *2 ft. Aug.–Oct. 2 ft. sq.*

Mrs. Ralph Woods, large rosy-pink florets. *2½ ft. Aug.–Oct. 2 ft. sq.*

Nocturne, a fairly new variety characterised by exceptionally strong growth and large rosy-lavender flowers. *2½ ft. Aug.–Oct. 2 ft. sq.*

Red Fire, of German origin this variety is also known as Rotfeur. The flowers are a good red, perhaps the deepest in shade in the group. *2 ft. Aug.–Oct. 2 ft. sq.*

Rudolf Goethe (syn. 'Queen Mary'), large, pale mauve. *2½ ft. Sept.–Oct. 2 ft. sq.*

Sonia, lovely shade of rosy-pink. *2 ft. July–Aug. 1½ ft. sq.*

Ultramarine, deep violet-blue. This is a very old variety but still holds its own in a mixed border. *2 ft. July–Aug. 1½ ft. sq.*

A. cordifolius: Blue Wood Aster. N. America. Received its common name from the fact that in its native habitat the plant likes to grow in light shade under trees. Another old American name for it is Beeweed, doubtless referring to the attraction the flowers have for bees and insects. The leaves are heart-shaped and roughly hairy, although the flowers as individuals are extremely small, varying from ½ to ¾ inch in diameter. However, as many thousands of these blooms are carried on dense arching sprays from a single plant, the general effect is very striking.

The following varieties merit attention:

Ideal, pale blue. *3 ft. Aug.–Sept. 3 ft. sq.*

Photograph (*Plate XIV, p. 241*), pale blue. *3½ ft. Aug.–Sept. 3 ft. sq.*

Silver Spray, arching sprays of pale lilac flowers. *5 ft. Sept.–Oct. 3 ft. sq.*

A. dracunculoides. (*Plate 29, p. 128*.) Russia. Also known as a variety of *A. acris*; small flower heads, purple; linear oblong leaves.

2 ft. or more. Aug. 1½ ft. sq.

A. ericoides. Heath Aster. E.N. America. This is a species which will live and thrive in much drier conditions than most of the genus. The habit is so attractive—with fresh, heather-like foliage and long arching sprays of tiny flowers—that it deserves to be more widely grown. When cut the sprays last several weeks in water and make delightful contrast with the larger flowered kinds.

There are several garden varieties, the height of which varies from $1\frac{1}{2}$ to 4 ft. The taller of these need staking as the flower sprays are often very heavy. All must have plenty of sun and like a well-drained soil.

Blue Star, pale lilac. *2½ ft. Aug.–Sept. 2 ft. sq.*

Brimstone, sprays studded with tiny yellow florets. *2½ ft. Aug.–Sept. 2 ft. sq.*

Chastity, white. *2½ ft. Aug.– Oct. 2½ ft. sq.*

Delight, graceful sprays studded with tiny, white, golden-eyed flowers. *2½ ft. Aug.–Sept. 2 ft. sq.*

Enchantress, bluish-pink. *3 ft. Aug.–Sept. 2½ ft. sq.*

Perfection, pale lavender blue. *3½ ft. Aug.–Sept. 3 ft. sq.*

Ringdove, rosy lavender. *3 ft. Aug.–Sept. 2½ ft. sq.*

Star Shower, pale lilac. *2½ ft. Aug.–Oct. 2½ ft. sq.*

White Heather, white. *2½ ft. Aug.–Oct. 2½ ft. sq.*

A. farreri. Tibet. Named after Reginald Farrer the great plant collector who introduced it in 1914. The plant forms tufts of rough, oblong narrow leaves and bears several stems each of which carries a large, single, bright violet-blue flower with a golden centre. It blooms best in poor soil, being apt to make too much leaf in a rich medium.

12–15 in. May–June. 1 sq. ft.

A. farreri var. ' *Berggarten* '. An improved form of the type with exceptionally large flowers. These are good for cutting.

1½–2 ft. May–June. 1½ ft. sq.

A. × frikartii. A name coined for a group of seedlings of *A. thomsonii* × *A. amellus.* These were raised by a Mons. Frikart of Switzerland, and although they do not set fertile seed, can be easily propagated from slips or division. Their chief merit is freedom of flowering, the plants being in bloom almost continuously from July until late September. The type has sky-blue flowers with yellow eyes. The blue is deeper in the variety ' Wonder of Staffa '. *2½ ft. July–Sept. 2 ft. sq.*

A. grandiflorus. Christmas Daisy. E. United States. The latest flowering species, blooms even persisting into November and December in more sheltered parts of the country. It produces stiff, reddish, hairy and leafy stems crowned with branches. Each of these carries a single 2-inch, deep violet flower at their extreme tip.

2–2½ ft. Sept.–Nov. 2 ft. sq.

A. linosyris. Yellow Aster, Goldilocks. Europe, incl. Britain. A good autumn perennial with bright yellow flowers, often without ray florets, which associates happily with the blues of other species. It is not fastidious, growing well anywhere; propagation by division.

1½–2 ft. Aug.–Sept. 1 ft. sq.

Plate 19: DAYLILIES, *Hemerocallis*—1. SANDSTONE.   2. PINK LADY.   3. HIAWATHA.
4. PAUL BOISSIER.   5. *fulva.*   6. *forrestii*

Plate 20: 1. PERUVIAN LILY, *Alstroemeria ligtu.* 2. QUEEN OF THE PRAIRIE, *Filipendula rubra venusta magnifica.* 3. GIANT THRIFT, *Armeria gigantea.* 4. HOLLYHOCK, *Althaea rosea.* 5. GIANT DEADNETTLE, *Lamium orvala*

Plate 21: 1. MASTERWORT, *Astrantia carniolica.* 2. BABY'S BREATH, *Gypsophila paniculata* 'Rosy Veil'. 3. PRAIRIE MALLOW, *Sidalcea malvaeflora* 'Rose Queen'. 4. BLANKET FLOWER, *Gaillardia aristata.* 5. HIMALAYAN CINQUEFOIL, *Potentilla atrosanguinea* 'Gibson's Scarlet'

Plate 22: 1. Rose Himalayan Knotweed, *Polygonum campanulatum roseum*. 2. Bears' Breeches, *Acanthus spinosus*. 3. Japanese Burnet, *Sanguisorba obtusa*

A. novae-angliae. New England Aster. United States. A tall-growing species distinguished from *novi-belgii* by its rough leaves and greater number of ray florets. The type has given rise to several good varieties, all of which are useful for back of the border work. They come into flower just after the *amellus* section and last well into the autumn. Staking is not generally necessary; the blooms are not so good for cutting as the *novi-belgii* types, since they show a tendency to close in artificial light.

Named varieties are:

Barr's Blue, purple-blue, resembling ' Barr's Pink ' in habit. *3½ ft. Aug.–Sept. 2½ ft. sq.*

Barr's Pink, a very old plant with bright rose-purple flowers. These have a prominent gold centre and are attractive to Red Admiral butterflies. *3½–4 ft. Aug.–Sept. 2½ ft. sq.*

Crimson Beauty, rich rose-crimson with gold eye. *4½ ft. Oct. 2 ft. sq.*

Harrington's Pink (*Plate 29, p. 128*), the first really pink Aster, introduced from America between the World Wars. The blooms are a warm rose shade. *4 ft. Aug.–Sept. 3 ft. sq.*

Incomparabilis, a dwarf variety from America with bright cyclamen-purple florets. *2½ ft. Aug.–Sept. 2½ ft. sq.*

Mrs. S. T. Wright, rosy-mauve, deepening to purple; gold eye. *4 ft. Sept.–Oct. 2½ ft. sq.*

Red Cloud, deep rosy-red. *4 ft. Aug.–Sept. 3 ft. sq.*

Snow Queen, the only white in this section. *3½–4 ft. Aug.–Sept. 3 ft. sq.*

Survivor, another American variety with rose-pink flowers which come later than most of the section. *2½ ft. Sept.–Oct. 2 ft. sq.*

A. novi-belgii. New York Aster. E. United States. A tall blue, September flowering species which has given rise to a large number of named sorts. These vary between 6 in. and 5 ft. in height and show a wide range of colours. Some will need staking, particularly in exposed situations. They will grow in any good garden soil.

The following make good border perennials:

Ada Ballard, a show variety with well-shaped, large mauvy-blue flowers. *3 ft. Sept.–Oct. 2½ ft. sq.*

Alaska, an American variety with large pure white flowers. *2–2½ ft. Sept.–Oct. 2½ ft. sq.*

Alderman Vokes, fresh salmon-pink. *3 ft. Sept.–Oct. 2½ ft. sq.*

Amethyst, deep mauve, semi-double. *3–4 ft. Sept. 3 ft. sq.*

Apple Blossom, creamy-white, overlaid pink, semi-double. *4 ft. Sept. 3 ft. sq.*

Archbishop, large deep purple-blue, semi-double. *3 ft. Sept.–Oct. 3 ft. sq.*

Beechwood Beacon, compact habit, deep rosy-crimson. *3 ft. Sept.–Oct. 3 ft. sq.*

Beechwood Challenger, an old variety with garnet red flowers. It is subject to mildew in some seasons. *2½ ft. Sept.–Oct. 2 ft sq.*

Beechwood Glow, bright rosy-red. *3 ft. Sept.–Oct. 2½ ft. sq.*

Beechwood Rival, deep cyclamen-purple. *3–4 ft. Sept.–Oct. 3 ft. sq.*

Bishop, very large flowers, reddish-purple. *3½ ft. Sept.–Oct. 2½ ft. sq.*

Blandie, white, semi-double. *4 ft. Sept.–Oct. 3 ft. sq.*

Blue Eyes, large, soft lavender-blue, small centre, single. *4 ft. Sept.–Oct. 2½ ft. sq.*

Blue Gown, large, clear, light-blue self. One of the last to flower. *4–5 ft. Oct.–Nov. 3 ft. sq.*

Chequers, a new and good dwarf variety with large, rich purple flowers. *2 ft. Sept.–Oct. 1½ ft. sq.*

Choristers, a good white kind with large starry flowers. *2½–3 ft. Sept.–Oct. 2½ ft. sq.*

Climax, a very old variety, with large, light-blue flowers with gold eyes. *5 ft. Oct. 3 ft. sq.*

Colonel F. R. Durham, clear mauve, double. *4 ft. Sept. 2 ft. sq.*

Crimson Brocade, a new kind with bushy growth and red flowers which are double on first opening, but later reveal the soft gold centre. *3 ft. Sept.–Oct. 2½ ft. sq.*

Daphne Ann, rich rose, almost double, strong growing and erect. *3½ ft. Sept.–Oct. 2 ft. sq.*

Dean, large, single, rich carmine-pink. *3½ ft. Sept.–Oct. 3 ft. sq.*

D. M. Harrison, deep rose. *4 ft. Sept.–Oct. 2 ft. sq.*

Erma, an American variety with clear orchid-pink flowers. *1½ ft. Sept.–Oct. 1½ ft. sq.*

Esther, clear rose-pink, a very old variety. *2½ ft. Sept.–Oct. 2 ft. sq.*

Eventide (*Plate 29, p. 128*), one of the late Ernest Ballard's finest introductions. The flowers which are so large that they weigh down the branches are of a striking violet-blue shade. Staking is advisable. *3½ ft. Sept.–Oct. 3 ft. sq.*

Festival, semi-double, orchid-mauve, compact. *4 ft. Sept.–Oct. 2½ ft. sq.*

Fontaine, tawny-pink with an orange eye. *2½ ft. Sept.–Oct. 2 ft. sq.*

Gayborder Blue, rich, bright blue. *4 ft. Sept.–Oct. 3 ft. sq.*

Gayborder Royal, glowing petunia-purple, semi-double. *3 ft. Sept. 2 ft. sq.*

Gayborder Supreme, large, semi-double, rich rose. *3–4 ft. Sept.–Oct. 2½ ft. sq.*

Harrison's Blue, deep amethyst-blue, a very fine colour. *3½ ft. Sept.–Oct. 3 ft. sq.*

Hilda Ballard, large, rosy-lilac. *4 ft. Sept. 2 ft. sq.*

Janet McMullen, semi-double, very large, clear pink flowers. *3½ ft. Sept.–Oct. 3 ft. sq.*

Lady Paget, lively orchid-purple. *3 ft. Sept. 2 ft. sq.*

Little Boy Blue, a very old favourite but still widely grown. Bright blue flowers are carried on sturdy, compact bushes. *2½ ft. Sept.–Oct. 1½ ft. sq.*

Little Pink Lady, a slightly

taller counterpart of 'Little Boy Blue' with pink florets. *2½–3 ft. Sept.–Oct. 1½ ft. sq.*

Little Pink Pyramid, light pink, semi-double, flowers large for its size. *1½–2 ft. Sept.–Oct. 1½ ft. sq.*

Little Red Boy, a pale-red kind of similar habit to 'Little Pink Lady'. *2½ ft. Sept.–Oct. 1½ ft. sq.*

Marie Ballard, an outstanding variety with soft powdery-blue flowers, which are very large and very double. *3 ft. Sept.–Oct. 2 ft. sq.*

Melbourne Belle, orchid-purple semi-double. *2–2½ ft. Sept. 2 ft. sq.*

Melbourne Magnet, double flowers of a fine shade of soft heliotrope. *4 ft. Sept.–Oct. 2½ ft. sq.*

Mother of Pearl, large single flowers of silvery mauve. *5 ft. Sept.–Oct. 3 ft. sq.*

Mount Everest (*Plate 29, p. 128; XIV, p. 241*), a free-flowering variety with pure white florets of large size. These are borne on open sprays. *4 ft. Sept.–Oct. 2½ ft. sq.*

Mulberry, mulberry-red, semi-double. *3–4 ft. Oct. 2½ ft. sq.*

Olga Keith, semi-double, rosy-pink, compact. *3½–4 ft. Sept.–Oct. 2½ ft. sq.*

Peace (*Plate 29, p. 128*), very large lilac-pink flowers, needs staking. *3½ ft. Sept.–Oct. 3 ft. sq.*

Phyllis, a pale pink form of Climax. *4 ft. Sept.–Oct. 2 ft. sq.*

Picture, reddish-carmine with gold centre, good for cutting, late. *4 ft. Oct. 2 ft. sq.*

Plenty, semi-double, light mauve. *3½ ft. Sept.–Oct. 2½ ft. sq.*

Pride of Colwall, claret-purple. *2½ ft. Sept.–Oct. 1½ ft. sq.*

Prosperity, deep rose-pink. *3½ ft. Sept.–Oct. 2½ ft. sq.*

Red Rover, compact bushy habit, deep rosy-red. *3 ft. Sept.–Oct. 1½–2 ft. sq.*

Red Sunset (*Plate 29, p. 128*), glowing rosy-red flowers. *3 ft. Sept.–Oct. 2 ft. sq.*

Royal Velvet, gleaming violet. A very good variety which is mildew resistant. *3 ft. Sept.–Oct. 1½ ft. sq.*

Ruth Bide, deep rosy-purple. *4 ft. Sept.–Oct. 3 ft. sq.*

Strawberries and Cream, shell-pink and white. *3½ ft. Sept. 2½ ft. sq.*

Tapestry, pink, very compact. *2½ ft. Sept.–Oct. 2 ft. sq.*

The Archbishop, semi-double, deep purple-blue. *3 ft. Sept.–Oct. 3 ft. sq.*

The Cardinal, rich, rose-red, vigorous and free-flowering. *3½ ft. Sept.–Oct. 2 ft. sq.*

The Sexton, a fine early-flowering variety with very large, single, rich blue flowers. *3½ ft. Sept.–Oct. 2½ ft. sq.*

Winston S. Churchill, glowing ruby red. *2½ ft. Sept.–Oct. 1½ ft. sq.*

The following dwarf varieties also come in this section and are particularly useful for the front of the border or edging work.

Audrey, forms a compact bush smothered with lilac-mauve flowers. *1 ft. Oct. 1½ ft. sq.*

Autumn Princess, semi-double, soft lavender-blue. *14 in. Sept.–Oct. 1½ ft. sq.*

Blue Peter, bright blue. *16 in. Sept.–Oct. 1½ ft. sq.*

Countess of Dudley, shell pink, semi-double. *1 ft. Oct. 1 ft. sq.*

Court Herald, soft rosy-lilac. *14 in. Sept.–Oct. 1½ ft. sq.*

Lady in Blue, semi-double, rich blue. *12 in. Sept.–Oct. 1½ ft. sq.*

Lilac Time, lilac, very free. *1 ft. Sept.–Oct. 1 ft. sq.*

Margaret Rose, bright rose pink. *¾ ft. Oct. 1 ft. sq.*

Nioke, an excellent white variety. *1–2 ft. Sept.–Oct. 1 ft. sq.*

Pink Lace, semi-double, pink. *14 in. Sept.–Oct. 1½ ft. sq.*

Queen of Sheba, pink, suffused soft lilac. *10 in. Sept.–Oct. 1½ ft. sq.*

Rose Bonnet, misty pink. *10 in. Sept.–Oct. 1½ ft. sq.*

Rosebud, apple-blossom pink fading to mauve. *1 ft. Sept. 1 ft. sq.*

Snow Sprite, white. *12 in. Sept.–Oct. 1½ ft. sq.*

A. ptarmicoides. White Upland Daisy. N. America. An extremely hardy and free-flowering species which is much prized for indoor decoration. The rigid stems require no staking and are closely branched, carrying small white daisy flowers.   *2 ft. July–Sept. 1 ft. sq.*

A. thomsonii. The first Aster to obtain an Award of Garden Merit from the Royal Horticultural Society, chiefly on account of its freedom of flowering in a sunny well-drained situation. Plants happily situated may bloom from July until November. Once established they may be kept three or more years in position and then should be divided, in spring. The flowers are a pleasing lavender-blue, and the leaves soft and somewhat heart-shaped.

2 ft. Aug.–Oct. or longer. 1 ft. sq.

A. tradescantii. Michaelmas Daisy. N. America. A particularly interesting species on account of its historical association (see page 94) but attractive also for its slender, leafy stems and white, half-inch flowers. In Tradescant's time (c. 1633, when the plant was introduced) Michaelmas fell later than it does now, which gave point to its English name. Although grown for hundred of years in Britain, its garden worthiness was only appreciated in 1951 when it received an Award of Merit from the Royal Horticultural Society.   *2½ ft. Autumn. 2 ft. sq.*

A. yunnanensis. W. China. Produces several stems each carrying a single pale bluish-mauve daisy flower. The species is important for its variety ' Napsbury ', a large-flowered form raised some years before World War II at the Mental Hospital of that name. The blooms are 2½–3 in. across and the ray florets are intense purplish-blue. Flowers best in well-drained soil, and must not lie wet during the dormant period. Plant and divide in spring.   *15 in. June. 1 ft. sq.*

ASTILBE (*Saxifragaceae*): False Goat's Beard. From *a* (Gk) ' without ', *stilbe* ' brilliance ', referring possibly to the smallness of the individual florets.

Astilbes are amongst the most beautiful of herbaceous perennials and will grow in any good garden soil, providing that this has reasonable reserves of moisture during the summer months. Sun is not essential and the plants do well in partial shade, but dryness is a very real enemy. In light land peat or leaf-mould should be incorporated with the soil at planting time, and in after years an annual mulch of well-rotted dung or compost should be provided about April. It should be appreciated that the roots of these plants always remain near the surface, so that such mulches feed the plants as well as retain moisture.

Astilbes occupy an important place in late planting schemes, for the light feathery plumes of flowers and handsome palmate foliage lend character and grace to the border. The colours, too, are very distinctive, especially the cerise and deep pink forms. These associate particularly well with white or silver plants like *Artemisia stelleriana* or *Stachys lanata*.

Astilbes are also useful plants for growing in a woodland setting, or close to water in association with Primulas, Ferns and the moisture-loving Irises.

Seed is produced by some species, but named varieties must be propagated by division in spring. Established plants may be moved in autumn or spring.

Although a number of species can be grown in the border, most gardeners will welcome the *arendsii* hybrids, a race of brilliantly coloured varieties raised by the late George Arends of Ronsdorf. These were obtained from continually crossing and recrossing *A. japonica*, *A. thunbergii*, *A. astilboides* and *A. davidi*.

Mons. Lemoine of Nancy also raised several fine garden varieties.

A. × *arendsii*. These are of garden origin as already mentioned, but have a compactness and colour range invaluable for border work.

Apple Blossom, soft pink. *2½ ft. July–Aug. 2 ft. sq.*

Avalanche, white. *3 ft. July–Aug. 2 ft. sq.*

Betsy Cuperus, pale pink on long graceful, drooping sprays. *2½ ft. July–Aug. 2 ft. sq.*

Bonn, rich rose-pink. *2½ ft. July–Aug. 2 ft. sq.*

Burgkristal, thick branching stems with white, coconut ice-like flowers. *3 ft. July–Aug. 2 ft. sq.*

Cattleya, rich orchid-pink. *3 ft. July–Aug. 2 ft. sq.*

Ceres, pink. *3 ft. July–Aug. 2 ft. sq.*

Cologne, deep carmine-rose. *2 ft. June–July. 2 ft. sq.*

Deutschland, pure white. *2 ft. July–Aug. 2 ft. sq.*

Dusseldorf, rosy-lilac. *2 ft. July–Aug. 2 ft. sq.*

Erica, large open trusses of pink flowers. *2¾ ft. June–July. 2½ ft. sq.*

Etna, deep glorious red. *2 ft. July–Aug. 2 ft. sq.*

Fanal, deep garnet red, reddish foliage. *2 ft. July–Aug. 2 ft. sq.*

Federsee, bright rosy-red, useful on light soils as it is more tolerant of dry conditions. *2½ ft. July–Aug. 2 ft. sq.*

Fire, brilliant rose-red. *2 ft. July–Aug. 2 ft. sq.*

Gertrude Brix, deep crimson. *2½ ft. June–July. 2 ft. sq.*

Gloria, soft pink. *2½ ft. June–July. 2 ft. sq.*

Gloria purpurea, dark crimson with brownish-green foliage. *3½ ft. July–Aug. 2½ ft. sq.*

Glut, new variety of glowing red. *2 ft. July–Aug. 2 ft. sq.*

Granat, crimson. *3 ft. June. 2 ft. sq.*

Hyacinth, lilac-pink. *2½ ft. July–Aug. 2 ft. sq.*

Irrlicht, snow-white, very free. *1½ ft. July–Aug. 1½ ft. sq.*

Jo Orphorst, ruby-red. *2 ft. July–Sept. 2 ft. sq.*

King Albert (*Plate I, p. 192*), creamy-white. *4 ft. July–Aug. 3 ft. sq.*

Koblenz, rosy-red. *2½ ft. July–Aug. 2 ft. sq.*

Meta Immink, delightful deep pink. *2½ ft. July–Aug. 2 ft. sq.*

Montgomery, of recent introduction, intense deep red. *2 ft. July–Aug. 2 ft. sq.*

Prof. v.d. Wielen, pure white, loose sprays. *4 ft. July–Aug. 2 ft. sq.*

Queen Alexandra, rose, *2½ ft. July–Aug. 2 ft. sq.*

Red Sentinel, intense red, a new variety. *2 ft. July–Aug. 2 ft. sq.*

Rhineland, brilliant pink. *2½ ft. July–Aug. 2 ft. sq.*

Rubin, rosy-red. *3 ft. July–Aug. 2 ft. sq.*

Salland, deep rose. *3 ft. July–Aug. 2 ft. sq.*

Salmon Queen, vigorous, salmon-rose. *3½ ft. July–Aug. 2 ft. sq.*

Tamarix, tall, late, pink. *July–Sept. 2 ft. sq.*

Venus, silver-pink. *2½ ft. July–Aug. 2 ft. sq.*

Vesuvius, glowing salmon-red. *2 ft. July–Aug. 2 ft. sq.*

William Reeves, dark crimson with bronze foliage. *2½ ft. July–Aug. 2 ft. sq.*

A. astilboides. Goat's Beard Astilbe. Japan. A fine species with handsomely cut foliage, the leaflets toothed and slightly hairy. The flowers are white, in congested and divided heads.

2–3 ft. June. 2 ft. sq.

A. chinensis. China. Branching habit; flowers white tinged with red on short spikes in clustered panicles. *2–3 ft. July–Aug. 2½ ft. sq.*

A. davidi. China. A tall species for the back of the border. The flowers are crimson magenta, often in 2 ft. long spikes, whilst the leaflets, which are arranged in feathered fashion on long stems, are individually somewhat like elm leaves. An excellent plant for partial shade but it needs plenty of moisture. *6 ft. or more. July. 4 ft. sq.*

A. japonica: Silver Sheaf. Japan. A species much used for forcing purposes. White flowers in dense plumes and three or five divided leaves.

2 ft.   May–June.   1½ ft. sq.

A. japonica var. *foliis purpureis.* Similar to *A. japonica* except that the leaves and stems have a purple tinge.   *3–4 ft.   June–July.   2 ft. sq.*

A. rivularis. W. China. A moisture-loving species, unsuited to light soil. Flowers yellowish-white on spiky branches.

3–4 ft.   June–July.   2 ft. sq.

A × *rosea.* Hybrids of garden origin derived from *A. chinensis* and *A. japonica.* Vars. ' Peach Blossom ' pink, and ' Queen Alexandra ' rose, succeed in moist soil.   *2–3 ft.   July–Aug.   2 ft. sq.*

A. rubra. India. A front of the border plant with handsome divided leaves and dense panicles crowded with small rose flowers.

2 ft.   July–Aug.   2 ft. sq.

A. thunbergii. Japan. Yellowish-green, divided leaves, and small, white flowers on erect, branching sprays.   *1½ ft.   May.   1½ ft. sq.*

ASTRAGALUS (*Leguminosae*): Foxtail Milk Vetch. Ancient Greek name.

A very large family, of which only the following is used in the border.

A. alopecuroides. Spain to Siberia. An erect plant with silky, hairy leaves made up of 50 or more small opposite leaflets. Individual flowers are small, and soft yellow, packed together on small, stalkless spikes in the axils of the leaves. They bear some resemblance to a large clover head. Well-drained soil and sun constitute the plant's chief requirements. Propagation by seed.   *3½ ft.   June.   2 ft. sq.*

ASTRANTIA (*Umbelliferae*): Masterwort. From *astron* (Gk) ' star ', referring to the star-like flower heads.

Strangely fascinating little plants with green and rose whorls of blossom, aromatic black roots and palmately lobed or dissected leaves. They will grow in partial shade or sun, providing only that the soil does not dry out in summer. Propagation by division in spring or autumn, or from freshly gathered seed.

A. biebersteinii. Caucasus. Has silvery white flowers and toothed, three-lobed leaves.   *1–2 ft.   June.   1 ft. sq.*

A. carniolica (Plate 21, p. 96). Europe, Asia. White or blush-pink flowers with a ring of white bracts, each having a green midrib and tinged with red. In var. *rubra* the flowers are redder.

1 ft.   July–Aug.   2 ft. sq.

A. major. Europe. A taller species, the flowers more pinkish.
2 ft. July–Aug. 2 ft. sq.

A. maxima (syn. *A. helleborifolia*): E. Caucasus. An attractive species with pink, bristly flowers and tripartite leaves. Var. *major* is larger in all its parts.
1–2 ft. June. 1 ft. sq.

BAPTISIA (*Leguminosae*): False or Blue Indigo. From *bapto* (Gk) 'to dip'; an extract from the flowers was at one time used as a substitute for indigo.

Baptisias grow well in any soil but do best in a sunny situation. Propagation is by division or seed.

B. alba. S.E. United States. An attractive summer-flowering perennial with straight stems of white, leguminous flowers and pea-like leaves.
2–4 ft. June. 1½ ft. sq.

B. australis (*Plate 11, p. 64*). N. America. Deserves a place in every border. Blooms in early summer with Vetch-like leaves and rich blue, pea-like flowers. The habit is reminiscent of a Lupin.
4–5 ft. June. 2 ft. sq.

B. tinctoria. E. United States. Has short terminal racemes of yellow flowers.
2–3 ft. July. 1 ft. sq.

BARBAREA (*Cruciferae*): Europe and Asia. Herb of St. Barbara. Latin name derived from St. Barbara to whom it was dedicated in ancient times.

A small family which includes *B. praecox* (Land Cress) sometimes used for winter salads. The best variety for garden purposes is *B. vulgaris*, particularly the beautiful form *flore-pleno*, which is also known as the Double Yellow Rocket. This has cut leaves rather like a dandelion in shape, and branching heads of small, double, silvery-yellow flowers. Var. *variegata* has golden mottling of the leaves which is attractive in early spring. To preserve the beauty of the latter, gardeners frequently nip off the flowers so that the leaves persist beyond the normal spring season.

In Sweden the leaves of the type plant are sometimes boiled as greens. Barbarea will grow in any good garden soil providing it does not dry out too much in the summer. Propagation by cuttings or division.
10–18 in. May. 9 in. sq.

BERGENIA (*Saxifragaceae*): Pig Squeak; Megasea. Named after Karl August von Bergen, 18th-century botanist and physician of Frankfort.

A useful genus of early flowering perennials with thick leathery leaves, fleshy rootstock and spikes of pink or white flowers. Bergenias make good edging subjects, or can be grown in clumps at vantage points in either sun or shade. They are not particular as to soil and may be propagated by seed or division.

B. cordifolia (syn. *Megasea, Saxifraga cordifolia*) (*Plate 2. p. 17*). Has round, thick leathery leaves very much like those of a Water Lily and short spikes of deep pink flowers. The top growth is almost perennial, only being killed in severe winters. There is also a fine red-leaved form known as *foliis purpureis*. Other varieties show variation in the colour of the flowers; var. *alba* white, *purpurea* purplish-pink, *rosea* bright pink.

1 ft. March–April. 1 ft. sq.

B. crassifolia. Siberia. A fleshy leaved plant with thick and woody rootstock and branching panicles of large red flowers. A showy front of the border subject. Var. *aureo-marginata* has variegated leaves; var. *media*, rosy flowered with metallic green foliage; var. *orbicularis*, pink flowers; var. *rubra*, deep red. *1 ft. Mar.–April. 1 ft. sq.*

B. ligulata. Nepal. An attractive plant with heart-shaped, toothed leaves and pale pinkish, forked spikes of flowers. These are substantial and make a brave show. Var. *speciosa* has crimson flowers.

1 ft. March–May. 1 ft. sq.

B. stracheyi. Himalayas. Somewhat lower growing than *B. ligulata*, with rounded or wedge-shaped leaves and much branched heads of flowers. The individual blooms of these are fairly large ($\frac{3}{4}$ to 1 in. across) and weigh down the spikes so as to give these a drooping effect. Var. *alba* has reddish-bronze leaves and white flowers.

6–12 in. March. 1 ft. sq.

B E R K H E Y A (*Compositae*). Named after M. J. de Berkhey, a Dutch botanist.

Thistle-like plants with long leaves green above and greyish beneath, and heads of flowers enclosed in a spiny involucre. Well drained soil and sun are necessary. Propagation by division in spring.

B. adlamii. Transvaal. Hardy in Britain; the largest species, with yellow flowers $3\frac{1}{2}$ in. across *4–5 ft. July. 2 ft. sq.*

B. macrocephala. S. Africa. Has large, golden yellow flowers and Thistle-like leaves. *2½–3 ft. July 2½ ft. sq.*

B. purpurea. S. Africa. Hardy perennial with purple flowers and Thistle-like leaves. *3 ft. July. 1½ ft. sq.*

B O L T O N I A (*Compositae*): False Chamomile. Named after James Bolton, an 18th century English botanist.

Handsome Michaelmas Daisy-like plants which deserve to be better known. They would probably repay the attention of plant breeders. All are very easy to grow in any type of soil and need no staking. Propagation by division.

B. asteroides. N. America. Suitable for a back row position this plant has narrow, lance-like leaves, which come without stalks from the flower stems. The flowers are white, pink or purple and resemble small Michaelmas Daisies. *5-6 ft. Aug.–Sept. 2 ft. sq.*

B. latisquamata. N. America. Much smaller than *B. asteroides,* but with brighter flower heads of bluish violet, which are more showy in habit. *3-4 ft. Aug.–Sept. 2 ft. sq.*

BORAGO (*Boraginaceae*): Borage. Name believed to be corrupted from *cor* (L) heart, *ago* to act, an allusion to its early medicinal use as a stimulant. It is still used in some fruit cups.

The plants noted below are useful for naturalising in fairly dry places and may be grown in most soils. They are propagated by division in spring or by cuttings. Seed may also be sown outside from March to May.

B. laxiflora: Corsican Borage. (*Plate 6, p. 33.*) Corsica. A useful bee plant, much prized for its handsome blue or purple racemes of flowers. The foliage and stems are extremely hairy. Both leaves and flowers are at times used in salads. *1 ft. May–Aug. 2 ft. sq.*

B. officinalis. Europe. Has sprays of light blue, five petalled flowers very like Anchusa, but characterised by prominent purplish black anthers. The leaves are rough, oblong and hairy. This is the common Borage, the blossoms and young shoots of which are used in soups. *2 ft. May–Aug. 2 ft. sq.*

BOYKINIA (*Saxifragaceae*): Named after Dr. Boykin, 19th century American field botanist.

A small group of woodland plants suitable for the rougher parts of the border or wild garden. The leaves resemble Heuchera or Saxifrage, being somewhat heart-shaped and much cut at the edges. The flowers are small, mostly white and borne on branching stems. Propagation by seed or division.

B. aconitifolia. Aconite Saxifrage. E. United States. A front of the border plant with rounded leaves on long stems and branched panicles of white flowers. *1-2 ft. May–June. 1 ft. sq.*

BRUNNERA (*Boraginaceae*): Named after Samuel Brunner, 19th century Swiss botanist.

B. macrophylla. Siberian Bugloss. (*Plate 1, p. 16.*) Siberia. Long known and grown in gardens as *Anchusa myosotidiflora* this pretty flowering perennial has large, rough, heart-shaped basal leaves on long stalks and sprays of small, blue, Forget-me-not flowers. It will grow most satisfactorily in damp soil and does not mind a little shade. Propagation by division or root cuttings. *1-1½ ft. June. 1 ft. sq.*

BULBINELLA (*Liliaceae*): From Bulbine, an allied species.

Herbaceous perennial with thick fleshy roots, narrow grassy leaves and simple sprays of white or yellowish flowers. Treatment and general cultivation as for Anthericum q.v. p. 88. Propagation by seed or division.

B. hookeri. New Zealand. Bright yellow flowers and grassy leaves.

$1\frac{1}{2}$–$2\frac{1}{2}$ *ft.* *June.* *1 ft. sq.*

B. rossii. New Zealand. A strong plant but one which needs some winter protection. Well-drained but moist soil and light shade suits it well. The flowers are orange and in dense racemes, male and female on separate plants, the former more showy. *2–3 ft.* *June.* *1 ft. sq.*

BUPHTHALMUM (*Compositae*): Yellow Ox-Eye. From *bous* (Gk) ' ox ' and *opthalmos* ' eye ', referring to the shape of the disc or centre florets in the flowers.

Showy border plants of coarse habit with quantities of solitary, golden yellow, daisy-like flowers. The plants do well in any garden soil providing they are in full sun. Propagation by division of the roots in spring.

B. salicifolium. Willow-leaf Ox-Eye. Austria. A useful plant for front of the border work, with large round yellow heads of daisy-like flowers. The leaves are coarse and slightly hairy, somewhat lance-shaped.

$1\frac{1}{2}$–*2 ft.* *June–July.* *3 ft. sq.*

B. speciosum (syn. *Telekia speciosa*): Heart-leaf Ox-Eye. S. E. Europe. A more robust plant which is quite magnificent when well grown, as at the margin of a pool, etc. It can be included in the mixed border but must be watched and kept within bounds. The flower heads are very large, solitary and of a rich gold colour; the leaves large, heart-shaped at the bottom, and oval on the leaf stems. The whole plant has a strong aromatic scent. *2–4 ft.* *July–Sept.* *4 ft. sq.*

CALAMINTHA (*Labiatae*): From *kalos* (Gk) ' beautiful ', *mintha* ' mint '.

A family of low-growing annuals and perennials with aromatic foliage which are grown for their flowers and use as culinary herbs. They will thrive in practically any soil and can be propagated by division, seed and soft cuttings.

C. alpina (syn. *Satureia orontia*): Alpine Savory. S. Europe. Has hairy, nettle-like leaves and whorls of purple sage-like flowers.

6 in. *July.* *1 ft. sq.*

CALLIRHOE (*Malvaceae*): Poppy Mallow. Greek legendary name for the daughter of the river God Achelous.

A small genus of plants, all native to America. Poppy Mallows are easy to cultivate and so bright and attractive when in flower that they deserve to be better known. They like sunshine and a light soil and are propagated by cuttings.

C. papaver. A scrambling or sometimes erect growing perennial with reddish-purple, large, poppy-like flowers and delicate mallow-like leaves. *2 ft. July–Aug. 2 ft. sq.*

CAMPANULA (*Campanulaceae*): Bellflower. From *campana* ' bell ', referring to the shape of the flower.

A large genus containing some of our most popular garden plants, nearly all originating from the northern hemisphere, especially the Mediterranean Region. Few genera show such diversity of form and habit, for whilst many are important subjects for the rock garden, a number of the border kinds may reach as much as 5 ft. in height. The latter will grow in practically any garden soil where the drainage is good. Others are tolerant of shade conditions. Indeed, when well established in light woodland a few species such as *C. persicifolia* have to be watched lest they become too rampant. Occasionally staking is necessary, and for best effects in the border, varieties of the same kind should be grouped in clumps of 3, 5 or more. A watchful eye must be kept for stray seedlings which may embarrass the grower or in some instances become useful to him for naturalising purposes. Apart from sowing seed, propagation may be effected by division of the roots in spring or autumn, or from softwood cuttings taken in March. A number of species have edible roots, but right through the ages the plants have been chiefly grown for the beauty of their flowers.

C. alliariifolia. Spurred Bellflower. (*Plate XI, p. 240.*) Caucasus. A perennial with a creeping underground rootstock and basal growths of heart-shaped leaves, which are toothed, and white beneath. The flowers are creamy-white in colour, about 2 in. long and borne in arching sprays. *1½–2 ft. June–July. 2 ft. sq.*

C. betonicifolia. Asia Minor. Has much branched stems carrying about three purplish-blue flowers with yellow bases. The leaves are hairy, oval and slightly toothed. *1½ ft. July–Aug. 2 ft. sq.*

C. bononiensis. Siberia. Carries numbers of small (¾-in.) bluish-violet flowers on long, willowy racemes. The leaves are oval, toothed, stalked at the base but clasping the stem above. The whole plant is somewhat hairy. Var. *alba* has white flowers. *2 ft. July. 2 ft. sq.*

C. burghaltii. A good border plant of garden origin, possibly a hybrid from *C. punctata.* Flowers large and pendant, in a beautiful shade of violet-grey. *2 ft. July–Aug. 2 ft. sq.*

C. carpatica. Carpathian Bellflower. E. Europe. A spreading perennial with leafy, branching stems carrying bright blue, open bell-shaped flowers. These may be 2 inches in diameter when well grown. This is a valuable species and has produced such worthwhile varieties as *alba* with white flowers; ' Isabel ' soft violet; ' White Star ' a good, large white; *turbinata* which is dwarf and more compact than the type; ' Riverslea ' deep violet-blue with very open flowers.

1 ft. June–Aug. 1 ft. sq.

C. collina. Caucasus. This has rather hairy stems with a few deep blue-purple, hanging bell-shaped flowers on each. Leaves oval oblong and rough to the touch. *1 ft. June. 1 ft. sq.*

C. glomerata: Danesblood. (*Plate 15, p. 80.*) Europe including Britain. This is one of the best border perennials of the genus and worth a place in every garden. It grows in all soils, but forms larger heads and taller stems when the ground is moist and in good heart. The funnel-shaped, rich violet flowers are borne in a clustered head at the top of a terminal stem. Garden varieties worth noting are *alba* white; *superba* rich violet-blue and later than the type; *dahurica* deep violet-purple. *1–2 ft. June–Aug. 1 ft. sq.*

C. × hendersonii. A garden hybrid with terminal racemes of mauvy-blue flowers. It can be rather tricky and is apt to die out after the first season. *1 ft. July–Sept. 1 ft. sq.*

C. lactiflora. Milky Bellflower. Caucasus. A fine, free-flowering sort, with rigid stems 5–6 ft. high carrying loose or dense panicles of white or blue tinged flowers. Individual florets are about an inch long. It forms a thick, fleshy, much branched rootstock and the best specimens come from self-sown seedlings or seed sown where it is to flower.

Although happiest in a full sunny position the plant will flower comparatively well in partial shade. Deep, rich soil is essential and plenty of moisture during the growing season. Var. *alba* is more dwarf (4 ft.), with pure white flowers. *4–6 ft. June–July. 2 ft. sq.*

C. lactiflora ' Loddon Anna '. (*Plate VI, p. 209.*) A beautiful garden variety of recent origin, with spreading racemes of mushroom-pink pendant blossoms. In association with blue Delphiniums and red-flowered Heuchera this plant looks particularly fine. ' Prichard's Variety ' is a good form with deep-blue flowers (3 ft. in June and July) and ' Pouffe ', a low-growing variety (6–9 in.) with light-blue flowers which are in character for weeks. (June–Sept.) Both require a planting space of approximately 2 ft. *3–4 ft. June–July. 2 ft. sq.*

C. latifolia. Great Bellflower. Europe to Kashmir, including Britain. An imposing species with erect stems, sometimes reaching to a height of 5 ft. These, however, are so strong, that in spite of their height they require no staking. The leaves are egg-shaped and lanceolate, tapering, toothed and rough to the touch, the flowers large and pendant, bluish-purple and hairy within. Var. *alba* has white flowers;

macrantha purplish-blue blossoms which are rather more open than the type. Named varieties worth noting are ' Brantwood ', purple, 4 ft.; ' Burghaltii ', pale blue, 3 ft.; ' Highcliffe variety ', large deep violet flowers, 3 ft. *4–5 ft. July. 4 ft. sq.*

C. latiloba (syn. *C. grandis*): Olympic Bellflower. Siberia. Forms a neat rosette of long, smooth, strap-shaped and mostly toothed leaves which are narrow at both ends. From the centre of these rise stout, leafy stems bearing large, flat, circular flowers about 2 in. across. These may be blue or white and either carried singly or in threes. It will grow in any soil in full sun or semi-shade and is easily propagated by self-sown seedlings or division. Var. *alba*, white.

1–3 ft. July–Aug. 2 ft. sq.

C. persicifolia. Peach-leaved Bellflower. (*Plate 15, p. 80.*) Europe, including Britain. A low-growing plant which does equally well in sun or semi-shade, producing slender spikes of wide open bell-shaped flowers and narrow peach-like leaves. It is also called by gardeners the Paper Bellflower, from the stiff, though delicate texture of the blossoms. Among the best of the named varieties are:

alba (*Plate 15, p. 80*), single white.
alba flore pleno, a very good white, double.
Beechwood, soft blue, *2 ft.*
Boule de Neige, double white.
coerulea flore pleno, semi-double, blue.
Delft Blue, china-blue, double.
Fair Mile, rich blue.
Misty Morn, a semi-double American variety, frosted blue, reputed to be excellent for cutting.
Moerheimii, semi-double, white.
Pride of Exmouth, semi-double, rich lavender.
Snowdrift, single white.
Telham Beauty, syn. *maxima*, large, china-blue flowers, twice as large as the type. It should be noted that if it is left too long in one place the plant deteriorates, but division is easy in autumn or spring. It is also easily raised from seed which for preference should be sown where the plants are to flower.
Wirral Belle, a fine deep blue double-flowered variety of recent introduction. *1–3 ft. May–July. 2 ft. sq.*

C. phyctidocalyx. Armenia. Rather similar in habit to *C. persicifolia*, but shorter. Flowers violet-blue. *2 ft. July. 2 ft. sq.*

C. poscharskyana (*Plate 15, p. 80*): Dalmatia. An attractive, strong-growing perennial for the front of the border, or the base of the rock garden. It is a rampant creeper and takes advantage of any shelter provided, so that, although normally of trailing habit, it may reach a height of several feet. The plant is happy in either sun or partial shade and has a long flowering season. Blooms are small but very numerous and of a lavender blue shade, the leaves smooth and heart-shaped and mostly toothed.   *1 ft. June–Nov. 2 ft. sq.*

C. punctata (syn. *C. nobilis*): Spotted Bellflower. E. Siberia and N. Japan. An attractive species which does well on light soils. In heavier land it is apt to die off in winter, therefore avoid letting excessive damp collect round the crowns at that season. It has thin, wiry, erect flower stems carrying a few large, very long, tubular creamy bells. These may be 2 inches in length and speckled inside with purplish dots. The leaves are leathery, oval and soft to the touch.
1½ ft. June–Aug. 1 ft. sq.

C. pyramidalis. Chimney Bellflower. Dalmatia. Perhaps the most majestic member of the genus, forming thick, carrot-like roots with rosettes of heart-shaped leaves on long stalks. The flowers are carried on stately spikes rising to a height of 5 ft. or 6 ft. and bear wide-open bells which are pale blue with a darker centre. The shades vary in the type, however, and there is a pure white form. Generally speaking this species is best treated as a biennial or propagated each year from the non-flowering side shoots which appear close to the ground. It requires a deep, rich soil and a long season of growth.
5 ft. July–Sept. 2 ft. sq.

C. rapunculoides. False Rampion. Europe, including Britain. A species which spreads rapidly and must be so placed that it will not crowd out other nearby plants. It is a straight, tall subject 3–4 ft. high with large, drooping, funnel-shaped flowers. These are rich deep violet and slightly bearded inside. The basal leaves are rough, wedge-shaped with mostly toothed edges, whilst the stem leaves have no stalks and are oblong ovate. It is a plant to watch but nevertheless is extremely beautiful in a wild or rough state. The roots are edible. Var. *janisensis* has larger flowers.   *3–4 ft. June. Spreading.*

C. rhomboidalis. Europe. An erect plant, branching near the top of the stem into short stems, each carrying several drooping blue, bell-shaped flowers.   *1½–2 ft. July. 1 ft. sq.*

C. sarmatica. Caucasus. Resembling *C. alliariifolia* with pale blue, velvety, hairy blooms.   *1–2 ft. July–Aug. 1 ft. sq.*

C. stricta. E. Mediterranean. Has a woody rootstock and bristly stems with narrow leaves and tubular, stalkless, blue flowers. Var. *libanotica* is smaller.   *1–1½ ft. July–Oct. 1 ft. sq.*

C. trachelium: Coventry Bells. (*Plate 15, p. 80.*) Europe including Britain. A well-known British plant which is easily distinguished from other species by its leaves, which are shaped like those of the common nettle. It is a rough plant bearing a stem about 2 ft. high with rather large, deep purple flowers. This plant as well as some other species, was formerly used for throat complaints and so shares with these the name of Throat Wort. Both purple and white forms occur and there are also double forms of each colour. It is best kept in the wild garden or in uncongenial places in the large border. Var. *alba* is white; *alba plena* double white; *caerulea plena* double blue.

1–3 ft.   July–Sept.   1½ ft. sq.

C. × van houttei. An excellent border plant, probably of garden origin, which is referred to *C. punctata* by some authorities. Of tufted habit, this is a front of the border subject and chiefly characterised by the dark blue flowers, which may be 2 inches in length.

9–12 in.   July.   1 ft. sq.

C. versicolor. Greece. An upright smooth perennial with heart-shaped basal leaves, slender pointed stem leaves and variable blue or violet flowers. Var. *tenorei* is an improved form (1 ft.) and var. *tomentella* is softly hairy on stems and leaves.   *3–4 ft.   July–Sept.   1 ft. sq.*

CARDAMINE (*Cruciferae*): Bittercress. From *cardia* (Gk) ' heart ', *damao* ' to fortify ', referring to its supposed medicinal properties.

Moisture-loving perennials only suited to the heavier types of soil. They bloom in spring or early summer on slender, leafy stems, the flowers being four-petalled and usually purple or white. The leaves are simple or feathery (pinnate) and the roots often tuberous or rhizomatous.

C. asarifolia. S. Europe. A pretty little plant for damp light shade. The rather large rounded leaves have wavy edges and the flowers are white.

1–1½ ft.   May–June.   1 ft. sq.

C. pratensis. Cuckoo Flower. Europe including Britain. A well-known plant with small lilac flowers arranged on the stems like a wallflower. The leaves are very pungent and were once relished as a salad herb. Gardeners will prefer to grow the double form *pratensis flore pleno* which is much more spectacular. Propagated by division or from leaf cuttings in moist soil.   *12–15 in.   April–May.   1 ft. sq.*

CARDUNCELLUS (*Compositae*): Diminutive from *Carduuculus* (L) ' thistle '.

Thistle-like plants which in light soils and full sun become compact clumps, but in rich soils are apt to become weedy. Propagation by division.

C. caeruleus. Greece. Leathery leaves, oblong lanceolate and blue Thistle flowers *1–1½* in. across.   *1–1½ ft.   June–July.   1 ft. sq.*

C. multifidus. Algeria. Finely cut leaves and Cornflower like heads of blue flowers.   *1–2 ft.   June–July.   1 ft. sq.*

Plate 23: 1. Bearded Penstemon, *Penstemon barbatus.* 2. Crimson Monkey Flower, *Mimulus cardinalis.* 3. Turtle Head, *Chelone lyoni.* 4. Maltese Cross, *Lychnis chalcedonica.* 5. Giant Mallow, *Malva setosa*

Plate 24: 1. Tree Lavatera, *Lavatera olbia.* 2. Mexican Bergamot, *Agastache mexicana.*
3. Clary, *Salvia sclarea.* 4. Big Betony, *Stachys macrantha.* 5. Rose Shamrock, *Oxalis lasiandra*

Plate 25: 1. Cardinal Flower, *Lobelia fulgens.* 2. White Scabious, Pincushion Flower,
Scabiosa caucasica alba. 3. Scabious, *S. caucasica* 'Clive Greaves'. 4. White Cupid's
Love Dart, *Catananche caerulea alba.* 5. Cupid's Love Dart, *C. caerulea major.*
6. African Lily, *Agapanthus africanus*

Plate 26: 1. SEA LAVENDER, *Limonium latifolium* 'Violetta'. 2. MONKSHOOD, *Aconitum wilsonii* 'Barker's Var.' 3. MEALYCUP SAGE, *Salvia farinacea*. 4. SEA HOLLY, *Eryngium* x *oliverianum* 'Violetta'. 5. STOKES'S ASTER, *Stokesia laevis*. 6. TORREY'S NIGHTSHADE, *Solanum torreyi*

C. pinnatus. N. Africa. Large terminal, lilac flower heads and feathery foliage.   *9 in. June–July. 1 ft. sq.*

CARLINA (*Compositae*): Carline Thistle. Named to commemorate Charlemagne, whose army smitten with a fearful pestilence is reputed to have been cured with this plant.

Plumeless Thistles with stalkless, spiny leaves and the typical mauve Thistle flowers. They will grow in any ordinary soil in a dry, open position but on account of their seeding propensities are best relegated to the wild garden, or else should have the flower heads removed immediately these finish. Planting should take place in spring, and propagation is effected by seed sown outside in spring where the plants are to flower.

C. acanthifolia. S. Europe. A stemless perennial with deeply lobed leaves which are downy on the underside. Flower heads white.

           2 ft. June. 2 ft. sq.

CATANANCHE (*Compositae*): Cupid's Love Dart. From *katanangke* (Gk) literally ' strong urge '. (It was used in early days for making love philtres.)

An effective front of the border perennial with quantities of cornflower-like blooms and narrow, hairy, grass-like leaves. The plants do best in a light soil but can be induced to grow in heavy land by planting them on a slope or in raised beds (see p. 36). Some of the best plants we have ever grown were treated in this fashion and made specimens between 3–4 ft. tall. Propagation by root cuttings, division or seed. Plant in spring. Catananches must have full sun and look particularly well associated with purple Lythrums, *Echinacea* ' The King ' and yellow Day-lilies.

C. caerulea. Mediterranean Region. Has mauve, semi-double, daisy-like flowers protected at the back by silvery, papery bracts. The type is largely passed over in favour of its variety *major* (*Plate 25, p. 112*) which is larger and finer in all its parts. The flowers can be cut and dried for winter bouquets. It is possible to extend the season of flowering right into autumn by growing two clumps and cutting one down as it comes to flower as suggested for Anthemis. Var. *alba*. (*Plate 25, p. 112.*), is a silvery-white form raised at Enfield just before the war. It is less sturdy than the blue *major*. Var. *bicolor* has blue and white florets.   *2 ft. June–Aug. 2 ft. sq.*

CELSIA (*Scrophulariaceae*): Named after Olaus Celsius, an 18th-century professor in Upsala University.

A small genus of plants mostly native to the Mediterranean region and Southern Asia. The flowers are borne in loose terminal spikes like those of a Verbascum, whilst the leaves are deeply cut and divided. All favour good, well-drained soil but need plenty of sunshine. Propagation by half-ripe cuttings or seed sown in the open border in spring.

C. arcturus. Bear's Tail Mullein. Crete. A shrubby perennial, doubtfully hardy in some areas but worth trying in warmer parts of the country. The plant when in flower resembles a dwarf yellow Verbascum, each flower bearded with purple hairs. There is an improved form, *linnaeana.* *2–3 ft. June–July. 1½ ft. sq.*

C. bugulifolia. A smaller and hardier species than *C. arcturus.* Flowers yellow with greenish-purple anthers. Crosses have been made between this species and *Verbascum phoeniceum.* *1 ft. July–Aug. 6 in. sq.*

CENTAUREA (*Compositae*): Centaury, Knapweed. Named after the Centaur Chiron who is said to have used it in the healing of his wounds, and later taught Man the value of plants and medicinal herbs.

Although the best-known member of this genus is *C. cyanus,* the annual blue Cornflower, there are several useful and attractive plants amongst the herbaceous perennials. These are easily grown in ordinary garden soil, but (in the case of *C. montana* varieties particularly) they should not be given too rich a medium lest they spread excessively. They will grow in sun or partial shade. The flowers are all of the typical cornflower shape, varying in colour according to species, but a few are grown primarily for their beautiful silver foliage. Propagation of the perennial kinds is usually effected by division in spring or autumn. Most species need to be lifted and divided every third or fourth year.

C. babylonica. Syrian Centaurea. E. Mediterranean. A fine plant with silvery foliage and many small yellow flowers on 4 or 5 ft. stems in summer. Under exceptionally good conditions it may grow even 10 or 12 ft. tall and in a light soil the roots go down 3 ft. or more. A well-drained sandy loam is the best planting medium. This kind can be propagated from seed. *4–10 ft. July–Sept. 3 ft. sq.*

C. clementei. Spain. A fine foliage plant with silvery woolly leaves, which are most attractive for edging purposes or as a foil for brightly coloured plants behind. The blooms are best removed, as they detract from and spoil the fine effect of the leaves. When allowed to bloom they are yellow. *3 ft. July. 2 ft. sq.*

C. dealbata. Persian Centaurea. Asia Minor. A graceful plant with pinnate leaves, which are somewhat silvery beneath. The flowers, which are borne on long stems, are thistle shaped, rosy-purple and deeply fringed at the margins.

There is a variety known as *Steenbergii* in which the blooms are a bright cyclamen shade. This needs to be carefully placed and looks best in association with greens and silvers. *1½ ft. June–Oct. 2 ft. sq.*

C. depressa. Persia. Another silvery-leaved species which forms congested or basal growths. The blossoms are blue, margined with white or black. Makes an attractive and bold edging for borders.

1 ft. Summer. 6 in. sq.

C. glastifolia. (*Plate 33, p. 144.*) Asia Minor. A vigorous species with rough stems which are much branched and carry soft yellow, cornflower heads. The leaves are oblong and attractively scalloped at the edges.

3-4 ft. June–Sept. 3 ft. sq.

C. gymnocarpa. Velvet Centaurea. S. Europe. A half-shrubby plant with intensely silver, velvety leaves which are beautifully cut. It forms a bush about 2 ft. high with strong branching stems. The flowers are rosy-violet or purple but are practically hidden amongst the leaves. The species is useful for edging purposes, or can be attractive if grown as a specimen plant in a bright sunny position.

1½ ft. July–Aug. 2 ft. sq.

C. macrocephala. Yellow Hardhead; Yellow Hardweed. (*Plate 16, p. 80.*) Armenia. An extremely handsome perennial too rarely seen in gardens. A strong plant may throw up between 20 and 30 stems 3 to 4 ft. tall, each surmounted with a golden head of bloom as large as a clenched fist. Part of the attraction of this blossom lies in the rough brown calyx, which looks like a fur coat protecting the inner florets. Rough, oblong leaves closely clothe the stem, and as they have no stalks give it a very dense appearance. This is a plant which looks well as an individual and is best situated in a mid-border position. It needs full sun and a light, sandy loam. *3-4 ft. July. 3 ft. sq.*

C. montana. Mountain Knapweed. Europe. A free-flowering but somewhat straggling species, which needs a little careful staking and tying if the blooms are to be seen to best advantage. Flowers come in great profusion with large, Cornflower heads; *alba* white; *carnea* flesh; *coerulea* blue; *grandiflora* blue; *purpurea* purplish-blue; *rubra* reddish; *sulphurea* pale yellow; ' Violette ' deep blue. The foliage is rough, oblong lanceolate and silvery-grey in colour.

1½ ft. April–June. 1 ft. sq.

C. orientalis. Caucasian Centaurea. Siberia. Has an erect, branched habit, and light yellow Thistle-like heads. *2-3 ft. Summer. 2 ft. sq.*

C. pulcherrima (syn. *Aethiopappus pulcherrimus*): Rose Centaurea. Caucasus. An attractive plant with deeply cut leaves which are silvery-grey in appearance; flower heads a bright rose. *2 ft. May–July. 2 ft. sq.*

C. pulchra. Kashmir. A handsome plant with large silver foliage and rosy purple flower heads. Var. *major* is larger but inclined to be tender. *1 ft. Aug. 1 ft. sq.*

C. ruthenica. E. Europe. Has attractively cut leaves and branching stems carrying pale yellow flowers. *2-3 ft. June–July. 2 ft. sq.*

C. rutifolia (syn. *C. candidissima*): Mediterranean Region. A foliage plant with silvery-white leaves, useful for planting near bright blues or reds. The pale purple flowers are less interesting than the leaves.

2–3 ft. July–Aug. 1½ ft. sq.

CEPHALARIA (*Dipsaceae*): Giant Scabious. From *kephale* (Gk) ' head ', from the shape of the flowers.

Attractive hardy plants of branching habit, mostly with yellow flowers, which are very similar to the blue Scabious (*Scabiosa caucasica*). They do well in any good garden soil, *C. gigantea* making a particularly useful back of the border subject. The foliage is also attractive and the blooms excellent for cutting. Although happiest in sun they do well in semi-shade. Planting should take place in spring. Propagation by seed sown outside in April or division in spring.

C. alpina. S. Europe. Back of the border subject with quantities of soft yellow flowers at the ends of the branchlets, and deeply cut leaves.

5 ft. June–July. 3 ft. sq.

C. gigantea (syn. *C. tatarica*): Giant Scabious. Caucasus. The most attractive species. Yellow flowers; the leaves are large, soft green and paler beneath.   *5–6 ft. Summer. 4 ft. sq.*

CHAMAENERION (*Onagraceae*): Rosebay; Willow Herb; Fire Weed. Name from *chamae* (Gk) ' ground ', *nerion* ' oleander '; significance uncertain.

Formerly known as Epilobium, but now referred to above genus.

Handsome but prolific perennials which need to be introduced with caution to the garden. The chief nuisance of the plant comes from the fur or down which surrounds the seeds; this tangles all neighbouring growth.

E. angustifolium. This plant should definitely *not* be introduced to the garden. It is the type species with sprays of pink flowers and smooth oval oblong leaves. However, it has two varieties which seed rarely and are therefore valuable for the border. Var. *album* (*Plate XVI, p. 257*) has pure white blossoms studding the wand-like stalks. The foliage is small and oblong in shape. Var. ' Isabel ' is a shell-pink form which is worth a place in any sunny border. Propagation by division.   *2–3 ft. July–Sept. 2 ft. sq.*

CHEIRANTHUS (*Cruciferae*): Wallflower. Derivation doubtful.

Well-known plants which are really perennial although usually grown as biennials. They are particularly useful for early work in the border both for their attractive flowers and sweet scent. Named or special coloured varieties can be kept true by taking soft cuttings, under handlights in spring, in a light sandy soil. The whole family prefers a dry or well-drained soil during the winter months and is also partial to a little lime.

C. cheiri. Best treated as a biennial. Varieties with variously coloured flowers are offered in the trade and come true from seed. This should be sown in a nursery bed in May or June, and the young plants put into their flowering positions in September or October. They will bloom the following spring.

Cloth of Gold, yellow, *1–1½ ft.*
Fire King, orange red, *1–1½ ft.*
Harpur Crewe, double yellow, *9 in.*
Rose Queen, terra cotta, *1–1½ ft.*

CHELIDONIUM (*Papaveraceae*): Greater Celandine. Swallow-wort. From *chelidon* (Gk) ' swallow ', probably because it flowers at the time of the coming of that bird.

C. majus. W. Asia and Europe including Britain. A rather weedy plant only suitable for the wild garden. It has attractive, coarsely toothed and cut foliage, small yellow flowers in branching sprays and hairy stems which emit a bright yellow juice when broken. The best form for the garden is the double flowered *flore-pleno.*

1–2 ft.   May   1 ft. sq.

CHELONE (*Scrophulariaceae*): Turtlehead. From *chelone* (Gk) ' tortoise ', from the supposed resemblance of the flower to a turtle's head.

N. American perennials closely related to Pentstemons which grow most happily in a rich, well-drained soil. The blooms, however, though bright and freely produced, are rather lumpy and not excessively useful in the border. The plants are tolerant of light shade and may be increased by seed, cuttings or division of the roots.

C. glabra: Snake Head. United States. Has Pentstemon-like leaves, toothed at the margins and white, or rose tinged, Antirrhinum-like heads crowded into terminal spikes. Var. *alba (Plate XV, p. 256)* is white.   *1–2 ft.   July–Sept.   1 ft. sq.*

C. lyoni. (Plate 23, p. 112.) S.E. United States. Forms a dense mass of stems with deep green leaves and carries packed clusters of showy pink flowers.   *2–3 ft.   July–Sept.   1½ ft. sq.*

C. obliqua. United States. Taller than *C. lyoni*, with rosy-purple blooms.
2 ft.   Aug.   1 ft. sq.

CHRYSANTHEMUM (*Compositae*): Ox-Eye. From *chrysos* (Gk) ' gold ' and *anthos* ' flower '; Linnaeus named the genus from the Corn Marigold *C. segetum.*

Well-loved plants now almost as popular in the west as the Orient. In 1754, the first Oriental species was introduced into England. But it was to be some 70 years later before it established itself as a florist's flower, and cultivation spread to the cottager's window and the more sheltered parts of the garden.

In the hardy border, however, most florists' Chrysanthemums are of little value. They are killed by winter frosts, or flower too late, and it was not until the years between the wars that they were seriously considered as border perennials in their own right. This period coincided with the introduction of the Korean hybrids, which derived from the native Korean Chrysanthemum (*C. coreanum*), a hardy wild species, with white daisy-like flowers.

Chrysanthemum rubellum, the other hardy garden group, started life as *C. erubescens*. The original plant, a straggling ragged petalled species with pale pink flowers, seems to have turned up first in a public garden in Llandudno, but passed unnoticed in gardens until Kew exhibited it in 1935 at a Royal Horticultural Society meeting, under the name of *C. erubescens*. It received an Award of Merit, but in 1938, as it could not be related to any known species was renamed *rubellum*. *Rubellum* can be distinguished from the Korean types by the rootstocks. In the former these run underground like couch grass, but remain compact in the latter. They also come into bloom earlier and stand more severe winters.

Both these types are invaluable in the autumn border. They blend particularly well with Michaelmas Daisies, providing colour shades lacking in the latter genus. They grow practically anywhere, but flower most freely in well-drained loam and in full sunshine. Division of the roots should take place every other year, early in the spring. When replanting give a change of soil if possible and do not let them dry out during the summer months.

Also included under Chrysanthemums are two other useful groups of garden plants. *C. coccineum* includes the Pyrethrum and *C. maximum* the Ox-Eye or Shasta Daisy. Pyrethrums are particularly useful as they give periodic (especially early summer and autumn) displays throughout the season. They need a good rich soil which will not dry out, and benefit from annual mulches of compost or rotted dung. After the first crop of flowers is done the plants may be cut down to encourage later displays. The plants should be lifted every other year for division, in spring.

The Shasta Daisies are excellent for cutting but need a well-drained soil which will not dry out. They are useful mid-border subjects and flower between seasons, that is in July and August. Propagate by spring division.

C. arcticum. Arctic Europe, Asia and America. A low-growing humpy species, which is remarkably hardy. The flowers are single, white shading to pink when mature.

12–15 in.   June–July.   1 ft. sq.

C. coccineum (syn. *Pyrethrum roseum*): Pyrethrum. Persia, Caucasia. A variable species with large flower heads, white to red, and sometimes tipped with yellow. This is the parent of many good garden

Royal Command, semi-double, rich wine purple. *2½ ft.*

White Wedgewood, semi-double, white. *2½ ft.*

C. uliginosum. Giant Daisy, Moon Daisy. (*Plate VIII, p. 224.*) Hungary. An erect plant which branches somewhat at the top of each stem, and carries single white flowers with green centres. These are between 2 and 2½ in. across. This is a fine back of the border plant which deserves to be more widely grown. *4½–5 ft. Sept.–Oct. 3 ft. sq.*

CICHORIUM (*Compositae*): Chicory. Ancient Arabic name.

A bright native plant from 2–5 ft. high which in summer bears beautiful light blue flowers. It is worth a place in the border providing the seedlings are not allowed to get out of hand. The blanched leaves are also useful for winter salads. One drawback to chicory as a garden plant is the fact that the flowers close early and in dull weather, but on a fine day, the blue of the blossoms studding the long stems presents a handsome and unforgettable sight. Propagated by root cuttings or seed.

C. intybus: Chicory, Succory. (*Plate 11, p. 64.*) S. Europe including Britain. A thick rooted perennial with broad oblong leaves which become smaller towards the top of the flower stem, and wand-like branches packed with bright azure flowers each about 1½ in. across. Var. *album* (*Plate X, p. 225*) has white blooms, var. *roseum*, clear rose pink. *2–5 ft. July–Aug. 2 ft. sq.*

CIMICIFUGA (*Ranunculaceae*): Bugbane. From *cimex* (L) 'bug', *fugo* 'to drive away'.

Tall, handsome, late summer flowering perennials with beautiful buttercup-like leaves and erect, feathery plumes of creamy-white flowers. The one drawback is the unpleasant smell which emanates from the plant at close quarters. The plants are however, admirably suited to a mid to back position in the border, and prove especially useful in partially shaded sites. Although they thrive in most soils, better quality spikes are obtained when the roots grow in good, deep, rich vegetable soil. Propagation by seed sown as soon as gathered, or division of the roots in spring or autumn.

C. americana (syn. *C. cordifolia*): American Bugbane. (*Plate XV, p. 256.*) E. & N. America. A slender species, with creamy-white flowers on an elongated branching stem, and much divided leaves. The leaflets of the latter are almost round, particularly at the base, which gives it a distinguishing characteristic from other species. It associates well with Phlox and Red Hot Pokers.

2–4 ft. Aug.–Sept. 2 ft. sq.

C. dahurica. Dahuria and Japan. Creamy flowers characterised by the outer stamens which are enlarged and almost petal-like. Deeply cut leaves which are lobed and toothed. It is taller and more branched than *C. americana*. *4 ft. Late summer. 2 ft. sq.*

C. foetida. Kamchatka Bugbane. Russia, Siberia to Japan. This species has some importance from an economic point of view for it is used as an insect deterrent, chiefly in Russia. It is less commonly grown in borders than the other types mentioned, chiefly because of the offensive smell. It grows stiffly erect and has greenish-yellow flowers. *5 ft. July–Aug. 2 ft. sq.*

C. japonica. Japanese Bugbane. Japan. A beautiful variety with very large leaves and heavy racemes of white flowers. *3 ft. Aug.–Oct. 2 ft. sq.*

C. racemosa. Black Snake-root. E. & N. America. Has feathery sprays of creamy-white flowers borne on branching stems. These droop most gracefully and present an Astilbe-like appearance. The flowers have an offensive odour but they are certainly beautiful for late summer work. *3–6 ft. July–Aug. 2½ ft. sq.*

C. racemosa var. *dissecta*. Has attractive much cut leaves and small white flowers. It often continues in bloom until September. Var. *simplex* produces the most handsome flowers of the genus and has particularly clean white blossoms on erect spikes. By some authorities this is given specific rank whilst others refer it to *C. foetida*. 'White Pearl' is another varietal form and reaches 4 ft. in height. *3 ft. July–Aug. 2 ft. sq.*

CLAYTONIA (*Portulacaceae*): Spring Beauty. Named after John Clayton of Virginia, an 18th-century American botanist.

A genus of small, smooth, rather succulent plants, sometimes used for damp spots in borders or wild gardens. They have tuberous root-stocks, which divide easily in spring to produce new colonies, or new plants may be propagated from seed. A damp peaty soil provides the best planting medium.

C. sibirica. Siberia. Produces slender, succulent leaves from a deep rounded corm and carries loose sprays of white or pale rose flowers. As it seeds very easily it should not be planted amongst border plants, but rather in the wild or rougher parts of the garden. *6 in. Mar.–April. 1 ft. sq.*

C. virginica. E. & N. America. A taller growing perennial, the white flowers tinged with pink. These are very often, five-petalled. *8 in. Mar.–April. 1 ft. sq.*

CLEMATIS (*Ranunculaceae*): Traveller's Joy. Greek name for a climbing plant.

Although this genus is chiefly noted for its handsome climbing shrubs, there are a few border perennials worth noting. The stems of these die down in autumn and are of a bushy but non-climbing habit. Although tolerant of most soil types they prefer a chalky, well-drained loam. Where this is not available, a little hydrated lime can be introduced during the initial planting. Plant the roots in spring or autumn and when frost spoils the foliage cut the stems hard back, and give the plants a good mulching of well-rotted manure. Propagation by seed or root division.

C. douglasii. N. America. Low growing species suited to the front of the border, with solitary terminal flowers on rather downy stalks. They are bell shaped with the sepals curved back, blue at the back and deep purple inside.   *1 ft. June. 2 ft. sq.*

C. fremontii. N.W. America. Somewhat smaller in all its parts than *C. douglasii.* It has simple leaves which are oval lance-shaped and heavily veined, and single flowers borne on rather stiff stems. These are tubular, purple and somewhat downy at the edges.
1½ ft. May–June. 1½ ft. sq.

C. heracleifolia. Tube Clematis. (*Plate 11, p. 64.*) China. An erect but sturdy plant with large, Cow-Parsnip-like leaves and short stalked clusters of tubular flowers of a purplish-blue colour.
2–3 ft. Aug.–Sept. 2 ft. sq.

C. heracleifolia var. *davidiana.* A fine hybrid with deep blue flowers produced in great profusion. These are sweetly scented. It does well in a shady position and is a good garden plant. Var. ' Cote d'Azur ' is sky-blue.
2–2½ ft. Aug. 3 ft. sq.

C. heracleifolia var. ' Edward Prichard '. (*Plate XIV, p. 241.*) A fine modern variety with cobalt blue flowers. *2–2½ ft. Aug.–Sept. 3 ft. sq.*

C. integrifolia. S. Europe. A mid-summer blooming variety with handsome, oval, stalkless leaves and branches carrying solitary, deep blue flowers.   *2 ft. June–Aug. 2 ft. sq.*

C. recta. S. & E. Europe. Is somewhat of tufted growth and has slender, straggling stems carrying pinnately divided leaves. The flowers are very numerous, borne on branching sprays at the head of the stem. They are white and very sweetly scented, each about an inch across. This species is best trained up twiggy peasticks or it will sprawl in untidy fashion in the border. So treated it makes a very handsome perennial. Var. *flore-pleno* has double flowers; var. *grandiflora* pure white fragrant starry flowers; var. *purpurea* is similar but has purple foliage.   *3–4 ft. June–July. 3 ft. sq.*

C. recta var. *manchurica.* Makes an exceptionally good plant for cutting and when established sends up flower spikes about 3 ft. high. In the

border it forms an attractive clump which associates well with plants like *Aster yunannensis* ' Napsbury ', Red Hot Pokers and *Salvia* × *superba*.
3 ft. July–Aug. 3 ft. sq.

CLINTONIA (*Liliaceae*). Named after De Witt Clinton, a Governor of New York State.

A group of low-growing herbaceous plants with running, underground rhizomes and a few broad, shining leaves. The flowers are usually borne on smooth long stems in umbels. The genus thrives best under woodland conditions in leafy soil and shaded sites. These are front of the border subjects and sometimes useful in difficult situations. Propagation by division in spring.

C. andrewsiana. California. Has smooth, broadly oblong leaves which are sharply pointed and clusters or umbels of deep rose, bell-shaped drooping flowers. These are followed in autumn by blue berries.
1½ ft. June. 1½ ft. sq.

C. uniflora. Queencup. California. Has leaves similar to Lily of the Valley, and one (or rarely two) drooping white flowers on each stem. These are followed by the blue berries typical of this genus.
6 in. June. 1 ft. sq.

CODONOPSIS (*Campanulaceae*): Bellwort. From *kodon* (Gk) ' bell ', *opsis* ' like ', referring to the shape of the flowers.

A small genus related to the Campanula family, chiefly characterised by the beautiful colouring inside the bell-like flowers. These are the typical Campanula shape outside, usually blue, but the interior is beautifully marked with various shades of green, chocolate, orange and blue. Because of this the plants are best grown on a raised bed so that the interior as well as the exterior of the flowers can be seen. They all favour a well-drained loam and full sunshine. The plants may be raised from seed or soft cuttings. The following are the most important species.

C. clematidea. Asia. Has flowers bluish-white externally, and slender, oval leaves.   *3–4 ft. Summer. 1 ft. sq.*

C. convolvulacea. Upper Burma and W. China. Climbing species with smooth leaves alternately arranged on the stems. The flowers are large, blue, bell-shaped and between one and two inches across. Staking is necessary to prevent the plant sprawling.
2–3 ft. Aug. 2 ft. sq.

C. meleagris. China. One of the most attractive species and when well grown reaches a height of approximately 1 ft. The drooping bell-shaped flowers are of rare beauty, being pale, porcelain blue outside, heavily marked inside with bright zonings of chocolate, purple and green. The rootstock is extremely fleshy. *9–15 in. Aug. 1 ft. sq.*

C. ovata. Himalayas. A plant of spreading habit, close to the ground, but with the older branches becoming erect later. The leaves are oval, small and very rough to the touch, the flowers pale blue, speckled inside with gold and green markings.   *6–12 in. Aug. 1 ft. sq.*

C. tangshen. China. This plant needs to be grown well back in the border, for it is of climbing nature and should be staked with peasticks. The flowers are greenish without and brightly striped with purple inside. Grow in groups of three.   *6–10 ft. Summer. 3 ft. sq.*

COMMELINA (*Commelinaceae*): Blue Spiderwort, Day Flower. Named after J. and K. Commelin, 17th century Dutch botanical writers.

A variable family, the herbaceous species of which grow upright or procumbent, rather similar in manner to Tradescantia. The nodes or joints are swollen and often root from these areas. Commelina is not always hardy in exposed situations or on cold, wet soil and in such districts should be protected with a mulch of well-weathered ashes in autumn, or the roots may be lifted and stored, like Dahlias. In well-drained or sandy soils which are warm in winter it often grows extremely freely.

C. coelestis, 'Mexico'. Has hairy backs to the delightful sky blue flowers. The joints or nodes are very pronounced, the oblong leaves clasping the stems. It is such a beautiful shade of blue that it is sometimes grown alone in a small bed. It should be looked upon as half-hardy except in most favoured areas. Propagation is from division of the tubers in spring or from seed. Var. *alba* has white flowers, var. *variegata* is a bicolour form.   *1½ ft. June. 1 ft. sq.*

C. erecta. S.E. United States. A sturdy plant, very hardy with large, rough, oblong lanceolate leaves. Flowers blue and white.
    2–4 ft. Summer. 2 ft. sq.

CONVALLARIA (*Liliaceae*): Lily of the Valley. From *convallis* (L) ' valley ', in allusion to the habitat.

Well-loved flowers native to but not common in Great Britain, with sweet scented sprays of handsome bell-like flowers.

The roots do best in leafy loam in light shade, planting the crowns in early autumn immediately after the foliage dies down. When once established they should be left undisturbed for several years. The finest garden form is ' Fortin's Giant ' which has larger flowers and is much more robust in growth than the common kinds. Propagation from the ' pips ', or rootstock division.

C. majalis. The common Lily of the Valley. Europe. Has a running rootstock, and large oval oblong leaves arranged in pairs. Flowers extremely fragrant, borne in pendulous sprays. Var. *rosea* has soft

pink flowers; var. *variegata*, white striped foliage; var. *prolificans*, double white blooms. There is also a new garden form worth noting called ' Everest ' which like ' Fortin's Giant ' is larger than the type.
6 in. Spring. 6 in. sq.

COREOPSIS (*Compositae*): Tickseed. From *coris* (Gk) ' bug ', *opsis* ' similar to ', referring to the appearance of the seed.

Showy N. American plants valuable for their cut blooms; although if intended for this purpose they should be grown in small beds away from the border. Most of the perennial kinds are untidy in growth and need some support from peasticks. To stimulate more blooms seed should be prevented by constant removal of the spent flowers. Coreopsis will grow in any ordinary garden soil providing the position is in full sun. Propagation by seed sown outside in April or side shoots taken from the base in autumn.

C. auriculata. S. United States. Long-flowering perennial with large flower heads and very wiry stems. The petals or rays are yellow, with zonal bands of purplish-brown around the central disc. There is an improved form of this ' Astolat ' with deeper coloured blossoms; also *superba*, characterised by a plum-purple blotch at the base of each petal. *1–1½ ft. June–Aug. 2 ft. sq.*

C. grandiflora. S. United States. A smooth perennial, leafy in all the branches, with bright golden flower heads 1–2½ in. across. These are borne on long stems, excellent for cutting. Var. ' Badengold ' is a recent introduction with much finer, larger and more brightly coloured flowers. It is inclined to be disappointing at times, and in some soils produces an abundance of leaves but few or no blooms. A starvation diet or rather poor soil is recommended in such instances. Var. ' Mayfield Giant ' is the tallest growing garden form with extra large flowers on longer stems. This characteristic makes it a first-class plant for cutting. Staking is necessary. *3 ft. June–Aug. 2 ft. sq.*

C. grandiflora, ' Perry's Var.' (*Plate 27, p. 128.*) Introduced in the early 1920's; one of the first breaks in the species. It is a shorter plant with semi-double flowers of deep yellow.
2–2½ ft. June–Aug. 2 ft. sq.

C. lanceolata. E. United States. Differs from *C. grandiflora* ' Perry's Var.' chiefly by reason of the leaves, which are much cut in basal specimens, but entire on the flower stems. The blooms are bright yellow and the branching stems usually carry one flower on each branchlet.
3 ft. June–Sept. 2 ft. sq.

C. rosea. N. America. Likes a moister soil than the other species and has a creeping rootstock and small pink or rosy flowers.
1 ft. Aug.–Sept. 1 ft. sq.

C. tripteris. Cent. United States. A smooth perennial with slender, upright growth and yellow flowers just over an inch across.

3½–4 ft. June–Sept. 2 ft. sq.

C. verticillata. E. United States. A distinctive species by reason of the foliage, which is finely divided into thread-like segments. The flowers are tiny but produced in great profusion. This is a first-class front of the border plant for it has an extremely long season. The variety ' Golden Shower ' is richer and brighter than the type and the best kind to seek for the herbaceous border. *2 ft. June–Sept. 1½ ft. sq.*

CORYDALIS (*Papaveraceae*): Fumitory. From *korydalis* (Gk) ' lark ', from the fancied resemblance of the flower to the spur of a lark.

C. cheilanthifolia. China. Has beautiful basal, much cut leaves and loose sprays carrying many yellow, tubular flowers.

1 ft. May–June. 1 ft. sq.

C. lutea. Europe. A well-known, long-flowering, dwarf plant which produces its blooms in almost any situation. The foliage is beautiful, cut like a fern, whilst the bright yellow flowers are borne in crowded clusters. The species has the great merit of growing where nothing else will, in cracks in walls, between stones, or even on a gravel path. If not kept under control it may become troublesome. Propagation from seed. *1 ft. All Summer. 1 ft. sq.*

CRAMBE (*Cruciferae*): Sea Kale. From *crambe* (L) ' cabbage '.

One of the noblest and largest leaved herbaceous plants, producing striking blossoms when grown in rich soil. Usually one plant is all that is required, as most species attain a height of 5–6 ft. and spread over an area almost as great. The leaves are large, heart-shaped, greyish-green, somewhat like the common Sea Kale, whilst the small white flowers are borne in thousands on dense branching sprays. In seasons of infestation from Cabbage White Butterflies this plant may be as subject to attack as any other member of the Brassica family. Propagation by root cuttings or seed. Flowers come from seed in three years.

C. cordifolia. Caucasus. The best-known species with wide heads of Gypsophila-like flowers. It is not long-lasting and needs to be periodically renewed. Var. *grandiflora* has larger flowers, darker foliage, is taller and more robust. Var. *kotschyana* also has large flowers. *6 ft. June–July. 6 ft. sq.*

CROCOSMIA (*Iridaceae*): Coppertip. From *crocus* (L), ' saffron ', *osme* ' smell '; the dried flowers soaked in water smell of saffron.

Handsome herbaceous plants with narrow, strap-like leaves and funnel-shaped yellow or orange-scarlet flowers. The two species have been crossed and produced some very fine colour forms with large, open flowers. Hardy in favoured situations and well-drained soil, it pays to lift the corms in colder districts and store them in damp peat in a frostproof shed until March or April. Light rich soil suits them best. Propagation by offsets or seed sown as soon as ripe.

C. aurea. Golden Coppertip. S. Africa. Has golden-yellow flowers with orange or brown hairs. Var. *flore pleno* has double blooms; *imperialis*, fiery orange-red; *maculata*, orange, spotted on the inner petals with chocolate. *2–3 ft. July–Oct. 1 ft. sq.*

C. × *crocosmiiflora.* A name which embraces most of the garden varieties between *C. aurea* and *C. pottsii.* The flowers may be yellow, orange, orange-scarlet, chocolate or vermilion. They make good cut flowers. Varieties worth noting are:
    Aurora, rich orange-yellow.
    Citronella, clear lemon-yellow.
    Herbert Perry, large flowers, deep orange-scarlet.
    Lady Wilson, clear orange, tall.
    Nimbus, gold with crimson base.
    Prometheus, orange flushed crimson, spotted centre.
    Queen Adelaide, red and deep orange.
    Queen Alexandra, chrome-yellow blotched with carmine.
    Star of the East, pale orange-yellow.
    W. D. Houghton, large clear scarlet.
$1\frac{1}{2}$–3 ft. July–Sept. 6 in. sq.

C. pottsii. S. Africa. Flowers bright yellow flushed with red.
3–4 ft. Aug. 1 ft. sq.

CYNOGLOSSUM (*Boraginaceae*): Chinese Hound's Tongue. From *kynos* (Gk) 'dog', *glossa* 'tongue', alluding to the shape of the leaves.
    Rough-stemmed perennials with beautiful funnel-shaped flowers, often of a fine blue, although sometimes these vary through rose, blue and purple in the same plant. Plants grow well in ordinary soil providing it is well drained, and are easily raised from seed. The majority are short-lived perennials but may be sown where they are to flower.

C. amabile. China. A beautiful species best treated as a biennial, raising fresh stock each year from seed sown in March or April in a cold frame. The drooping funnel-shaped flowers are a delightful shade of blue, pink or white. *2 ft. July–Aug. 1 ft. sq.*

C. grande. Western N. America. Bright blue with oval hairy leaves.
1–2$\frac{1}{2}$ ft. Spring. 1 ft. sq.

C. nervosum. Himalayas. A handsome plant which sends up branching sprays of small, intensely blue forget-me-not like flowers. The leaves are rough, oblong and narrow. This is a plant which needs a moderately rich loam and full sun. *2 ft. June–July. 1 ft. sq.*

Plate 27: 1. TICKSEED, *Coreopsis grandiflora* ' Perry's Var.' 2. RED HOT POKER, *Kniphofia hybrida* ' Royal Standard '. 3. PERENNIAL SUNFLOWER, *Helianthus decapetalus flore pleno.* 4. ROUGH HELIOPSIS, *Heliopsis scabra.* 5. TREASURE FLOWER, *Gazania* hybrids

Plate 28: 1. JOE PYE WEED, *Eupatorium purpureum.* 2. HEDGEHOG CONEFLOWER, *Echinacea purpurea.* 3. CALIFORNIAN FUCHSIA, *Zauschneria cana.* 4. KAFFIR LILY, *Schizostylis coccinea.* 5. OBEDIENT PLANT, *Physostegia virginiana* 'Vivid'

Plate 29: MICHAELMAS DAISIES, *Aster*—1. PEACE (*A. novi-belgii*). 2. MOUNT EVEREST
(*n-b*). 3. KING GEORGE (*A. amellus*). 4. HARRINGTON'S PINK (*A. novae-angliae*). 5. *A. dracun-*
culoides. 6. EVENTIDE (*n-b*). 7. RED SUNSET (*n-b*)

Plate 30: 1. GIANT RAGWORT, *Ligularia japonica.* 2. JAPANESE FLEECE-FLOWER, *Polygonum reynoutria* hort. 3. PURPLE-LEAVED ICE PLANT, *Sedum maximum atropurpureum.* 4. CUP PLANT, *Silphium perfoliatum.* 5. VINE-LEAVED WINDFLOWER, *Anemone vitifolia*

C. virginianum. Eastern N. America. Light blue, tubular flowers.

1–1½ ft. July. 1 ft. sq.

DELPHINIUM (*Ranunculaceae*): Perennial Larkspur. Name from *delphis* (Gk) 'dolphin', the flower buds before expansion being thought to resemble that fish.

No really representative collection of hardy plants can be complete without Delphiniums. There are no other herbaceous perennials so stately and magnificent. Most people love blue flowers and the shades of colour which come in the large-flowered perennial forms defy imitation or description.

Delphiniums are greedy plants. To get good results you must give them plenty of nourishment—a deep, rich soil, and quantities of rotted manure. Established specimens are often prodigal with flower spikes, and these should be reduced when a few inches high to 3, 6 or 8 (according to the size of the plants). Slugs and snails should be kept from the young shoots in spring, by covering the crowns with sharp, well-weathered ashes, and by using poison bait.

Whilst the Bouquet (*D. grandiflorum*) and the Garland Larkspurs (*D. belladonna*) need grouping for spectacular effects, one well-grown specimen of the Candle or Bee Larkspur (*D. elatum*) can often stand alone.

All Delphiniums are sun lovers. They should be propagated by seed sown in April or May under glass or in the open; the young seedlings may be grown on in boxes or drills and planted in their permanent positions about September. Named varieties should be increased from the young basal shoots, taken with a piece of the old rootstock in March. The wounds made should be dusted with charcoal, and the cuttings rooted in a cold frame. Generally speaking new Delphinium plants should be established in spring. They may survive autumn transplanting, but mature specimens often fail to root until spring and, lying in cold wet soil, tend to rot off if the winter is a hard one. Delphiniums are particularly good associates for Foxtail Lilies (Eremuri) early-flowering Red Hot Pokers and Madonna Lilies (*Lilium candidum*).

D. belladonna. Delphinium, Garland Larkspur. (*Plate 6, p. 33.*) A garden race of unknown parentage, referred by some authors to *D. cheilanthum* var. *formosum*. It originated about 1880, the type having light blue flowers, although seedlings may come up in blue, purple or deep blue. A white form 'Moerheimi' appeared in 1906 in a Dutch nursery, and has not been improved upon even to this day.

The following are good garden plants in this group and flower between June and July. Each needs a planting area of about 2 ft. sq.

Blue Bees, Cambridge blue with a white eye, *3 ft.*

Cliveden Beauty, sky blue, *3 ft.*

Lamartine, deep purplish-blue, *3 ft.*

Naples, a rich gentian blue, $3\frac{1}{2}$ ft.

Semi-plena, azure blue tinted pink, $2\frac{1}{2}$ ft.

Theodora, single electric blue, $3\frac{1}{2}$ ft.

Wendy, deep cobalt blue flecked with purple but very bright; a good cut flower, 3 ft.

D. × *ruysii* (syn. ' Pink Sensation '). The gardening world knew that the late B. Ruys of Dedemsvaart in Holland had set his heart on a pink Delphinium, and to that end had even employed a scientist in 1906. As parent he used the somewhat tender, red-flowered, and rather indifferent species *D. cardinale*, but the pink Delphinium did not materialise and Mr. Ruys gave up the quest. Then, in the late 1930's, at Ruy's own nurseries, a chance seedling came up in a seed bed, and the flowers were pink. This became ' Pink Sensation ' and in turn has given rise to ' Rose Beauty ' which is even richer in colour. Because of its low stature and general habit it is believed that *D. nudicaule* was one of the parents. *2–3 ft. June–July. 2 ft. sq.*

LARGE FLOWERED HYBRIDS (*D. elatum*). (*Plate 17, p. 80.*) The large-flowered hybrids are also of uncertain lineage, the parentage of many good garden sorts being completely lost. Most of them are derived from *D. elatum* the Candle or Bee Larkspur. The following varieties may be grown as individuals or planted in threes in a mid to back border position. Each needs a ground area of approximately 3 ft. sq.

Alice Artindale, long tapering spikes of fully double, rosy-mauve flowers edged with azure blue. The only true double, this should be included in every collection. *5 ft. June–July.*

Ann Miller, rich gentian blue, very robust with flowers nearly 4 in. across. *$4\frac{1}{2}$ ft. June–July.*

Anne Page, fine large flowers of a rich cornflower blue on exceptionally strong stems. *$5\frac{1}{2}$ ft. June–July.*

Anona, very pale blue lightly touched with mauve, white eye. Mildew resistant. *5 ft. June–July.*

Beau Nash, dark mauve-purple with black and gold eye. *5 ft. June–July.*

Blackmore's Blue, sky blue, white eye. *$4\frac{1}{2}$ ft. June–July.*

Blackmore's Glorious, mauve flushed pale blue, white eye; very vigorous. *$5\frac{1}{2}$ ft. June–July.*

Blue Gown (*Plate 36, p. 160*), rich deep blue. *5 ft. May–June.*

Brutus, rich blue and wine-purple, black and gold eye. *5 ft. June–July.*

Cambria, soft mauve-blue, semi-double; an old favourite. *4–5 ft. June–July.*

Charles F. Langdon, clear blue with black eye. *$6\frac{1}{2}$ ft. June–July.*

Charon, dark blue with brown eye, dwarf habit. *4 ft. June–July.*

C. H. Middleton, broad tapering spikes, large semi-double rich blue flowers with yellowish-white eye. *5 ft. June–July.*

Crystal, long broad spikes, semi-double, sky-blue flowers with white centres. *5 ft. June–July.*

Daily Express, clear sky-blue with brown eye; mildew resistant and robust. *5 ft. June–July.*

Dame Myra Curtis, long tapering spikes clothed with sky blue flowers which have blue and black eyes. *5 ft. July.*

Guy Langdon, very long flower spikes, florets deep violet, with violet and white eye. *5½ ft. June–July.*

Jack Tar, very rich dark blue. *5 ft. July.*

Jennifer Langdon, mauve, tinged pale blue, black eye. *5½ ft. June–July.*

Julia Langdon, mauve and pale blue, white eye, very stout spikes. *5 ft. June–July.*

Kingswood, pale blue, suffused mauve. *5½ ft. June–July.*

Lady Eleanor, sky blue suffused with mauve. *6 ft. June–July.*

Lady Guinevere, large flowers of soft mauve; robust habit. *6 ft. June–July.*

Marathon, lavender-mauve tinged with rich gentian, very large spikes. *7 ft. June–July.*

Melora, light mauve, white eye. *5 ft. June–July.*

Minerva, very dark violet with black and gold eye. *6 ft. June–July.*

Natalie (*Plate 36, p. 160*), rich cornflower blue, with deep violet blue shading. *4 ft. June–July.*

Peacock, deep blue and purple, black eye, strong constitution. *5½ ft. June–July.*

Purple Ruffles, deep purple tinged with royal blue, double, the tips of the petals fluted and frilled, making this quite unlike any other variety. *5½ ft. June–July.*

Pyramus, rich blue, shaded mauve. *5 ft. June–July.*

Royalist, very vigorous with large, deep blue flowers. *6 ft. June–July.*

Ruffles, pale blue and mauve. *5½ ft. June–July.*

Silver Moon, large silvery-mauve with creamy-white eye. An outstanding variety. *5 ft. June–July.*

Startling, deep violet, white eye. *6 ft. June–July.*

Sylvia, light blue with white eye. *5½ ft. June–July.*

Tesse, silvery-mauve with white eye. *5½ ft. June–July.*

Tyrian, deep violet with white eye; long tapering spikes which cut well. *5 ft. June–July.*

Weeley White (*Plate VI, p. 209*), fine larger-flowered white variety with black eyes. *5 ft. June–July.*

Welsh Boy, sky blue and mauve. *5 ft. June–July.*

Wild Wales, gentian blue flushed pinkish, deep black eye. *5 ft. June–July.*

'PACIFIC STRAIN HYBRIDS'. A fine race of American origin which show a wide range of colour from white or the palest shade of blue to indigo blue and royal purple with many intermediate shadings. The large flowers are excellent for cutting and many are double. Seed gives excellent results as all the seedlings will be good. The plants, however, are not as long lived as most of the named sorts already described.

DELPHINIUM SPECIES

D. cardinale. Cardinal Larkspur. California. A somewhat tender species which needs deep, rich yet well-drained soil. If seed is sown under glass in February the young plants will flower the same year. The blooms are bright red and borne somewhat sparsely up the stems.

2–3 ft. July–Aug. 1 ft. sq.

D. grandiflorum. Bouquet or Siberian Larkspur. (*Plate 6, p. 33.*) Siberia. Western N. America. An attractive species with slender branching stems clothed with delicately poised, long spurred flowers. These are violet-blue in the type but a number of varieties have been named and show varying colour breaks. The leaves are very handsome and deeply cut.

The following named sorts will probably be preferred to the type for border work: Var. *album*, white; ' Azure Fairy ', pale blue; ' Blue Butterfly ', rich blue with a brown spot on each petal; ' Blue Gem ', deep blue, about 1 ft. tall. *1–3 ft. July–Aug. 1½ ft. sq.*

D. nudicaule. Orange Larkspur. California. A smooth species with deeply cut leaves and red and yellow flowers. Varieties from this species include *aurantiacum*, orange; ' Lemon Gem ', yellow; *purpureum*, purplish, and possibly ' × *ruysii* ' (' Pink Sensation '). (See p. 130.)

1–1½ ft. April–June. 1 ft. sq.

D. tatsienense. Szechwan. A handsome but not spectacular species for the front of the border or rock garden pocket. The flowers are deep violet. *1½ ft. July. 1 ft. sq.*

D. zalil. Yellow Larkspur. Persia. An uncommon species with narrowly cut, dark green leaves and straight spikes of lemon-yellow flowers. It is not a good perennial in cold wet soils.

1–2 ft. May–Aug. 1½ ft. sq.

DENTARIA (*Cruciferae*): Coral Root. Toothwort. From *dens* (L) ' tooth ', an allusion to the shape of the roots.

Plants closely related to the Cardamines with smooth, palmately cut leaves and racemes of small, somewhat drooping flowers. Their value to the gardener lies in their early blooms and a readiness to grow in semi-shaded situations. All do best in rich, moist, yet well-drained soils, and may be propagated by division. Seed is not freely produced.

D. bulbifera. Bulbous Coral Root. A rare native plant with pale purple flowers, somewhat resembling the Cuckoo Flower, *Cardamine pratensis*, but easily distinguishable from the latter by the small dark buds which grow on the upper parts of the stems, and which when ripe, fall off to produce new plants. The creeping roots are very fleshy and resemble a piece of coral. *1½–2 ft. April–May. 1 ft. sq.*

D. diphylla. Pepper Root. Nova Scotia. The common name derives from the fact that the long, crisp, succulent roots taste like Watercress.

The leaves are shaped somewhat like those of a Strawberry, whilst the flowers which resemble the Cardamine are white with a slight pinkish colour on the outside of the sepals. *1 ft. June. 1 ft. sq.*

D. laciniata. Cut Toothwort. *(Plate II, p. 193.)* N. America. Has the leaves arranged three in a whorl on short stalks, each segment being finely cut or jagged. The flowers on opening are rose but pale to almost pure white. They are larger than most of the family.

1 ft. April. 1 ft. sq.

DIANTHUS *(Caryophyllaceae)*: Garden Pinks, Border Carnation. From *dios* (Gk) ' divine ', *anthos* ' flower ', ' flower of the gods '.

This large and beautiful family is chiefly represented by rock garden plants; small, compact often delightfully fragrant. A few of the larger kinds, however, prove useful for border work, not only on account of the long season and beauty of the flowers, but because the neat silver foliage sets off the shape and shades of other nearby plants. The most important group are the Garden Pinks, for they flower practically the whole of the summer, and apart from making useful subjects for weaving into the border pattern, have a special value for edging purposes.

Border Carnations are derived from a different species, and in the main are slightly more difficult than Pinks. They have thicker and more succulent stems, a larger habit and are further characterised by the absence of an ' eye ', or circular zone of darker colouring in the centre of the flower. This latter feature is present in most Pinks.

Pinks and Border Carnations should be grown in a situation which is open and sunny, but not draughty. Good drainage is important, and they appreciate some lime. Whilst feeding makes good plants, care must be taken over the choice of humus material. Rotted manure is excellent, but both peat and leaf-mould seem to have a definitely harmful effect and may cause rotting of the stems. It should be appreciated also that the Pink family is of suffruticose habit, that is to say the leaves and stems are woody and persist in winter, but new growth comes from the growing parts of these stems. In this way they differ from shrubs, which break from the bottom and so can survive very hard cutting back. If one cuts too far back into the old growth of a Pink it often fails to shoot again. This point must be borne in mind during the spring and autumn tidying.

Neither Pinks nor Border Carnations need stopping, although exhibitors sometimes reduce blooms of the latter to one per stem for show purposes. Staking, however, will be necessary for some varieties although the supports should be light (cane or wire) and unobtrusive.

Propagation is effected by layers or cuttings, but seed can be used for species or where colour and other variations are unimportant.

The two following species should be considered the most important for border work, but if show and colour are required they will themselves be passed over for named varieties, the main groups and recommended kinds of which are also listed.

D. caryophyllus. Clove Pink, Carnation, Clove Gillyflower. W. Europe, naturalized in Britain. The parent of our modern Carnations (including border varieties), this species is characterised by slender, smooth silvery leaves, solitary flowers with notched petals, and a spicy fragrance. *1–2 ft. July–Aug. 1½ ft. sq.*

D. plumarius. Pink. S.E. Europe. This is the parent of the Garden Pinks, a hardy species, rather variable, with twin-flowered stems, the former pink, red or rarely white. *1–2 ft. May–July. 1 ft. sq.*

BORDER CARNATIONS. Height 1 ft. 1–2 ft. sq.
    Beauty of Cambridge, pale yellow.
    Consul, apricot.
    Diplomat, salmon pink flecked with deeper colour.
    Downs Clove, crimson, richly scented.
    Harmony, grey-mauve overlaid cerise.
    Lavender Clove, heliotrope.
    Madonna, white.
    Pink Pearl, pink.
    Royal Mail, scarlet.

GARDEN PINKS. This group has large flowers which often split the calyx. They flower in June only. Propagation by cuttings. Height 10 in. 1–2 ft. sq.
    Dad's Favourite, white with chocolate edging to petals.
    Dusky, dusky-pink, double, fragrant.
    Earl of Essex, rose-pink, fringed, double.
    Her Majesty, white, large, double, fragrant.
    Ice Queen, white with red eye, fringed, scented.
    Inchmery, pale pink.
    Lilac Musgrave, pink with fawn eye ringed with crimson, single.
    Mrs. Sinkins, white, an old favourite.
    Musgrave's Pink, white with green eye, fringed, single.
    Paddington, pink with purple eye, dwarf, double.
    Pink Mrs. Sinkins, pink with maroon eye.
    Sam Barlow, purplish-black and white.
    White Ladies, fragrant, white.

ALLWOODII PINKS. Raised by Allwood Brothers in the 1920's from a cross between a Perpetual Carnation and the white Garden Pink

' Old Fringed '. Apart from being perfectly hardy the plants bloom
several times in a season. They are propagated from layers or cuttings.
Height 8–10 in.   1½ ft. sq.

Alice, white fringed with carmine centre.
Arthur, maroon red with darker eye, double.
Barbara, crimson.
Betty, white with red centre; semi-double.
Daphne, pink with darker eye.
Derek, ruby crimson.
Freda, rosy purple.
Ian, double, rich crimson.
Isobel, cherry-red with darker eye.
Jean, white with violet centre, semi-double.
Monty, fragrant, rose pink with chocolate eye.
Philip, purple with deeper purple fleckings.
Thomas, deep red with darker eye.
Winston, bright crimson, fragrant, double.
Vera, pale pink with blood-red eye and waxy petals.

ALLWOOD'S SHOW PINKS.   Nearly as free-flowering as the Allwoodii
Pinks but many require staking; they are propagated in the same way.
Height 1½–2 ft.   2 ft. sq.

Bridesmaid, soft pink with salmon eye.
Crimson Glory, rich crimson with serrated petals, fragrant, double.
Fortune, fuchsia rose.
Leader, rose-pink with red eye.
Show Beauty, deep rose-pink with maroon eye.
Show Lady, salmon rose.
Show Pearl, white.
Show Portrait, cardinal red, very free-flowering.

LONDON PINKS.   Raised by Mr. F. R. McQuown from Allwoodii and
Garden Pinks. Many are ' laced ' or have a loop or lacing right round
the petal, of the same colour as the eye. Height 10–14 in. 1½ ft. sq.

London Fire, white, with rich red eye and lacing.
London Poppet, white, flushed pink, eyed and laced with ruby red.

EXHIBITION VARIETIES, IMPERIAL PINKS and HERBERT'S PINKS are
all allied to the above groups and require similar treatment.

SWEET WIVELSFIELD (Hyb.). Very dainty yet sweet scented pinks, both
single and double. ' Rainbow ', ' Loveliness ', ' Dianthus Sweetness '
and ' Blue Dianthus ' (a lavender-blue Sweet William) can all be
recommended. They are usually raised from seed, but vary considerably in colour.

D. fragrans. N. Caucasus. Another name used at times for sweet scented
Pinks of mixed parentage. The true type plant, white tinged with rose,

is sometimes grown, but not as frequently as its double form var. *plena* (*Plate VIII, p. 224*).   *1–1½ ft.   May–June.   1 ft. sq.*

DICENTRA (syn. Dielytra) (*Papaveraceae*): Bleeding Heart. From *dis* (Gk) ' two ', *kentron* ' spur ', the flowers having twin spurs.

Old-fashioned perennials. The species have fleshy, brittle roots and finely cut, fern-like foliage, whilst the flowers hang in pendant fashion from slender, arching sprays. Many books and writings express the view that Dicentras should grow in light shade, but the best specimens of *D. spectabilis* I ever saw were raised and grown in full sunshine in an open border. Here they attained a height of over 4–5 ft., flowering profusely in early summer and making magnificent specimens. It is my opinion that they are capable of standing much more sun than is usually believed, but they must have a deep, cool root run. Mulches of rotted manure or compost around the crowns of the plant in spring increase stature, and quality of flower. Propagation by division, and occasionally from seed.

D. eximia. Fringed Bleeding Heart. (*Plate 2, p. 17.*) United States. A fine border plant which combines attractive, fern-like foliage with rosy-purple blossoms on long drooping racemes. Equally at home in sun or shade it can be introduced to many corners of the garden and is perfectly hardy anywhere.

1–1½ ft.   Freely in May and September and intermittently between these months.   1 ft. sq.

There is also a good white form known as *D. eximia alba* (*Plate V, p. 208*). A hybrid of recent introduction, ' Bountiful ', is vastly superior to the type, growing 18 in. high with blue-green, handsomely cut foliage and spikes festooned with as many as 30 or 40 fuchsia red flowers. These are double the size of the type. The variety comes into bloom in early May and lasts well into July. A few intermittent blossoms are produced throughout the summer but in early autumn it flowers again as freely as in spring.

D. formosa. W. & N. America. Another species which is long-flowering providing the roots do not become dry during the growing period. Of tufted habit, it has coarser foliage than *D. eximia* and the flowers are pink or light red.   *1–1½ ft.   May–June.   1 ft. sq.*

D. spectabilis. Bleeding Heart, Dutchman's Breeches. (*Plate 3, p. 32.*) Siberia, Japan. An elegant plant which will grace any garden. It has finely cut foliage and arching sprays festooned with hanging, heart-shaped flowers. These are rosy-pink with pure white tips which glisten when the blossoms are fresh. The plant forces well. Propagation by division of the roots in autumn. There is a white variety, *alba.*

Normally 1½–2 ft. but in exceptional circumstances up to 4 ft.   May–June.   2 ft. sq.

DICTAMNUS (*Rutaceae*): Burning Bush. From old Greek name *diktamnos* ' ash leaved ', probably alluding to the foliage.

An old-fashioned herbaceous perennial which when once established, may be left in the same spot for several generations. The compound leaves are smooth, light green and not unlike those of an ash tree; the flowers, large and attractive, are borne in spikes up stiff erect stems. In the type species these are white but there is also a form commonly grown (var. *purpureus*) which has pink blooms lightly striped with red. In general habit the flower spikes may be said to resemble those of a very large single stock.

From an interest point of view Dictamnus is worth growing on account of the volatile oil which it secretes. On a sultry windless day it is sometimes possible to ignite this with a lighted match. All parts of the plant, but particularly the old flower heads are extremely rich in this secretion. This phenomenon, which was first discovered by Linnaeus, has earned the plant the name of ' Burning Bush ' in England and ' Gas Plant ' in America. It is also deemed a most sacred plant by the fire-worshippers of India on account of this strange happening. When gently rubbed the plant emits a fragrant scent, like lemon peel.

Dictamnus grows easily in any well-drained garden soil, and once established should be left undisturbed. It will do in some shade but flowers better in full sunshine. Propagation by division, or seed sown directly after gathering in the open ground. The seedlings flower about the third year.

D. albus (syn. *D. fraxinella*): Burning Bush, Dittany, Fraxinella. (*Plate VIII. p. 224.*) E. Europe, Asia. Has glossy compound foliage and showy terminal spikes of large, fragrant white flowers. The blooms are excellent for cutting. Var. *purpureus* (*Plate 18, p. 81*) has purplish blossoms; var. *giganteus* (syn. var. *caucasicus*) is a particularly large rosy-purple form with blooms carried on stems twice the height of the normal varieties.   *1½–2 ft. June–July. 2 ft. sq.*

DIERAMA (*Iridaceae*). From *dierama* (Gk) ' funnel ', referring to the shape of the flowers.

A small genus hardy in southern England but doubtfully so in the north. The plants need a deep, rich but well-drained soil. Although tall growing the graceful pendulous flower stems are not obstructive, so that a position fairly near the front of the border can be provided. Propagation by division or seed.

D. pendulum (syn. *Sparaxis pendula*). Long narrow grassy leaves and arching sprays of white, pink or purple flowers. *3 ft. June–July. 1 ft. sq.*

D. pulcherrimum (syn. *Sparaxis pulcherrima*). A larger and stronger plant with pendant, wand-like sprays of bright purple flowers. The best garden forms include *album*, white; ' Heron ', rich wine-red; ' Kingfisher', soft pink; 'Port Wine', rich purple; 'Skylark', purplish violet.   *4–6 ft.   Sept.–Oct.   1½ ft. sq.*

DIGITALIS (*Scrophulariaceae*): Foxglove. From *digitus* (L) 'finger', the flower being shaped like a gloved finger.

The woodland Foxglove *D. purpurea* is a biennial. With a rosette of basal leaves and spikes of pink and brown spotted flowers it is almost too well known to need description. It is, however, a plant which can take its place in any garden, its clean straight lines and erect habit looking particularly beautiful when associated with various shades of green. In shady areas Foxgloves are invaluable and provide a rich colouring. There are several true perennial species worth noting for the shady border. These will grow in ordinary garden soil providing it contains sufficient organic material to prevent drying out in summer.

The plants can be increased from seed sown outdoors in shallow drills about April or May or can be divided in spring.

D. ferruginea. S. and S.E. Europe. Syria, Persia. Another perennial which is best grown as a biennial. The leaves are smooth or slightly downy, the flower spikes long and thickly packed with rust-red flowers. These are downy outside and netted with darker brown inside.

4–6 ft.   July.   2 ft. sq.

D. grandiflora (syn. *D. ambigua*): Yellow Foxglove. Europe, W. Asia. A poor perennial best grown as a biennial. The leaves are oblong lanceolate, notched at the edges and clasped to the stem; the flowers large, about 2 in. long, pale yellow blotched with brown. The whole plant is somewhat hairy.   *2–3 ft.   July–Aug.   1 ft. sq.*

D. lanata. Grecian Foxglove. Greece. A fine species, very free-flowering. The leaves are deep green, oblong and covered with silvery hairs; the blooms rather small (1–1½ in. long), soft creamy-yellow with deeper coloured veining, in dense, many-flowered spikes.

2–3 ft.   July–Aug.   1½ ft. sq.

D. lutea. Straw Foxglove. (*Plate 14, p. 65.*) S.W. and Cent. Europe. N.W. Africa. A smooth perennial species, with oblong, toothed leaves and densely flowered racemes of primrose yellow flowers. These are small but the general effect is most attractive. *2 ft.   July.   1 sq. ft.*

D. orientalis. Asia Minor. Has pale creamy-yellow flowers similar to *D. lanata*, with less marking. The leaves, however, are much longer and somewhat narrower.   *2½ ft.   July–Aug.   1½ ft. sq.*

D. thapsi. Spain. A perennial species with mauve and red spotted flowers. It is very similar in general appearance to *D. purpurea*, the common Foxglove and sometimes referred to this genus. The leaves are oval oblong and somewhat wavy at the edges. *2–4 ft. June–Sept. 1½ ft. sq.*

DIMORPHOTHECA (*Compositae*): Cape Marigold. From *dis* (Gk) ' two ', *morphe* ' shape ', *theca* ' fruit ', there being two forms of seed.

Dimorphothecas are only half-hardy except in very favoured parts of the country, but the bright daisy flowers are so beautiful and persist so long in character that plants wintered in frames are often introduced to the border for the summer months. Most species are annual, but the type usually grown, *D. aurantiaca*, is perennial and may be propagated from cuttings or raised from seeds sown outside about April in the places where they are to bloom. A light, well-drained soil suits the family and they must have plenty of sun. The blooms show a tendency to close in bad weather and also fold their petals during the late afternoon.

D. aurantiaca. S. Africa. A perennial which is usually treated as an annual. The stems are somewhat shrubby and carry a number of branches, each of which terminates in a large daisy flower. These vary considerably in the varieties but the type is bright orange with a deep dark brown disc tipped with metallic blue. This species has given rise to a number of hybrids which range in colour from white to red and soft yellow, orange and salmon. Particularly good forms can be kept true by means of cuttings. The leaves are 2–3 in. long, narrowly oblong and somewhat toothed. This is one of the finest and most useful plants in a hot, dry summer. Among the best of the named varieties are:

Glistening White, silvery white.
Lemon Queen, lemon, with prominent black central zoning.
Orange Glory, large, brilliant orange.
Salmon Beauty, orange-salmon.   *1–1½ ft.   June–Sept.   1 ft. sq.*

DISPORUM (*Liliaceae*): Fairybells. From *dis* (Gk) ' two ', *sporon* ' seeds '.

Perennial plants very similar to Smilacina or Uvularia with smooth, pleated leaves and bunches of drooping flowers from the leaf axils. Disporums deserve to be better known for they grow in partially shaded situations. They should be propagated by seeds or division about March, and need a moist vegetable soil.

D. lanuginosum. S. Carolina, Canada. Grows about 1 ft. high with forking stems. The leaves are oval oblong, narrowly pointed, smooth above and downy beneath. Flowers yellow and green, tubular shaped and drooping.   *1 ft.   May.   9 in. sq.*

D. menziesii. California. Carries clusters of greenish flowers and has tiny pointed leaves.   *1–3 ft.   May.   1 ft. sq.*

D. pullum. China, India. Perhaps the best species, with bunches of nodding, bell-shaped purplish-green, white or deep purple flowers. These may be very variable in a batch of seedlings.

1½ ft.   May.   1 ft. sq.

DODECATHEON (*Primulaceae*): Shooting Star, American Cowslip. From *dodeka* (Gk) ' twelve ', connection obscure.

Dodecatheons are small perennials with turned back, Cyclamen-like flowers and smooth, ground hugging leaves. They need similar conditions to Primroses, that is light shade and a leafy soil. When allowed to spread, a colony in early spring presents a most attractive sight. Apart from the shady border and wild garden Shooting Stars are suitable for front row positions in the shrubbery and may also be used as cold greenhouse plants. In the latter instance roots should be lifted in November, potted on and kept outside in a cold frame until March, and then brought into a cool house. An open, well-drained soil, which is unlikely to dry out during the summer, suits the genus. The plants are propagated by division or seeds, although the latter method is somewhat slow.

D. *hendersonii*. California. Has smooth, deep green and rather small leaves. The flowers are fewer in number than some species and are of a dark purple colour with a yellow base. The anthers are also purple.   *1 ft. May–June. 1 ft. sq.*

D. *jeffreyi*. California. Larger growing plant with bold, erect, slightly sticky leaves and flower spikes which contain many starry, reddish-purple flowers. These have prominent dark purple stamens which join together at their tip to form a sharp point.

1–2 ft. May–June. 1 ft. sq.

D. *meadia*. Shooting Star. (*Plate 2, p. 17.*) N. America. The best-known species with slender, erect stems terminating in umbels of about 20 rosy, backward-pointing flowers. The anthers are bright yellow and protrude to a point, giving the bloom a somewhat starry appearance. The leaves are borne in rosettes close to the ground. They are individually oval oblong and about 6 in. in length.

1–2 ft. May–June. 1 ft. sq.

DORONICUM (*Compositae*): Leopard's Bane. From *doronigi*, the Arabic name.

Golden flowered, daisy-like plants invaluable for early work in the border. They are among the first perennials to flower, usually blooming with the late Daffodils. Doronicums will grow in sun or partial shade but should always have a deep, cool root run. For best effects plant them in groups of six or more and divide the roots every third year. The plants have bright green, heart-shaped leaves which disappear during the summer when the plant is dormant. The flowers are excellent for cutting; if spent blooms are removed, a second crop of flowers is often produced in autumn. The root is reputed to be poisonous, the old name Leopard's Bane being derived from the fact that the juice of one species was used at one time to tip arrows when hunting leopards.

D. austriacum. Austria. A small hairy plant with rough toothed leaves and narrow petalled daisy flowers. It is less spectacular than some of the other species. *2 ft. April–May. 2 ft. sq.*

D. carpetanum. N. and Cent. Spain. A good plant for cutting with golden yellow flowers 1–2 in. across and rounded to heart-shaped leaves. It spreads by underground stolen roots. *1 ft. April–June. 2 ft. sq.*

D. caucasicum. Europe, Asia. Has kidney-shaped, serrated foliage and solitary 2-inch golden flower heads. Var. *magnificum* is slightly larger. *1 ft. April–May. 1 ft. sq.*

D. clusii. S. Europe. Has oval, downy leaves and solitary flowers which come later than *D. austriacum.* *1 ft. May. 1½ ft. sq.*

D. plantagineum: Leopard's Bane. W. Europe including Britain. Has hairy, heart-shaped leaves, somewhat toothed, the upper ones clasping the stem. Flowers yellow, between April and June; the later ones are usually taller. The species is largely passed over by gardeners in favour of its garden varieties, particularly var. 'Harpur Crewe' (*Plate 4, p. 32*). A good plant of this may produce individual flowers almost 3 in. across on branching stems 2½ ft. tall. Another good garden form is 'Miss Mason'. *2 ft. April–May. 2 ft. sq.*

DRACOCEPHALUM (*Labiatae*): Dragon's Head. From *drakon* (Gk) 'dragon', *kephale* 'head'.

Hardy herbaceous plants; the perennial species are easily cultivated in any well-drained loamy soil. A partially shaded situation is best as in a sunny position the flowers soon pass. The blooms resemble Catmint to some extent, being similarly arranged on long spikes. The foliage is mostly entire, but sometimes toothed or deeply cut. The perennial kinds are best increased by root division or soft cuttings taken in April or May.

D. hemsleyanum. China. An erect plant with a branched and leafy stem terminating in a loose spike of purplish-blue, Sage-like flowers. Five to seven blooms are carried on each stem and the individual florets vary between 1 to 1½ in. in length. The leaves are oblong, up to 2 in. in length and have no leaf stalks. *1½ ft. June. 1 ft. sq.*

D. isabellae. W. China. Has large violet-blue flowers on long spikes, and deeply cut leaves. The stem is densely covered with white hairs. *1–1½ ft. July–Aug. 1 ft. sq.*

D. ruyschianum: Siberian Dragon's Head. (*Plate 12, p. 64.*) Siberia. The best-known species with oblong smooth leaves and broken spikes of purplish-blue or purple flowers. Var. *japonicum* is a finer plant and has white flowers shaded with blue. *1½–2 ft. July–Aug. 1 ft. sq.*

D. sibiricum (syn. *D. stewartianum*, *Nepeta macrantha*). Siberia, Mongolia.

A fine robust border plant which resembles, but is more impressive than a giant Catmint; the foliage is the same silvery-green and the flowers lavender-violet. It does not winter well in damp low-lying localities, but may be helped considerably by being grown on raised beds (see p. 36). This draws away excessive moisture from the crowns.   *1½–3 ft. July. 2 ft. sq.*

D. wilsonii. Yunnan. Has the habit of *D. sibiricum* but is not so free-flowering. The flowers are bluish-violet.   *1½–2 ft. July. 1½ ft. sq.*

ECHINACEA (*Compositae*): Purple Coneflower. From *echinos* (Gk.), ' hedgehog ', referring to the sharply pointed scales at the back of the flower heads.

Strong-growing perennials closely related to Rudbeckia but with the flowers mostly rose, purple or crimson (in Rudbeckia they are nearly always yellow or orange). Although somewhat coarse in appearance, the unusual coloration is not unattractive in the border, particularly when the late afternoon sun touches the petals. Cone-flowers should be grown in rich soil which is well-drained and they prefer a warm and sunny site. They are propagated by division and should not be disturbed more often than is necessary when happily established.

E. purpurea. Hedgehog Coneflower. (*Plate 28, p. 128.*) E. and N. America. Has oval, lanceolate leaves which are sharply cut and purple-crimson flowers sometimes 4 in. or more across. Var. ' The King ' is a fine garden form 3–4 ft. tall with flowers 5–6 in. across. These are wine-crimson with a deep mahogany-red centre to each bloom. The flowers cut well. This variety should be planted with *Aster yunnanensis* ' Napsbury ' or *Catanache caerulea major* for contrasting effects. *E. purpurea* ' White Lustre ' has white flowers. Var. ' Abendsonne ' is an extra strong deep wine-red variety with darker centre, 3½ ft.
2–2½ ft. Aug.–Sept. 2 ft. sq.

ECHINOPS (*Compositae*): Globe Thistle. From *echinos* (Gk) ' hedgehog ' *ops* ' like ', from the appearance of the flowers. Handsome, coarse-growing perennials of easy culture, with pinnate or spiny foliage which is woolly underneath, and large, round, Thistle-like flowers. They will grow in sun or shade in almost any soil. Echinops in the garden should be grown at the back of the border in association with plants of different habit such as Macleaya or Hollyhocks. The blossoms are attractive to bees; they are sometimes dried (before fully open) for winter bouquets. Plant in spring or autumn. Propagation is by division of the roots or root cuttings.

E. bannaticus. Hungary. Has thin, Thistle-like leaves which are downy on the undersides, and round, globe heads of blue flowers.
2–3 ft. July–Aug. 2½ ft. sq.

E. horridus. Caucasus. A spiny and strong-growing species with rough leaves which are densely covered with cobwebby hairs; slate-blue flowers. This is a handsome plant and deserves to be better known.
6–7 ft. July–Aug. 3 ft. sq.

E. ritro. Steel Globe Thistle. (*Plate 37, p. 160.*) E. Europe. A tall, rough plant with pinnately divided leaves which, like the stems, are downy on the undersides and cobwebby above. The round, Thistle heads are steely-blue and somewhat variable in colour. There are several garden varieties of which perhaps the most spectacular is ' Taplow Blue '. The blooms of this are intense metallic blue. It is very free-flowering and looks particularly handsome against a clump of white or pink Phlox. *3–5 ft. July–Aug. 2 ft. sq.*

E. sphaerocephalus. Europe, W. Asia. Has silvery-grey flowers and green and grey pinnate leaves which are downy underneath.
6 ft. July–Aug. 3 ft. sq.

E. tournefortii. S. Europe. A handsome but scarcely known species with vigorous branching stems (the whole leaves and stem covered with white hairy, net-like film). The flowers are pale blue.
3–4 ft. Sept. 2 ft. sq.

EOMECON (*Papaveraceae*): Dawn Poppy, Snow Poppy. E. China. From *heòs* (Gk) ' dawn ', *mekon* ' poppy ', referring to the habitat.

An attractive perennial with white, Poppy-like flowers on slender branching stems. There is only one member in the genus, *E. chionan-thum.* It needs a little protection in exposed parts of the country and should be grown in a cool, retentive soil in a position which misses the strong midday sun. Propagation by division in spring. The leaves are heart-shaped, pale grey-green and rise on long spikes from a creeping rhizome. The milky-white blossoms are about *1½* in. across.
1 ft. May–June. 2 ft. sq.

EPIMEDIUM (*Berberidaceae*): Barrenwort, Bishop's Hat. Name given by Dioscorides and retained by Linnaeus.

A genus of creeping, rhizomatous perennials with handsome foliage, which forms a dense ground cover, particularly useful in shaded situations. Sometimes this grows so densely that it kills all other vegetation, especially weeds, but it is dry underneath and this may encourage field mice. I once sustained a lot of damage to bulbs through mice who made their home under Epimedium leaves. A cool, woodland soil suits the family best, although they thrive in sun providing the soil does not dry out in summer. Epimediums retain their foliage in winter, particularly under trees and, as this foliage is often brightly splashed with purple and green markings, it makes a welcome patch of colour during the dullest days of the year. Propagation by division after flowering.

E. alpinum. Europe naturalized in Britain. Has compound leaves, each leaflet of which is divided into shield-like and finely toothed segments. These are shining green. The flowers are rose-purple, drooping on branching stems.   *6–9 in. June. 1 ft. sq.*

E. grandiflorum. Japan. One of the finest species, with oval, heart-shaped leaflets, green in colour, 2–3 in. long, and variable flowers which may be white, pale yellow, deep rose or violet. Two varieties worth noting are 'Rose Queen' with crimson-carmine flowers, and *violaceum* in which the flowers are light violet.

8–15 in. June. 1 ft. sq.

E. perralderianum. Algeria. A fine foliage form; the young leaves have rich bronze markings, and are just as attractive as the pale yellow blooms which appear in early summer. The leaves remain throughout the winter.   *14 in. June. 1 ft. sq.*

E. pinnatum. Barrenwort. (*Plate 4, p. 32.*) Persia. Has bright yellow flowers and more deeply cut leaves than most other species.

8–12 in. June–July. 1 ft. sq.

E. × versicolor var. *sulphureum.* A plant of garden origin with pendulous pale-yellow flowers and spiny toothed leaves which are red when young.   *1 ft. May. 1 ft. sq.*

E. × youngianum. Snowy Barrenwort. Japan. A slender plant with heart-shaped, tooth edged leaflets and a few nodding, white flowers tinged with green. Var. *niveum* (*Plate III, p. 208*) is dwarf (6 in.) and of more compact habit. The flowers are pure white.

6–12 in. April. 1 ft. sq.

EREMURUS (*Liliaceae*): Foxtail Lily. Desert Candle. From *eremos* (Gk), 'solitary', *oura* 'tail', alluding to the flower spike.

Magnificent garden plants which should be represented in every herbaceous border. The roots are uniquely shaped, being somewhat like an octopus, or in the smaller species, the open fingers of a hand. The plants do best in an open, sunny situation and appreciate a fairly heavy loam with some lime. The roots can be moved in October and should be planted about 10 in. deep, or they can be stored over the winter months and replanted in spring. In wet areas it is advisable to set them at all times in a bed of sand to deter slugs and snails, the chief enemies of these beautiful plants.

The dangerous period for Eremuri is about March or April when the noses break through the soil, for if wet weather is succeeded by frost at this time, they can be irreparably damaged. The first season or so therefore it pays the grower to cover the crowns with a light mulch of leaves to protect the young shoots. Although the flower spikes rise high in the border the foliage forms flat rosettes which hug the ground. This characteristic makes Eremuri suitable for a mid-border position,

Plate 31: Chrysanthemum rubellum—1. LADY IN PINK, 2. QUEEN OF SCOTS. 3. DUCHESS OF EDINBURGH. 4. MARY STOKER. 5. RED ENSIGN. 6. ANNE LADY BROCKETT. 7. CLARA CURTIS. 8. ROYAL COMMAND

Plate 32: 1. GOLDEN GROUNDSEL, *Ligularia clivorum* 'Othello'. 2. PERENNIAL SUNFLOWER, *Helianthus decapetalus* 'Capenock Star'. 3. PURPLE DISC SUNFLOWER, *Helianthus atrorubens* 'The Monarch'. 4. CONEFLOWER, *Rudbeckia nitida* 'Herbstsonne'. 5. BLACK-EYED SUSAN, *Rudbeckia speciosa*. 6. SNEEZEWEED, *Helenium hybridum* 'Crimson Beauty'

Plate 33. top CENTAURY, *Centaurea glastifolia; bottom* SNEEZEWEED, *Helenium hybridum; left* 'The Bishop', *right* 'Moerheim Beauty'

Plate 34: top KANSAS FEATHER, *Liatris pycnostachya; centre* FLEECE-FLOWER, *Polygonum amplexicaule* var. *atrosanguineum; bottom* PRAIRIE MALLOW, *Sidalcea* 'Sussex Queen'

where the foliage is unseen but the wands or spears of blossom (always in pale pastel shades) stand out to greater advantage.

The Foxtail Lilies associate happily with Delphiniums and Iris. Although the stems wave in the breeze, they should not need staking, but the plants are not suitable for exposed windy situations. Propagation is by division and seed. They increase rapidly and should be divided about every third year. If left in the same position indefinitely the height becomes less and the clump more congested.

E. bungei. Persia. One of the smaller growing species with slender flower spikes closely packed with small bright yellow blossoms and green sword-shaped leaves. There are several varieties from this species, notably 'Highdown Gold' with flowers of pure gold, and 'Dawn', deep pink with black stems. *2–3 ft. June. 1 ft. sq.*

E. elwesii. A beautiful plant of uncertain origin with long wands tightly packed with soft pink flowers. Var. *albus* is white.

6–9 ft. May. 2 ft. sq.

E. himalaicus. Himalayas. One of the tallest growing species with enormous roots sometimes over 2½ ft. across. These should be carefully planted by setting the crown on a mound of sand with the octopus-like roots falling away in a slightly descending circle. The flowers are white and very densely arranged on the stems. This is the first Eremurus to flower. *5–6 ft. May–July. 3 ft. sq.*

E. olgae. Turkestan. Has narrow leaves and starry white flowers with particularly long stamens. It is very graceful and handsome.

4 ft. July. 2 ft. sq.

E. robustus. Turkestan. A magnificent species which Sir Frederick Stern (an authority on this genus), records as growing in his garden at Highdown to 10 ft. in height with 3 ft. spikes of soft pink flowers. In most gardens, however, 5–8 ft. is a more usual height. The variety '*elwesianus*' flowers earlier than the type and has white blossoms tinged with pink. This is not as robust as its parent.

6–10 ft. June. 4 ft. sq.

E. × shelford. A fine race of garden origin, which is particularly free-flowering and shows a wide colour range of orange, buff, pink, pale yellow, bright pink and white. *4½–6 ft. June. 3 ft. sq.*

E. × tubergenii. Of garden origin with pale yellow florets.

1½ ft. May. 1½ ft. sq.

ERIGERON (*Compositae*): Fleabane. From *eri* (Gk) 'early', *geron* 'old man', possibly alluding to the early appearance of the seed heads.

A useful family if only on account of its long flowering season, some varieties blooming intermittently throughout the whole of the summer. In addition the plants, with the exception of *E. aurantiacus*, are of the easiest culture thriving in most soils either in sun or light shade. A circumstance to avoid is a water-logged soil during the dormant season, otherwise there are no cultural problems, but the plant stays in character longer where it receives shade from the midday sun. Young plants grow quickly—small divisions in spring making good specimens by autumn. Fleabane is reputed to repel insects but the original name refers to a tropical species which has a particularly strong odour.

E. aurantiacus. Orange Daisy. Turkestan. This plant at first glance might be mistaken for a Hieracium, for in contrast to most of the family it has orange instead of white or mauve flowers. The blooms are semi-double and of a vivid orange shade. This species requires light, well-drained soil and full sun. It is not too hardy or robust and sometimes disappears in exposed or very cold situations. Var. ' Asa Gray ' is of garden origin, with buff-yellow flowers.

1–2 ft. June–July. 1 ft. sq.

E. hybridus. Includes a number of garden varieties of uncertain origin. Of these the best are:

Amos Perry, good mauve, flowers 2–2½ in, across; good for cutting; greyish foliage; needs staking.

1 ft. June–Sept. 2 ft. sq.

B. Ladhams, rose-pink with deep green foliage.

1½–2 ft. May–July. 2 ft. sq.

Charity, clear soft pink. *2 ft. June–Aug. 2 ft. sq.*

Darkest of All, of German origin with very deep violet-blue flowers. *2 ft. June–Aug. 2 ft. sq.*

Dignity, violet-mauve deepening to purple, flowers 2 in. across. *2 ft. June–Aug. 2 ft. sq.*

Dimity, dwarf, bright pink with gold eyes. *10 in. June–Aug. 1 ft. sq.*

Elsie, mauve-pink, free-flowering. *1 ft. June–Sept. 1 ft. sq.*

Felicity, clear pink. *1½–2 ft. June–Aug. 2 ft. sq.*

Festivity, very fine petals, flowers 2½ in. across, lilac-mauve. *2 ft. June–Sept. 2 ft. sq.*

Frivolity, rose-lavender, loose habit. *2 ft. June–Sept. 2 ft. sq.*

Gaiety, bright pink. *2½ ft. June–Sept. 2 ft. sq.*

Integrity, warm rose-pink, bright gold centre. *2 ft. June–Aug. 2 ft. sq.*

Merstham Glory (*Plate 6, p. 33*), deep mauve, long flowering. *2 ft. June–Sept. 1 ft. sq.*

Mesa-grande, deep violet-blue. *1½ ft. July–Aug. 1½ ft. sq.*

Mrs. H. F. Beale, violet-blue with golden centre. *1 ft. June–Sept. 1 ft. sq.*

Serenity, very deep mauve, good for cutting. *2½ ft. June–Sept. 2 ft. sq.*

Sincerity, large petals of light mauve, golden centre. *2½ ft. June–Sept. 2 ft. sq.*

Unity, bright pink, over 2 in. across with very thick ray petals.
1½ ft. June–Aug. 1 ft. sq.
Wupperthal, a fine Continental variety, violet-mauve, very sturdy.
2½ ft. June–Aug. 2 ft. sq.

E. mucronatus. Bony-tip Fleabane. Mexico. A sometimes rampageous
subject which is excellent for planting at the corner of steps or in the
front of the rock garden or border. Small pink and white flowers,
throughout most of the summer. *8 in. Summer and autumn. 1 ft. sq.*

E. multiradiatus. Himalayan Fleabane. N. India. Has solitary terminal
flowers about 2 in. across with many purplish ray florets and a yellow
central disc. *6 in.–2 ft. Summer. 1 ft. sq.*

E. philadelphicus. N. America. A plant which needs to be carefully
watched lest it becomes invasive. Of slender branched habit, it has
narrow oblong leaves and numerous pale flesh coloured or reddish
purple blossoms. *2 ft. June–Aug. 1 ft. sq.*

E. speciosus. W. & N. America. Has produced many fine garden varieties
all of which are long-flowering and useful for cutting. The type has
violet-blue flowers with very many narrow petals. Amongst horticultural forms the following are worth noting; *grandiflorus* with larger
flowers; ' Quakeress ', many petals which are more rosy than the
type; ' White Quakeress ' (*Plate VIII, p. 224*) a good white; *superbus*,
with improved blossoms. *1½–2 ft. June–July. 1½ ft. sq.*

ERODIUM (*Geraniaceae*): Heronbill. From *erodius* (Gk) ' heron ', the
seed pods resembling the head and beak of that bird.
Erodiums are plants for a sunny, well-drained border and valuable
both for their flowers and foliage. They have no special cultural
problems and are propagated by seed or root cuttings.

E. manescavi. Pyrenees. A dainty plant with divided leaves which are
somewhat like those of the scented Geranium. The flowers are large
—up to 2 in. across—rich purplish-red with darker spots on the upper
petals. Several flowers are carried at one time on the naked stems.
1–2 ft. Spring to autumn. 2 ft. sq.

ERYNGIUM (*Umbelliferae*): Sea Holly. From *eryngos* (Gk) ' thistle-
like '.
Sea Hollies in the border provide individual and strong flower and
foliage contrasts which increase the value of neighbouring plants.
The habit is attractive, the leaves being either toothed or deeply cleft
and somewhat spiny, and the flowers Teazle-shaped. The stems also
are singularly beautiful, having vivid steel-blue tints, a character
which is shared by the involucre or prickly, much cut base of the
flowers.

There is great diversity in the shape of the leaves, from the great sword-like foliage of *E. pandanifolium* to the small, Thistle-like leaves of *E. spinalba*. As a general rule those with large leaves are less hardy than the others, possibly because of their succulent nature, and may be damaged in wet situations in very severe weather. Damp is the enemy of these plants. They will stand any amount of exposure as long as the drainage is good. A sunny situation is accordingly to be preferred and a light soil. Sea Hollies also take kindly to a biennial dosage of Kainite. This manure contains potash but also has a high salt content and Sea Hollies are naturally denizens of the sea-shore. Propagation is best undertaken by root cuttings, although the species will also come true from seed, or they can be carefully divided in spring.

E. agavifolium. Argentine. One of the tallest species and suitable for a key or corner situation on account of its handsome sword-like leaves. These may be up to 5 ft. long, somewhat fleshy and spined at the edges like the back of a shark. The flowers are greenish-white and carried in large branching sprays. 　　*5–6 ft. July–Aug. 4 ft. sq.*

E. alpinum. Europe. Has deeply cut and toothed foliage and branching heads of 10 or 20 beautiful blue Teazle flowers. The whole of the upper part of the plant is also tinged with blue. Unlike the rest of the family this species will grow in a shady spot, and stiff clay soil. 　　*1½–2 ft. July–Sept. 2 ft. sq.*

E. amethystinum. Europe. Has basal leaves which are deeply cut and somewhat feathery in shape, and branching heads of round, small, amethyst blue flowers. 　　*1–2 ft. July–Sept. 1½ ft. sq.*

E. bourgati. Pyrenees. This species branches at the top of the stem and carries blue flowers, protected by spiny bracts on light blue flower stems. The leaves are divided and spiky. 　*1–2 ft. July–Aug. 2 ft. sq.*

E. giganteum. Caucasus. Although this plant is monocarpic (i.e. it dies after flowering), it usually leaves sufficient seedlings to ensure continuance providing the grower is not too assiduous in weeding. It is, however, so beautiful that it should not be passed over on account of its bad perennial habit. The plant needs a sunny situation and well-drained soil, and flowers best in a dry season. Leaves, flowers and stems are a uniform and striking shade of silvery blue. Gathered before the plants come to full fruition, the stems make excellent winter bouquets. 　　*2–2½ ft. Aug.–Sept. 2 ft. sq.*

E. × *oliveriarum.* A hybrid, possibly of natural origin, and a strong grower. It has rounded leaves cut into 3–5 segments and many rich blue, Teazle-like flowers which are very spiny. There are several varieties of which the best are Var. *superbum*, rich, almost light navy-blue, and ' Springhill Seedling ' which has extra large heads in a steel blue shade. Var. 'Violetta' (*Plate 26, p. 113*) is an improved form with violet-blue flower heads and stems. It grows 3 ft. tall.

3–4 ft. July–Sept. 3 ft. sq.

E. pandanifolium. Sword-leaved Sea Holly. (*Plate XI, p. 240.*) Monte Video. A noble species, of the same habit as *E. agavifolium*, with quantities of small, rounded purplish flowers on large branching stems, and long pointed spiny leaves. *4–6 ft. July–Sept. 4 ft. sq.*

E. planum. E. Europe. A small growing species for the front of the border with blue flowers and heart-shaped leaves divided into 5 segments.

2 ft. July–Aug. 2 ft. sq.

E. spinalba. Europe. Has bluish-white flowers which are rather small, on branching stems, and Thistle-like foliage.

2½ ft. July–Sept. 1½ ft. sq.

E. tripartitum. Origin unknown, possibly a hybrid. This variety has smaller flowers than the majority but produces greater quantities on its very branched stems. They are grey-blue in colour. The leaves are less spiny than most species and smaller in size.

2 ft. July–Sept. 1½ ft. sq.

E. yuccaefolium (syn. *E. aquaticum*): Button Snakeroot, Rattlesnake Master. N. America. Another species allied to *E. agavifolium*, with long, broadly sword-shaped leaves, spiny at the edges, and branching heads of small, round, white or very pale blue flowers. *2–3 ft. July–Sept. 2 ft. sq.*

EUPATORIUM (*Compositae*): Hemp Agrimony, Thorough-wort. Named after Mithridates Eupator, King of Pontus, who used it as an antidote against poisoning.

A large genus, mostly perennials, of which only a few can be considered for garden use. The exceptions, however, are quite ornamental in the wild garden or at the back of the border, and grow easily in ordinary garden soil. Propagation by division.

E. ageratoides. White Snakeroot. (*Plate XVI, p. 257.*) N. America. One of the best of the hardy summer-blooming species, this has thin, long stalked, oval leaves which grow on opposite sides of the stem, and a profusion of white Thistle-like flowers in dense flat heads.

2–4 ft. Summer. 2 ft. sq.

E. cannabinum. Common Hemp Agrimony. Europe including Britain and Asia. In gardens the type is usually passed over in favour of the double form var. *plenum*, which makes a handsome perennial with large showy heads made up of many small, dull purple flowers. The leaves are arranged oppositely on the stems and are slightly downy and deeply cut into 3 or 5 segments. This plant does well in a heavy clay or moist situation. *3–4½ ft. Aug.–Sept. 2 ft. sq.*

E. purpureum. Joe Pye Weed. (*Plate 28, p. 128.*) N. America. A tall, striking plant, useful for creating bold effects in the shrubbery or back of the border. The flowers are pale purple, arranged in flat plate-like heads and the leaves 3 to 5 in a whorl. It grows best in moist soil.

3–6 ft. Aug.–Sept. 3 ft. sq.

EUPHORBIA (*Euphorbiaceae*): Milkweed, Spurge. A classical name said by Pliny to have been given this plant in honour of Euphorbus, King Juba's physician.

The chief value of Spurges in the border is in early spring as many bloom in March or April when flowers and colour are scarce. The decorative parts are really the bracts, for the flowers themselves are usually small and inconspicuous. But, when grouped together and set off by the golden bracts they become quite showy.

The plants are also characterised by a milky sap which is poisonous and drips from the cut stems and stains the hands. When the blooms are gathered the loss of this latex weakens their constitution and they quickly die. It is therefore advisable to apply a styptic to the cut ends as soon as possible after picking. This can be effected either by applying a taper to the tip or by dipping it into boiling water or glacial acetic acid for a few moments.

Garden Spurges grow readily in practically all garden soils but *E. wulfenii* needs a sheltered position against a fence or a wall. A careful watch has to be kept on some species as they are apt to become invasive.

Propagation by division in spring or autumn, with the exception of *E. wulfenii*, which must be increased from seed or by soft cuttings taken in early spring.

E. cyparissias: Cypress Spurge. Europe including Britain. A rather invasive species which spreads by means of underground roots. It is readily known by its slender grass-like leaves and small, greenish-yellow flowers which are surmounted by heart-shaped, yellow bracts. The plant possesses powerful and dangerous properties and is very poisonous if taken internally in any quantity.

1 ft. April–May. 2 ft. sq.

E. epithymoides (syn. *E. polychroma*): Cushion Spurge. Europe. Has rounded heads of flowers surmounted by bright gold bracts. When seen *en masse* a group of this Spurge is most attractive in early spring.

1 ft. April–May. 2 ft. sq.

E. wulfenii. Europe. A handsome plant and one which should be included in every garden if only for its striking habit and early flowers. The strong stems are densely clothed with oblong, bluish green, somewhat hairy leaves and terminate in large heads of yellowish-green flowers. When gathered in spring and associated with Pheasant's Eye Narcissus and pink Cherry blossom, they present a very beautiful arrangement.

4 ft. May–June. 4 ft. sq.

FERULA (*Umbelliferae*): Giant Fennel. From '*ferula*' (L) 'rod', an allusion to the stems.

Majestic, herbaceous perennials much prized for their finely cut and graceful foliage. Although the plants will grow in practically any soil, they should be planted out young as they do not take kindly to being moved later. Ferulas are good plants for separating two bright neighbours, for example, a vivid patch of Phlox and another of bright blue Salvias. A solitary, well-grown specimen also looks attractive in its own right in the shrubbery, wild garden or by the stream.

Propagation is from seed sown outside directly after gathering.

F. communis. Common Giant Fennel. Mediterranean Area. A robust plant with light green leaves which are very finely cut and protected at their base by large, pale straw-coloured sheaths. The flowers, which are yellow and borne in branching umbels, are rather less attractive than the foliage. In practice it is wiser not to let the plant bloom in the garden as the seedlings can become a nuisance.

8–12 ft. June. 5–6 ft. sq.

F. tingitana. N. Africa. This plant is not too hardy in gardens and for this reason should always be set in a sheltered position. Of branching habit, the leaves are very deeply cut and toothed and have a polished appearance. When well grown they look like massive plumes of filmy ferns. The flowers are yellow, borne many together in large terminal umbels. Gum ammoniac is obtained from one species.

6–8 ft. June. 6 ft. sq.

FILIPENDULA (*Rosaceae*): Dropwort. From *filum* (L) 'thread', *pendulus* 'hanging'. In *F. hexapetala* the root tubers hang on slender thread-like roots.

Handsome Spiraea-like plants with attractive pinnate or palmate foliage and fluffy flower heads made up of many individual florets. The plants are surface rooting so need coolness and moisture during the summer months. A mulch of well-rotted organic material takes care of both contingencies, except on light soil. With the exception of *F. hexapetala* all species need some such help unless they are grown in the vicinity of water. They will grow in sun or partial shade. Propagation by division or seed, sown in pans under glass, in autumn.

F. camtschatica (syn. *Spiraea gigantea*). Manchuria. A noble species with large, white fragrant flower plumes and huge palmate leaves. There are variable forms, var. *carnea* and *rosea*, with flesh pink and rose flowers.

4–8 ft. July. 2½ ft. sq.

F. hexapetala (syn. *Spiraea filipendula*): Dropwort. (*Plate XII, p. 240.*) Europe, including Britain; Asia. A beautiful border subject with tufts of fern-like foliage and creamy-white flower heads. Var. *grandiflora* is an improvement on the type and may reach 3 ft. in height. There is also a good double-flowered form, *flore pleno*, which does not exceed 18 in. in height. Given sun, this species will grow in almost any soil.   *2–3 ft. June–July. 2 ft. sq.*

F. palmata. Siberia. Has five lobed leaves which are often covered with white hair on the undersides, and pale pink plumes of flowers which fade with age to white.   *2–3 ft. July. 2 ft. sq.*

F. purpurea (syn. *Spiraea palmata*): Japan. This is a handsome plant when grown in moist soil, with large lobed leaves and heavy plumes of fluffy carmine pink flowers. The stems are crimson—Var. *alba* has white flowers and var. *purpurascens* purple tinted leaves.
      2–4 ft. June–Aug. 2½ ft. sq.

F. rubra (syn. *Spiraea lobata; S. rubra; S. venusta*): Queen of the Prairie. E. United States. A most attractive species with feathery plumes of deep peach flowers borne on tall branching stems. The plant is particularly suited to the wild or bog garden. Var. *venusta magnifica* (*Plate 20, p. 96*) has deep pink or carmine flowers.
      4–8 ft. June. 2½ ft. sq.

F. ulmaria. Meadow Sweet, Queen of the Meadows. Europe, including Britain; Asia. The type is one of our most beautiful natives, and since it is usually found in the vicinity of water, must have moist, drought-free conditions in the garden. The leaves are beautiful being 3–5 lobed, white downy beneath; the creamy flowers are densely packed on branching heads. There is a double form *flore-pleno*, and also one with variegated leaves, var. *aurea*, for those who favour parti-coloured foliage.   *2–3 ft. June–Aug. 2 ft. sq.*

FOENICULUM (*Umbelliferae*): Fennel. Old Latin name.

Handsome foliage plants similar to and requiring the same treatment as Ferula (p. *151*). The flowers are less attractive and should not be encouraged or the seedlings may become a nuisance. Propagation by seed.

F. vulgare. Fennel. S. Europe including Britain. The leaves are used for flavouring food, especially fish, and the seeds medicinally. Leaves much cut into threadlike segments, flowers yellow in umbels.
      4–5 ft. Aug.–Oct. 2 ft. sq.

GAILLARDIA (*Compositae*): *Blanket Flower*. Named after Gaillard de Marentonneau, a French patron of botany.

Showy annuals and perennials with bold daisy heads, very suitable for the border or cutting. All favour a light, well-drained soil with plenty of sunshine; in cold wet land they do not always survive the winter. I have known gardeners on heavy London clay to have success with Gaillardias and other sun-loving plants by growing them on raised flower beds (see p. 36).

Being of untidy habit Gaillardias need some form of support.

Peasticks are most useful in this respect. The roots should be planted 12–18 in. apart in bold clumps. The perennial kinds are propagated by division, stem and root cuttings and seed. The seedlings, however, do not always come true.

G. *aristata.* (*Plate 21, p. 96.*) W. & N. America. Is the parent of most of the garden forms. It blooms the first year from seed and has a very variable habit. A number of forms worth noting are the following, which bloom almost continuously from June to November.

Burgundy, rich wine-red. *2 ft. 2 ft. sq.*

Copper Beauty, orange-yellow shading to copper-brown. *2 ft. 2 ft. sq.*

Firebrand, flame-orange, very robust. *2½ ft. 2 ft. sq.*

Ipswich Beauty, large orange and brown-red flowers. *2½ ft. 2 ft. sq.*

Mrs. H. Longsten, large golden-yellow with red centre. *2½ ft. 2 ft. sq.*

Nana Nieske, dwarf with true yellow and red flowers. *1–1½ ft. 1 ft. sq.*

The King, red, tipped yellow. *2 ft. 2 ft. sq.*

The Prince, very large flowers, yellow with deep crimson centre. *2½ ft. 2 ft. sq.*

Wirral Flame, tangerine-red, with trace of gold at tip of petals. *2 ft. 2 ft. sq.*

GALAX (*Diapensiaceae*). From *galakto* (Gk) ' milk '; connection obscure.

This genus contains only a single species, although it had much wider representation in geological times. The leaves are used extensively in America for decorative purposes, particularly at Christmas time.

G. *aphylla.* Wand-flower, Galax. (*Plate X, p. 225.*) Eastern N. America. A low-growing, ground-covering plant, especially adapted to the shady border or front of the shrubbery. A Rhododendron soil, a deep, cool, peaty loam, suits it well. The round, heart-shaped leaves are very handsome, and although they remain green in very dense shade develop beautiful reddish bronze tints in lighter situations, especially when frosts appear. They remain evergreen throughout the winter. The white flowers are borne on long, slender, wand-like spikes. *1–2 ft. June–July. 1 ft. sq.*

GALEGA (*Leguminosae*): Goat's Rue. From gala (Gk) ' milk ', from the plant's reputed power to stimulate milk production.

Goat's Rue should be planted towards the back of the border as it is of untidy habit and needs other subjects to conceal it after flowering. The small mauve Sweetpea-like flowers are borne in axillary spikes and present a shade rather uncommon in the spring border. The plants will grow in practically any soil and can be propagated by seed or division.

G. officinalis. (*Plate IX, p. 224.*) S. Europe, W. Asia. Has soft green, pinnate leaves and spikes of white or mauve pea-shaped flowers. Being of compact habit it does not require frequent division. Var. *alba* has white blooms; another very desirable variety is *hartlandii*, with large mauvy-lilac blooms. Other good garden varieties from this species are *carnea plena* with double, pinkish flowers; ' Her Majesty ', soft lilac-blue flowers; ' Lady Wilson ', mauve and white; ' Duchess of Bedford ', mauve and white.   *3–5 ft. June–July. 3 ft. sq.*

GAURA (*Oenotheraceae*). From *gauros* (Gk) ' superb '.

 G. lindheimeri from Texas is sometimes seen in garden borders where it provides slender spikes of rosy-white flowers from July to August. It is a graceful plant, preferring a light soil, and can be raised from seed sown in spring in a sheltered border and transferred in autumn to its flowering situation. The leaves are lance-shaped.

3–4 ft. July–Aug. 2 ft. sq.

GAZANIA (*Compositae*): Treasure Flower. (*Plate 27, p. 128.*) From *gaza* (Gk) ' riches ', referring to the splendid floral colourings.

 Mostly perennial plants, which are frequently used for bedding out at the front of the herbaceous border. Although only hardy in more sheltered areas, such as Devon and Cornwall, they are so attractive and long blooming that many will feel the trouble of wintering them well worth while. The plants are easily kept from year to year by taking side shoots from the base of the plants during July and August, rooting these in sandy soil in a close frame.

 Gazanias have a wide colour range—from pure white to yellow, orange, scarlet, black, tangerine and green. Some of these are selfs but more generally the flowers are made up of combinations of several shades. Most of the varieties grown in gardens to-day are of hybrid origin, having narrow grassy leaves which are deep green on the upper surface and greenish white underneath. The majority grow from 6–12 in. high and flower almost continuously from June to October. They should be planted about 1 ft. apart, after the middle of May. Apart from their use in the border, Gazanias make good pot plants and can also be planted as dry wall subjects.

GENTIANA (*Gentianaceae*). Named after *Gentius*, King of Illyrica who is credited with the discovery of the medicinal value of the roots.

 A large genus of mostly alpine plants with a few species suitable for the herbaceous border. It is difficult to generalise over the cultivation of this family, since individual members of the genus vary considerably. But, as far as the border types are concerned, these thrive best in a rich vegetable soil, and a position which receives a certain amount of shade during the hottest part of the day. Propagation by seed, sown directly after harvesting. The following are the best and most easily grown of the taller Gentians.

G. asclepiadea. Willow Gentian. S. Europe. Produces long arching stems carrying willow-like leaves and spikes of dark purple tubular flowers. The colour varies in seedlings between pale blue, violet and white. (The white form *alba* (*Plate IX, p. 224.*), also known as the White Milkweed Gentian, does reproduce true from seed.) This species will live in shade or half-shade and likes a rich, moist vegetable soil. Left to itself in a woodland setting it often becomes naturalized.

$1\frac{1}{2}$ *ft.* *Aug.–Sept.* $1\frac{1}{2}$ *ft.*

G. lutea. Europe, Asia Minor. A fine yellow-flowered species for any rich, moist spot in a sunny situation. It is reproduced from seed and the young plants must be carefully transplanted without damaging the roots. The star-shaped flowers are grouped on tall, sturdy stems, the foliage forming a wide rosette of large, crinkled basal leaves, with small simple leaves on the stems. *G. lutea* yields the bitter tonic Gentian root, which has long been used in medicine. It is collected chiefly in Central and Southern Europe. *3 ft. July–Aug. 2 ft. sq.*

G. pneumonanthe. Marsh Gentian. N. Hemisphere including Britain. Normally found in marshy situations, this plant requires deep, cool soil which is very rich in humus and completely lime free. It does particularly well when planted near water. The flowers are a deep purplish-blue, funnel-shaped, and grouped several together on the same stalk. There is also a white form, var. *alba*; ' Styrian ' is taller, and has paler blue flowers than the type. *6–12 in. Aug. 6 in. sq.*

GERANIUM (*Geraniaceae*): Cranesbill. From *geranos* (Gk) ' a crane ', because of the resemblance of the seed pod to a crane's bill.

A widely distributed genus of easy cultivation, although some of the species are inclined to become weedy if allowed to drop their seeds indiscriminately. They flower freely in any light, well-drained soil in a sunny situation. Propagation by seed or in the majority of cases by division of the roots. (The Geraniums of gardens do not belong here, but to Pelargonium.)

G. endressii. Pyrenees. Has small, five-lobed, buttercup-like leaves and pale pink, five-petalled flowers which are lightly marked with red. It is in flower practically the whole of the summer and deserves wider cultivation. In sun or semi-shade the plant forms close and compact growth, almost smothering any germinating weeds. ' Wargrave Variety ' has clear pink flowers without the red of the type; ' Russell Prichard ' is of trailing habit with rich rose flowers.

9–12 in. Summer. 1 ft. sq.

G. grandiflorum. Lilac Cranesbill. (*Plate 12, p. 64.*) N. Asia. Has very large flat flowers of rich blue-veined with red. The leaves are rounded and five-lobed, on very long stalks. Var. *alpinum* is more dwarf (10–12 in.) with larger flowers. *12–15 in. July. 2 ft. sq.*

G. ibericum. Iberian Cranesbill. Caucasus. Forms an erect leafy stem, with large showy violet flowers, and five- to seven-lobed leaves. Var. *album* has white blooms; 'Johnson's Blue', bright blue.

2 ft. July–Aug. 1½ ft. sq.

G. macrorrhizum. S. Europe. Forms a compact plant with a somewhat woody stem and very large roots. The leaves are five-lobed and the flowers deep red or bright purple. Var. 'Ingwersen' (15 in.) is suitable for light shade, with large, clear pink flowers.

1–1½ ft. May–July. 2½ ft. sq.

G. pratense. Blue Meadow Cranesbill. This is the largest of our native species and a very handsome subject, with beautiful open blue flowers over an inch across. It is a valuable garden plant with long-stalked leaves, divided into seven lobes. There are varieties, *album* (*Plate III, p. 208*), with white flowers; *bicolor* and *striatum*, blue and white; also mauve, pink and purple, both single and double-flowered (*plenum*).

1½–3 ft. July–Sept. 2 ft. sq.

G. psilostemon (syn. *G. armenum*): Armenian Cranesbill. (*Plate 2, p. 17.*) Armenia. An extremely fine species with brilliant magenta flowers, each petal of which has a black spot on its base. The foliage is silvery, broadly heart-shaped and cut into five divisions. This is probably the most handsome garden plant of the family.

2–3 ft. June–July. 2 ft. sq.

G. sanguineum. Bloody Cranesbill. Europe. Noted for its very long-flowering period and intense magenta coloured blossoms. The foliage is divided into seven parts. There is also a good white form, var. *album.*

1–1½ ft. June–Aug. 2 ft. sq.

G. sanguineum lancastriense. Is a more dwarf variety than *G. sanguineum*, with rose-pink flowers. An extremely good front of the border subject.

1 ft. June–Aug. 2 ft. sq.

G. wallichianum. Himalayas. A good front of the border plant, which must not, however, be exposed to a very hot, dry situation. It is of prostrate trailing habit, the leaves covered with silky hairs, the foliage pale green and divided into three or five lobes. The flowers are large and violet-blue. The variety 'Buxton's Blue' is even deeper in colour, each flower having a white eye.

1 ft. Aug.–Sept. 2 ft. sq.

GEUM (*Rosaceae*): Avens, Herb Bennett. From *geuo* (Gk) 'to taste'. Most Geums have a clove-like fragrance in the roots and for this reason were used for flavouring wines and ales.

A family of easily-grown perennials much prized for the brightly coloured chalice-shaped flowers. Many are in bloom practically the whole of the summer, but because of their vivid shades should not be placed in close proximity to Oriental Poppies or Pentstemons, otherwise discordant colour clashes will result. The foliage forms close rosettes to the ground with the individual leaves irregularly lobed.

Geums grow in any good garden soil, either in sun or light shade. The roots should be divided every two or three years, preferably after flowering. The various species and varieties cross readily, so that a number of good garden forms are available. Propagation by division or seed.

G. × *borisii*. Is of branching habit and carries numbers of vivid orange-scarlet flowers. *1 ft. June–Sept. 1 ft. sq.*

G. *bulgaricum*. Bulgarian Avens. Bulgaria. A summer-flowering perennial with bright yellow nodding flowers and hairy, toothed leaves.
1–1½ ft. June–Aug. 1 ft. sq.

G. *chiloense*: Scarlet Avens. (*Plate 3, p. 32.*) Chile. Although this species is not often seen in gardens to-day, it is probably the parent of the majority of the garden hybrids, including the well-known ' Mrs. Bradshaw '. This variety has become one of the most popular garden plants of the century.

The history of this plant has some connection with my husband's family, according to the following story which my father-in-law, the late Amos Perry, used to tell. Apparently in the early 1900's he had a nursery at Winchmore Hill, and amongst a number of keen nearby amateur gardeners was one John Bradshaw of the Grove, Southgate. Bradshaw and he often used to exchange plants and amongst several items which changed hands on a particular morning in 1906 were some Violas and a box of Geum seedlings. And it was one of the seedlings from this box, grown by his gardener Mr. G. Whitelegg, which produced the fine semi-double variety which became ' Mrs. Bradshaw '. It comes practically 100 per cent true from seed and has fine, semi-double, scarlet flowers of good size and substance.
2 ft. All summer. 2 ft. sq.

Dolly North, a free-flowering sort with glowing orange flowers. *2 ft. June–July. 2 ft. sq.*

Fire Opal, has single blossoms of orange overlaid with a warm reddish glow. *1½ ft. June–July. 1½ ft. sq.*

Golden West, rich golden-yellow. *1½ ft. May–Aug. 1 ft. sq.*

Lady Stratheden, an excellent counterpart for ' Mrs. Bradshaw ' with rich, golden-yellow, double flowers. *2 ft. All summer. 2 ft. sq.*

Orangeman, large orange flowers. *2 ft. May–June. 1 ft. sq.*

Prince of Orange, bright orange. *2 ft. June–Aug. 1 ft. sq.*

Princess Juliana, semi-double, with deep golden-orange blossoms. *2 ft. June–July. 2 ft. sq.*

Red Wings, another semi-double form with bright scarlet blossoms. *2 ft. July–Aug. 2 ft. sq.*

G. × *heldreichii*. Of doubtful origin, but presumably a garden hybrid.

It makes a fine plant with rich orange flowers on long branching stems. Various forms are offered including *magnificum*, *splendens* and *superbum*, the latter with blossoms almost 2 in. across.

1–1½ ft.   June–Oct.   1½ ft. sq.

G. rivale. Water Avens. N. Hemisphere including Britain. A plant which does best in a damp situation, this has nodding, reddish flowers on hairy stems, and feathered basal leaves. The roots have been used medicinally, both in this country and N. America. It has given rise to garden varieties, including ' Leonard's Variety ', in which the blossoms are pink with orange tints, and *superbum*, a large-flowered form. *1 ft.   May–Sept.   1 ft. sq.*

GYPSOPHILA (*Caryophyllaceae*): Chalk Plant. From *gypsos* (Gk) ' chalk ', *phileo* ' to love '.

Well known and loved garden plants with feathery masses of small flowers, which are much appreciated for their gossamer quality, particularly when associated with larger blooms. They make useful subjects for masking the untidy after-flowing effects of such subjects as Papaver and Anchusa. The leaves are small and insignificant, the whole charm of the plant being associated with its cloudy branching flower heads.

As the name implies, Gypsophilas are chalk-lovers, but that does not mean that they need to be grown in a limy soil. Practically any situation which affords a deep root run will suit them, but they are gross feeders and the roots go well down after food. For this reason it is best to prepare the soil adequately before planting, enriching it with some good vegetable material and digging the ground deeply. They must have a well-drained situation, however, and full sun.

It is unwise to disturb established specimens (which will probably die after moving), but young plants set out in spring soon start to grow and last for a number of years in the same position. Propagation is effected by seed, sown in gentle heat in pots or pans in February, or outside in the open border from March onwards. Nearly all seedlings sown one year will flower during the next. Cuttings can also be taken from varieties which do not come true, such as ' Bristol Fairy ', but these must be from young spring growths and from plants specially grown under glass. Rarely do they strike from the harder cuttings produced out of doors. These cuttings are taken with a heel and rooted in a sandy compost in pans in the greenhouse. The chief commercial method of propagating named forms of Gypsophila, however, is by root grafting, as described on p. 67.

G. paniculata. Baby's Breath. E. Europe, Siberia. A strong-rooted perennial with small, grass-like leaves and myriads of tiny white, or sometimes pinkish, flowers in large, loose, branching 3-ft. panicles. The best garden varieties from this are *flore pleno* which has tiny double

white flowers, even more attractive than the single ones ($3\frac{1}{2}$–4 ft.);
nana alba (*Plate VII, p. 224*), Dwarf Gypsophila, which is nearly
prostrate (9–12 in.); and ' Bristol Fairy ' (*Plate VII, p. 224*) more
robust than *flore pleno* and consequently more widely grown (3 ft.).
There is also a new form, ' Bristol Fairy *perfecta* ' (3 ft.) which is finer
still. ' Rosenchleirer ' also known as ' Rosy Veil ' (*Plate 21, p. 96*)
has small double flowers which start white and later turn rose pink.
It is of semi-prostrate growth, about 9 in. high. ' Flamingo ', a new
fine pink Gypsophila, with large double flowers which open pink,
makes an excellent cut flower ($2\frac{1}{2}$ ft.).   *June–Aug.   2–3 ft. sq.*

HELENIUM (*Compositae*): Sneezeweed. Old Classical name of
uncertain origin.

A genus of N. American plants invaluable for late summer and
autumn work in the border. The sturdy stems are well clothed with
leaves, and carry on branching heads quantities of large daisy flowers,
usually in typically autumn shades, of yellow, bronze and red. The
central disc of these is extremely prominent—a characteristic of the
whole family.

Heleniums will grow in practically any garden soil but do best in
a fairly stiff loam. Some varieties have an untidy habit, and sprawl
on the ground, particularly after heavy rain. These should be staked.
The plants like full sun, and can be easily propagated by division in
spring or autumn, or from seed.

H. autumnale. Canada, E. United States. This is the parent of a whole
range of garden varieties (*Helenium hybridum*), most of which make
good border plants and excellent cut flowers. The following are the
best of the present-day varieties. All flower between July and Sept.

Altgold, large flowers, yellow with bronze reverse.   *4 ft. 3 ft. sq.*
autumnale rubrum, bronze-crimson.   *4 ft. 3 ft. sq.*
Baron Linden, bright orange shaded with bronze, large.
                                                      3 ft. 2$\frac{1}{2}$ ft. sq.
Baudirektor Linne, a new variety with large deep orange-red
flowers on 4 ft. stems.   *2$\frac{1}{2}$ ft. sq.*
bigelovii aurantiacum, early bright yellow.   *2 ft. 2 ft. sq.*
Chipperfield Orange, yellow, streaked and splashed crimson.
                                                      4 ft. 3 ft. sq.
Copper Spray, copper-red.   *3$\frac{1}{2}$ ft. 2 ft. sq.*
Crimson Beauty (*Plate 32, p. 144*), bronze-crimson. *2 ft. 2$\frac{1}{2}$ ft. sq.*
Gartensonne, bright golden-yellow.   *4 ft. 2$\frac{1}{2}$ ft. sq.*
Golden Fox, very large, rich orange-brown. A good variety.
                                                      3 ft. 2 ft. sq.
Golden Youth, large, rich butter-yellow.   *3 ft. 2 ft. sq.*
Goldlackzwerg, gold and copper red.   *2$\frac{1}{2}$ ft. 2 ft. sq.*
July Sun, golden-orange.   *3 ft. 2$\frac{1}{2}$ ft. sq.*
Karneol, rich bronze.   *2$\frac{1}{2}$ ft. 2 ft. sq.*

Madame Canivet, yellow with dark brown centre,

3 ft. 2 ft. sq.

Moerheim Beauty (*Plate 33, p. 144*), warm glowing bronze-red.

3 ft. 2½ ft. sq.

pumilum magnificum, very free-flowering, rich deep yellow

2½ ft. 2 ft. sq.

Red Indian, a new reddish-bronze variety   *3½ ft. 2½ ft. sq.*

Riverton Beauty, yellow.   *5 ft. 2½ ft. sq.*

Riverton Gem, rich crimson streaked with yellow.

4½ ft. 2½ ft. sq.

Spatrot, the best bronze-red.   *4 ft. 2½ ft. sq.*

The Bishop (*Plate 33, p. 144*), large, rich buttercup yellow with
dark centre. Although an old variety this is still one of the best.

3 ft. 2½ ft. sq.

Waltraud, large-flowered, golden-brown.   *3½ ft. 2 ft. sq.*

Wyndley, erect growth, copper-orange.   *2 ft. 2 ft. sq.*

H. hoopesii. Orange Sneezeweed. Rocky Mountains. The earliest
flowering species; bright yellow flowers with golden centres.

1–3 ft.   May–Sept.   1½ ft. sq.

HELIANTHUS (*Compositae*): From *helios* (Gk) ' sun ', *anthos* ' flower '.
A large and somewhat coarse genus of annuals and perennials,
the latter useful for back of the border work or the wild garden. All
bloom in late summer and autumn. The roots are voracious feeders
and quickly exhaust the ground, so should be lifted and divided every
third year. Whilst they will grow in practically any soil, the best
results come from a rather stiff loam in full sun. Propagation by
division in spring.

H. atrorubens (syn. *H. sparsifolius*): Purple Disc Sunflower, Darkeye Sunflower (*Plate 32, p. 144*). S.E. United States. This has become well
known chiefly on account of its wonderful garden variety ' The
Monarch '. This is one of our best late autumn border perennials
and makes a first-rate background subject. In a good season the stems
will grow 6–7 ft. high, branching freely at the top into a number of
long rough stems each carrying a round, golden, semi-double and
substantial flower the size of a man's hand. When cut these last about
five weeks in water. Unfortunately ' The Monarch ' is not hardy in all
situations but can be kept from year to year by lifting some of the
tubers in autumn and storing them away from frost, until the following
spring.   *6–7 ft.   Sept.–Oct.   4 ft. sq.*

H. decapetalus. Perennial Sunflower. N. America. Makes a bushy plant
of branching habit, with long, oval-lanceolate, very rough leaves
which are sharply toothed at the edges. The flowers may be 2 to 3
inches across and are light yellow.

2–5 ft.   July–Sept.   3½ ft. sq.

Plate 35: CINQUEFOIL, *Potentilla nepalensis* ‘ Miss Willmott ’

Plate 36: CANDLE LARKSPUR, *Delphinium—left* 'Natalie'; *right* 'Blue Gown'

Plate 37: top GLOBE THISTLE, *Echinops ritro*; *centre* WHITE BALLOON FLOWER, *Platy-codon grandiflorus albus*; *right* BALLOON FLOWER, *Platycodon grandiflorus*

Plate 38: PHLOX VARIETIES, *Phlox paniculata—top* 'Newbird'; *right* 'Graf Zeppelin';
bottom 'Le Mahdi'

A number of garden varieties have been raised from this species. It is worth noting that unless the double varieties are divided fairly frequently they tend to revert to singles.

Capenock Star (*Plate 32, p. 144*), large, single, lemon-yellow flowers which are excellent for cutting. *5 ft. 4 ft. sq.*

flore pleno (*Plate 27, p. 128*), double flowers. *4 ft. 3 ft. sq.*

Loddon Gold, rich double yellow blossoms. *5 ft. 4 ft. sq.*

Soleil d'Or, sulphur-yellow flowers, the petals fluted and quilled rather like a Cactus Dahlia. This is an old variety and very widely grown. *4½ ft. 4 ft. sq.*

Triomphe de Gand, large golden-yellow flowers with ball-shaped centres. *5 ft. 4 ft. sq.*

H. salicifolius (syn. *H. orgyalis*). Central United States. A late bloomer with small flowers and narrow-leaved foliage which is not nearly as coarse as that of most other species. The stems are leafy up to the flower heads, which are extremely numerous and of a deep golden-yellow shade. *6–8 ft. Sept.–Oct. 4 ft. sq.*

H. tomentosus. S.E. United States. A species chiefly noted for its silvery and downy stems and leaves. The flowers are bright yellow, hairy at the back, and rather sticky to the touch. *4 ft. Sept. 3 ft. sq.*

HELIOPSIS (*Compositae*): Orange Sunflower. From *helios* (Gk) 'sun', *opsis* 'like'.

Sunflower-like perennials needing similar treatment to Helianthus, q.v. The general habit is somewhat smaller and more compact, however, whilst the blooms are brighter in colour. Propagation by division in spring.

H. scabra. Rough Heliopsis. (*Plate 27, p. 128.*) N. America. A plant with numerous flower heads and very rough stems and leaves. In preference to the type gardeners frequently grow some of the varieties such as *major* which is larger in all its parts; *incomparabilis*, with rich double yellow blooms (3 ft.); *gigantea*, large, golden, semi-double; 'Goldgefieder', full double blooms having yellow rays and green centres (3½ ft); 'Gold Greenheart', a popular variety in the United States with double, buttercup-yellow flowers which show an emerald green heart as the buds open: this disappears when the blooms mature: excellent for cutting (3 ft.); 'Orange King', a fine showy plant with bright orange flowers; *patula*, semi-double, with three rows of pointed incised petals on the large, rather flat flowers (3½ ft.); 'Light of Loddon', bright yellow (3 ft.); 'Summer Sun', clear orange-yellow (3 ft.). All bloom from July to September and need a planting area of about 2 ft. sq.

HELLEBORUS (*Ranunculaceae*): Christmas Rose, Lenten Rose, Hellebore. From *helein* (Gk) 'to injure', *bora* 'food'; the roots are poisonous.

Invaluable border plants, early-flowering and long-lasting. The blooms often persist for months. This latter trait is probably due to the fact that the flowers are not constructed in the usual manner, for in Hellebores the sepals are the ornamental part of the bloom, the petals being converted to smaller tubular nectaries which stand just behind the stamens. These sepals may be red, green or white, the last group probably the most important as it contains the beautiful Christmas Rose (*H. niger*).

The plants are not strictly herbaceous as they hold their foliage during the winter, but this will be thought an advantage by most gardeners. A well-drained soil is essential, and it pays to prepare their planting sites rather carefully. Take the soil out to about 2 ft. depth and replace it with equal parts of fibrous loam and well-rotted manure, and half these quantities of both coarse sand and peat. A sheltered position where relief can be found from the midday sun suits the plants best, indeed many Hellebores do well in a shady situation amongst shrubs and associate particularly happily with ferns. The fronds of the latter prevent soil being splashed on the goblet-shaped flowers.

Once established they should be left undisturbed as they are sensitive to changes. Slugs often seek out the juicy stems and must be kept at bay with metaldehyde or a proprietary slug killer.

In early December the flowers of the Christmas Rose should be protected against mud, either by top dressing the soil around with peat or placing a piece of canvas or handlight over them. The blooms are attractive when cut, but should have the ends burned with a taper or dipped for a second or two in glacial acetic acid before being placed in a vase. The blooms of Lenten Roses (*H. orientalis*) will not stand when cut but may be used as floating flowers in a bowl. Both types force well if the roots are gradually immured to a warm temperature.

Propagation by division (but do not have the divisions too large or they may not settle in), or by seeds sown after ripening in boxes, or in the open ground. The seedlings flower the third season.

H. abchasicus. Caucasus. Winter flowering, with smooth evergreen leaves and dull red, nodding flowers. These are sometimes green within. Var. *coccineus* is wine-crimson and var. *venosus* has dark veining on rosy-purple.   *1 ft.   Jan.–Mar.   2 ft. sq.*

H. corsicus. Corsican Hellebore. (*Plate V, p. 208.*) Corsica. A most handsome species. The flowers are borne in large clusters and are of a strange pea-green shade; they remain in character for six months of the year. There may be 15–20 blooms on a single spike. The leaves are beautiful and of a glaucous green colour, armed with spines, and divided into imposing segments.

2–3 ft.   March–April (hanging to Aug.)   2 ft. sq.

H. foetidus. Setterwort, Stinking Hellebore. (*Plate I, p. 192.*) Europe including Britain. A strong-smelling and poisonous species. The powered roots, mixed with meal, have been used as bait for mice in country areas. The blooms appear early and are pale green tipped with purple. The evergreen foliage is beautifully cut, and divided—almost—but not quite to the centre of each leaf.

2 ft. Feb.–May. 2 ft. sq.

H. niger. Black Hellebore, Christmas Rose. Central and S. Europe. It has deep green leaves which are divided into oval segments, toothed at their apex. The flowers are a very clean white, saucer shaped, with bright golden anthers. Unfortunately the stalks of the true species are rather short so that most gardeners will seek to grow the longer-stemmed variety, *altifolius*. Another good white form of recent introduction is known as 'Keesen Variety'. *1–2 ft. Jan.–Feb. 2 ft. sq.*

H. × nigricors. A fine hybrid derived from crossing *H. niger* and *corsicus*. It has the handsome foliage of *H. niger* and many pale green blooms.

1½ ft. Feb. 2–3 ft. sq.

H. orientalis. Lenten Rose. Greece and Asia Minor. A very variable species which has given rise to a number of good garden varieties. The coloured perianths or flowers of these may be cream, green, purple, pink, rose or almost black, and many of them are spotted with several shades. It differs from *H. niger* by having branched flower stems, and in very exposed districts the leaves disappear in winter. In warmer districts however, the leaves are usually held throughout the season. *2 ft. March–April. 1½ ft. sq.*

H. viridis: Green Hellebore. Europe, parts of Ireland. This plant is remarkable for the pale green tints of the flowers which show in pleasing contrast against the darker shades of the foliage. It is not averse to a little lime in the soil and contains much honey which is said to be poisonous. *1½ ft. March–April. 1½ ft. sq.*

HEMEROCALLIS (*Liliaceae*): Daylily. From *hemera* (Gk) 'day', *kallos* 'beauty'; the individual flowers only last one day.

Few plants surpass in vigour and beauty a well-flowered clump of Hemerocallis, and its graceful, arching foliage and tall, stout flower scapes lend enchantment to any garden. Hardy, dependable and long lasting the plants will grow in practically any soil or situation—in sun or shade, at the edge of the shrubbery, in the herbaceous border, by the lakeside, or even in the water itself. They can be left in the same position for many years. Propagation by division in spring. As cut flowers also they are most desirable, the buds open well in water and emit a most delightful fragrance.

Nevertheless recognition of the Day Lilies as good garden plants has been slow. Possibly the short duration of the individual flowers, especially in the species, accounts for this neglect, but modern varieties last not one but two or three days and produce such a succession of blossom that the plants are in character for weeks or months at a time.

When not in flower the foliage is worth its place and remains a fresh cool green, even in a town border. All the following are good garden plants:

C. P. Raffill, maroon-pink, shaded with apricot.

2½ ft. July–Aug. 3 ft. sq.

Desert Song, a unique colour combination, the large Lily-like flowers are a delicate shade of orange-apricot with a chestnut banding in the throat. *2½ ft. July–Aug. 3 ft. sq.*

forrestii (Plate 19, p. 96), a Chinese species with thin, grass-like foliage and wiry branching stems, which carry many somewhat small, light golden-yellow flowers.

2 ft. June–July. 2½ ft. sq.

fulva (Plate 19, p. 96), S.E. Asia. The large open flowers are a pleasing shade of tawny-red with an apricot line through each petal. *2½ ft. July. 3 ft. sq.*

Garnet Robe, dark blood-red, rather thin flowers.

3 ft. July–Aug. 3 ft. sq.

George Yeld, rich orange suffused orange-scarlet, very open flowers. *2 ft. July–Aug. 2½ ft. sq.*

Gipsy, brilliant deep orange flowers on branching stems, a beautiful plant for small borders or town gardens.

3 ft. July–Aug. 2½ ft. sq.

Hesperus, soft citron yellow. *4 ft. July–Aug. 3 ft. sq.*

Hiawatha *(Plate 19, p. 96)*, an exceptionally free-flowering variety. The medium-sized flowers are a brilliant dark copper-crimson with a golden-yellow base. *3 ft. July–Aug. 2½ ft. sq.*

Hyperion, broad attractive foliage and stout branching stems, bearing large, golden-yellow, Lily-like flowers.

2½ ft. July–Aug. 2 ft. sq.

Klondyke, the large, well-expanded brilliant golden-orange flowers are over 5 in. across, each segment charmingly crimped and slightly reflexed. *3 ft. July–Aug. 2½ ft. sq.*

Marcus, rich orange overlaid bronze, very robust, with large recurving flowers. *2½ ft. July–Aug. 2½ ft. sq.*

Margaret Perry, orange-scarlet with a yellow base and prominent yellow line running through each petal.

3½ ft. July–Sept. 3 ft. sq.

Paul Boissier *(Plate 19, p. 96)*, rigid stems, carrying somewhat crowded heads of large open flowers. These are a combination of light bronze and yellowish-copper, with a faint red zone in the throat. *2½ ft. July–Aug. 2 ft. sq.*

Pink Damask, salmon-pink, sturdy. *2¼ ft. July–Aug. 2½ ft. sq.*

Pink Lady *(Plate 19, p. 96)*, arching, narrow foliage and graceful thin stems. The flowers which are carried in Lily-like clusters are a warm amber pink with a soft buff midrib and a cool ice-yellow throat. *3 ft. July–Aug. 3 ft. sq.*

Royal Ruby, rich crimson-red. *3 ft. July–Aug. 3 ft. sq.*

Sandstone (*Plate 19, p. 96*), broad, overlapping petals and large, open, cup-shaped flowers of bright lemon-yellow with a faint reddish zone. *2½ ft. July. 2 ft. sq.*

St. Agnes, the somewhat small flowers of this compact growing variety are a pleasing combination of rich bronze-red and golden-yellow. *2½ ft. July–Aug. 2 ft. sq.*

The Doctor, deep red with velvety petals.
2½ ft. July–Aug. 3 ft. sq.

W. B. Cranfield, the attractive, light bronzy-red flowers are carried on stout branching stems. The plant is very vigorous and grows well in light shade. *3½ ft. July–Aug. 3 ft. sq.*

HESPERIS (*Cruciferae*): Sweet Rocket. From *hesperos* (Gk) 'evening'; the Night Scented Stock belongs to this family.

Old-fashioned perennials and biennials, with fragrant flowers and smooth, oblong toothed leaves. They are bad perennials and seem to exhaust the soil more quickly than most plants. The roots should therefore be lifted, divided and transplanted to a fresh site at least every other year. They will, however, naturalise happily in situations where they are left undisturbed and make showy plants in light shade, or at the edge of shrubberies and in the wild garden.

H. matronalis. Damask Violet. Sweet Rocket. S. Europe, Siberia. Has a profusion of long spikes of four-petalled, white, mauve or purple flowers in early summer. These are fragrant and useful for cutting. Seedlings vary considerably and any of the above shades may appear; especially good plants should therefore be divided in order to perpetuate the desired trait. There are several good garden forms with double flowers, such as *alba plena*, double white and *flore pleno*, double purple, and a fine white single, *candissima*. *2–3 ft. June. 1½ ft. sq.*

HEUCHERA (*Saxifragaceae*): Alumroot, Coral Bells. Named after J. H. Heucher, an 18th-century German Professor of Medicine.

Low-growing perennials with heart-shaped, evergreen leaves and slender stalks of small, hanging, bell-shaped flowers. These are quite useful for cutting and bloom spasmodically from spring until late autumn. Unfortunately many of the species have a tendency to die out even in good soils and consequently must be frequently divided and given fresh situations. Special care is necessary also in dry seasons for they will not tolerate drought. Many of the seedlings raised from the species are more tractable and will be grown in preference to the form. All are easily raised from seed but seedlings will show much variation and only the best should be kept. They can also be propagated by division in spring.

The first Heucheras were introduced by the late Thomas Ware of Tottenham Hale Nurseries, an establishment very famous in its day, and where many of the older generation of nurserymen in Europe and Britain were trained. About 1885 Dr. Murray brought over from Mexico six plants of *H. sanguinea* in an open basket, and these, surviving the rigours of a long journey by sail, gave such pleasure to English gardeners that they were carefully tended and from their progeny all the plants of *H. sanguinea* have been raised. The roots have been used medicinally.

H. sanguinea. Coral Bells. (*Plate 2, p. 17.*) Mexico, Arizona Has heart-shaped or roundish, five- or seven-lobed leaves. These are slightly hairy. The spikes of flowers are graceful and airy; the individual blooms are bright red. The following varieties should be noted:

    alba, white.
    Apple Blossom, soft pink with rosy buds.
    atrosanguinea, dark red.
    Freedom, large, bright rose-pink.
    Gaiety, glowing carmine red.
    Huntsman, scarlet.
    Jubilee, rose.
    Oakington Jewel, coral-pink suffused copper.
    Pearl Drops, almost white.
    Pluie de Feu, cherry-red.
    Red Spangles, rich scarlet-crimson.
    Snowflakes, pure white.
    Souvenir of Wolley Dod, turkey-red.
    Sparkler, carmine and scarlet.

1–1½ ft.   June–Sept.   1½ ft. sq.

Readers should also note that there is another race of Heucheras (sometimes known as *H. brizoides*) which have been derived from crossing Heuchera varieties with *Tiarella cordifolia*. For this reason the plants are also known as *Heucherella*. These have very fine mottled and lobed leaves and dainty spikes of hanging, bell-shaped flowers. There is a white form, *alba*; Bloom's Variety, rich coral-red; Coral Plume, coral-red; Edge Hall, pink; *gracillima*, rosy-crimson. All grow about 1½ ft. tall.

In 1956 a new varietal cross called ' Bridget Bloom ' received the R.H.S. Award of Merit. It grows about 2 ft. high and has rich pink flowers which begin to bloom in May and continue for eight months.

HIERACIUM (*Compositae*): Hawkweed. From *kierax* (Gk) ' hawk ', because it was supposed that these birds of prey used the plant to strengthen their vision.

Perennial plants with dainty heads of small yellow or orange daisy-like flowers and ground-hugging foliage. This is often silvery. The plants will grow in practically any soil but favour a well-drained situation and must be watched lest they become too weedy. Propagation by division.

H. aurantiacum. Devil's Paintbrush. Europe naturalized in Britain. Has bright orange flowers and is a good plant if kept in bounds. The stem is covered with short black hairs, which earned it the name 'Grim the Collier' in some parts. *1–1½ ft. June–Sept. 1 ft. sq.*

H. villosum. The Shaggy Hawkweed. Central Europe. Has silvery leaves and shaggy, bright yellow flowers. *1 ft. June–Aug. 1 ft. sq.*

HOSTA (syn. Funkia) (*Liliaceae*): Plantain Lily. Named after Nicolaus Thomas Host, a 19th-century Austrian physician.

Attractive Asiatic plants with beautiful foliage and handsome spikes of flowers. They can be most satisfactorily employed in key positions, where fine foliage effects are wanted—as in stone vases, by a woodland seat, at the corner of the shady border, or flanking the water garden. Here they are seen in their full beauty, the leaves smooth, frequently crimped and in some instances variegated in attractive shades of green and cream and white. The clumps improve with age and should be left in the same position if happily situated. They need a soil which is rich in vegetable material and unlikely to dry out. Full sun overhead is detrimental as it burns out the clumps and the foliage soon becomes shabby. Propagation is effected by division when growth starts in the spring.

H. albomarginata. Japan. A small-leaved species with dull matt green leaves and violet, funnel-shaped flowers. Var. *albomarginata* has white edges to the foliage. *1–1½ ft. July–Sept. 1½ sq. ft.*

H. decorata var. *decorata:* Blunt Plantain Lily. Japan. Has oval leaves which are margined with white and rather dark blue, drooping flowers. *1½–2 ft. May. 1½ ft. sq.*

H. fortunei. Plantain Lily. A group name covering a number of good garden plants, all of hybrid origin. Var. *rugosa* has beautiful heart-shaped leaves of rich bluish-green; the flowers are pale lilac. Var. *variegata* has variegated foliage; var. *albopicta* has yellowish leaves edged with green. *1½–2 ft. May. 2 ft. sq.*

H. glauca (syn. *Funkia sieboldtiana*). Japan. Has handsome, corrugated, blue-green leaves some 12 in. long and pale lilac flowers. *1½ ft. June. 2 ft. sq.*

H. lancifolia. Lanceleaf Plantain Lily (*Plate VII, p. 224*). Japan. A small species of tufted growth with lance-shaped leaves which narrow at both ends; flowers pale lilac. *1½–2 ft. July–Sept. 1½ ft. sq.*

H. plantaginea. China, Japan. Oval, heart-shaped leaves and white, trumpet-shaped fragrant flowers. Var. *grandiflora* has larger blooms. *2 ft. Aug.–Sept. 2½ ft. sq.*

H. tardiflora (syn. *H. lancifolia* var. *tardiflora*): Japan. A distinct and useful plant characterised by a dwarf habit and late flowers. The latter are pale purple, the leaves dark green and glossy.

1 ft. Sept.–Oct. 1 ft. sq.

H. undulata. Wavy-leaved Plantain Lily. Japan. A handsome plant with large oval leaves, heavily splashed with white; the flowers pale lilac. Var. *erromena* is completely green. *2½ ft. Aug. 2 ft. sq.*

H. ventricosa (syn. *H. coerulea, Funkia ovata*): Blue Plantain Lily. E. Asia. Has elongated, heart-shaped leaves about 9 inches long and 6–8 inches wide. The blades are deep bluish-green and the flowers lavender-blue striped with a paler shade. Several of these hang on each stem, the individual florets being about 2 inches long and funnel-shaped. Var. *marginata* has white-edged leaves. *2–3 ft. May. 2½ ft. sq.*

INCARVILLEA (*Bignoniaceae*): Chinese Trumpet Flower. Named after Pierre d'Incarville, a French missionary in China and botanical correspondent with Jussieu, Director of the Jardine Botanique of Paris in the mid-18th century.

Handsome, almost exotic looking perennials with fuchsia coloured, Gloxinia-like flowers and striking, pinnate leaves. The plants should be grown in light, sandy loam enriched with well-rotted manure or compost. They need full sun and a sheltered background; protection should be given in exposed situations, although the plants are hardier than their looks lead one to believe. I have seen them in cold London clays flowering freely. In any case it is a wise precaution to heap a little bracken round the roots or cover them with a pane of glass during the worst of the winter. Slugs are attracted to the stems and leaves and the plants must be protected against them. Propagation by seed sown after ripening, in pans or pots (they come to bloom in about three years), or by division in spring.

I. compacta. Dwarf Trumpet Flower. N.W. China. A plant of compact habit but rather shy blooming. The flowers are bright rose-pink, funnel-shaped and about 2½ in. in length. *1 ft. May–June. 1 ft. sq.*

I. delavayi. Chinese Trumpet Flower. (*Plate 13, p. 64.*) W. China. A vigorous and handsome perennial with ash-like leaves and large, bright rose-red flowers, five to six blooms on each stem. The garden variety ' Bees Pink ' has blossoms of a paler shade.

1–1½ ft. May–June. 2 ft. sq.

I. grandiflora. W. China. Is more dwarf than *I. delavayi* with extremely large, rich, rosy-red flowers, often 3–4 in. across. They have a yellow throat. Var. *brevipes* is brighter in colour, being a deep rose-purple.

1 ft. May–June. 1½ ft. sq.

INULA (*Compositae*): Ancient Latin name.
Coarse but showy perennials with large, brightly coloured, daisy

flowers 2–4 in. across. Whilst some are only suited to the wild garden, others may be planted in any moist situation, such as the margin of a stream, and several can be grown in the herbaceous border. Their cultivation does not present difficulties, providing the soil does not dry out in summer. They all favour plenty of sunshine. Propagation by seed or division.

I. ensifolia. Caucasus. A front of the border plant with small, solitary yellow flowers. *9 in. Aug. 1 ft. sq.*

I. grandiflora. The earliest flowering variety; the habit of the plant is more dwarf than *I. helenium.* *2 ft. June. 2 ft. sq.*

I. helenium. Elecampane. Europe including Britain; N. Asia. A vigorous plant with a stout stem and coarse leaves, suitable for associating with other foliage plants in the border or it can be planted in the bog or water garden. The flowers are bright yellow and resemble small Sunflowers. The rather large leaves are bitter and aromatic, also the roots, the latter containing a white starchy powder termed Inuline, also a volatile oil, a resin and a bitter extract. All of these have been much used medicinally. *3–4 ft. June–Aug. 3 ft. sq.*

I. magnifica. E. Caucasus. A robust perennial, with purplish striations on the roughly hairy stems. It has coarse oval, toothed leaves which may be 10–12 in. long and 6–7 in. across. The bright golden-yellow flowers are borne in terminal heads and have rather ragged florets.
5–6 ft. June–Aug. 3 ft. sq.

I. oculis-christi. E. Europe. A strangely beautiful plant with large bright, golden-yellow flowers with shaggy petals. The cushion central part of these is covered when young with a whitish substance which looks like wax, and gives it the appearance of an eye—hence the specific name. The leaves are rather small and lance-shaped.
1 ft. Summer. 1 ft. sq.

I. orientalis (syn. *I. glandulosa*): Caucasian Inula. (*Plate 14, p. 65.*) Caucasus. The best-known species, with wavy edged, large orange flowers 4–5 in. across and large, striking leaves. It is not coarse. The flowers are useful for cutting. There are two garden varieties, var. *laciniata*, with thread-like, ragged petals and var. *superba* in which the flower heads are larger than the type. *2–3 ft. June–Aug. 2 ft. sq.*

I. royleana. Himalayas. A striking Himalayan species with large orange flowers on unbranched stems; the buds are black with a green collar.
2 ft. Aug.–Oct. 2 ft. sq.

IRIS (*Iridaceae*): From *Iris* (Gk) ' rainbow ', from the bright colours of the flowers.

A large and important family of perennials with rhizomatous, bulbous or creeping rootstocks. Although the blooms are not individually long-lasting, a succession of flower buds ensures several weeks of colour, and their poise, shape and bright rainbow hues are other compensatory virtues. By careful selection, the genus may be represented in bloom for almost twelve months of the year. The foliage is neat—either thin and grass-like or erect and lance-shaped, the habit good, and many have fragrant flowers or rootstocks.

June flowering Irises (*I. barbata*) are particularly handsome, the flowers embracing such a wide range of colour that they are often known as 'Rainbow Irises'. Their foliage is also attractive, being silver-grey, erect and always tidy, a combination of circumstances which sometimes leads gardeners to plan borders entirely of Irises. When in bloom such borders can be really striking, but in three to four weeks the flowers are done and the colour gone. A useful way of prolonging the interest is to interplant the Iris with Gladioli. The foliage is complementary, and when the blooms of the former are done, one can still look forward to the bright spears of the Gladioli.

When considering soil conditions there are no overall rules. Some species like lime, others detest it, a few want sun baked, rather dry soil, and a minority bog or even aquatic conditions. One cannot even generalise over situations, for whilst *I. barbata* requires full sun to give of its best, it will nevertheless exist in shade. *I. foetidissima*, on the other hand, prefers woodland conditions.

I have therefore thought it expedient to include cultural details with each group or species, and would only repeat that care should be exercised in siting individuals, bearing in mind the fact that 'One man's meat', etc., is particularly applicable to Irises.

For the sake of cultural convenience the family has here been divided into five groups.

GROUP I. THE GERMAN OR BEARDED IRIS

This section which is either referred to as *I. barbata* or *I. germanica* is chiefly characterised by bearded appendages on the petal falls. These are the best and most widely grown Irises and possess long, banana-like or rhizomatous rootstocks which should be left half-exposed at planting time. All like full sun (and must have it to flower freely), well-drained soil and lime. In ground naturally deficient in the latter, a little hydrated lime can be sprinkled round the roots after planting. These Irises grow quickly and need dividing every second or third season, an operation which should be carried out immediately after flowering (July), as spring or autumn disturbance often loses a season's bloom.

As border plants, members of the group should be given a front to mid-position (according to height) and are best grouped in colour blocks of 5 or 6 plants. Varieties are legion, in colours varying from white to yellow, blue, purple, mauve, pink, red and combinations of more than one shade. They flower in May and June and can be propagated from seed (which usually comes to flower the third season) or by division.

A representative collection of the best varieties is given below; they should be planted $1-1\frac{1}{2}$ ft. apart.

Aline, fragrant, pure azure blue, *3 ft.*

Amigo, standards clear lavender; rich, velvety-purple falls with narrow white margins, $2\frac{1}{2}$ *ft.*

Arabi Pasha, intense royal blue, *3 ft.*

Arctic Snow, pure white, of branching habit, *3 ft.*

Belle Meade, white, plicated or veined with violet-blue, *3 ft.*

Benton Baggage, rose standards, reddish-lilac falls, $3\frac{1}{2}$ *ft.*

Blue Valley, flax-blue with darker veining. Fragrant, *3 ft.*

California Gold, massive heads of large deep golden-yellow flowers on strong stems. One of the best yellows, $3\frac{1}{2}$ *ft.*

Childhood, a charming combination of bronze-pink and blue, $3\frac{1}{2}$ *ft.*

Cliffs of Dover, ruffled white petals, *3 ft.*

Elmohr, exceptionally large flowers in a beautiful shade of mulberry-purple. Increases rapidly. Of American origin, *3 ft.*

Golden Hind, clear chrome-yellow with golden beard on falls, *3 ft.*

Great Lakes, probably the best all blue Iris, crispy-texture, very free-flowering, $3\frac{1}{2}$ *ft.*

Gudrun, creamy-white with brilliant gold beard, $2\frac{1}{2}$ *ft.*

High Command, yellow and velvety-crimson, free-flowering, *3 ft.*

Indiana Night, deep rich velvety purple—almost black. This variety makes a good contrast against white or pale yellow forms, *3 ft.*

Joan Long, rich orange-yellow, vigorous, *3 ft.*

Lady Mohr, standards oyster-white, large and slightly fluted with strong mid-rib. Falls pale chartreuse with prominent veining. Possibly a hybrid with Oncocylus variety, *4 ft.*

Lambent, large flowers, with golden standards and maroon falls, *3 ft.*

Louvois (*Plate 9, p. 48*), warm velvety-brown and maroon, *4 ft.*

Mabel Chadburn, a very fine self-yellow, *3 ft.*

Mary Randall, deep rose-pink with orange beard, *3 ft.*

Mrs. J. L. Gibson, rich indigo purple-blue, flowers early and of fine form and habit, *3 ft.*

Nightfall, falls velvety, rich dark pansy-purple, standards a few shades lighter making a very striking colour combination, $3\frac{1}{2}$ *ft.*

Ola Kala, deep yellow, almost orange, petals heavily ruffled, well-branched stems, *3 ft.*

Prairie Sunset, solid, extra-large flowers in a wonderful combination of peach-apricot, rose, copper and gold, *3 ft.*

Radiation, orchid pink with deep tangerine beard, very fine, $2\frac{1}{2}$ *ft.*

Ranger, late-flowering, very dark crimson-red. The long standards are closed and cone-shaped, the falls smooth and like rich velvet, *3 ft.*

Red Torch, falls deep red, with standards or upright petals glowing buff-gold, 2½ ft.

Sable, flowers of thick texture, a uniform shade of deep blue-black violet with blue beard, *3 ft.*

Solid Mahogany, colour aptly described by the name, a deep bronzy gold beard ac-centuates the richness of the plush-like falls, *3 ft.*

St. Agnes (*Plate 9, p. 48*), free-flowering, branching, flowers greyish-white with a gold beard, 2½ ft.

The Red Douglas, gigantic flowers rich deep purple-red. The bright orange beard is softened by a slight flush of brown, 3½ ft.

Wabash, large, slightly ruffled flowers, standards pure white, petals rich velvety violet bordered white, 3½ ft.

I. pallida Sweet Iris. A species of uncertain origin, but distinguished from *I. barbata* by reason of its silvery foliage and flower bracts. It is scented like the elder and has large pale mauve flowers. Var. *argentea* (*Plate 9, p. 48*) has silver striped foliage, and *aurea fol. var.* golden. *2–4 ft. May–June. 1 ft. sq.*

GROUP II. JAPANESE IRIS

These are lime haters and moisture-loving. *I. laevigata* and its varieties, being really aquatic, need standing water always over the roots, but *I. kaempferi* need moisture during the growing season and drier conditions in winter. It is possible to grow *I. kaempferi* really well in a border if the site is deeply dug and prepared with well-rotted manure. Apart from feeding the plants, the latter conserves moisture during the summer months. Many of the kaempferi hybrids are most colourful, and as well as selfs in blue, purple, white, pink or red, the large flat flowers come up in combinations of several shades, often blotched, stippled or striated as well in fantastic patternings. These varieties can often be bought under the original Japanese names, but it is just as satisfactory (and certainly much cheaper) to buy a mixed batch of seedlings, for all the hybrids are good.

Kaempferi Iris flower in July and grow 2 ft. tall. They should be planted 2 ft. apart.

Good named varieties, if these are preferred are:

Akashi, reddish-violet with white veining.

Aoigata, violet self.

Gei-sho-ui, reddish-purple with yellow spots.

Glamour, flowers 8 in. across, violet-purple and yellow.

Gofukushoshu, violet-red veining on a grey background.

Illumination, purple with lighter veining and golden beard.

Kyo-kanoko, rich violet veined with white.

Momyi-no-taki, reddish-purple striated greyish-white.

Morning Mist, white with yellow markings, petals bordered with violet.

Nagisa-no-umi, white streaked with violet-blue.

Tomo-shiraga, white.

Yeso-niskiti, deep violet, double.

GROUP III. THE BEARDLESS IRIS (APOGON)

Most of this group again are moisture loving, but only in the sense that they should not go short in the growing season. The chief species are as follows:

I. crocea (syn. *I. aurea*). Kashmir. A fine hardy plant of noble proportions. The 3 to 4 ft. stems are topped by spikes carrying several tiers of rich golden, crimped petalled flowers. The foliage dies down completely in autumn, but reappears again in mid-winter. Propagation by spring division.   *3–4 ft. Late June. 2 ft. sq.*

I. delavayi. China. A deep violet-purple *sibirica* type Iris (see p. *174*) which nevertheless needs wetter conditions than that species. Propagation by spring division.   *3–4 ft. June. 2 ft. sq.*

I. douglasiana, The Douglas Iris. (*Plate 9, p. 48*.) California. A good front of the border plant which when happily situated forms thick mats of grassy foliage. It should be grown in lime free soil and have an annual mulch of leaf-mould round the roots. The flowers are variable, from mauve or lavender, to apricot and cream. Propagation by spring division.   *1 ft. May. 2 ft.*

'Margot Holmes' (*Plate 9, p. 48*), a hybrid derived from this plant and *I. chrysographes* (a Chinese species) is outstandingly beautiful with rich plum-purple flowers picked out in gold on the falls. Raised at Enfield it received every possible award both in Gt. Britain and the United States in 1927, the year of its introduction. This variety should be grown in soil which remains moist during the summer. Propagation by spring division.   *1½ ft. June. 1½ ft. sq.*

I. forrestii. Yunnan Iris. (*Plate 9, p. 48*.) W. China. Has good, clear yellow flowers and narrow grassy leaves. Unless grown in a really moist situation it should be mulched each spring with rotted manure or compost; *forrestii major* has flowers larger than the type. Propagation by spring division.   *12–15 in. July. 1½ ft. sq.*

I. ochroleuca. Yellowband Iris. (*Plate 9, p. 48*.) Asia Minor. A noble plant with wide, firm, strap-like leaves and flower stems up to 5 ft. high with several tiers of large yellow and white flowers. Var. *ochroaurea* is deeper in colour. Propagation by spring or autumn division.   *4–5 ft. June–July. 3 ft. sq.*

I. sibirica. Siberian Iris. Central Europe, Russia. A most important species with thin grassy leaves and strong, slender stems, carrying 2 or 3 attractive flowers. In the type, these are bluish-purple but there are a number of good garden varieties all of which grow taller when in the vicinity of water, but nevertheless give a very good account of themselves even in a fairly dry border. Propagation by division in early autumn or late spring.

Caesar, rich violet-purple, *3 ft.*

Caesar's Brother, a darker tone than ' Caesar ', *4 ft.*

Emperor, deep violet-blue, *3 ft.*

Eric the Red, appealing shade of dark purplish-red, *2½ ft.*

Heavenly Blue, rich azure, *4 ft.*

Marcus (*Plate 9, p. 48*) deep Oxford blue, *2½ ft.*

Margaret, Cambridge Blue, *3 ft.*

Pembina, purple, edged white, *3 ft.*

Perry's Blue, very free-flowering, a beautiful china-blue variety, *3 ft.*

Pickanock, royal blue, falls suffused white, *3½ ft.*

Snow Queen, large freely produced flowers of snowy whiteness, *3 ft.*   *2½–4 ft. June. 1½ ft. sq.*

I. wilsonii. W. China. *A. sibirica* type species, with pale yellow blossoms which have a light-brown throat. Propagation by spring division.

2 ft. June. 1 ft. sq.

Group IV. Dwarf Iris

A large group which includes many only suited to the rock garden and others extremely difficult for the average garden. The handsome Oncocylus, with strange, mauve, brown or blackish flowers belong here. But these need to be grown in warm, sunny situations, and must be kept covered with lights whilst the foliage dies down (from July until October) to prevent rain touching the rhizomes. They must also be protected from excessive wet in autumn and winter, a combination of requirements which really makes them unsuitable for the average border.

For narrow beds or a front row position, however, the varieties of *I. pumila* and *I. chamaeiris* are most satisfactory. The latter has been crossed with *I. barbata* and produced a fine range of colourful hybrids, midway between the tall June flowering Bearded kinds and the dwarf *I. pumila.* These are often catalogued as *I. intermedia.*

I. chamaeiris. S. Europe. Often confused with *I. pumila* but distinguished from this species by having a true stem. The flowers may be blue, purple, yellow or whitish, all with bright orange beards. Propagation by division.   *6–10 in. April–May. 1 ft. sq.*

I. pumila. S. Europe and Asia Minor. Has a long perianth tube (but no stem), with mauve, yellow, cream or reddish-purple flowers. Propagation by division.   *3–5 in. April. 6 in. sq.*

Named varieties derived from *I. chamaeiris* and *I. pumila* are:

Amber Queen, amber-yellow, *6 in.*
atroviolacea, purple-violet, *5 in.*
Blue Mascot, lilac-blue, large, *5 in.*
Burgundy, claret-purple, *10–12 in.*
Heatherbloom, rosy-red, *6 in.*
Moongleam, creamy-yellow, *7 in.*
Orange Queen, soft yellow with orange beard, *8 in.*
The Bride, milky-white, yellow beard, *10 in.*

GROUP V. SHADE LOVING IRIS

The chief representative in this group is *I. foetidissima* the Stinking Gladwin. Native to W. Europe including Britain, it has handsome grassy leaves and bluish-lilac flowers. In autumn the seed pods open to reveal rows of bright orange seeds, which are very ornamental. The species is useful for any moist, shady border or in woodland areas. The plant has a singular odour, and whilst it is untouched this is not unpleasant, reminding one of roasted meat. In country areas it is sometimes called Roast-beef Plant, but, if bruised or broken the smell becomes most unpleasant. *1–1½ ft.   June–Aug.   1 ft. sq.*

ISATIS (*Cruciferaceae*): Woad. From *isazo* (Gk) ' to equalise ', because it was supposed to smooth out all roughness on the skin.

This plant has particularly interesting associations with Great Britain, for it is presumed by some authors to be reponsible for the very name of Britain. The early peoples of these islands are believed to have stained their bodies with the indelible juices of *I. tinctoria* and the old Celtic name for paint was Brith. Brithon signified a stained man, a fact which has led some historians to assume that Britain or Britannia was derived from this noun. Woad is still cultivated in some places in England, for the dye from its leaves can be used as a substitute for indigo, but it is becoming less common as the years go by. The plants succeed in any ordinary garden soil and can be propagated by seed; it is best treated as biennial.

I. glauca. Asia Minor. A poor perennial with panicles of bright yellow, four-petalled flowers. These are somewhat reminiscent of a flowering cabbage head; the leaves are oblong and about one inch long.
2–4 ft.   June.   1½ ft. sq.

I. tinctoria. Common Dyer's Woad. Europe, including Britain. Is sometimes grown in borders but being of rampant habit is passed over by most gardeners in favour of the more attractive *I. glauca*. The flowers are very similar. *2–4 ft.   June.   1½ ft. sq.*

KENTRANTHUS (syn. Centranthus) (*Valerianaceae*): Spur Valerian. From *kentron* (Gk) ' spur ', *anthos* ' flower '.

A genus of annuals and perennials, the latter making good border plants in any ordinary garden soil and a variety of situations. One of the most attractive uses of the plant I have seen was during the war, when large quantities were employed to cover the raised mounds over air-raid shelters used by schools in Middlesex. Travellers in the south of England will have noticed it flowering freely on the railway cuttings, and the plant will also grow on walls, in rock gardens or close to the path in the border. Although *K. ruber* is not a British species it has become naturalized in many situations. It has a variety of garden names such as Pretty Betty, but in olden days was also called Setewall. In Southern Europe and Sicily the leaves are commonly eaten in salads and the seeds of one species were at one time used for embalming the dead. The chief disadvantage of the plant is an obnoxious catty smell, when the leaves are bruised. Propagation by seed sown in March out of doors.

K. ruber. Europe, naturalized in Britain. Has smooth pointed leaves and bold clusters of white, pink or red flowers. The type is usually a rosy-mauve but there is a white variety, *albus* (*Plate III, p. 208*) (White Valerian), also var. *atrococcineus*, deep red.

1½–3 ft.   June and throughout the summer.   1 ft. sq.

KIRENGESHOMA (*Saxifragaceae*): Yellow Waxbells. From *ki* (Jap.) 'yellow', '*rengeshoma*', the native name of *Anemopsis macrophylla*, a plant which it somewhat resembles.

A monotypic genus, the species *K. palmata* (*Plate 16, p. 80*) being native to Japan. It is a beautiful plant, vigorous and hardy with dark, smooth stems about 3 ft. high carrying slender, Sycamore-like leaves which are slightly hairy. The stems terminate in clusters of long, drooping, bright yellow flowers, the petals of which are so fresh that they look like wax. The plants thrive best in light shade and should be supplied with moist, leafy soil. On no account must this become dry during the height of the summer. Propagation by seed and division.   *3–4 ft.   Sept.–Oct.   2 ft. sq.*

KNIPHOFIA (syn. Tritoma) (*Liliaceae*): Red Hot Poker, Torch Lily. Named after J. H. Kniphof, an 18th century German professor of medicine.

A genus of handsome plants mostly from South and East Africa, with smooth, heavy stems surmounted by quantities of drooping, elongated, brightly coloured flowers. As these are often scarlet, orange or yellow and borne closely together at the top of the stem, they resemble a burning torch, which probably accounts for their common name. At one time Kniphofias were believed to be tender in Britain, chiefly because of wrong methods in handling during the dormant season. The plants hold their foliage during winter but spread it out over the ground, thus exposing the crowns to the elements. During showers these become filled with moisture, which freezes in severe weather. This causes expansion inside the core, which damages the

Plate 39: PHLOX VARIETIES, *Phlox paniculata—top right* ' Mrs. Ethel Prichard '; *top left* ' Caroline van der Berg '; *bottom* ' Daily Sketch '

Plate 40: KOREAN CHRYSANTHEMUM, *Chrysanthemum korean* ‘Venus’

membranes and later kills the plants. The best measure of protection is obtained by pulling the leaves above the crown in autumn and fastening them together with a rubber band or raffia tie. They thus cover and protect the vital crown beneath.

Very many garden hybrids have been raised in recent years so that the family may be had in flower from May until October. Many of these hybrids are hardier and sturdier than the type species.

Kniphofias need a rich soil for they are hungry plants, and the ground should be well prepared with rotted manure before planting. In later seasons mulches applied in mid-April serve to maintain the vigour of the clump, which can remain for years. Plant Red Hot Pokers in clumps, 2–3 ft. apart. They associate well with Michaelmas Daisies and any white flowers like Gypsophila, Marguerite Daisies and white Phlox.

There are also several species of more woody nature which are best grown as individuals, in some spot where the nobility of the foliage and flowers can be seen to best advantage. These are propagated by beheading, that is the tops (which remain above ground) are cut across so that they develop a number of offshoots. When these have made a few roots they are separated and kept in a close frame for a time and then potted up in a sandy compost. Species to be treated in this way are *caulescens* and *northiae*. All other kinds can be reproduced by division in spring or autumn, or from seed.

K. caulescens. S. Africa. Has very glaucous leaves emanating from a woody trunk, rising 5–6 in. above the ground level. This may be as thick as a man's arm, and from the centre rises a stem 4–5 ft. tall with a dense 6-in. spike of flowers. These are salmon-rose on opening but gradually pale to greenish-yellow. The foliage is metallic blue, the leaves having a serrated edge like the sides of a saw. Although the blooms are less striking than some of the stemless garden kinds, the plant is nevertheless magnificent when well grown, and should be considered for any corner site or situation, where it can dominate the surrounding vegetation. It must be propagated by beheading (see above) if suckers or short basal growths do not arise naturally. In severe winters or in northern districts a mulch of straw or leaves will protect the crowns during winter. *4–5 ft. Autumn. 5 ft. sq.*

K. comosa. Abyssinia. A graceful, slender plant for well-drained soil and a sheltered position. The grassy leaves are bright green and stand well above the ground. The flowers are yellow. This Abyssinian species has bright yellow flowers and where there is only one spike the upper flowers open first—thus reversing the normal procedure. Where there are lateral spikes, however, that is two or three from the same stalk, the blooms open from the base upwards. It is not suitable for very windswept districts. *1–2 ft. Aug. 1 ft. sq.*

K. corallina. A garden hybrid between *K. uvaria* and *K. macowanii* which has tangerine-red flowers on slender stems. Var. *superba* has brighter flowers. *2–3 ft. June–Sept. 2½ ft. sq.*

K. × *erecta.* A strange garden hybrid of uncertain origin which is particularly ornamental by virtue of the fact that none of the flowers really fade in the normal way. Instead, after the lower ones have passed they turn upwards and meet the young downward pointing buds. This eventually makes a diamond effect. The variety is not as hardy as some forms and needs the protection of leaves or straw during the worst of the winter. *4 ft. July–Aug. 3 ft. sq.*

K. foliosa. Abyssinia. Very similar to *K. caulescens* but growths spring directly from the base on distinct stems, instead of from a trunk. In many ways this is one of the most oustanding members of the family, and may be distinguished by its bright leaves which form a dense tuft at the top of a stem 1–3 ft. high. These are broad at the base and taper to a long point. The flowers are borne in a dense head, 10–12 inches long, and are bright yellow, tinged with red. *2–3 ft. Aug. 3 ft. sq.*

K. galpinii. Transvaal. A miniature Torch Lily excellent for cutting and front of the border work. It needs a sheltered position and must be protected during the winter months and in exposed situations. The flowers are a vivid flame colour, quite distinctive in this genus.
2½ ft. July–Sept. 2½ ft. sq.

K. gracilis. Natal. A slender, delicate looking plant, with narrow, grassy leaves and small heads of drooping, whitish flowers. There are a number of garden forms from this—all of which are excellent for cutting. *2 ft. July–Aug. 2 ft. sq.*

K. leichtlinii. Abyssinia. A hardy species with many narrow, grassy leaves 3–4 ft. in length. The flowers are bright yellow but sometimes speckled with red. Var. *aurea* has golden-yellow flowers.
4 ft. Aug. 4 ft. sq.

K. multiflora. S. Africa. A splendid plant with 7 ft. stems carrying quantities of small white flowers. It looks like a white torch.
7 ft. Oct.–Nov. 6 ft. sq.

K. nelsoni. S. Africa. Has very narrow toothed leaves with bright scarlet flowers tinged with orange. It needs a sunny situation and is a striking garden plant useful for cutting. *2 ft. Aug.–Sept. 2 ft. sq.*

K. northiae. S. Africa. Closely related to *caulescens* but with broader leaves and without the saw edge. The flowers are yellow below and red above, in very dense flower heads over 6 in. long. *4–5 ft. Aug. 3 ft. sq.*

K. rooperi. British Caffraia. A slender plant with woody, dark green leaves, which are toothed at the edges, and orange-red flowers which turn yellow with age. It requires a little protection during severe winters. *2 ft. Nov. 2 ft. sq.*

K. snowdenii. Uganda. Most distinct, with coral-scarlet, widely-spaced
flowers on 4–5 ft. stalks. It bears some resemblance to a large
Lachenalia. The plant is hardy in sheltered parts of Britain but needs
winter protection elsewhere.   *4–5 ft. July–Aug. 4 ft. sq.*

K. tuckii. S. Africa. Has wide, channelled, Yucca-like leaves with saw
edges and bright red flowers which pale with age to a soft yellow.
                                                 4 ft. June–Aug. 2½ ft. sq.

K. uvaria (syn. *K. aloides, K. hybrida*): For border work one cannot do
better than grow some of the hybrids from this species. The type
plant is often known as *aloides* or *alooides* and comes from the region
of the Cape. Much of the early work of hybridising Kniphofias was
carried out by Max Leichtlin of Baden Baden, who received the
greatest impetus to his labours from the introduction of *K. comosa* q.v.
    Good forms from *K. uvaria* include:
    August Gold, large heads of rich golden-yellow.
                                             Aug. and Sept. 4½–5 ft.
    Autumn Queen, greenish-yellow, flushed bronze, *Aug. 3–4 ft.*
    Bee's Lemon, citron yellow and green.   *July. 2½–3 ft.*
    Gold Else, golden-yellow flowers on slender spikes. *Aug.–Sept. 2 ft.*
    grandiflora, bright orange-scarlet and yellow   *July. 4 ft.*
    John Benary, rich-orange red.   *Aug.–Sept. 4 ft.*
    July Glow, buttercup-yellow overlaid apricot. *July. 2½ ft.*
    Kathleen greenish-yellow.   *Aug.–Sept. 4 ft.*
    Lord Roberts, bright red.   *July–Aug. 3 ft.*
    Maid of Orleans (*Plate XVI, p. 257*), dense spikes of flowers which
        open a delicate straw shade, but change almost at once to a
        beautiful ivory-white. Looks particularly well associated with
        red Phlox or blue Delphiniums, stands extremely hard weather
        and flowers practically the whole summer.   *3–3½ ft.*
    maxima, massive heads of brilliant crimson-scarlet flowers on 6–7
        ft. stems.   *Aug.–Sept.*
    Mount Etna, intense scarlet.   *Aug.–Sept. 5 ft.*
    Nobilis, sturdy spikes, rich orange-red.   *July–Sept. 6 ft.*
    Red Chief, bright red.   *July–Sept. 3 ft.*
    Royal Standard (*Plate 27, p. 128*), bright red and yellow.
                                                   July. 3½ ft.
    Sir C. K. Butler, rose-red and yellow.   *June–July. 3 ft.*
    Springtime, creamy-buff and reddish-orange. *July–Aug. 3 ft.*
    Star of Baden, stout spikes, rich yellow.   *Aug. 5 ft.*
    Yellow Hammer, yellow, free-flowering.   *July–Sept. 3 ft.*

LACTUCA (*Compositae*): Blue Lettuce. From *lac* (L), 'milk', an
    allusion to the milky juice in the stems.
    Most members of the Lettuce family are unsuitable for the flower
garden but L. *bourgaei* (*Plate 12, p. 64*) (syn. Mulgedium) is not

without charm as a back of the border subject. It likes a deep, well-drained soil and produces tall sturdy stems, crowded with bristly leaves and corymbs of small, soft blue flowers. Although the plant will stand many years in the same place, it sometimes starts to die out after five or six seasons and should then be transplanted to a fresh spot. Propagation by seed or division in spring. *5–6 ft. July–Aug. 3 ft. sq.*

LAMIUM (*Labiatae*): Dead Nettle. From *laimos* (Gk) ' throat' from the shape of the flower.

Perennial plants, mostly extremely weedy and unworthy of a place even in the wild garden, but the following exceptions are not without attraction at the front of the border and will also grow in light shade. They are easily propagated by pieces of the underground roots taken in spring and will grow in any ordinary garden soil.

L. maculatum. Spotted Deadnettle. Europe, including Britain. A plant with the habit of the common white Deadnettle (square stems, serrated heart-shaped leaves and axillary flowers), except that the leaves have bold white stripes covering the main veins and sometimes blotches as well; the flowers are usually purple. Var. *aureum* has golden foliage, and in damp situations makes a useful edging plant.

1 ft. May–July. 1 ft. sq.

L. orvala. Giant Deadnettle. (*Plate 20, p. 96.*) Italy, France. Has bright rose flowers in early summer and is larger than *L. maculatum.*

2 ft. May–July. 1 ft. sq.

LATHYRUS (*Leguminosae*): Old Greek name for the Pea.

A well-known genus, the most familiar member being the Sweetpea. In the border those species without tendrils (which were formerly referred to *Orobus*) are particularly useful by reason of their accommodating habit and early blooming traits. They succeed best in deep sandy loam and sheltered situations. Propagation by seed or division of the roots.

L. grandiflorus. Everlasting Pea. S. Europe. A perennial climber with similar foliage to, and fuchsia coloured flowers as large as the annual Sweetpeas. Twiggy sticks or similar supports should be provided, and the plants used either as background subjects or individually in beds to themselves. Although the flowers last only a day, the plants are so floriferous that there is bloom practically all summer. Although it may occur I have never seen fertile seed on *L. grandiflorus*, so the roots must be divided for propagation purposes.

5–6 ft. June–Aug. Several together 3 ft. sq.

L. latifolius. Perennial Pea. S. Europe. A very handsome climbing perennial for a corner site or the back of the border, with neat, elliptic leaves and long-stemmed sprays of large, many-flowered rosy blossoms.

There is a white form *albus*, which has given rise to an improved variety
' Snow Queen ', and a rich rose form *roseus*. Some supports must be
provided for the plants to climb during the summer.

2–8 ft. July–Aug. In groups of 3 at 2 ft. spacing.

L. luteus (syn. *Orobus luteus*): Has 4 to 5 pairs of leaflets and small yellow
flowers. Var. *aureus* has yellow and brown flowers.

1–2 ft. June. 1–2 ft. sq.

L. montanus. Bitter Vetch. Europe including Britain. Makes erect plant
with pairs of pea-like leaves without tendrils and bunches of large,
crimson flowers which fade to blue. This species makes a good mid-
border plant and will stand a considerable amount of shade.

2–3 ft. June–July. 2 ft. sq.

L. niger. Black Pea, Black Bitter Vetch. S. Europe. A delicate species
characterised by small purple flowers. *1–2 ft. June–July. 2 ft. sq.*

L. vernus (syn. *Orobus vernus*): Spring Bitter Vetch. A vigorous species for
light shade or a sunny situation; has light green, pea-like leaves and
bluish-violet, nodding, pea-like flowers. Var. *albus* has white flowers.

1–2 ft. May–June. 2 ft. sq.

LAVATERA (*Malvaceae*): Tree Mallow. Named after the two
brothers Lavater, 18th century naturalists and doctors of Zurich.

Vigorous strong-growing annuals, biennials and perennials, some
of the latter being shrubby. Only one species is really suitable for the
border.

L. olbia. Tree Lavatera. (*Plate 24, p. 112.*) S. Europe, naturalised in
Britain. Really of shrubby habit but usually employed in the
herbaceous border rather than the shrubbery. A single plant makes
a fine specimen when grown in a favourable situation, with branching,
woody stems studded with large, reddish-purple, Hollyhock-like
flowers and long-stalked, vine-like leaves. It must be grown in full
sun and have a well-drained but rich garden soil. Propagation by
seed or soft cuttings taken in spring. Var. *rosea* has pure rose-
coloured blossoms, more delicate than the type.

5–6 ft. June–Oct. 3 ft. sq.

LIATRIS (*Compositae*): Kansas Feather, Gayfeather, Button Snakeroot.
Origin of name unknown.

Unusual N. American perennials for the late summer and autumn
border, with straight spikes of closely packed flowers which resemble
miniature paint brushes without handles. These are of a brilliant
fuchsia pink shade and need to be carefully grouped against other
plants. The foliage is small and strap-like, forming a rosette close to
the ground although the stems too are leafy. The flowers are good for

cutting and dry well for winter bouquets. These plants need to be grown in very poor soil, with plenty of sun; they do not appreciate looseness at the roots. Propagation from basal buds, potted on, or from seed sown in pans in early spring.

L. callilepis. United States. A tall leafy plant with narrow basal leaves and bright carmine flowers on long straight spikes.

$1\frac{1}{2}$–*2 ft. July–Sept. 1 ft. sq.*

L. graminifolia. Grassleaf Gayfeather. E. United States. Has a tuberous rootstock with oblong, pointed leaves and purple flowers. It is a good plant for dry soils. *2–3 ft. Sept. 1 ft. sq.*

L. pycnostachya. Kansas Feather, Cat tail Gayfeather. (*Plate 34, p. 145.*) Central United States. Has densely flowered spikes 6–8 in. long, crowded with purple blossoms. *3–5 ft. Aug.–Oct. 1$\frac{1}{2}$ ft. sq.*

L. scariosa. E. & N. America. Closely resembles *L. pycnostachya* with cyclamen-purple flower heads and rather narrow spoon-shaped or oblong leaves. Var. *alba* is white. *2–4 ft. Sept. 1$\frac{1}{2}$ ft. sq.*

L. spicata, Spike Gayfeather. E. & S. United States. Will grow in more moist situations than other species and is handsome in the vicinity of a bog garden, or in a border on heavier soil. The flowers are reddish-purple and last a long time in character. Var. *alba* has white flowers.

3 ft. Sept. 1$\frac{1}{2}$ ft. sq.

LIBERTIA (*Iridaceae*): Named after Marie Libert, a 19th-century Belgian botanist.

A small genus with delicate flowers and grassy foliage which retains its colour and substance throughout the winter. All thrive in peaty or leafy borders but tend to exist rather than thrive on soils which are not to their liking. In cases where growth seems stationary therefore it would be wise to mulch the roots with plenty of peat or leaf soil. They are not too hardy and require a sheltered position and full sun.

L. formosa. Chile. A neat, compact plant with the largest flowers of the genus. They lie close together on the stems and are pure white. The leaves are sword-shaped and rather rigid. *16 in. May. 1 ft. sq.*

L. grandiflora. N. Zealand. Another handsome evergreen species with starry white flowers studding the stems and strap-like leaves.

2–3 ft. May–June. 2 ft. sq.

LIGULARIA (*Compositae*). From *ligula* (L) ' strap ', alluding to the shape of the ray florets.

Handsome foliage perennials sometimes included with Senecio in older gardening books. The hardy species mentioned below thrive in a deep, cool soil in full sun. Propagation is mostly by division, although seed is produced freely in most cases.

L. clivorum (syn. *Senecio clivorum*): Golden Groundsel. Japan, China. Has large heart-shaped leaves 1 ft. or more across and sturdy, much-branched heads of large (*2–3* in.) orange-yellow flowers. Each of these has a brown centre. It makes a particularly fine subject at the edge of a water garden or in a corner site in the wild garden. Var. ' Othello' (*Plate 32, p. 144*) is one of the best garden varieties, with purplish leaves (4 ft.); also *hessei*, rich yellow (*5–6* ft.); ' Greynog Gold ', golden flowers with bronze centres (3 ft.). *3–4 ft. July–Aug. 3 ft. sq.*

L. intermedia. N. China, Japan. Has kidney-shaped leaves about 9 in. long and 15 in. across, on long stalks close to the main stem. The flowers are yellow, 4–5 on a head. *1½ ft. Aug. 1½ ft. sq.*

L. japonica (syn. *Senecio japonicus*): Giant Ragwort. (*Plate 30, p. 129.*) Japan. One of the noblest kinds with the leaves nearly 1 ft. across divided up into 7–11 segments. The flower stems are slightly branched and carry blooms of a rich orange colour in autumn. This is a plant which must never lack moisture, and in its native country (close to streams) is reputed to reach 15 ft. in height. *5 ft. Aug.–Sept 4 ft. sq.*

L. tussilaginea (syn. *Farfugium*). A handsome perennial with creeping under-ground rootstock and nearly round, much toothed leaves. The flower heads are carried on a branched, woolly stem and are light yellow. Var. *aureo maculata*, known in America as Leopard Plant, has golden, white and pink variegated leaves. This is not as hardy as the type and needs winter protection in almost all areas. Var. *argentea* has white margined leaves. This also needs protection.
2 ft. Aug. 1½ ft. sq.

L. veitchiana. China. One of the handsomest species with massive leaves between 1 and 2 ft. wide and almost as long. They are roughly heart-shaped with long stems. The deep golden-yellow flowers are very striking and borne in quantity on branching stems.
3–6 ft. July–Sept. 4 ft. sq.

L. wilsoniana. China. A plant of bold habit well suited to waterside gardening or the woodland; has kidney-shaped leaves 1½ ft. long, with tiny stems, and golden-yellow flowers densely packed on tall stalks. This species is very similar to *veitchiana*; it is distinguished by the fact that the leaf-stalks of the former are hollow, instead of solid.
5–6 ft. June. 4 ft. sq.

LIMONIUM (syn. Statice) (*Plumbaginaceae*): Sea Lavender. From *leimon* (Gk) ' meadow ', an allusion to the habitat of many of the species.

A genus of annuals and perennials of graceful habit, characterised by dainty, paper-textured flowers which may be dried for winter bouquets. The perennial kinds rival Gypsophila in the lightness of the branching sprays of bloom. In the front of the border, in association with Phlox or other brightly contrasting subjects Limoniums can look most effective and will thrive in any well-cultivated, light, well-drained soil. Propagation is usually effected by seed or from careful division in spring. *L. latifolium* can also be raised from root cuttings. If the blossoms are to be used for indoor decoration, they should be gathered just before they are fully open and dried in bunches hanging upside down in a shady, airy shed.

L. elatum. S. Russia. Produces strong basal growths with leaves 4–8 in. long, bright green, smooth and slightly sticky. The much-branched flower-heads are smothered with tiny blue flowers.

2 ft. July. 1½ ft. sq.

L. gmelinii. E. Europe and Siberia. Has rosettes of oval oblong leaves 2–5 in. long and 1–2 in. wide, and branched heads of tiny, pinkish tubular flowers. *1–2 ft. July–Aug. 1½ ft. sq.*

L. incanum. Siberia. A low-growing species with rose-pink flowers and narrow pointed leaves. Var. *dumosum* with pink flowers is the best form. *1 ft. June–Aug. 1 ft. sq.*

L. latifolium. Bulgaria, S. Russia. Perhaps the most popular garden sort with bright cobwebby masses of deep lavender-blue flowers and rosettes of elongated leaves. In recent years a particularly fine form ' Violetta ' (*Plate 26, p. 113*), has been introduced, with deep violet flowers. Var. *grandiflorum* is deep lavender-blue; ' Grittleton Variety ' has large sprays of light lavender-mauve flowers; also ' Chilwell Beauty ', deep violet-blue, very large flowers, and ' Blue Cloud ', large mauve florets. *2 ft. July–Sept. 1½ ft. sq.*

L. mouretii. Morocco. Only hardy in sheltered locations. An elegant plant with rose or purplish flowers and tapering, oblong lanceolate leaves. *1½–2½ ft. Aug.–Oct. 1½ ft. sq.*

LINARIA (*Scrophulariaceae*): Toadflax. From *linum* (L) ' flax ', from the appearance of the leaves.

A large genus, many only suitable for the rock garden or annual border. There are, however, a few perennials which are useful, if only on account of their long-flowering habit. These grow in practically any well-drained soil, in full sun or light shade. They are propagated by division in spring or autumn. The yellow native Toadflax, *L. vulgaris*, is a common weed of light soils.

L. dalmatica. Dalmatian Toadflax. S.E. Europe. Has erect or sprawling leafy stems. The foliage is oblong-lanceolate, with golden-yellow Snapdragon-like flowers, large, and loosely arranged at the ends of the branches. *3–4 ft. June–Sept. 2 ft. sq.*

L. genistifolia. Europe, Asia Minor. A rare plant with pale yellow or orange flowers, and stem-clasping grassy leaves.

2–4 ft. June–Oct. 2 ft. sq.

L. macedonica. Macedonia. Very similar to *L. dalmatica* but with bolder and longer flower stalks. These are a richer yellow with each bloom nearly an inch long. Var. ' Nymph ' has cream flowers.

3–4 ft. June–Sept. 2 ft. sq.

L. purpurea. Purple Toadflax. (*Plate 13, p. 64.*) S. Europe, naturalized in Britain. Grows 2–3 ft. high, carrying slender spires of purplish-blue flowers which are touched with white at the throat. It flowers for a very long time and is easily raised from seed. It has produced an excellent garden variety ' Canon Went ' with bright pink blooms, touched with orange. A light soil suits it best.

2 ft. July–Sept. 1 ft. sq.

L. repens. Creeping Toadflax. Europe, including Britain. A smooth plant of running habit with whorls of lanceolate leaves on slender stems. Flowers white, veined with pale purplish-blue. Var. *alba* is white (*Plate XII, p. 240*), about 1 ft. tall. *2½ ft. June–Sept. 1 ft.*

L. sagittata. Morocco. Of rather weedy habit but sometimes used at the back of the border, where it should receive some support. The flowers are yellow. *6–7 ft. June. 2 ft. sq.*

L. triornithophora. Spain. A smooth, branching species, with oval leaves and purple and yellow flowers. It is only half-hardy and needs winter protection. *3 ft. June–Sept. 2 ft. sq.*

L. vulgaris. Toadflax. Europe including Britain. An erect plant with yellow and gold flowers, attractive but inclined to become weedy. A double flowered form is known. *1–3 ft. All summer. 6 in. sq.*

LINDELOFIA (*Boraginaceae*). Named after F. von Lindelof, a German botanist.

The one species mentioned is hardy and grows well in good garden soil. It can be raised from seed, the plants flowering the second season, or can be propagated by division of the roots in spring.

L. longiflora (syn. *L. spectabilis*): Himalayas. Has rough, long lanceolate leaves and small, bright blue, Forget-me-not-like flowers. The whole plant is somewhat hairy. *1½ ft. May–Aug. 1 ft. sq.*

LINUM (*Liniaceae*): Flax. From *lin* (Celtic) ' thread '.

An invaluable genus, important economically as the source of linen and linseed oil. The flowers are extremely beautiful, mostly in a rich shade of blue. Give the plants a well-drained situation and as warm and sheltered a spot as possible. They are sun lovers and in shady situations or on dull days they remain closed. New plants are raised from seed sown outside in April, half-ripe cuttings, taken in July, or by careful division of the roots in spring.

L. arboreum. Crete. This is really a shrub as the growth persists and is woody, but its low stature makes it a useful front of the border subject. The flowers are large and golden yellow. Some protection should be given in winter and it should only be grown in warm, well-drained soil.   *1 ft.   May–June.   1 ft. sq.*

L. austriacum. Austrian Alps. An erect plant with soft blue flowers. Var. *album* is white.   *1–2 ft.   June–July.   6 in. sq.*

L. flavum. Germany to Russia. Needs some winter protection in very cold, exposed areas but is worth growing if only on account of its bright, open golden flowers which are borne profusely on branching stems. Var. *compactum* is a more free-flowering form.

1–1½ ft.   June–Aug.   1 ft. sq.

L. narbonense. (*Plate 12, p. 64.*) S. Europe. Has slender, arched and branching stems, covered with simple, rich blue flowers. The leaves are small and narrow and held very erect. A number of garden forms have been derived from the species including ' Peto's Variety ', which is perhaps the finest of all the Flaxes. In sheltered situations the foliage remains evergreen during the winter, but severe or prolonged cold spells kill off the top foliage, which breaks from the base again the following year. Another good garden form is ' June Perfield' and again is a far better plant than the type. Var. ' Heavenly Blue ' is a soft pale blue; ' Six Hill's Variety ', sky blue.   *1½ ft.   May–June.   2 ft. sq.*

L. perenne. Europe, including Britain. Is less attractive than *L. narbonense* but bears quantities of sky blue flowers; *lewisii* is a taller variety; var. *album* has white flowers.   *1–1½ ft.   May–July.   1 ft. sq.*

LITHOSPERMUM (*Boraginaceae*): Boragewort. From *lithos* (Gk) ' stone ', *sperma* ' seed ', an allusion to the toughness of the seeds.

Beautiful blue flowered plants mostly suited to the rock garden, although *L. purpureo-caeruleum*, the purple Gromwell, is useful for shady situations in the border. It is native to Europe, including Britain, and has erect flower stems about 1 ft. high clothed with narrow, alternate leaves and nodding 5-petalled flowers. These open red and then turn blue. The seeds are particularly hard and in winter become bright and glossy; it is very difficult to break them. They present a most singular appearance. Propagation by seed or cuttings.

9–12 in.   June.   1 ft. sq.

LOBELIA (*Campanulaceae*). Named after Matthias de L'Obel, physician to King James I.

Distinctive and much prized plants, the perennials almost without exception, requiring deep, rich and rather moist soil. The roots must never suffer from drought during the growing season and to ensure adequate moisture at this time, incorporate plenty of peat or leaf-mould in the soil when planting. The scarlet-flowered forms, particularly *L. fulgens*, are doubly valuable by reason of their handsome foliage. The rich crimson shades of these associate well with silver leaved plants like *Veronica incana argenta* or *Artemisia stelleriana*. Unfortunately some of the best kinds are not reliably winter hardy, but they can be preserved without heat by lifting the roots in their entirety towards the end of September and setting these in a cold frame packed round with soil and leaves. During the worst of the winter glass can be kept over them, and about mid-May the plants should be broken into convenient divisions and replanted in the border. During the winter resting period they should be kept rather dry. Propagation by division or seed raised in gentle heat in February.

L. cardinalis. Cardinal Flower. N. America. Has smooth, oblong-lanceolate leaves, both from the base of the plant and on the flower stems. The blooms are very showy, brilliant scarlet, borne on thickly-clothed spikes. This plant is often confused with *L. fulgens*, but one striking difference is that whilst the foliage of *L. cardinalis* is green, that of *L. fulgens* is generally crimson. There is a white-flowered form. The plant will do very well in a partially shaded situation. Var. ' Russian Princess ' is pale pink. *3 ft. Aug.–Oct. 1 ft. sq.*

L. fulgens. Cardinal Flower. (*Plate 25, p. 112.*) A beautiful and precious plant for the garden, with long narrow leaves of rich wine-red which contrast strikingly with the spikes of pillar-box scarlet flowers. The stems are stouter and larger than in *L. cardinalis*, with broad, hanging petals. This species may be kept in a cold frame during the winter and propagated by soft cuttings early in the year. It has given rise to a number of splendid garden forms, of which the following are especially worth noting: ' Queen Victoria ', deep purple leaves and crimson flowers; ' The Bishop ', rich velvety scarlet, bronze foliage; ' Huntsman ', brilliant red blooms; ' Jack MacMasters ', a hybrid with *L. syphilitica*, violet-blue flowers and dark purple foliage; ' Purple Emperor ', purple flowers. *1–3 ft. May–Sept. 1 ft. sq.*

L. × gerardii. A garden hybrid between *L. cardinalis* and *L. syphilitica* with very fine spikes of large pink to violet-purple flowers.
4–5 ft. July–Sept. 1½ ft. sq.

L. × rivoirei. Of similar origin to *L. × gerardii*, but with rose-pink flowers.

L. syphilitica. Blue Cardinal Flower (*Plate 12, p. 64*). E. United States. A handsome perennial for moist soil, either in the vicinity of the water garden or in heavy loam in the border. When well grown it makes a really beautiful plant and, for some years now, we have had bold beds of both this and its white form in the garden. In good soil the plants reach 3 ft. in height. We grow them in heavy clay, enriched with decayed cow manure and some peat.

The long spikes of light blue flowers and narrow oblong leaves make fitting associates for the scarlet *L. fulgens* or Eupatorium varieties, or they look well with various lilies. There is a white variety, *alba* (*Plate IX, p. 224*), Large White Lobelia, and the type has been crossed with *L. cardinalis* and *L. fulgens*.

The plant has poisonous properties according to Feuillee, who says that even the odour of the flower causes excessive vomiting, whilst, applied to the skin it excites violent inflammation and pain. Lest any be deterred from growing this handsome species on this account, I may say that I have handled the plant for a number of years with no ill effects. *1–3 ft. July–Oct. 1 ft. sq.*

L. tupa. Chile. A rare perennial with leafy stems and huge spikes of large, brick-red flowers. The whole plant is somewhat downy and not hardy except in very favoured situations or near the sea. It will, however, winter in the south, if grown against a south wall, and protected with sifted ashes or gravel during the winter months.

3–5 ft. July–Sept. 3 ft. sq.

LUPINUS (*Leguminosae*): Lupin. (*Plate 3, p. 32.*) From *lupus* (L) ' wolf'; Lupins were once supposed to destroy the fertility of the soil in which they grew.

Thirty or so years ago Lupins were very ordinary plants in the garden. They made useful back of the border subjects, but the colour range was not extensive and varied mostly between blue and purple to reddish-purple and white. The chief species grown was the old *Lupinus polyphyllus*, a North American perennial of sturdy nature, able to hold its own in any garden soil or situation.

To-day this plant is rarely seen. All garden forms previously grown were superseded when George Russell introduced the Russell hybrids. The large blossoms, shapely spikes and extensive range of shades provided a brilliance hitherto unknown in the early border.

Nevertheless, Russell Lupins have not the stamina of the old-time species, possibly because of mixed parentage. In his quest for brighter colours and larger blooms Russell bought Lupins from all over the world, including a race of annuals from a German grower, and the bright shades and bicolor forms which came from his seedlings seem to indicate that annual forms such as *L. laxiflorus*, *L. lepidus*, *L. nootkatensis*, *L. mutabilis*, and *L. leucophyllus* played a part in their inheritance. This may account for some degree of reduced permanency.

In order to keep the plants, therefore, never allow all the spikes to make seed. Remove old flower heads as soon as spent and grow the plants in a light, sandy loam soil. Lime should not be provided, they do better in slightly acid conditions. Plant them firmly in sun or light shade. Finally, be prepared to renew the plants every third or fourth season, either from cuttings, taken with a piece of the old rootstock in a frame in March, or from seed. They will flower in twelve months.

The following list includes a fair selection of some of the most up-to-date varieties. For best results they should be planted in spring, and in bold clumps of one colour. Mixed shades grown together can never look as effective, as several groups, each made up of one hue.

General heights are $2\frac{1}{2}$–3 ft., the plants bloom in June–July and each root needs an area of approximately $2\frac{1}{2}$ ft.

Alicia Parrett, extra large, pale cream flowers.

Apple Blossom, a delightful uniform shade of soft pink.

Betty Astell, rose-pink.

Billy Wright, deep pink and white.

Bishopsgate, rose-pink deepening to red.

Blue Jacket, flowers deep blue at the base. In the young stage the standards are yellow but turn white when fully developed.

Blushing Bride, soft yellow, with slightly deeper standards.

Canary Bird, bright canary-yellow.

Celandine, yellow.

Charmaine, orange-salmon.

Cherry Pie, bright cherry-red.

City of York, a combination of bright and deep red. One of the best dark reds.

Commando, deep mauve and yellow.

Cynthia Knight, violet and white.

Daydream, a beautiful combination of peach-pink and bright golden-yellow.

Dusky Minstrel, a distinctive bicolor; large plum-apple bells, and vivid yellow standards.

Eleanor Richards, sturdy with large individual flowers, deep yellow and salmon-orange.

Elsie Waters, pink and white.

Firedrake, well-clothed spikes of large, rosy-orange flowers, with standards of a similar shade touched with gold at the base.

Fireglow, orange and yellow.

Flaming June, orange self.

Freedom, mauvy-blue and white.

Gaiety Girl, yellow and rose.

George Russell, coral-pink bells, and creamy-yellow standards edged with pink.

Golden Gleam, pale salmon-rose with a little yellow on the centre of the standards.

Goldfinch, rich golden yellow.

Happy Days, rose-pink and yellow.

Heatherglow, rich wine-purple with a flush of bronze overlaying the standards.

Jane Ayr, violet-blue and white, very large.

Josephine, slate-blue and gold.

Lady Fayre, deep rose.

Lady Gay, extra large spikes of charming pale yellow flowers.

Lilac Time, rosy-lilac and mauve.

Maud Tippets, deep orange-red.

Melody, vivid carmine-red, with a trace of ivory at the base of the standards.

Monkgate, blue and white.

Mrs. Garnet Botfield, bold

spikes of beautiful yellow flowers lightly shaded with buff.

Mrs. Mickelthwaite, rich salmon-pink.

Mrs. Noel Terry, pale pink, deepening with age.

Nellie B. Allen, salmon-orange.

Patricia of York, primrose yellow.

Radiant, vivid orange-red, overlaid with soft yellow.

Rita, pale red deepening to wine.

Simon Henry, fuchsia pink and white.

Susan of York, yellow and brick-red.

Sweetheart, orange and pink.

Thundercloud, dark violet-blue, very good.

Tom Reeves, yellow.

Torchlight, an unusual and pleasing combination of rich apricot and bright golden-yellow.

York Minster, pale rose and cream.

LYCHNIS (*Caryophyllaceae*): Campion. From *lychnos* (Gk) ' lamp ', referring to the brightness of the flowers.

A genus of vividly coloured perennials with open, Dianthus-like flowers. All grow well in well-drained soil, enriched with manure or compost. They can be propagated by division or seed.

L. chalcedonica. Maltese Cross. (*Plate 23, p. 112.*) E. Russia. An old border plant with large rounded heads of brilliant scarlet flowers and rough oval leaves. There is a white variety var. *alba,* and a double form *alba plena*; *carnea,* flesh-pink; *salmonea,* salmon-rose; also var. *rubra plena* with double red flowers. The latter is extremely rare to-day and only likely to be found in old gardens. The type plant is easily raised from seed but the double forms must be perpetuated from cuttings. 2–3 ft. June–Aug. 1½ ft. sq.

L. coronaria (syn. *Agrostemma coronaria*): Rose Campion. S. Europe. A well-known plant with silvery stems and foliage, and a softly furry effect, caused by a thick coating of fine silvery hairs which practically covers the whole plant. Only the flowers are exempt from this protective wrapping and these stand out in a startling cerise shade. Var. *atrosanguinea* (*Plate 13, p. 000*) is brighter in colour, and var. *alba* (*Plate X, p. 225*), white. ' Abbotswood Rose ' is brilliant rose-crimson. 1½–2½ ft. July–Aug. 2 ft. sq.

L. flos-cuculi. Ragged Robin. Europe, including Britain, W. Asia. The type plant with its ragged petalled flowers is well known to country people, being found wild in hedgerows, banks or light shady woods. In gardens the double variety *pleniflora* makes a good border plant. 1–2 ft. May to autumn. 1 ft. sq.

L. flos-Jovis. Flower of Jove. Central Alps. A plant with very woolly stems and leaves, and purple or scarlet flowers about the size of a half-penny. ' Hort's Variety ', has bright pink flowers and grey foliage. 1–2 ft. June–July. 1 ft. sq.

L. × *haageana.* By crossing *L. fulgens* with a form of *L. coronata* plant breeders have obtained a large-flowered and brilliantly coloured race of Lychnis. Seedlings vary considerably, so that varieties may appear with blooms 2 in. across, in orange, scarlet, crimson or white. The plants must be watched in winter or slugs will destroy them. They dislike cold, wet soil and should be given a well-drained sandy aspect, with shade from the midday sun. The beautiful scarlet-flowered Lychnis *arkwrightii* belongs here. *1 ft. June–July. 1 ft. sq.*

L. viscaria. German Catchfly. Europe, including Britain. Derives its English name from the glutinous stalk, from which alighting insects cannot disengage themselves. It is a British plant, with long, grassy leaves and many showy, rosy-red flowers on branching stems in early summer. The variety *splendens plena* is particularly brilliant and worthy of cultivation. Some botanists now refer this to a separate genus, *Viscaria viscosa.* The plants are easily propagated by seed or division, or half-ripe cuttings can be taken in early summer.
1½ ft. May–July. 1½ ft. sq.

LYSIMACHIA (*Primulaceae*): Loosestrife. Named after King Lysimachus of Thracia, who first discovered the plant's medicinal virtues.

Accommodating perennials which are happiest in damp situations, but adaptable enough to grow in practically any garden conditions in sun or semi-shade. Some of the species are native to Britain. It is sometimes called Yellow Willow Herb. Propagation from seed or division, but the plant must be watched when grown amongst more delicate perennials lest it becomes invasive.

L. clethroides. (*Plate X, p. 225.*) Japan, China. Long, nodding, rather dense spikes of white blossoms and oval leaves which assume brilliant tints in autumn. The flowers are good for cutting.
1½–3 ft. July–Sept. 1½ ft. sq.

L. fortunei. China, Japan. Loose spikes of yellow flowers and elegant, narrowly lanceolate alternate leaves. *2–2½ ft. July–Sept. 2 ft. sq.*

L. punctata. Asia Minor. The best known species with straight stems carrying whorls of bright yellow flowers.
2–3 ft. June–July. 1½ ft. sq.

L. thyrsiflora. Water Loosestrife. North temperate regions including Britain. An erect plant with small, yellow, axillary flowers and tapering stalkless leaves. *1–2 ft. June–Aug. 1 ft. sq.*

L. vulgaris. Yellow Loosestrife. A showy plant for a moist border or at the waterside, with leafy spikes carrying panicles of yellow and orange flowers. *2½ ft. June–Aug. 1 ft. sq.*

LYTHRUM (*Lythraceae*): Purple Loosestrife. From *lythron* (Gk) 'black blood', referring to the colour of some of the flowers.

The cultivated varieties of Loosestrife give some of our brightest and gayest late-summer perennials. They look particularly fine associated with certain shades of mauve, such as Cupid's Love Dart or Catmint. They are happiest in heavy or moisture-retentive soil and should be given a front to mid-way position in the border. Plant them in good bold clumps as very indifferent effects are obtained if only one or two plants are grown. Propagation by cuttings.

L. salicaria. A plant of wide distribution in the northern hemisphere, including Great Britain, and also native to Australia.

Hybrids from this species provide the best border plants. The type is rarely grown. Good forms are:

atropurpureum, deep purple.

Brightness, rosy-pink.

Lady Sackville, brilliant rose.

Morden's pink, rich deep pink.

Prichard's Var, rich rose, *4 ft.*

Robert (*Plate 13, p. 64*), erect spikes of bright rosy-carmine, very showy for the front of the border as it only grows 2 ft. high.

Rose Queen, long branching spikes of bright rose flowers.

roseum superbum, bright magenta red.

The Beacon, deep rose-red, very packed spikes.

2–4 ft.   June–Sept.   1½ ft. sq.

L. virgatum. Taurus. Has spikes of purple flowers borne in threes in the leaf axils. The leaves are lanceolate. Not to be placed near scarlets or orange because of colour clashing. Var. ' Rose Queen ' has graceful spikes of rich rose flowers.   *2–3 ft.   June–Sept.   2 ft. sq.*

MACLEAYA (syn. Bocconia, (*Papaveraceae*): Plume Poppy. Named after Alexander Macleay a 19th-century Secretary of the Linnean Society.

Handsome and impressive plants with beautiful foliage, admirably suited to the back of the border. The leaves are roughly Fig-shaped, attractively cut and silvery beneath, whilst the small yellow flowers are carried in feathery plumes high above the foliage. The whole plant secretes a yellow juice which stains the fingers. For this reason Plume Poppies do not last well when cut, and unless a styptic (of boiling water or glacial acetic acid) is applied to the ends immediately after gathering, they soon fade. The plants increase rapidly by means of underground roots and can become a nuisance unless kept rigidly within bounds. Plume Poppies may be grown at the back of the mixed border or as individual specimens in a small bed on a lawn, where they show to particular advantage. They can also be used to mask an untidy shed or shelter in the garden. They grow in most soils but make better plants where the ground is a little rich. Sun or light shade. Propagation from seed or by pieces of the underground rootstock or suckers.

Plate I: 1. ASTILBE, *Astilbe* x *Arendsii* ' King Albert '. 2. SNEEZEWORT, *Achillea Ptarmica.*
3. SNOWDROP WINDFLOWER, *Anemone sylvestris.* 4. SETTER-WORT, *Helleborus foetidus.*
5. SAXIFRAGE, *Saxifraga* ' James Bremner '

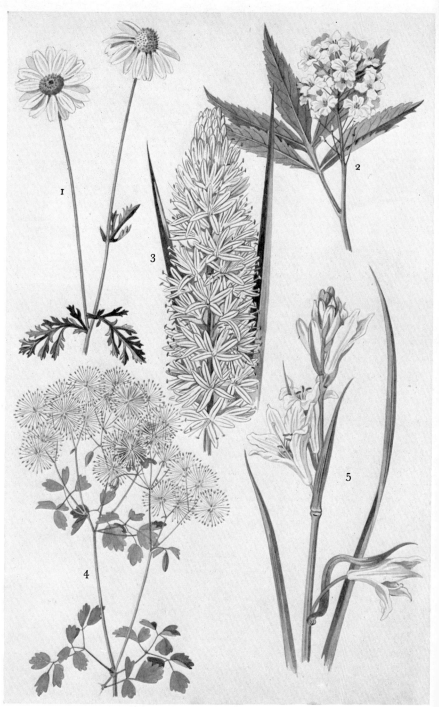

Plate II: 1. WHITE CHAMOMILE, *Anthemis montana.* 2. CUT TOOTHWORT, *Dentaria laciniata.* 3. ASPHODEL, *Asphodelus albus.* 4. WHITE MEADOW RUE, *Thalictrum aquilegiifolium album.* 5. ST. BRUNO'S LILY, *Paradisea liliastrum*

M. cordata (syn. *Bocconia cordata*). (*Plate VII, p. 224.*) China, Japan. The species most widely grown, makes a noble subject with pinkish-apricot plumes of flowers. 'Kelway's Coral Plume' has rich coral-pink flowers. *5–8 ft. July–Sept. 3 ft. sq.*

M. microcarpa. China. A beautiful Chinese variety with conspicuously veined leaves and loose-spreading panicles of small, rose-coloured buds which later develop into copper-yellow flowers. *7 ft. July–Sept. 3 ft. sq.*

MALVA (*Malvaceae*): Musk Mallow. From *malacho* (Gk) ' to soften ', the leaves have emollient qualities.

Most people know the general Hollyhock character of the rose-coloured flowers of this lovely genus, for a number of varieties may be found growing wild in Europe, Africa and Asia, and they have been naturalised in N. America. The perennial kinds here listed may be propagated from cuttings or seed.

M. alcea. Europe. Large, soft rose-purple, widely open flowers on terminal and axillary flower spikes. The leaves are heart-shaped, light green and lobed. Var. *fastigiata*, which originated in Italy, is characterised by red flowers and somewhat toothed leaves. *3–4 ft. July–Oct. 2 ft. sq.*

M. moschata. Musk Mallow. Europe, including Britain. A handsome plant with finely-cut, Buttercup-like foliage and wide, soft pink flowers. The leaves when bruised emit a pleasing musk odour especially towards evening. Var. *alba* (*Plate X, p. 225*) has white flowers. *1–2 ft. May–Oct. 1½ ft. sq.*

M. setosa. Giant Mallow. (*Plate 23, p. 112.*) Italy. Stately stems bearing a profusion of large, cup-shaped flowers, rich rose. *6 ft. Aug.–Oct. 3 ft. sq.*

MALVASTRUM (*Malvaceae*). From ' *Malva* ' and ' *aster* '.

A small family of Malva-like plants of which *M. coccineum* from the United States is hardy in well-drained, sandy soil. The plant has a running, woody rootstock, silvery-grey, prettily cut leaves and terminal racemes of scarlet, 5-petalled flowers. Propagation by cuttings or seed. *1 ft. July–Oct. 3 ft. sq.*

MECONOPSIS (*Papaveraceae*): Himalayan Poppy, Welsh Poppy. From *mecon* (Gk) ' poppy ', *opsis* ' like '. The plants are sometimes known as Poppyworts.

Beautiful plants, the majority from the Himalayas although several are native to Europe, including Britain. Practically all the species need similar treatment to Primulas, that is, a moist vegetable soil unlikely to dry out in summer, and shade from the strong midday sun. Perhaps the most prized species is the fabulous *M. betonicifolia (baileyi)*, which was collected by Frank Kingdon-Ward in the Himalayas in 1924.

Most of the genus can be propagated by seed, which must be sown directly it is gathered, as it deteriorates rapidly when stored. Sow in pans of equal parts of sand, loam and sifted peat and keep these in in slight warmth (50–60° F.). Seedlings can be pricked off into small pans or boxes as soon as they are big enough to handle and kept in a cool house until spring. A few species like *M. quintuplinervia* or *M. grandis* can be propagated from side shoots or division. Meconopsis should always be grown in association with plants needing similar conditions, like Primulas (particularly the candelabra types), Ferns and Trilliums. Visitors to the woodland garden at Wisley who have seen such associations cannot fail to be struck by the ' rightness ' of the general effect.

M. betonicifolia (syn. *M. baileyi*): Himalayan Blue Poppy. (*Plate 1, p. 16.*) Tibet, Yunnan. The fabulously beautiful plant which all gardeners crave to grow. At their best the flowers are a delightful sky blue, 2 in. across, nearly round, lightly crimped on the perianth segments and with an iridescence which makes the bloom look mauve in some lights. It is in fact very like taffeta, the changing lights affecting the shades. The boss of yellow stamens in the centre of the flower throws up this beautiful blue. The leaves and stems are hairy.

Usually the plant dies after flowering. For this reason, the amateur is advised to treat it always as monocarpic. It comes up readily from seed and tries to flower the first year but the developing spikes should be pinched out and the plant left to form a bigger leaf rosette. When it blooms in the second season the spikes will then be good and later, seed can be collected and the plant perpetuated. I have never known it do well as a perennial, and indeed only seen one really old plant. This was in Messrs. Ruy's Nurseries at Dedemsvaart where a specimen 17 years old flowered freely every year. It is interesting to note that seedlings from the stock plant failed to show the perennial habit of the parent. Seed should be saved annually from the good blue forms. This is a variable plant and only the best shades should be kept.

2–5 ft. according to locality and the clearness of the atmosphere. In Scotland, for example, it usually makes far finer plants than in the south.

June–July. 1 ft. sq.

M. cambrica. Welsh Poppy. W. Europe, including Britain. A perennial with grey-green leaves and solitary, orange or yellow Poppy-like flowers. These are in bloom practically all the summer and seed readily so that the plant soon naturalizes itself. There are double forms of each shade, *flore pleno* (*Plate 16, p. 80*), which are reckoned to be better garden plants.　　　　　*1 ft. June–Sept. 1 ft. sq.*

M. grandis. Nepal, Tibet, Bhutan. A good perennial of tall habit with uncut, oblong-lanceolate leaves and solitary purple flowers of fine glossy texture. *2 ft. May–June. 2 ft. sq.*

M. integrifolia. Yellow Chinese Poppy. A plant from the high mountains of S.W. China and Tibet, where they are reputed to be found with flowers 7–10 inches across. Like *M. betonicifolia* the plant should be grown as a biennial. It has rich yellow blooms and oval uncut leaves covered with soft silky hairs. *1–1½ ft. July. 1 ft. sq.*

M. napaulensis (syn. *M. wallichii*): Satin Poppy. Central Asia. A monocarpic species with red, purple, blue or occasionally white flowers. The blue kinds are the ones worth preserving and from which seed should be collected. The leaves are densely covered with bronze hairs. *4–6 ft. June–July. 3 ft. sq.*

M. quintuplinervia. Hairbell Poppy. Tibet, W. China. Should be grown in a sheltered spot or in a rock garden pocket. It forms basal rosettes of rough, bronze, hairy leaves and carries solitary, large hanging flowers which are lavender-blue, tending to deepen in shade towards the base. It increases by means of the underground stems and so can be readily divided in spring. *1–1½ ft. May–June. 1 ft. sq.*

M. regia. Nepal. A monocarpic plant with rich yellow flowers and extremely handsome foliage and leaves. The latter are narrowly spoon-shaped, 18–20 inches long and densely covered with bronzy-gold hairs, a colour which associates particularly well with the yellow blooms. The first season the dormant rosette, with its silver or golden haired foliage is extremely beautiful and worth having for its own sake. It usually flowers the second season and then dies. *4–5 ft. June–July. 2 ft. sq.*

M. × sheldonii. A fine deep-blue flowered hybrid between *M. betonicifolia* and *M. grandis. 3 ft.*

MELITTIS (*Labiatae*): Bastard Balm. Name from *melissa* (Gk) ' bee ', referring to its attraction for bees.

Plants of the Salvia family, with several Nettle-like flowers in white with wine-purple lower lips. These have a faint musk fragrance. The foliage is rough, somewhat puckered and broadly oval with a heart-shaped base. The plants grow in good garden soil but are particularly suited to light shade amongst shrubs or in the mixed border. Propagation from seed.

M. melissophyllum. S. Europe. White and wine-purple flowers in the leaf axils. Var. *album* is white; *grandiflorum* is a larger-flowered variety. *1 ft. May–June. 1 ft. sq.*

MERTENSIA (*Boraginaceae*): Virginian Cowslip. Named after F. Karl Mertens, a 19th-century German Professor of Botany.

Beautiful blue-flowered plants of the Borage family, suitable for partial shade and sheltered positions in rich loamy soil. Propagated from seed sown as soon as it ripens or by division in autumn.

M. ciliata. N. America. Large, oval oblong leaves and bright blue, bell-shaped flowers on long hanging sprays. The buds of these are pink.
2 ft. May–June. 2 ft. sq.

M. sibirica. Siberia. A beautiful plant both in habit and colour which grows readily in any moisture-retaining soil. The small bell-shaped flowers are borne in drooping clusters, and are soft rosy-pink when young, turning purplish and blue in maturity.
1–1½ ft. May–July. 1 ft. sq.

M. virginica. Virginian Cowslip. (*Plate 1, p. 16.*) Virginia. The best known species, with drooping heads of purplish-blue Forget-me-not-like flowers and soft, bluish-grey leaves. It must have plenty of moisture during the growing season. *2 ft. May. 1 ft. sq.*

MIMULUS (*Scrophulariaceae*): Musk, Monkey Flower. From *mimo* (Gk) 'ape', referring to the shape of the corolla.

Plants with brightly coloured Antirrhinum-like flowers and simple hairy leaves.

Although this family is generally associated with the environs of the water garden, several species bloom richly and for weeks on end in ordinary garden soil. They must, however, have plenty of moisture during the summer months and to ensure this organic material should be incorporated with the soil at planting time. In most parts of the country they are not too hardy, for which reason it is usual to perpetuate some of the better named sorts by means of cuttings in late summer, wintering these in a cold frame. They can also be raised annually from seed, or again may be covered with glass during the worst of the weather. When sowing Mimulus seed it is important not to cover it with too much soil as it germinates badly if deeply buried. Many gardeners use only a light covering of sphagnum moss, and remove this on germination. In southern England, however, and the warmer parts of America, they may be left outside to naturalise themselves. Few plants will be brighter in the front of the border in high summer.

M. cardinalis. Crimson Monkey Flower. (*Plate 23, p. 112.*). N. America. A showy plant with white, pink or deep crimson Antirrhinum-like flowers. Var. *grandiflorus* is larger. Good varieties are: ' Rose Queen ', bronzy-scarlet, 1–1½ ft.; ' Cerise Queen ', bright cerise, 9 in.
2–4 ft. June–July. 1 ft. sq.

M. cupreus. Chile. A species with coppery-orange flowers which has given rise to a number of brilliantly coloured garden varieties. The best of these are:

Bee's Dazzler, brilliant pillar-box scarlet.
Bonfire, bright scarlet.
Chelsea Pensioner, scarlet.
Fire Flame, flame red.
grandiflorus, yellow and scarlet.
Leopard, yellow spotted with orange-brown.

Plymtree, cherry pink.
Queen's Prize, pink, salmon, rose and yellow.
Red Emperor, bright crimson-scarlet.
Whitecroft Scarlet, scarlet.

All these varieties must be propagated from cuttings if they are to be kept true and should be afforded some protection in the winter. They will do in full sun providing there is plenty of moisture at the roots but they are equally happy in light shade.

8–12 in. June–Sept. 1 ft. sq.

M. lewisii. British Columbia. A species closely related to *M. cardinalis* but with old rose flowers, freely spotted maroon. Var. *albus* is white.

1½ ft. June–Aug. 1 ft. sq.

M. luteus. Monkey Musk. Chile. N. America, naturalized in Britain. This species with its hybrids has greater need of moisture than most of the group and must never dry out during the summer months. The free-flowering propensities and large blooms render them highly ornamental, so that they are frequently grouped and used in bedding schemes. Among a number of interesting varieties mention should be made of *duplex* which is also known as *Hose in Hose* because one flower sits inside another; *guttatus*, yellow blossoms spotted with purple-brown, and *luteus maculatus* which has large yellow flowers spotted with red. *1 ft. May–Aug. 1 ft. sq.*

MONARDA (*Labiatae*): Bee Balm, Bergamot. Named after Nicolas Monardes, a 16th-century Spanish botanist.

Easily grown border perennials which must have moist soil for successful cultivation. In their native haunts Monardas grow along the banks of streams, so that dry gravelly situations should have plenty of organic material incorporated to retain the moisture. The plants have square stems, extremely aromatic nettle-like leaves and brightly coloured flowers borne in close heads or whorls on stems 2–3 ft. high. The fragrance is as compelling and the blossom more arresting than Lavender. Monardas associate happily with *I. sibirica* and Daylilies and should be planted in bold groups in spring or autumn.

They will grow in full sun or partial shade, and if the ground is poor and not well prepared, it pays to mulch the plants in time of drought.

Growth is usually rapid, so the roots need frequent separation. Every second or third year split the clumps and replant; even the tiniest piece of rootstock will grow. Spring is the best time for the operation, as autumn disturbance could prove fatal in heavy soil and bad winters.

M. didyma. N. America. A robust plant well adapted either for the sunny border or naturalising in light shade. The flowers are bright scarlet. A number of good garden forms have been derived from this species, the best being:

Adam, ruby-red.

alba, white.

Beauty of Cobham, clover pink.

Burgundy, dark blue-purple.

Cambridge Scarlet (*Plate 18, p. 81*), more brilliant than the type.

Croftway Pink, rich rose-pink.

Kalmiana, deep crimson.

Mahogany, Indian Lake red.

Mrs. Perry, dark crimson-red.

Perfield Crimson, crimson.

Perfield Glory, which will suceed in a drier spot than the type.

violacea superba, purple-red.

2–3 ft. June–Sept. 2 ft. sq.

M. fistulosa. Wild Bergamot. N. America. A robust plant with variable flowers which may be anything from white to light red. Var. *violacea* has deep violet-purple flowers. *2–4 ft. June–Aug. 2 ft. sq.*

MONTBRETIA (*Iridaceae*). Named after A. F. Conquebert de Montbret, an 18th-century French botanist.

A small genus of South African plants closely related to Tritonia, which in well-drained soils bloom freely and profusely in late summer and autumn. In heavy clays and similar conditions they are best grown in raised beds. The majority of garden Montbretias, however, are Crocosmia varieties, q.v. Propagation by division.

M. laxifolia. S. Africa. Has linear, grassy leaves and erect spikes bearing a dozen or so funnel-shaped cream and orange flowers.

6 in.–1½ ft. Autumn. 6 in. sq.

MORINA (*Dipsaceae*): Himalayan Whorlflower. Nepal. Named after L. Morin, a 17th-century French botanist.

M. longifolia. (*Plate 18, p. 81.*) A particularly handsome perennial from Nepal too rarely seen in gardens. The large spiny leaves are reminiscent of the better forms of Thistle, with the flowers, borne on long spikes, arranged round the stem in whorls. Individual florets (enclosed in spiny bracts) are pink, red, yellow or white, with long, tubular blooms and gaping mouths. The plants should be grown in full sun in well-drained sandy loam. Shelter is necessary from spring winds. Propagation by division carried out immediately after flowering or from seed sown soon after ripening.

2–3 ft. June–July. 1 ft. sq.

MYOSOTIDIUM (*Boraginaceae*): Giant Forget-me-not. Name from Myosotis, the flowers somewhat resembling the Forget-me-not.

A genus of one species, *M. hortensia* (syn. *M. nobile*), a plant native to the Chatham Islands. It is not easy to grow except perhaps for those living in sheltered areas with a cool damp soil, preferably near the sea. When established it makes a thick stem, 12 or 18 inches long, with large, fleshy, somewhat puckered leaves, and dense sprays of blue Forget-me-not-like flowers. Propagation is by seed. This is definitely not a plant for everyone, but is rather for the connoisseur. When happily situated it resents disturbance. Mulching with seaweed is beneficial.   *12–18 in. Spring. 1 ft. sq.*

NEPETA (*Labiatae*): Catmint. Origin of name uncertain.

Catmint, the so-called *N. mussinii* is a useful edging plant, its mauve flowers and silvery foliage associating either with stone or brightly-coloured perennials like Phlox, Anthemis or Geum. It is one of those strange plants which have been grown in gardens for years under a wrong name. There is a species *N. mussinii*, but it is a poor thing, and only seen in botanic gardens or collections of plants. The garden *mussinii* is really of hybrid origin. It sets no seed and originated in the garden of a Dutch grower called Faassen. For this reason it should really be called *N. faassenii* but tradition dies hard, and probably the plant will always be known to gardeners under the old name.

For propagation purposes, Nepeta should be cut to the ground after flowering, in July. This action will encourage the growth of young shoots from the base, which can then be taken as soft cuttings and struck in sandy soil in a cold frame. The cuttings soon root and can be planted out the following spring. Nepeta likes well-drained soil and is resentful of moisture standing round the roots in winter. In heavy land, therefore, it pays to sprinkle sand or gritty material over the surface in winter or to grow them on a raised bed.

N. × faassenii (syn. *mussinii*). (*Plate 11, p. 64.*) Small grey serrated leaves and soft lavender blue flowers.   *1–1½ ft. May–Sept. 1½ ft. sq.* There is a fine tall-growing Nepeta of garden origin called ' Six Hills Giant ' which may fit into this family or Dracocephalum. Violet-blue. *2½ ft. 3 ft. sq.*

N. nervosa. Kashmir. has green lanceolate leaves and clear blue flowers which make an attractive display when in full flower.

1–2 ft. July–Sept. 1 ft. sq.

OENOTHERA (*Onagraceae*): Evening Primrose. Name from *oinos* (Gk) ' wine ', *thera* ' taste ', the roots are said to induce a thirst for wine.

Many Evening Primroses are biennial or monocarpic, that is they die after blooming, but there are a few perennial species available for the border. Here they are useful, not only on account of the long-flowering habit, but because—unlike the biennial forms, which only open their blossoms at night—they are in character during the day as well. Although the rich fragrance of the biennial kinds is not so marked in the perennials, there are one or two with a pleasant scent. Oenotheras should be grown in sandy, well-drained soil, and given full sun or a light shady situation. They are propagated by seed or division of the roots in spring. Cuttings taken in May in sandy soil usually root readily.

O. caespitosa. Tufted Evening Primrose. Western N. America. An almost prostrate species suitable for the front of the border because of its long flowering habit. The blooms, which are practically stemless are large and fragrant, white, deepening with age to pink. Var. *eximea* is taller.
1 ft. May–Aug. 1½ ft. sq.

O. californica. California. Has narrow toothed leaves and white or pinkish flowers with yellow centres. Fragrant. *6 in. July. 1 ft. sq.*

O. erythrosepala (syn. *O. lamarckiana*). Apparently of garden origin this is a floriferous form with red stems, broad, crinkled stalkless leaves and quantities of golden flowers 2–3½ in. across, which turn reddish with age. The buds are very hairy. The variety 'Afterglow' has more reddish flowers. *4 ft. June–Autumn. 2 ft. sq.*

O fruticosa. Sundrops. Nova Scotia. This species and its varieties are among the most attractive of all the lemon-coloured border plants. The flowers are showy and on erect leafy stems. There are a number of varieties including *major* (*Plate 16, p. 80*), which has larger flowers, and 'Youngii' which has many reddish-brown, branching stems and flowers in terminal clusters. These are tinged with red in the bud stage, but open to bright yellow blooms, 1½ in. across. This needs a mid-border position. 'William Cuthbertson' grows 12–15 in. high, making a bushy plant with wiry, branching stems and bright, pale yellow flowers. Var. 'Yellow River' has large yellow flowers in abundance, 1½ ft. *2 ft. June–Autumn. 2 ft. sq.*

O. missourensis. Ozark Sundrops. S. Central United States. One of the best species, which gained an Award of Merit at the R.H.S. in 1935. It blooms in July and forms a spreading plant with reddish stems and bright funnel-shaped flowers. These are 2–2½ in. across, and bright silver-yellow. The buds are often spotted with red.
6–9 in. July. 3 ft. sq.

O. odorata. Southern N. America. Of branching habit with wavy-edged, lanceolate leaves and fragrant, night-blooming yellow flowers which deepen to red. *1½ ft. April–June. 1 ft. sq.*

O. perennis. Eastern N. America. Has loose, leafy spikes of yellow flowers which open during the day. *1–2 ft. July. 1 ft. sq.*

O. speciosa. S. Central United States to Mexico. A handsome plant with many large fragrant flowers. These are flat, basin-shaped and pure white with pale greenish-cream centres. As the blooms pass they change to a soft rose shade. It is a true perennial, suitable for the front of the border or pockets in the rock garden.

14–18 in. July–Sept. 2½ ft. sq.

O. speciosa rosea. Is of garden origin and originated in Winchmore Hill in 1900. To-day it is almost lost to cultivation. The flowers are pale pink but deepen to rich rose, with white and yellow bases. It is a lovely plant, wonderfully free and makes a handsome addition to the herbaceous border. *2 ft. July–Sept. 2 ft. sq.*

O. tetragona. E.N. America. The species has small yellow flowers and is of branching habit. Var. *fraseri* is an improved form, also var. *riparia* which is useful on account of its long-flowering habit.

1–2 ft. All summer. 1 ft. sq.

OMPHALODES (*Boraginaceae*): Navelwort. From *omphalos* (Gk) ' navel ', *oides* ' like ', from the shape of the calyx.

An attractive plant with Borage or Forget-me-not-like flowers and entire leaves. It is suitable for the front of the border, particularly in light shady situations. In deep shade plants grow too prolifically and the colour of the flowers is less intense. A cool soil is essential but this must be well drained. Slugs attack the young foliage in spring and should be deterred with some repellent. Propagation by division or seed.

O. cappadocica. Dogwood Navelseed. Asia Minor. Has dark green, heart-shaped leaves and a creeping rootstock. The flowers are borne in graceful sprays and resemble large, deep blue Forget-me-nots.

1 ft. June–Aug. 1 ft. sq.

O. verna. Blue Eyed Mary. S. Europe. Has running underground roots and oval or heart-shaped leaves on long stalks. The flowers are blue with a white throat with several borne on each slender stem. It likes a light shaded situation or will grow at the fringe of woodland.

6–9 in. March–May. 1 ft. sq.

ONOPORDON (*Compositae*): Cotton Thistle. Old Greek name of ancient origin.

Stately, Thistle-like plants, valuable in exposed places, to use mixed with shrubs or wild plants, or as individual specimens in small beds. For the border the best kind is *O. acanthium*, which is native to Europe, including Britain, and makes a sturdy branched, woolly-stemmed plant 4–5 ft. high. The leaves are Thistle-shaped and densely covered with long, whitish web-like hairs. The branches terminate in large heads of rich purple flowers. The Cotton Thistle will grow in ordinary garden soil but is more suited to the larger border or any prominent key position. It can be propagated by seeds, sown outside in well-drained soil about April. *4–5 ft. July. 3 ft. sq.*

OROBUS (*Leguminosae*): Bitter Vetch. Name of uncertain origin. Modern reference books frequently refer this genus to Lathyrus and Vicia but long garden usage seems to present a case for its retention in the present volume under Orobus.

A handsome race of plants closely related to *Lathyrus* but of neater and more compact habit. The plants bloom in spring or early summer and have Sweetpea-like flowers and foliage. They succeed best in deep sandy loam in sheltered situations. Propagation by seed or division.

O. aurantiacus (syn. *Vicia aurantia*). (*Plate 4, p. 32.*) Europe. Has orange-yellow flowers closely arranged on upright flower spikes.

$1\frac{1}{2}$ *ft. May–June.* $1\frac{1}{2}$ *ft. sq.*

OSTROWSKIA (*Campanulaceae*): Giant Bellflower. Named after M. N. von Ostrowsky, a 19th-century Russian patron of botany.

A most beautiful border perennial but unfortunately not the easiest plant to grow. *O. magnifica*, Turkistan, is the only species. In situations to its liking it reaches striking proportions, the large fleshy roots going deeply into the ground. Individual stems may then be 4–6 ft. high, carrying attractive glaucous foliage, which grows in whorls, of 4 or 5 leaflets, all the way up the stem (a characteristic which distinguishes it from Campanula) and bearing also many fine, cup-shaped flowers, 4–6 in. across at the mouth. These are of a delicate light purple shade with darker veinings or markings. A deep, sandy loam suits the genus best and it likes lime. The ground must never be subjected to water-logging, and after the plant dies down in autumn the crown should be protected with a mulch of leaves or a piece of glass. It is resentful of disturbance when once well established, and should therefore be propagated from seed sown directly after ripening, the seedlings being transplanted to their flowering quarters as soon as possible. The seedlings come to bloom in three or four years. *4–6 ft. July. 2 ft. sq.*

OXALIS (*Oxalidaceae*). Named from *oxys* (Gk), ' acid,' from the acrid taste of the leaves.

A family of herbaceous and tuberous rooted plants, some of which are extremely woody, the majority more suited to the rock garden than the border. The species described, *O. lasiandra*, is valuable for a front-row position on account of its long-flowering habit. It blooms from May practically until the frosts come. It is a ' no trouble ' plant, rarely increasing, and may stay in the same position for years on end. The plant must have full sun and a well-drained situation. In cold wet clays it often succumbs to a winter frost. Propagation from the tubers at the base of established plants.

O. lasiandra. Rose Shamrock. (*Plate 24, p. 112.*) Mexico. Usually known to gardeners as *O. floribunda*. Makes small bulbs and has Shamrock-like leaves on slender, slightly hairy stems. The flowers, borne in umbels of a dozen or so, are cyclamen pink and about ¾ in. across.

1 ft. All summer. 1 ft. sq.

PAEONIA (*Ranunculaceae*): Paeony or Peony. Ancient Greek name used by Theophrastus, thought to be named for Paeon, a physician of the gods, who first used the plant medicinally.

This genius appears to possess all the attributes of a good plant. The blooms are early and substantial in size and texture; the colours rich with a wide variety of shades and the flowers last well in water. The perennial nature of Peonies makes them ideal subjects for permanent planting, and since the foliage is ornamental and naturally neat, one has no problems of dowdiness after flowering. Added to all this, the incidence of pest and disease is so remote as scarcely to merit consideration.

The plants are also particularly accommodating in the garden and will grow freely in full sun or partial shade. A position which catches the early morning sun is not always advisable, as morning frosts will injure the buds if these thaw out too quickly.

The common Peony of gardens is *P. officinalis*. This has three double forms, all well known. The commonest is a deep blood crimson, a favourite cottager's plant, whose origin is steeped in mystery although it was certainly known and described as far back as Pliny's time. Of the others, one is dark rose which gradually pales with age, and the other a poor white, which opens a flesh pink and fades to a dingy cream. It is sometimes known as *alba plena*. Although many Peonies have a delightful fragrance, these three possess a really unpleasant smell, a strong, penetrating odour.

Perhaps the most beautiful section for border work are the beautiful and fragrant Chinese Peonies, *P. lactiflora*. These should be planted between the middle of October and the middle of November. The roots start growing soon afterwards and should be left undisturbed so that the thick fleshy tubers go down deep into the ground. Plant them in deeply dug, rich soil. Like Roses, Peonies are gross feeders and appreciate generous treatment. Rotted stable dung, compost, old leaf soil and bonemeal are all beneficial, and in later years the plants should be mulched with similar material towards the end of February. The roots should never be short of water during the growing period, and in addition to supplying moisture during hot, dry spells, the application of liquid manure (just when the buds are swelling) pays dividends in flower returns.

The propagation of herbaceous Peonies is effected by division in early October, or (in the species) from seed. They will take approximately four years to flower.

P. emodi. N.W. India. Has fine, large, single flowers which are white (4–5 in. across) with golden stamens.   *1½–2½ ft. June. 2 ft. sq.*

P. lactiflora. Siberia, Mongolia. This species, which has large, white fragrant flowers is important as the parent of a great number of garden varieties. These are known as Chinese Peonies, chiefly because the first hybrids were raised in that country. The group is particularly valuable since the blooms appear after the European species are finished. The following are all worthwhile varieties:

$2\frac{1}{2}-3\frac{1}{2}$. *June. 2 ft. sq.*

Adolphe Rousseau, deep purple-red, double.

Albatross, white, with crimson flecks on centre petals, double.

Albert Crousse, double pink, sweetly scented.

Alice Harding, very large, creamy-white, double.

Avalanche, pure white, double.

Baroness Schroeder, double, blush-white, very large, fragrant, late.

Bunker Hill, crimson, semi-double.

Canary, cream with yellow centre, double.

Charles Leveque, pale pink, double.

Cherry Hill, cherry-red, double.

Claire Dubois, satiny pink, globular, large, fragrant, double.

Clairette, single, pure white with golden stamens.

Couronne d'Or, double white.

Duchesse de Nemours, rich creamy-white, double, scented.

Duchess of Portland, single white, with a rosy flush.

edulis superba, brilliant pink with silvery sheen, fragrant, double, early.

Eva, very late, single to semi-double, light pinkish-crimson.

Felix Crousse, double, brilliant rose.

festiva maxima, paper white with crimson splashes.

General MacMahon, glowing crimson, double.

Globe of Light, deep rose-pink, outer petals forming a cup, which is filled with many, narrow yellow petals.

Inspector Lavergne, double crimson with frilled petals.

Karl Rosenfield, double, dark wine-red.

Kelway's Glorious, double, blush-white, fragrant.

Lady Alexandra Duff, delicate pink, loose centres, large, fragrant.

Lady Bramwell, double carmine.

Le Cygne, pure milk-white with a touch of green, very fragrant, double.

Lemon Queen, creamy-white with a lemon centre, Japanese or anemone flowered.

Leoni (*Plate 5, p. 32*), double white.

Lord Kitchener, flesh pink, double.

Madame Calot, malmaison pink, sweetly scented.

Madame Emile Lemoine, pale pinkish-white, free, double.

Marechal McMahon, double, deep red.

M. Jules Elie, silvery lilac-pink, double.

M. Martin Cahuzac, deep purple, double.

Mons. Charles Leveque, flesh-pink with a darker centre,

fragrant, double, one of the best for cutting.

Mrs. Edward Harding, exceptionally large flowers, white and very double.

Neomie Demay, flesh pink with silvery flush, double.

Pink Delight, single, soft rose passing to pure white with golden stamens.

President Roosevelt, deep red, double.

President Taft (syn. Reine Hortense), large double flowers of a beautiful flesh pink.

Sarah Bernhardt, double, apple-blossom pink.

Solange, double, orange-salmon pale flesh pink centre.

Suzette, deep rose, double.

The Bride, pure white, single.

The Moor, single, maroon-crimson.

Thérèse, double, flesh colour with soft pink centre petals.

Thorbecke, blush pink, double.

Torpilleur, anemone flowered, carmine with golden centre petals.

Victoire de la Marne, dark crimson with a purple glow, double.

Victoria, single, deep crimson, with golden anthers.

Weisbaden, blush pink, early, double.

P. mlokosewitschi. Lemon Peony. (*Plate 5, p. 32.*) Caucasus. A particularly desirable species with attractive, broad-leaved foliage of bluish-green and large, single, citron-yellow flowers. This delicate shade is accentuated and set off by a boss of rich golden stamens. Later there is a second attraction in the seed pods, which in autumn spread wide to display a double row of shiny, blue-black seeds, interspersed with brilliant scarlet, infertile ovules. As they rest there, with the autumn tints of the leaves around, they seem as beautiful as a necklet of precious stones. $1\frac{1}{2}$ *ft. April. 2 ft. sq.*

P. officinalis: Common Red Peony. France to Albania. A very old species with solitary, scarlet flowers and deeply cut foliage. There are several double forms including *rubra plena* (*Plate 5, p. 32*), *alba plena*, and *rosea plena.* $2-2\frac{1}{2}$ *ft. May.* $2\frac{1}{2}$ *ft. sq.*

P. russi. Russo's Peony. (*Plate 5, p. 32.*) Corsica, Sicily. Has rose-red flowers with very rounded petals. $1-1\frac{1}{4}$ *ft. May. 2 ft. sq.*

P. tenuifolia. Fringed Peony. (*Plate 5, p. 32.*) Caucasus. A species characterised by the finely cut foliage, which gives the leaves a Fennel-like appearance. The cup-shaped flowers are deep crimson and about 3 in. across. There is a double form, *plena.*

$1-2$ *ft. May.* $1\frac{1}{2}$ *ft. sq.*

P. wittmanniana. Caucasus. A beautiful yellowish white species with red stigma and filaments. The leaves are broadly cut and shining green.

3 ft. April. 2 ft. sq.

PAPAVER (*Papaveraceae*): Poppy. From *papa* (Celtic) 'pap'; it was once given to fractious infants with their food, as a narcotic.

The most important species in this large and colourful family is undoubtedly *P. orientale*, for not only are the blooms large and showy, but they come when most wanted—in early summer. The type plant comes from S. Europe, where it follows the coast line down as far as Armenia. The flowers are brilliant scarlet, usually with a prominent purple-black blotch at the base of each petal. *P. orientale* is very similar to *P. bracteatum*, but the latter is distinguished by having leafy stems. They are always leafless in *P. orientale*.

Oriental Poppies will grow in any deep, well-drained soil and last for years in the same position. They are gross feeders and appreciate a fairly substantial mulch applied round the roots in April.

For best effects Poppies should be grown in bold clumps, and in mixed borders should be set in a midway position with later-flowering plants in front. These will mask the untidy, dying down effects in July and August. Suitable perennials for this purpose are *Artemisia lactiflora*, Gypsophilas, *Salvia azurea* var. *grandiflora*, some of the lower growing Solidagos, and *Chrysanthemum rubellum*. A few of the varietal forms show a tendency to sprawl so should be staked with peasticks early in the year, when the growths are only a few inches high.

Whilst the type may be raised very easily from seed, named and varietal forms are usually increased by root cuttings, as described on page 64.

Although *P. orientale* has been grown for very many years in Britain, it was not until 1906 that the first colour break appeared. My late father-in-law, Amos Perry, inspecting a bed of seedlings one day, found that one plant had rose—instead of scarlet—flowers. He named this ' Mrs. Perry ' after his wife, and then, feeling that the break might continue, hand pollinated the flowers hoping for a still paler form or even a white poppy. But all the seedlings flowered red.

Then in 1912 a client was making a pink-red border, and the plants were carefully chosen and graded so that the deeper shades were in the centre, and worked out gradually to the pale flesh tones at either end. Poppies were felt to give the brilliance of colour needed for the central focal point. But in 1913 Amos Perry received an irate letter. His client wrote to say that the plants had come to bloom, and, in the most conspicuous position, where the scarlet area was designed, one of the poppies had flowered—white. Eventually Amos Perry went to see the garden, and was amazed to see the new plant, which, exchanged for some Montbretia corms, in time became ' Perry's White '.

Later there came other shades and even double forms, and to-day a wide range of varieties are available. If these have smooth stems they have been derived from *P. orientale*, and if leafy, from *P. bracteatum*.

Barr's White, large, pure white flowers with purplish-black blotches.

Beauty of Livermore, immense blood-crimson.

Cowigan, an Australian variety with oxblood-red blooms.

Crimson Pompom, one of the earliest and certainly the best double variety to date.

Flowers rounded and rich red.

Ethel Swete, almost pure rose.

Indian Chief, deep mahogany-red; one plant contrasts well with the pink forms.

Mahony, very dark, blood-red.

Marcus Perry (*Plate 7, p. 48*),

a good late variety (July and Aug.) which does not need staking, bright orange-scarlet with a black base to each petal.

Mrs. Perry (*Plate 7, p. 48*), a beautiful shade of soft salmon-pink.

Orange King, brilliant orange-scarlet.

Perry's White (*Plate IX, p. 224*), large white, with maroon-purple blotches at the base of each petal.

Queen Alexandra, rose.

Salmon Glow, large, double, salmon-orange flowers, which are 8 in. across when grown in good soil.

Snowflame, deep orange at the top of the flower but with a pure white base. The white ring differs in width in individual flowers.

Stormtorch (Sturmfackel), fiery red, on erect stems.

Watermelon, large single, cherry rose. $1\frac{1}{2}$–*3 ft. May–June. 2 ft. sq.*

PARADISEA (*Liliaceae*): St. Bruno's Lily. S. Europe. Named for Count Giovanni Paradisi.

A genus of a single species, *P. liliastrum* (syn. *Anthericum liliastrum*) (*Plate II, p. 193*). This beautiful subject produces short rhizomes with rather thick roots and has long, strap-like leaves and spikes of white Lily-like flowers. Individually these are wide and about 2 inches long, and tipped with green on the outside of the petals. Var. *major* is taller and has larger flowers. *1–2 ft. June. 1 ft. sq.*

PATRINIA (*Valerianaceae*). Named after Mons. Patrin, an 18th-century traveller in Russia.

White or yellow Valerian-like plants, several of which make good hardy perennials for the early summer border. They are easily cultivated in any good garden soil and do particularly well in damp and shady places. Propagation by division of the roots, and seed.

P. triloba (syn. *P. palmata*): Japan. Has an erect, reddish stem and finely cut foliage. The flowers are closely packed together in rather loose clusters on short stems. They are bright golden-yellow and extremely fragrant. *1 ft. July. 1 ft. sq.*

PELTIPHYLLUM (*Saxifragaceae*): Umbrella Plant. From *pelta* (Gk) 'shield', *phyllon* 'leaf'; referring to the shape of the foliage.

A genus of a single Californian species, *P. peltatum* originally known as *Saxifraga peltata*. It is a handsome subject where spectacular foliage effects are required; the large, completely round, umbrella-like leaves topping 3 or 4 ft. stems. The blooms appear very early in the spring, before the foliage. They are white or very pale pink in dense clusters on stout stems. The plant makes a thick, fleshy rootstock and does best in deep, moist soil. Propagation by division or seeds.

3–4 ft. April. 2 ft. sq.

PENTSTEMON (*Scrophulariaceae*): Beard Tongue. From *pente* (Gk) ' five ', *stemon* ' stamen '; the flowers have five stamens.

A genus of brightly coloured flowers invaluable in late summer and autumn and particularly useful in sunny or dry situations, for they will stand drought better than most border perennials. Besides being showy, the blooms of many garden forms are large and resemble a Foxglove in shape.

Pentstemons thrive best in a border which has been enriched with well-rotted dung or leaf-mould earlier in the spring. They also appreciate a little lime in the soil but abhor frost and wet—particularly the latter. It is therefore essential to give them a well-drained situation, but apply water (or mulch the ground) during the summer. Being of doubtful hardiness it pays the gardener to perpetuate stock annually by taking cuttings from some of the basal shoots about September. These should be rooted in a cold frame and kept there until the following May or June when they may be planted outside again. It is possible to propagate from seed but the seedlings will be variable. Sow in February or March and prick the seedlings out into sandy soil, in a frame, for putting outside in May. In the herbaceous border the plants are suitable for a front to mid-row position.

P. barbatus (syn. *Chelone barbata*): Bearded Penstemon. (*Plate 23, p. 112.*) Mexico. A hardy species with small coral-red, tubular flowers about an inch long and rather smooth leaves on branching stems. The type has given rise to a number of good garden forms such as ' Rose Elf ', which is very prolific, carrying 10 or more flower spikes to a single plant. It grows about 18 in. high with clear shell-pink blossoms from June to August. ' Torreyi ' has bright scarlet flowers and is interesting by reason of the fact that there is no beard on the lower petal, as in most Pentstemons. *Salmonea* is a very good salmon-pink; *coccineus*, scarlet. *3 ft. June–Aug. 2 ft. sq.*

P. campanulatus. Mexico. Has slender toothed and pointed foliage and variable bell-shaped flowers of pink, dark purple or violet. Good varietal forms are *pulchellus*, lilac, *purpureus*, purple.

1–2 ft. June. 1 ft. sq.

P. glaber. Blue Pentstemon. S.W. United States. Has erect, rather glaucous stems which are not branched, and sprays of bright blue flowers. Var. *roseus* is similar except that the flowers are pink or rose. *1–2 ft. Aug. 1–2 ft. sq.*

P. hartwegii. Mexico. An erect plant with oval lanceolate leaves and scarlet or blood-red drooping, tubular flowers. This species is believed

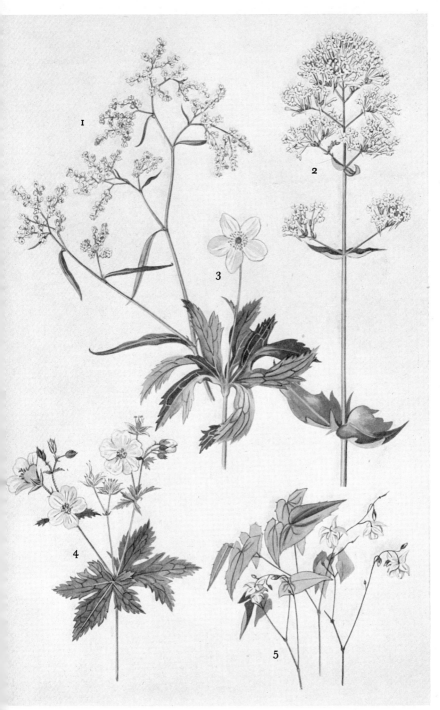

Plate III: 1. ALPINE KNOTWEED, *Polygonum alpinum.* 2. WHITE VALERIAN, *Kentranthus ruber albus.* 3. MEADOW ANEMONE, *Anemone dichotoma.* 4. WHITE MEADOW CRANES-BILL, *Geranium pratense album.* 5. SNOWY BARRENWORT, *Epimedium* x *youngianum niveum*

Plate IV: 1. SOLOMON'S SEAL, *Polygonatum multiflorum.* 2. SIEBOLD PRIMROSE *Primula sieboldii.* 3. FAIR MAIDS OF FRANCE, *Ranunculus aconitifolius flore plena* 4. MULLEIN, *Verbascum hybridum* 'Miss Wilmott'

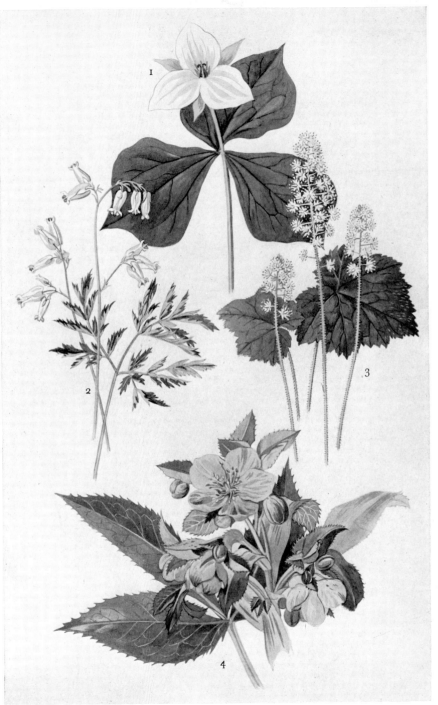

Plate V: 1. TRINITY FLOWER, *Trillium grandiflorum.* 2. WHITE FRINGED BLEEDING
HEART, *Dicentra eximia alba.* 3. FOAMFLOWER, *Tiarella cordifolia.* 4. CORSICAN HELLEBORE,
Helleborus corsicus

Plate VI: 1. DELPHINIUM, *Delphinium elatum* 'Weeley White'. 2. MILKY BELLFLOWER, *Campanula lactiflora* 'Loddon Anna'. 3. PYRENEES CHRYSANTHEMUM, *Chrysanthemum maximum* 'Horace Read'

to be the parent of many florist's Pentstemons such as ' Southgate Gem ' (*Plate 7, p. 48*) which is very like its parent, and ' Myddelton Gem ' raised by the late E. A. Bowles, which has light crimson flowers. Other good varieties are:

Alice Hindley, pale blue shaded rose.

Cherry Red, a good red.

Firebird, also known on the Continent as 'Schonholzeri'; brilliant crimson flowers the size of a Foxglove; makes a good cut flower and blooms from June till November.

Majestic, violet-purple.

Newberry, light purplish-blue.

White Bedder, white.   *2 ft. July–Sept. 1–1½ ft. sq.*

P. heterophyllus. California. A semi-shrubby perennial with delightfully coloured flowers. These open a clear bright blue suffused with rose and then deepen to purple with age. Often they show considerable variation in the same plant. The leaves are small and grass-like. The plant does best in light soil and a warm sheltered position, but to ensure against winter losses it is best to take a few cuttings in autumn and winter these in a cold frame. ' Blue Gem ' is an attractive variety from this species with soft, gentian blue, campanulate flowers.

1–1½ ft. July. 1 ft. sq.

P. isophyllus. Mexico. A somewhat shrubby perennial, rather leafy, with red and white flowers. It is hardy only in very favoured situations.

2 ft. June–July. 1½ ft. sq.

P. ovatus. Central United States. A pretty plant with slender erect stems bearing bright green leaves and loose spikes of blue flowers which become purple with age.   *2 ft. July. 1 ft. sq.*

P. utahensis. The Utah Penstemon. (*Plate 7, p. 48.*) N. America. A robust species with tall, leafy, red-tinted stems. The large (¾-inch) well-shaped flowers are blue with a suspicion of mauve suffusing them when fully open.   *2 ft. July. 1 ft. sq.*

PEROVSKIA (*Labiatae*). (*Also spelt Perowskia.*) Named after V. A. Perovski, a Russian statesman.

A genus of deciduous, semi-shrubby plants which are almost invariably used in herbaceous borders instead of the shrub border. This is partly because of the delicate lacy growth texture and partly because of their diminutive size and late summer flowering. Perovskia makes a small plant (rarely more than 5 ft. even in extremely favourable conditions) and likes a well-drained soil. It is propagated from cuttings.

P. atriplicifolia. Afghanistan, Tibet. A handsome species with small oval lanceolate, coarsely toothed leaves of silvery-grey which contrast well with the spikes of soft blue, Nepeta-like flowers. The whole plant is aromatic, particularly when bruised, with a Sage-like odour. Grow it in a sunny position in well-drained soil. *3–5 ft. Aug.–Sept. 3 ft. sq.*

PHALARIS (*Gramineae*): Ribbon Grass. Old Greek name for grass.

P. arundinacea var. *picta*: Gardener's Garters. (*Plate VII, p. 224.*) Temp. N. Hemisphere. A handsome grass of perennial habit which will grow in practically any soil, in sun or shade. Its chief value lies in the beautiful variegation of the leaves which are striped longitudinally in green and white. This makes an admirable foil when arranged with brightly coloured subjects and the long stems are invaluable for cutting. Although not a true flowering herbaceous perennial, I would not willingly give up the use of this plant in the mixed border. When it dies down in winter, the foliage should be burned over lightly. Care must be taken to prevent it spreading too rapidly. Division about every third year keeps the plant in bounds. *2–3 ft. June–July. 2 ft. sq.*

PHLOMIS (*Labiatae*): Jerusalem Sage. Old Greek name of doubtful origin.

A group of shrubs and deciduous perennials belonging to the Sage family, interesting no less for the silvery foliage than the unusual flowers. The latter resemble giant dead-nettle blossoms, with their long tubular flowers, and are borne in conspicuous axillary whorls on stout stems. Usually they are yellow, but there are white and purple forms. Jerusalem Sage must have well-drained soil and does not mind a little dryness at the roots. It appreciates plenty of sunshine and should be planted in a mid to front position in the border. Propagation of the herbaceous kinds is by seed, cuttings, or division in spring or autumn.

P. cashmeriana. Kashmir. A striking plant with densely woolly stems and leaves and whorls of lilac-purple flowers. *2 ft. July. 2 ft. sq.*

P. fruticosa. Jerusalem Sage. Mediterranean area. A low-growing, branching shrub, with woolly hairy, wedge-shaped leaves and dusky-yellow flowers. It is more suited to the herbaceous border than the shrubbery. *2–4 ft. June. 4 ft. sq.*

P. herba-venti. Mediterranean region. Has showy purplish-violet flowers and hairy leaves and stems. *1–1½ ft. July–Sept. 2 ft. sq.*

P. samia. N. Africa. Plants for well-drained, warm situations, producing quantities of very woolly Sage-like leaves and small whorls of creamy white flowers, often tinged with green.
2–3 ft. May–June. 3 ft. sq.

P. tuberosa. E. Europe. Has larger leaves than most species, heart-shaped and wavy edged. The flowers are borne in impressive whorls and are purplish-rose and white. The roots are tuberous.
3–5 ft. July–Aug. 2 ft. sq.

PHLOX (*Polemoniaceae*). From *phlego* (Gk) 'flame', probably referring to the brilliance of the flowers.

Few border perennials are brighter in colour or possess more virile constitutions than the *paniculata* forms of garden Phlox. And yet, barely a century ago they were thought to be tender! It is interesting to recall also that (with one possible exception) the whole genus— which includes rock, greenhouse, annual and perennial species—are indigenous to North America. Notwithstanding this, it is almost entirely due to British and European hybridists that the demure, rather insignificant individuals of the parent species have produced such a handsome and useful race of garden plants.

The first break came when John Downie of Edinburgh raised an 'eyed' variety, a characteristic which makes so many modern varieties strikingly attractive. In later years Prichard, Baker and more recently Captain Symons-Jeune worked on the genus, so that to-day we have sturdy, free-flowering varieties in good clean colours and a wide range of shades.

As middle of the border subjects Phlox are indispensable for maintaining the flowering sequence, in that difficult period between the end of July and August. Given reasonable growing conditions, they remain in bloom 4–5 weeks, providing that one keeps the old laterals removed.

When growing Phlox in the garden always plant them in clumps. They like a fertile soil and must never become dry during the growing season. Phlox are almost the first plants in the border to show signs of drought. They will grow in sun or light shade, and it is desirable to thin out a few of the weaker shoots in order to obtain better and stronger flowers. Propagation is effected by division or root cuttings (see p. 65). The latter are best taken during the growing season, i.e. about the end of August.

P. × *arendsii*. This race comprises a group of hybrids between *P. divaricata* and *P. paniculata*, useful in the garden because they are usually shorter than the latter and therefore suitable for front of the border work. They have large, loose and fairly heavy trusses of flowers and come to bloom a little earlier than other garden Phlox. Representative varieties are 'Amanda', rich lilac with dark blue centres; 'Charlotte', white changing to lilac, with blue eye; 'Hilda', white overlaid lilac; 'Inge', clear rose and 'Marianne', rosy-lilac with a carmine centre.

14–24 in. June–July. 1½ ft. sq.

P. divaricata (syn. *P. canadensis*). Eastern N. America. A pretty species with slender stems terminating in corymbose heads of large lavender-blue flowers. Useful for the front of the border, rockery or as a pot plant. 'Perry's Variety' is similar but the flowers are an intense plumbago-blue; 'Violet Queen' is violet-blue.

1 ft. May–June. 1 ft. sq.

P. maculata. Eastern N. America. A vigorous perennial with hairy, red-spotted stems, narrow leaves and terminal heads of violet-purple flowers. This species must have a moist situation. In var. *purpurea* the stems are taller and the flowers purple.

2–3 ft. July–Sept. 1½ ft. sq.

P. paniculata (syn. *P. decussata*). Eastern N. America. From this species have been derived most of the garden varieties used to-day. Numbers of these are legion but the following are among the best of their kind. All these varieties are in character from the end of July until September, and they need approximately 2 ft. sq. planting area.

Aida, compact and bushy in growth, individual flowers of a glowing dark crimson with purple eye, 2½ ft.

Blue Boy, a first-class border plant with extra large trusses of bluish-mauve flowers, 2½ ft.

Caroline van den Berg (*Plate 39, p. 176*), deep lavender-blue with red flush at the eye, 3 ft.

Cecil Hanbury, glowing rich orange-salmon with vivid carmine eye, very compact in habit, 2½ ft.

Cinderella, pale mulberry-pink with bright carmine eye, very stocky in habit, 2½ ft.

Commander in Chief, large heads of fiery crimson flowers with dark red centres, 2½ ft.

Daily Sketch (*Plate 39, p. 176*), extra large flowers of salmon-pink with vivid crimson eye, 2½ ft.

Dresden China, exquisite soft shell-pink, tall and very free-flowering, 3 ft.

Early Gem, a dwarf compact plant of almost perfect habit. Flowers a soft pale pink with faint salmon sheen, 2 ft.

Europa, white with carmine centre, 3 ft.

Eva Foerster, large pyramidal trusses of deep crimson flowers with white eye, 2½ ft.

Eventide, a late-flowering variety with delicate lavender-blue flowers, 3 ft.

Fanal, rich, glowing flame-red, 3 ft.

Frau Ant. Buchner, enormous trusses of large, pure white flowers, 2 ft.

Graf Zeppelin (*Plate 38, p. 161*), an old variety with large white flowers with cherry-red centre, 3 ft.

Hampton Court, heliotrope-blue flowers and strikingly dark foliage, 3 ft.

Iceberg, a pleasing white with soft shading of violet, 3 ft.

Latest Red, compact heads of glowing rich carmine-red flowers, 2 ft.

Le Mahdi (*Plate 38, p. 161*), rich violet blue, sometimes suffused with white, 3½ ft.

Leo Schlageter, brilliant scarlet-carmine flowers with contrasting dark centre, 2½ ft.

Marie Jacob, an unusual shade of pale lilac with white centre, 2½ ft.

Mars, the well-formed flowers are a pleasing shade of orange-pink with a deep crimson eye, 2½ ft.

Mia Ruys, white, large, dwarf form, 2 ft.

Mrs. Askew, rose-pink with carmine centre, 3 ft.

Mrs. Ethel Prichard (*Plate 39,*

p. 176), pale violet flowers produced in profusion on large compact trusses, 2½ *ft.*

Newbird (*Plate 38, p. 161*), rich crimson, *3 ft.*

P. D. Williams, pyramidal trusses of soft apple-blossom pink with darker centre, *2 ft.*

Pink Gown, fine trusses of delightful pink flowers, *3 ft.*

Purple King, a strong free-flowering plant, with large trusses of rich purple-violet flowers, 3½ *ft.*

Salmon Glow, a plant of outstanding charm with salmon-pink flowers each with a pure white eye, 2½ *ft.*

Sam Pope, salmon-pink with scarlet eye, flowers not too large, *3 ft.*

Signal, very large, rich glowing red flowers, *3 ft.*

Sir John Falstaff, a recent introduction of exceptional vigour; the massive heads of flowers are a beautiful shade of rich salmon, *3 ft.*

Sunray, one of the first varieties to flower; extra large heads of salmon-pink blooms which are suffused orange, with white eyes, *3 ft.*

Symphony, an outstanding variety with strawberry-pink flowers, 3½ *ft.*

P. pilosa. Eastern N. America. Has very thin wiry leaves and loose sprays of rosy-purple flowers. Var. ' Attenberg ' has richer coloured dark rose blooms.   1½ *ft. May–July. 1 ft. sq.*

PHORMIUM (*Liliaceae*): New Zealand Flax. From *phormos* (Gk) ' basket '; the leaves have been employed for making baskets.

Fine foliage plants from New Zealand with sword-like leaves rising to a height of many feet. A specimen plant when well grown creates a striking and spectacular effect especially in a key position, as at the corner of a border, in an isolated situation on a lawn, at the waterside mixed with Bamboos and Gunneras or in the wild garden. In very cold winters even old plants may sustain mortal damage and the gardener should visit them at these times and protect the crowns with straw. However, the roots can take a good deal of punishment and even though the tops may be damaged they usually survive and throw up fresh shoots the next season.

New Zealand Flax likes a deep soil and plenty of sunlight but must never be short of moisture at the roots. Propagation by seed or root division.

P. colensoi. New Zealand. The smallest species with slender grassy leaves 2–3 ft. long and heads of yellowish flowers. It is hardier than *P. tenax.* A variety with cream leaf striations is known as var. *variegatum.*

         3–6 ft. Aug.–Oct. 3 ft. sq.

P. tenax. New Zealand. The best-known species; a tall stately plant with ridged, dark green leaves 8–9 ft. long and 4–5 in. wide. Frequently these split at the top. The light red flowers are borne on long spikes above the tops of the leaves. There are several varieties notably *atropurpureum* with bronzy-purple leaves; *variegatum*, striped yellow and green, and *veitchii*, variegated in white and green.

8–9 ft. July–Sept. 4 ft. sq.

PHYGELIUS (*Scrophulariaceae*): Cape Figwort, Cape Fuchsia. From *phyga* (Gk) ' flight ', *helios* ' the sun '; shade loving.

P. capensis. S. Africa. A shrubby plant, somewhat like Fuchsia, with candelabra heads of drooping scarlet flowers. It is happiest against a wall in a south position, and a well-grown specimen makes a fine background for late-flowering perennials. This is one of those border-line plants which are really shrubs but best grown with herbaceous perennials. The name derivation appears to indicate some need for shade, but, whilst this may be so in its country of origin, the plant should always be given a sunny situation in Britain. It stands heat and dryness extremely well and in exposed situations should be afforded some protection in winter. Propagation by seeds sown under glass in spring and then transplanted to a warm border, or from cuttings. *3–5 ft. Aug. 3 ft. sq.*

PHYSALIS (*Solanaceae*): Cape Gooseberry, Chinese Lantern. From *physa* (Gk) ' bladder ', referring to the shape of the calyx.

Plants more widely known for the fruit than the flowers, the dried and inflated calyx of the former being much used for winter decoration. Cape Gooseberries like a well-drained soil and flower more freely in warm than cold borders. They are not averse to light shade. As the plants increase considerably by means of underground stems a watchful eye must be maintained to keep them in bounds. Propagation by division.

In autumn, when the orange-red calices start to show colour the stems should be cut and dried. Tie them upside down in bundles in a light, airy shed. When the leaves dry these can be removed, leaving the fruits on the naked stems. Each of these in turn enclose a round berry-like fruit, about the size and colour of a cherry. These are good to eat in pies and salads or make a delectable jam.

P. alkekengii. Bladder Cherry. Caucasus to China. Has creeping root-stocks and straight stems well clothed with oval-pointed leaves and small white flowers. The latter give place to large scarlet fruits (which are edible) surrounded with the characteristic papery calices.

1 ft. July. 2 ft. sq.

P. franchettii. Japan. The most commonly grown species, and rather more robust than *P. alkekengii*. The foliage is very large. There are several varieties of this worth noting; var. *nana* which is similar in all its parts but smaller (9 in.); var. *monstrosa*, in which the deep orange calices are curiously cut and fringed, each segment shaped like a canoe (18 in.); var. *gigantea*, an improvement on the type with large scarlet

lanterns (3 ft.), and var. *orbiculare* in which the calices are spread out
flat like large saucers. *1½ ft. July. 2 ft. sq.*

PHYSOSTEGIA (*Labiatae*): Obedient Plant, False Dragonhead.
From *physa* (Gk) ' bladder ', *stege* ' covering ', referring to the shape
of the calyx.

A small, North American genus of which *P. virginiana* makes a
useful plant for the garden since it produces its bright showy blossoms
late in the year. It is a hardy perennial of sturdy habit, with leafy
stems and spikes of tubular flowers, twisted and puckered at the open
end like a Nettle flower of a fine fuchsia-rose shade. The long,
tapering leaves are toothed. A curious characteristic of the plant is the
way in which the blossoms may be moved from side to side on the
flower spikes and then remain as placed. This feature has earned it
the cognomen of ' Obedient Plant '.

Physostegias will grow in sun or light shade in any good soil but
should not suffer from drought during the growing season. Var.
' Vivid ' (*Plate 28, p. 128*) is particularly bright and glowing and not
so tall as the type. Var. *alba* (*Plate XV, p. 256*) has white flowers,
and there is a dwarf form *nana*. Propagation by division in spring.
1½–4 ft. Aug.–Sept. 2 ft. sq.

PHYTOLACCA (*Phytolaccaceae*): Pokeberry. From *phyton* (Gk)
' plant ', *lacca* ' varnish '; the fruits are brilliantly coloured.

The genus includes two useful species for border decoration, both
for foliage and floral effect. The plants are not spectacular enough
for the best positions in the mixed border, but will do well in light
shade or even in a wild garden situation. A deep, moist soil suits
them best.

Phytolaccas have very large roots, often as thick round as a man's
thigh, with smooth, much-branched stems and oval oblong leaves.
The flowers, borne at the tops of the spikes, are clustered closely
together. They are pink and green. Later these give place to long
clusters of berries of a dark purple, almost black shade, which contain
a rich, wine-red juice. Both root and berries have medicinal properties,
but since the whole of the plant is poisonous care should be taken in
siting it where children play. Propagation by seed or division.

P. americana (syn. *P. decandra*): Pigeonberry, Red Ink Plant, Virginian
Pokeweed. (*Plate 3, p. 32.*) Florida. Has large, fleshy, poisonous roots
and purplish stems with oval leaves. The flowers are white and
succeeded by dark purple berries which have a rich crimson juice.
The whole plant emits a disagreeable odour.
3–5 ft. May–Oct. 3 ft. sq.

P. clavigera. Yunnan, China. More ornamental than *P. americana* as the
flowers are pink with a green ovary. Berries deep black.
3–5 ft. May–Oct. 3 ft. sq.

PLATYCODON *Campanulaceae*): Chinese Bellflower, Balloon Flower. From *platys* (Gk) ' broad ', *kodon* ' bell '; from the inflated buds.

A monotypic genus native to China and Japan. The species *P. grandiflorus* (*Plate 37, p. 160*) makes a fine border plant for any well-drained, sunny situation. Staking is sometimes necessary. It is a good front of the border subject (rarely exceeding 2 ft. in height), with branching stems carrying numbers of large, open, bell-shaped flowers in a pleasing blue shade. These are inflated like a balloon in the bud stage but later the five petal segments split widely open to reveal the rich colouring of the bloom. Var. *mariesii* is more dwarf (12–18 in.) but has larger flowers of deep rich blue 2 in. or so across. Var. *albus* (*Plate 37, p. 160*) is white, and *plenus* semi-double.

1–2 ft.   Aug.–Sept.   1 ft. sq.

PODOPHYLLUM (*Berberidaceae*): May Apple. From *podos* (Gk) ' foot ', *phyllon* ' leaf '; the foliage of *P. peltatum* bears some resemblance to a duck's foot.

Shade-loving plants suitable for any rich vegetable soil. The foliage is generally very handsome and grows above rather open, cup-shaped flowers. Because of this Podophyllums are not spectacular but they will always find a place in the gardens of those who appreciate fine foliage plants or have suitable situations. The leaves and roots are extremely poisonous although used in present-day medicines. Liver Pills in particular are concocted from the roots. In N. America children know *P. peltatum* with its many-lobed leaves, as the ' Lady's Parasol ' and the small yellowish fruits are eaten with relish. They are also used in preserves and beverages. Propagation by division, or seed sown in cold frames as soon as ripe.

P. emodi. Himalayan Mayflower. India. Has large leaves cut into wedge-shaped lobes. These are a fine bronze-red in spring. The large flowers, white or pale rose, are succeeded in August by brilliant red fruits as large as a hen's egg. These are edible but not of an agreeable flavour.

6–12 in.   Spring.   1½ ft. sq.

P. peltatum. American Mandrake, May Apple. E. United States. Has poisonous roots and leaves but the berries are harmless. Less handsome than *P. emodi* it has glossy, wrinkled leaves carried aloft on long, bare stems. The fine waxy-white flowers are succeeded by yellowish-green, apple-like fruits.   *1–1½ ft.   May.   1½ ft. sq.*

P. versipelle. Chinese May Apple. (*Plate 10, p. 49.*) China. Has fine, Horse Chestnut-like leaves on long, smooth stems overtopping bunches of deep crimson, cup-shaped flowers. Although dark coloured fruits are reputed to succeed the flowers they rarely come to any size in Britain.   *2 ft.   May–June.   1½ ft. sq.*

POLEMONIUM (*Polemoniaceae*): Jacob's Ladder, Greek Valerian.

From *polemus* (Gk) ' war '; Pliny records that two kings, both of whom claimed the merit of discovering the virtues of this plant, went to war to settle the issue.

Hardy perennials with attractive, pinnate leaves arranged in orderly fashion on very long, leafy stalks. This regular patterning has suggested the colloquial name of Jacob's Ladder. The flowers are carried on branching stems in bold groups, the individual florets being 5-lobed, bell-shaped and usually blue or white. The plants do well in any good garden soil, providing only that it never becomes water-logged or bone dry during the growing season. They can be propagated by seed, or lifted and divided in autumn.

P. carneum. West N. America. Has light coloured flowers which are almost flesh shade and smooth, much divided leaves.
1–2 ft. April–Aug. 1 ft. sq.

P. coeruleum. Greek Valerian. N. Hemisphere including Britain. Has panicles of blue or white flowers and smooth, pinnate leaves. Var. *himalayanum* has richer blue flowers than the type, individually almost $1\frac{1}{2}$ in. across. *1–3 ft. June–Aug. 1 ft. sq.*

P. confertum. Colorado. A pretty plant with dense terminal clusters of rich blue flowers and narrow leaflets on the pinnate foliage. It will grow in light shade but may need some protection in a cold wet winter.
5–8 in. June–Aug. 6 in. sq.

P. flavum. Arizona. From a creeping, woody rootstock produces delicate pinnate leaves and sprays of open, bell-shaped, yellow flowers. It is not reliably hardy. *2–3 ft. July–Aug. 2 ft. sq.*

P. hybridum ' Blue Pearl '. A new variety for the front of the border with sprays of dangling deep blue bells. Finely divided, decorative foliage.
10 in. April–Sept. 1 ft. sq.

P. lanatum. Dwarf Polemonium. N. America. Suitable for the front of the border, with short spikes of bright blue flowers. This has given rise to several varieties including *humile*, which is an improvement on the type. *1 ft. July–Aug. 1 ft. sq.*

P. pauciflorum. Mexico. Only hardy in a sheltered situation but interesting because the flowers are yellow. *1–1½ ft. June–July. 1 ft. sq.*

P. reptans. Creeping Polemonium. Eastern N. America. Has bunches of blue or white drooping flowers and pinnate leaves. It spreads readily.
6 in.–1½ ft. April–May. 1 ft. sq.

POLYGONATUM (*Liliaceae*): Solomon's Seal. From *poly* (Gk) ' many ', *gonu* ' joint '; referring to the knotted joints of the root. The latter when cut across transversely, shows scars which some consider resemble the device known as Solomon's Seal (an Arabic six-pointed star), but later herbalists believe the name indicates the plant's virtues. In olden days the roots were said to seal or consolidate wounds.

Solomon's Seals are useful for shady situations in any good garden soil. They make good cut flowers early in the season and associate particularly happily with Foxgloves, Ferns, Lily of the Valley and other woodland subjects. Propagation by division.

P. commutatum (syn. *P. giganteum*). United States. Resembles the common Solomon's Seal but is very much larger and more robust in all its parts. The flowers are white.   *2–6 ft. June. 1 ft. sq.*

P. multiflorum. Common Solomon's Seal, Lady's Seal, David's Harp. (*Plate IV, p. 208.*) Europe, including Britain. A well-known plant with arching stems carrying opposite, oval oblong leaves and clusters of small white bells. There are a number of horticultural forms including *flore pleno* with double flowers and *striatum* with variegated leaves. The plant forces well if it is potted in November and afterwards plunged in old peat or leaf-soil until growth starts. The pots can then be taken inside to their flowering quarters.   *2 ft. June. 1 ft. sq.*

P. roseum. Central Siberia. Although less showy than *P. multiflorum* is interesting to a collector since the flowers are soft rose pink.

2 ft. May. 1 ft. sq.

POLYGONUM (*Polygonaceae*): Knotweed, Fleece-flower. From *polys* (Gk) ' many ', *gonu* ' joint '; referring to the jointed stems.

A variable genus, many too weedy or invasive to be introduced to the garden. The height varies from a few inches to 16 or 18 ft. Amongst border perennials those listed below are worth growing and will succeed in any good garden soil in sun or light shade. Propagation by division in spring or in some cases from seed.

P. affine. Himalayan Fleece-flower. Nepal. Forms close tufts of oval leaves and numerous spikes of closely packed, small pink flowers. Towards late summer the foliage becomes bronzy-red.

'Darjeeling' Red, with vivid crimson spikes is a good varietal form.   *9–12 in. Aug.–Oct. 1 ft. sq.*

P. alpinum. Alpine Knotweed. (*Plate III, p. 208.*) European Alps. A beautiful plant with numerous loose sprays of white flowers, which are very useful for cutting. The leaves are oval lanceolate and a deep green colour. The plant likes a moist situation.

2–3 ft. June. 1½ ft. sq.

P. amplexicaule. Mountain Fleece-flower. (*Plate 34, p. 145.*) Himalayas. Has a woody rootstock and pointed oval heart-shaped leaves. The flowers are bright crimson, in single or double spikes 2–6 in. long.

Var. *album* has white flowers: var. *atrosanguineum* very deep red, and var. *oxyphyllum* white flowers, delightfully fragrant.

2–3 ft.   Aug.–Oct.   2 ft. sq.

P. *bistorta*. Snakeweed. Europe, including Britain. A rare native for a moist situation, with spikes of beautiful soft pink flowers and oblong-oval leaves. It must be kept in bounds. Var. *superbum* is an improved form.   *1½ ft.   June–Sept.   1½ ft. sq.*

P. *campanulatum*. Himalayan Knotweed. (*Plate XI, p. 240*.) Himalayas. Makes a compact bush with simple oval leaves which are whitish beneath, and drooping clusters of pale pink fragrant flowers. Var. *roseum* (*Plate 22, p. 97*) has deeper coloured flowers.

2–3 ft.   July–Oct.   2 ft. sq.

P. *campanulatum* var. *lichiangense*, a Chinese form. Has lanceolate leaves, green above and grey beneath with creamy-white sprays of flowers.

2–4 ft.   July–Sept.   2 ft. sq.

P. *cuspidatum*. Japan. A handsome but invasive perennial best grown in a small bed by itself. The stout, smooth, bamboo-like stems carry large, oval leaves and sprays of feathery white flowers. In autumn, instead of cutting the reddish stems down, allow them to remain for winter decoration. Var. *compactum* (see also P. *reynoutria*) is sometimes referred here and var. *variegatum* has white striped leaves.

6–8 ft.   July–Oct.   6 ft. sq.

P. *emodi*. Bhutan. Very like P. *affine* with spikes of red flowers.

1 ft.   Aug.–Sept.   1 ft. sq.

P. *reynoutria* Hort. (By some authorities now referred to P. *cuspidatum* var. *compactum*): Japanese Fleece-flower (*Plate 30, p. 129*). Japan. A stiffly erect plant with branching stems which are somewhat grooved and spotted with purple. The leaves have a leathery texture and wavy margins. The flowers are pink with deep red buds and carried in very upright spikes in the axils of the leaves. I have found this makes an excellent ground cover, either in full sun or partial shade.

1–2 ft.   Aug.–Sept.   1½ ft. sq.

P. *sachalinense*. Sachalin Islands. A vigorous plant needing restriction. For this reason it is best grown in a bed by itself or away from more delicate species. The erect, angular stems are reddish and carry large oval oblong leaves which may be a foot or more long and half as wide. The greenish-white flowers are carried in the leaf axils.

8–12 ft.   July–Oct.   6–10 ft.

P. *vacciniifolium*. Himalayas. A front of the border plant, mat forming and useful on account of its late flowers. These are bright rose-red, and freely produced in upright spikes.

6 in.–1 ft.   Sept.–Oct.   1 ft. sq.

P. virginianum. Japan, Himalaya, N. America. Greenish flowers in long slender sprays and narrow, green and chocolate leaves.

2–5 ft.   Aug.–Oct.   3 ft. sq.

POTENTILLA (*Rosaceae*): Cinquefoil. From *potens* (L) powerful; from its reputed medicinal properties. At one time Cinquefoil was believed to be a cure for ague, and it was favoured as a heraldic device, the five leaflets answering to the five senses of Man.

Potentilla flowers resemble Geums but the foliage is possibly more attractive. The leaves are finely cut into finger-like segments and often have silver undersides. The border kinds are excellent perennials, growing well in dryish soil, in full sun or partial shade. Some are suitable for edging purposes but massed effects give the best results. Propagation by division in spring or autumn, or seed sown outside about April.

P. argyrophylla. Kashmir. A yellow-flowered species with heart-shaped, palmate leaves. These and the stems are covered with fine silky hairs.

2–3 ft.   May–Sept.   1½ ft. sq.

P. atrosanguinea. Himalayan Cinquefoil. Himalayas. The type has dark reddish-purple flowers but is rarely grown as a garden plant. Instead, a whole host of garden hybrids have sprung from the species, in a wide range of shades varying from scarlet and yellow to rich orange. In the border these are most effective when planted in association with Statice, Gypsophila or similar subjects of paler shades which set off their blooms to better advantage. The following are good garden forms: ' Gibson's Scarlet ' (*Plate 21, p. 96*), blood-red, single, June-Aug.; ' California ', golden-yellow, semi-double. ' Monsieur Rouillard ', double, blood-red and yellow probably belongs here, also ' Wm. Rollisson ', semi-double, vermilion and yellow and ' Yellow Queen ', bright yellow.

2 ft.   June–Sept.   2 ft. sq.

P. concolor. China. Large, deep yellow flowers with orange blotches at the base of the petals and finely hairy pinnate leaves.

1 ft.   July–Sept.   1 ft. sq.

P. fragiformis. N.E. Asia. A low-growing, softly hairy species with strawberry-like leaves and sparse yellow flowers.

9 in.   July–Sept.   6 in. sq.

P. × hopwoodiana. A good garden plant derived from *P. nepalensis* and *P. recta* with red and pink flowers, outlined in white.

1½ ft.   Summer.   1 ft. sq.

P. nepalensis (syn. *P. formosa*). W. Himalayas. Flowers practically all summer with bright, cherry-red blossoms on branching stems. Var. ' Miss Willmott ' (*Plate 35, p. 160*) (*1 ft.*) is an improved form of the

type, with bright rosy-crimson blooms, and var. ' Roxana ' (1½ *ft.*)
has orange-scarlet blooms. *2 ft. July–Aug. 1½ ft. sq.*

P. recta. Europe. An excellent border plant with stout stems, freely
branched and rather leafy, and terminal sprays of large (1 in.) yellow
flowers. Var. *sulphurea* is pale yellow, and *warrenii* rich yellow.
1–2½ ft. June–July. 1½ ft. sq.

PRIMULA (*Primulaceae*): Primrose. From *primus* (L), first, referring
to the early flowers of the common Primrose.

A vast family of alpine, perennial or monocarpic species, the great
majority of the border kinds needing moist—and in some instances—
boggy soil. It is useless to attempt to grow any of the candelabra
types in dry, sunny situations. They need to feel the influence of water
rather than its presence, and in the absence of a waterside border may
be grown with great success in any moist, partially shaded situation,
provided that the ground contains plenty of humus.

On the other hand, Primulas of the *juliana* type, Polyanthus and
the many varieties of *P. auricula* are invaluable for early work, and do
very well in most gardens, even in towns.

Because of a diversity of conditions it has been thought desirable
to include cultural directions and methods of propagation under each
genus.

P. alpicola. Tibet. This species has long, green tooth-edged leaves and
bunches of white, yellow, purple or violet fragrant flowers, arranged
Cowslip fashion on slender stems. There are several garden varieties
including *alba*, white; *luna*, yellow and *violacea*, purple. These may
be propagated from seed, sown as soon as ripe in shallow pans. The
whites and yellows will come true but the purple and violet varieties
are less dependable. This species does best in light shade and a moist,
vegetable soil. *1½ ft. June–July. 1 ft. sq.*

P. anisodora. Yunnan. An aromatic plant with toothed, Primrose leaves
and brownish-purple flowers with green eyes. These are funnel shaped
and arranged in whorls on stout stems. Seed. *2 ft. June. 1 ft. sq.*

P. aurantiaca. Yunnan. Has basal-toothed, oblong leaves and whorls of
reddish-gold flowers. Seed. *1 ft. July. 1 ft. sq.*

P. auricula. Common Auricula. European Alps. A handsome species
with stout, mealy stems and powdery oval leaves. The flowers are
bell-shaped, fragrant, borne in umbels, and golden yellow. The
florist's varieties of Auriculas are usually covered by the name *P.* ×
pubescens. These come into two main groups, the first, self-coloured
varieties, and those which have a white or yellow eye surrounded by
another shade. In both cases the flowers are smooth and not powdery.
In the second group both flowers and stems are densely coated with a

whitish meal. These again are sub-divided into selfs, and those with green, grey or white margins to the flowers.

Auriculas grow readily in most soils but need protecting against excessive drought. Humus in the soil helps in this respect and coolness at the roots can be maintained by placing stones nearby or mulching with screened leaf-mould.

Every second or third year the plants should be lifted and divided, in spring or early autumn. They may also be raised from seed sown in January in pans in the greenhouse. When large enough to handle these should be pricked out in rich soil in a shady border. Auriculas make good edging plants and are often sweetly scented. Particularly good varieties are ' Dusty Miller ', yellow and ' Red Dusty Miller ', red. *6–9 in. April–May. 9 in. sq.*

P. beesiana. W. China. A vigorous growing plant with velvety purple flowers, borne candelabra fashion on tall straight stems. A good perennial and a fine ornamental subject for the waterside or any deep, rich, moist border, it has been crossed with *P. bulleyana* and produced seedlings showing a fine range of colour, including rose, salmon and orange-red. Propagation, by seed, sown after gathering in pans, which can be wintered in a cold frame or merely covered with glass. After germination in spring, the seedlings should be pricked off in boxes and about August put into their flowering quarters. They should flower the following spring. *2 ft. May–June. 1½ ft. sq.*

P. bulleyana. W. China. A fine species, robust and handsome if provided with rich moist soil. The flowers are produced in whorls on stout stems, and vary in colour from bud to bloom between orange-scarlet, buff, orange and apricot. This is a good species to naturalise. Let the seed drop around the parent plant and do not weed too assiduously. The seedlings will appear in their dozens and soon make a fine colony. *2½ ft. May–June. 1½ ft. sq.*

P. burmanica. Upper Burma, Yunnan. Another candelabra species, needing similar cultivation to *P. beesiana.* The flowers are reddish-purple with clearly defined yellow eyes. *2 ft. June. 1 ft. sq.*

P. chionantha. Yunnan. A pretty plant with fragrant, white, tubular flowers, arranged in whorls on stout stems. The oblanceolate leaves are powdery white beneath. Seed. *1–2½ ft. May. 1 ft. sq.*

P. cockburniana. W. China. Forms a tuft of wrinkled, Primrose-like leaves, with slender stems carrying sparse whorls of large, deep orange-red flowers. Treatment as for *P. beesiana.* *1 ft. June. 9 in. sq.*

P. denticulata. Himalayan Primrose. Himalayas. A group of these Primroses at the front of the border in early spring presents a most attractive picture, the lilac or mauve, almost round heads of blossom resembling glorified, Dandelion ' clocks '. Primrose-like foliage is arranged in spreading fashion round the flower stems, and thickly powdered with a mealy farina. This is a variable species, the flowers differing in size and colour, from lavender and mauve to deep purple or crimson. Plants come readily from seed but exceptionally fine colour varieties are best perpetuated by means of root cuttings taken in December or January.

P. denticulata is a good perennial, but may sometimes be damaged by spring frosts. For this reason a sheltered situation is advisable and deep, moist rich soil. In very dry summers water the plants occasionally. They prefer a light shaded situation, but we grow them with great success in full sun by building up the humus content of the soil. Var. *alba* has white flowers; *rubra*, magenta red; ' Bengal Rose ', fuchsia-purple; ' Purple Beauty ', dark violet-purple; ' Stormonth's Red ', vivid orchid purple; ' *cachemiriana* ', large purple flowers, a vigorous variety; ' Red Emperor ', bright rose.

1 ft. March–May. 1 ft. sq.

P. florindae. Himalayan Cowslip (*Plate 8, p. 48*). S.E. Tibet. One of the tallest species with large, showy umbels of drooping, fragrant, sulphur-yellow flowers. The leaves are oblong or broadly lanceolate. This is a moisture-loving species and one that is happiest in the vicinity of water. In a drier soil the habit is smaller. Propagation by seed.

3 ft. June–July. 1½ ft. sq.

P. helodoxa. Yunnan, Burma. Another moisture-loving species with tapering, toothed leaves and whorls of golden flowers on long stems. Cultivation as for *P. florindae*.   *2–3 ft. June–July. 1 ft. sq.*

P. japonica. Japanese Primrose. A handsome and variable species with whorled tiers of white, rose or purplish flowers. Although included here, it should be remembered that this is a plant for the moist woodland border, or wet ditch. It is not suitable for mixed herbaceous borders. Propagation by seed which may be allowed to drop alongside the parent plants. Var. ' Miller's Crimson ' is dark crimson-purple and ' Postford White ', white.   *1½ ft. May–June. 1 ft. sq.*

P. juliae. Caucasus. Dwarf, early-flowering Primrose with a carpeting habit. Although low-growing the brightness of the blooms renders them highly conspicuous in March and April. Birds sometimes attack the flowers. Grow them in rich, light loam, in cool spots. Propagation by division. There are many good garden forms derived from this species including:

alba, white.	Old Port, wine-purple.
Betty Green, rich crimson.	Our Pat, double, dark purple.
Dorothy, pale yellow.	Pam, rich garnet-red.
E. R. Janes, rich cherry-red.	Snow Cushion, white.
Jewel, crimson-purple.	Wanda, claret-purple.
Mrs. McGillivray, old rose.	

4 in. March–April. 1 ft. sq.

P. poissonii. China. Has smooth green leaves and straight stems carrying several superimposed whorls of bright magenta flowers. It needs a rich moist soil and is propagated from seed.

$1\frac{1}{2}$–2 ft. *June–July.* 1 ft. sq.

POLYANTHUS PRIMROSES. These well-known and loved flowers are of garden origin, and chiefly derived from *P. veris* (Cowslip), *P. elatior* (Oxlip) and *P. vulgaris* (Common Primrose). They have Primrose foliage and the bunched flower heads of the Cowslip and Oxlip. The colours are variable, from white, cream and yellow to pink, rose, crimson and a variety of blue shades. Nurseries specialising in Primulas offer seed of Polyanthus in different colour groups; an arrangement which enables the gardener to plan his colour schemes. The blues are usually the most expensive. A good and unusual named variety is ' Garryarde Guinevere ' with purplish foliage and pale pink flowers.

Polyanthus are extremely hardy and will grow in practically any soil. If this is very poor a little decomposed cow manure or rotted leaf-mould helps to retain moisture and also feeds the plants. They are easily raised from seed, which for preference should be sown directly after ripening; or named and selected varieties can be divided about July. Whilst Polyanthus make a very brave show in spring, it is not always advisable to leave them all summer in their flowering quarters, particularly if this is hot and dry. The roots need resting in a shady reserve bed, so should be lifted about July, pulled to pieces if the clumps are too large, and replanted, for preference in a north facing bed. During the autumn tidying they can be brought back to the border and re-established.

9–12 in. March–April. 1 ft. sq.

P. pulverulenta: Silverdust Primrose. W. China. A robust species and one of the best for garden decoration. The long narrow leaves are frequently a foot in length, with stout flower scapes carrying tier after tier of large, Cowslip-like blossoms. This is an excellent plant for growing in woodland conditions, in a shady border amongst Mecconopsis and ferns or in the bog garden. The plants should be massed for maximum effect. Seed.

P. pulverulenta is a true perennial and may be relied upon to produce side offsets. Separating and replanting these is therefore a ready means of propagation. In addition they may be raised from seed, which is freely produced and germinates well if sown whilst fresh. Some selection of the seedlings will be necessary to keep the stock good.

Over a period of years the late G. H. Dalrymple developed a very fine strain of *P. pulverulenta*, with pink flowers. This is known as the Bartley Strain and groups of these interplanted with the blue Himalayan Poppy creates—to my mind—a picture of fairy-like loveliness. There are also several named garden varieties of exceptional merit.

Plate VII: 1. Dwarf Gypsophila, *Gypsophila paniculata nana alba*. 2. Lanceleaf Plantain Lily, *Hosta lancifolia*. 3. Gardener's Garters, *Phalaris arundinacea picta*. 4. Plume Poppy, *Macleaya cordata*. 5. Gypsophila, *Gypsophila paniculata* 'Bristol Fairy'

Plate VIII: 1. Giant Daisy, *Chrysanthemum uliginosum*. 2. White Fleabane, *Erigero speciosus* 'White Quakeress'. 3. Pink, *Dianthus fragrans plena*. 4. Woolly Betony, *Stach lanata*. 5. Burning Bush, *Dictamnus albus*

Plate IX: 1. WHITE ORIENTAL POPPY, *Papaver orientale* 'Perry's White'. 2. GOAT'S RUE,
Galega officinalis. 3. LARGE WHITE LOBELIA, *Lobelia syphilitica alba.* 4. WILLOW GENTIAN,
Gentiana asclepiadea alba

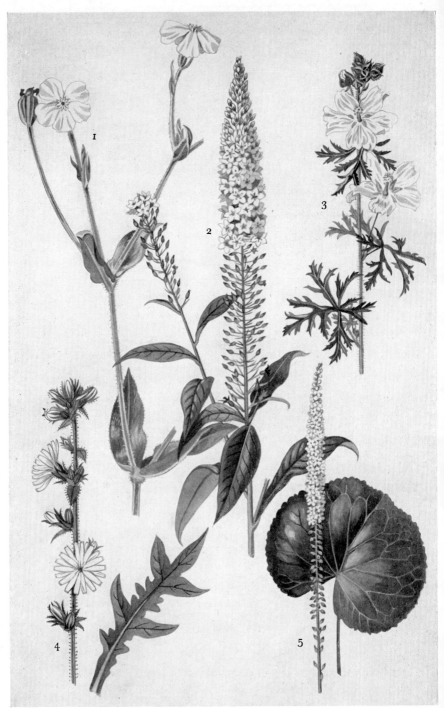

Plate X: 1. White Rose Campion, *Lychnis coronaria alba.* 2. Loosestrife, *Lysimachia clethroides.* 3. White Musk Mallow, *Malva moschata alba.* 4. White Chicory, *Cichorium intybus album.* 5. Galax, *Galax aphylla*

They include ' Lady Thursby ', which has bright rose-pink flowers with yellow eyes, ' Red Hugh ' and ' Aileen Aroon ', both bright red.
2½–3 ft. June–July. 1½ ft. sq.

P. rosea. N.W. Himalaya. Delightful early Primroses with brilliant rose flowers. This is a plant which must never become short of water and is particularly suited to the pondside. It will, however, grow well at the front of the border if planted in deep vegetable soil and kept watered during very dry weather. Var. ' Micia Visser-de-Geer ' is an improved form with rich magenta flowers. Division.
6 in. April. 1 ft. sq.

P. sieboldii. Siebold Primrose. (*Plate IV, p. 208.*) Although sometimes reputed to be doubtfully hardy, this has not been my experience with *P. sieboldii* in Enfield, for we have had several large clumps growing for years in a half-shaded situation, with little attention beyond an occasional top dressing of sifted leaf-mould. It is an attractive species with tufts of soft, heart-shaped leaves and slender spikes terminating in fragrant, often fringed, lilac, white or rosy-purple flowers. These are excellent for cutting. Given a sheltered, well-drained situation with some protection from summer suns and the worst of the winter weather, I see no reason why the plant should not be more widely grown. An old frame or light cloche would effectively guard the crown of the plant—its most vulnerable part—from winter's rains and frosts. Propagation by seed.
9 in. May–June. 9 in. sq.

P. sikkimensis. Burma, Sikkim, Tibet. A beautiful and distinct species with stout stems carrying numerous bell-shaped, fragrant pale yellow flowers. The foliage is neat and attractive, the leaves erect and oblong in shape. This is one of the best of the garden Primulas, but it must be grown in the damper parts of the border. Plenty of leaf-mould or peat in the soil helps to conserve moisture and it must also be protected from cutting winds and bright sunshine. In its natural habitat this Primrose is reputed to grow by the acre, usually in wet, boggy soil and at elevations from 12,000 to 17,000 ft. Propagation is most easily carried out by seed, sown directly after ripening. For maximum effects the plant is best treated as a biennial.
2–2½ ft. July–Aug. 1½ ft. sq.

P. vulgaris. Primrose. S. and W. Europe, including Britain. When dealing with shady borders our common Primrose must not be overlooked. It is a beautiful plant, particularly when allowed to naturalise itself in woodland surroundings, and has given rise to a number of garden varieties. Some of these have double flowers in shades of pink, cream, red, purple and even green, others are abnormal in the sense that the blooms sit one inside the other, e.g. ' Hose in Hose ', and there are varieties with variously coloured blossoms. Propagation by division or seed.
6 in. March–April. 9 in. sq.

PULMONARIA (*Boraginaceae*): Lungwort. From *pulmo* (L.) ' lung ';
the spotted foliage of *P. officinalis* was thought by the ancients to
resemble and even cure diseased lungs.

A useful genus for early work, the drooping clusters of bell-shaped
flowers appearing from March until May. The plants will grow in
practically any garden soil in sun or half-shade. Later in the season
the rather large, spotted leaves become somewhat overwhelming and
in their dying down processes, not only look ugly but are apt to flop
over and smother nearby plants. It is also apt to seed over freely and
throw stray plants in the border. For this reason the old flower heads
are best removed. Propagation by division in spring or autumn.

P. angustifolia. Cowslip Lungwort. (*Plate 1, p. 16.*) Europe, including
Britain. Has rough narrow leaves, which are unspotted, and bunches
of drooping, funnel-shaped flowers which open pink, then turn bright
blue. Var. *alba* has white flowers, and *azurea* sky blue. ' Munstead
blue ' is deep blue.   *1 ft.   March–April.   1½ ft. sq.*

P. officinalis. Jerusalem Cowslip, Lungwort, Spotted Dog. Europe,
including Britain. Has rosy flowers, turning to blue, and mottled
foliage. This is the most common species. *1 ft.   March–April.   1 ft. sq.*

P. rubra. S.E. Europe. Has bright green unspotted leaves and bright,
brick-red flowers. The latter are never blue or purple.
1½ ft.   March–April.   1 ft. sq.

P. saccharata. Bethlehem Sage. Europe. Has rough green leaves spotted
with white, and pink, funnel-shaped flowers which change to blue
with age.   *1½ ft.   March–April.   2 ft. sq.*

PULSATILLA (*Ranunculaceae*): Pasque Flower. Origin of name
uncertain.

A genus of beautiful, spring-flowering Anemone-like plants, which
are often included in that genus. They need well-drained soil, are
not averse to lime, and do best in a sheltered spot in which they miss
the worst of the March winds. When the Romans came to Britain
they brought *P. vulgaris* with them, and its British locations are still
in the vicinity of Roman ruins or earthworks. In olden days when
eggs were dyed at Easter time, the flowers were boiled with eggs to
turn the latter green. Propagation by seed.

P. alpina. European Alps. A beautiful plant, but it is short lived in
gardens, and should be frequently renewed from seed. The rootstock
is black, the flowers white, flushed with pink, violet or yellow outside
and fitted with golden stamens. Foliage, stems and bracts are densely
covered with silky hairs. The leaves appear after the flowers. Var.
burseriana is white with blue or reddish petal reverses, var. *sulphurea*
sulphur-yellow.   *1 ft.   May.   6 in. sq.*

P. halleri. Austria, Switzerland. Has large, open, purplish flowers which are succeeded by silky, shaggy seed heads.

1–2 ft. April. 6 in. sq.

P. patens. N. Europe. Pinnate, finely cut leaves and lilac or purple flowers with yellow stamens.

6 in.–1½ ft. March–May. 6 in. sq.

P. vulgaris. Europe including Britain (*Plate 1, p. 16*). A variable species with mauve, violet-purple or rarely white flowers and very prominent, golden stamens. The whole of the plant is covered in silky hairs. Var. 'Mrs. Van der Elst' is pink; var. 'Budapest' mauve and blue, like shot-silk taffeta.

6–9 in. April. 6 in. sq.

RANUNCULUS (*Ranunculaceae*): Buttercup. Name from *rana* (L) 'frog', which favours the same habitat.

A large family of world-wide distribution. A few make good border perennials, suitable for early work and a front row position. The genus will grow in practically any garden soil provided it does not dry out in summer, although a perennially moist situation gives best results. Propagation by division in spring, or seed.

R. aconitifolius. White Bachelor's Buttons. Europe. A mountain pasture plant, attractive for several weeks in early summer, with white flowers and shiny, palmately divided leaves. There is a double-flowered variety *flore pleno* (*Plate IV, p. 208*) which is usually known as Fair Maids of France. This has small, white, rosette-like blossoms.

6 in.–2 ft. May–June. 1 ft. sq.

R. acris. Bachelor's Buttons. Europe, including Britain. The double-flowered form of this species, *flore pleno* (*Plate 8, p. 48*), usually called Yellow Bachelor's Buttons, is a pretty plant for the front of the border, with button-like rosettes. It often flowers twice in a season. The leaves of this species are poisonous enough to cause a blistered skin if bruised and laid for any time on the body. *2 ft. June–August. 2 ft. sq.*

R. gramineus. S.W. Europe. A pretty plant with slender erect stems and narrow, grassy, bluish-grey leaves. The golden flowers are produced in great profusion during early summer, a characteristic which makes it useful for front of the border work. Var. *flore pleno* has double flowers. *1 ft. April–June. 1 ft. sq.*

RHEUM (*Polygonaceae*): Rhubarb. From *Rha*, old name of the River Volga, along whose banks the species grow wild.

Herbaceous plants of great vigour and fine foliage, but not suitable for small borders as they grow too rapidly. However, in a large garden an isolated specimen on a lawn, or in the vicinity of water, can become quite magnificent and create bold effects. The plants like deep rich soil and full sunshine or light shade. Propagation by seed, or by division in early spring.

R. alexandrae. China, Tibet. A fine plant, not as easy to cultivate as some species, with dark, yellowish-green, flopping leaves and a flower stem which is chiefly remarkable for the large reflexed, straw coloured bracts which roof the flowers. *3–4 ft. June–July. 4 ft. sq.*

R. emodi. Himalayas. A fine plant for grouping, with bronze-green, wrinkled leaves with large red veins, and purple plumes of flowers. *6–10 ft. June–July. 6 ft. sq.*

R. officinale. Tibet. A stately species with palmately lobed leaves 1–3 ft. across and giant spikes of greenish-white flowers. Var. *dissectum* has deeply cut leaves. *8–10 ft. June–July. 6 ft. sq.*

R. palmatum. Sorrel Rhubarb. China, Tibet. Is slower growing than most and has gigantic, deeply cut, 5-lobed leaves and tall panicles of creamy flowers. Var. *tanguticum* has more elongated leaves which are not so deeply lobed, whilst var. *atrosanguinea* has showy, dark red flowers. *5 ft. June–July. 6 ft. sq.*

RODGERSIA (*Saxifragaceae*): Bronze-leaf. Named after Admiral J. Rodgers of the United States Navy, who commanded an expedition in the 19th century during which *R. podophylla* was found.

Superb ornamental foliage plants from China and Japan for moist garden borders. They are perfectly hardy and should be given a sunny situation away from strong winds. Propagation by seed or division of the rhizomes in spring.

R. aesculifolia. China. Has glossy, bronze, crinkled foliage like that of a huge Horse-chestnut, and plumy spires of pinkish-white, fragrant flowers. It is a very handsome species and particularly adapted to the environs of the water garden.

3 ft. July. 2½ ft. sq.

R. pinnata. Feathered Bronze-leaf. China. A robust species with emerald green, sometimes bronze-tinged leaves, more finely divided than *R. aesculifolia*. The flowers are borne in large, much-branched panicles, and are of a rosy-pink shade which contrasts well with the foliage. Var. *alba* has creamy-white flowers, var. *elegans* (*Plate 18, p. 81*), rose-pink, and *rubra* deeper red. *3–4 ft. July. 2½ ft. sq.*

R. podophylla. (*Plate XIII, p. 240.*) Japan. Has heavily netted leaves divided into 5 deeply toothed lobes, and handsome sprays of yellowish-white flowers which resemble a Goat's Beard (*Aruncus*).

3–4 ft. June–July. 2½ ft. sq.

R. tabularis. China. A strange-looking plant with leaves like round trays standing on thick bristly stems. The flowers are creamy-white and carried well above the leaves. This is a handsome plant to grow in association with others of fine foliage. *3 ft. July–Aug. 2½ ft. sq.*

ROMNEYA (*Papaveraceae*): California Tree Poppy, Canyon Poppy. Named after Rev. T. Romney Robinson, an Irish astronomer who discovered the plant in about 1845.

A genus of two species, of magnificent herbaceous perennials. When happily established these produce fine blue-grey leaves, somewhat leathery in texture and huge white, Poppy-like flowers, 4–5 in. across. These have a prominent central boss of golden stamens which accentuates the whiteness of the petals. A good deep soil and a sunny situation suits the plants but they are impatient of disturbance and are difficult to establish. Although it is sometimes possible to propagate by means of the underground stems, usually the act of transplanting or the slightest damage to even one of the roots causes the plant to die. For this reason it is usually more expedient to grow the plant from seed in small pots, transplanting these without breaking the soil ball, into a prepared site. In winter the plants should be protected by throwing ashes or other covering over the roots. At all times it pays to give the plants the warmest and best drained position possible. It is one of our most beautiful perennials and worth a little trouble.

R. coulteri. Matilija Poppy. California. Has shapely sea-green or grey foliage and large, fragrant, single heads of white and gold flowers.
4–6 ft. July–Sept. 6 ft. sq.

R. trichocalyx. Tree Poppy. S.W. California. Very similar to *R. coulteri* but somewhat more slender; free flowering, but has a disagreeable odour. A fine distinct plant which when happily established can be left in the same position for years. *3 ft. July–Sept. 6 ft. sq.*

ROSCOEA (*Zingiberaceae*). Named after Wm. Roscoe, founder of the Liverpool Botanic Society in 1802.

A small genus of Asiatic perennials with clusters of fleshy roots. The flowers are extremely attractive and carried in terminal spikes at the ends of leafy stems. Individual blooms are 1½ to 2½ in. long, funnel-shaped, widening at the throat into unequally shaped flower segments; the lower lip or petal being very large (an inch or more), and hanging with frilly edges. The upper segments arch to form a kind of helmet. The plants grow best in well-drained, rich soil and make good front of the border subjects, or they can be used in pockets in the rock garden, or at the fringe of woodland. The late Lady Brocket at Fanhams Hall, Ware had a bed entirely devoted to *R. cautleoides* which was very striking. Propagation by division. The tubers should be planted 4–5 in. deep.

R. cautleoides. China. Has stemless, Lily of the Valley-like leaves surrounding several slender stems each of which supports a large, clear yellow orchid-like flower. Var. *Beesii* has paler flowers. *1 ft. June–Aug. 1 ft. sq.*

R. humeana. W. China. Smaller growing than *R. cautleoides*, with deep violet-purple blossoms. These are very spectacular.
8–12 in. June–July. 1 ft. sq.

R. purpurea. China. Similar to *R. cauletoides* but the flowers are a lighter purple shade. *1 ft. June–July. 1 ft. sq.*

RUDBECKIA (*Compositae*): Coneflower. Name commemorates Olaf Rudbeck and his son, 18th-century Professors of botany at Uppsala. A race of dependable autumn perennials, useful for cutting and indispensable for mid-season display. Closely related to Echinacea, they are characterised by a prominent central cone to the flowers. Rudbeckias grow in most soils and do particularly well on heavy land. On light soils add plenty of organic material at planting time. The plants should be set in bold groups, associated with such subjects as Michaelmas Daisies, Sidalceas or Lythrums. Propagation by division, or cuttings taken in spring.

R. hybrida. This includes a number of named varieties of uncertain origin, all useful for border work.

Autumn Sun, for the back of the border, with deep yellow, curved back flowers like *R. nitida*. *5–6 ft. Aug.–Oct. 3 ft. sq.*
deamii, fine deep yellow flowers with dark centres. Resembles *R. speciosa*. *2½–3½ ft. Aug.–Sept. 2 ft. sq.*
Golden Ball, nearly double, deep yellow, branching habit. *6 ft. Aug.–Sept. 3 ft. sq.*
Goldquelle, deep yellow, semi-double. *3 ft. Sept.–Nov. 2 ft. sq.*

R. laciniata. Canada. Has large, golden-yellow flowers with conical green discs, the leaves unevenly divided into deeply cut segments. This is the tallest of the Rudbeckias and will live for years in the same spot without undue spread or exhausting the ground. There are several garden forms of which *angustifolia* has narrower leaves and ' Golden Glow ' (*Plate 16, p. 80*) is a full double form.
5–8 ft. Aug.–Sept. 3 ft. sq.

R. nitida. N. America. Is characterised by rounded lance-shaped leaves, and large yellow flowers, which have the petals hanging back in the manner of Cyclamen so that the green central cone protrudes like a thimble from the middle of each bloom. Var. ' Herbstsonne ' (*Plate 32, p. 144*) is a better plant and usually grown in preference to the type.
6 ft. Aug.–Oct. 3 ft. sq.

R. speciosa (syn. *R. newmanii*): Black-eyed Susan. (*Plate 32, p. 144.*) N. America. A useful plant for the front of the border with striking golden-yellow flowers and high central discs of blackish-purple. The leaves are narrow and rather rough to handle. This makes an excellent cut flower. ' Sullivant's Variety ' (also known as ' Goldsturm ') is an improved form with much larger flowers. *2 ft. July–Oct. 2½ ft. sq.*

R. subtomentosa: Sweet Coneflower. N. America. Has soft, greyish foliage and rich golden flowers with a dark purple centre.
4 ft. July–Sept. 2½ ft. sq.

SALVIA (*Labiatae*): Sage. From *salveo* (L) ' to heal ', from its reputed medicinal properties.

Few plants are more striking for the late summer border than these, with their distinct and showy spikes of flowers. The Common Sage belongs here but several other species have aromatic foliage. As a general rule the plants should be given well-drained soil and a full sunny situation. They are dependable in a dry summer, but give a better account of themselves if the ground around is mulched. A few of those recommended for the border are monocarpic, usually flowering and dying after the second season. They are, however, easily raised from seed and so attractive that, having once grown them, few gardeners will mind this little extra trouble. Other species are propagated by division in spring or autumn, or soft cuttings.

S. argentea. Silver Sage. Mediterranean Area. A silvery-leaved, shaggy plant with pinkish-white flowers. Biennial. *2–3 ft. Sept. 1½ ft. sq.*

S. azurea. Azure Sage. N. America. A beautiful perennial with dense spikes of pale blue, Nettle-like flowers and oblong, toothed leaves. It is of vigorous constitution, with strong, straight flower stems. Several garden varieties are worth noting, especially var. *grandiflora* (syn. S. *pitcheri*) with downy leaves and dense spikes and var. *angustifolia*, with narrower leaves. *3–5 ft. Aug.–Sept. 3 ft. sq.*

S. beckeri. Caucasus. Blue and violet flowers in well-spaced whorls on short spikes, and oval leaves which are hairy beneath. *1½ ft. Aug.–Sept. 1 ft. sq.*

S. farinacea. Mealycup Sage. (*Plate 26, p. 113.*) Texas. Has many slender stems with narrowly oval, aromatic leaves and long slender sprays of deep violet-blue, Lavender-like flowers. It is attractive when grouped and the blooms are good for cutting. Var. *alba* has white flowers, and var. ' Blue Bedder ' is a deeper blue than the type. *3 ft. July–Aug. 2 ft. sq.*

S. glutinosa. Jupiter's Distaff. Europe. Central Asia. A sticky species with pointed, oval foliage and whorls of pale yellow flowers on slender stems. *2–3 ft. July. 1½ ft. sq.*

S. haematodes. Greece. A handsome plant which may be grown with advantage as a single specimen amongst lower-growing perennials. The leaves are large, heart-shaped, somewhat corrugated and more or less hairy all over; the bluish-violet, funnel-shaped flowers are borne on loose, spreading panicles. It is a poor perennial and best treated as biennial. *3 ft. June–Sept. 2½ ft. sq.*

S. involucrata. Roseleaf Sage. Mexico. Only hardy in favoured districts, this fine plant may be reproduced from cuttings and over-wintered in the greenhouse. The large, rosy-crimson flowers group together to form terminal spikes and the oval heart-shaped leaves are smooth and toothed. Var. *bethellii* has brighter flowers, which when in bud are surrounded by two large coloured bracts. Var. *deschampsiana*, raised in France, is bright rose with red bracts and may grow to more than 3 ft. *2–3 ft. Aug. 2 ft. sq.*

S. jurisicii. Serbia. A low-growing species with violet-blue flowers and curious foliage. The lower leaves are rounded with long stems and the upper cut into fine strips and on short stalks.

16 in. June. 1 ft. sq.

S. nutans. Nodding Sage. (*Plate 10, p. 49.*) E. Europe. A handsome species with spikes of violet-blue, drooping flowers, on somewhat hairy stems, and toothed and wrinkled, oval-oblong leaves.

2–3 ft. July. 1½ ft. sq.

S. patens. Gentian Sage. Mexico. One of the most beautiful plants in cultivation, but unfortunately not very hardy. The tuberous roots are, however, easily wintered like Dahlias, in a frost-proof frame or shed, from which they can be planted out again in the garden at the end of May.

The flowers are an intense deep blue, borne on sparse whorls and the foliage oval-oblong. Var. ' Cambridge Blue ' has paler flowers and var. *alba*, white. *1½–2 ft. Aug.–Sept. 1½ ft. sq.*

S. pratensis. Meadow Sage. Europe, including Britain. Has oblong, heart-shaped basal leaves and narrow pointed, stem leaves. These are wrinkled. The large purple flowers grow in whorls. The following varieties are sometimes obtainable: var. *alba*, white, *tenorii*, deep blue, *rosea*, rose-purple, *variegata*, blue and white.

2 ft. June–Aug. 1½ ft. sq.

S. przewalskii. China. A hardy plant with tall hairy stems, heart-shaped, toothed leaves and branching spikes of violet flowers.

3–4 ft. June. 2–3 ft. sq.

S. sclarea. Clary. (*Plate 24, p. 112.*) Europe. A biennial with hairy stems, large heart-shaped leaves and spreading panicles of bluish-white flowers. One specimen plant is usually enough in a border. Var. *turkestanica* has white flowers tinged with pink. Unfortunately both plants have an unpleasant smell when bruised.

3–3½ ft. Aug. 2 ft. sq.

S. × superba (syn. *S. virgata nemorosa*). (*Plate 17, p. 80.*) Origin unknown. One of the best Salvias for border work, perfectly hardy and in flower for weeks. The leaves are sage green and aromatic, the flowers violet with reddish violet calices, which persist after the petals have dropped. Var. *lubecca* (*compacta*) is similar but only grows 18 in. high. *2–2½ ft. July–Aug. 2 ft. sq.*

S. sylvestris. S. Europe. Long, narrow, somewhat branched racemes of purplish-blue flowers and grey-green oblong leaves, rounded at their base. Var. *alba* has white flowers. *2–3 ft. Aug. 1½ ft. sq.*

S. uliginosa. Bog Sage. (*Plate 17, p. 80.*) Eastern N. America. A tall and graceful plant with oblong, deeply toothed leaves and rich blue flowers. These often persist until the autumn frosts. In some localities this species is not always hardy and in this case the roots should be overwintered in a cold frame. *4–5 ft. Aug.–Oct. 2½ ft. sq.*

S. virgata. Oriental Sage. E. Mediterranean region. A much-branched species, with Nettle-shaped, toothed leaves and branching spikes of light blue, funnel-shaped flowers. These are borne in whorls. The foliage is pleasantly aromatic. *2 ft. July–Aug. 2 ft. sq.*

SANGUISORBA (*Rosaceae*): Burnet. From *sanguis* (L) ' blood ', *sorbere* ' stopping '; some of the species are reputed to have styptic qualities.

An attractive genus too rarely seen in gardens. At one time known as Poteriums, the plants have handsome, pinnate leaves and spikes of bottle-brush-like flowers. The border species grow in any good garden soil and should be afforded a front to mid-row position. They flower on and off for weeks at a time. Propagation by division or seed.

S. canadensis (syn. *Poterium canadense*): American Burnet. (*Plate XI, p. 240.*) Eastern N. America. A good border plant with deeply cut, grey-green foliage and rounded spikes of whitish flowers. These appear at the top of every developing shoot. The young leaves can be used as salad, and for flavouring beverages. They have the odour of freshly sliced cucumber. *3–4 ft. Summer. 2½ ft. sq.*

S. obtusa (syn. *Poterium obtusum*): Japanese Burnet. (*Plate 22, p. 97.*) Japan. A vigorous species producing handsome pinnate leaves which are pale green above, and somewhat glaucous beneath. The flowers in July, producing many arching branches of rosy crimson blossoms. These continue to look attractive until the end of summer. A cool soil suits this species better than a hot dry one. Var. *alba* has white flowers. *3–4 ft. Summer. 2½ ft. sq.*

SAPONARIA (*Caryophyllaceae*). From *sapo* (L) 'soap '; the leaves of some species lather like soap and have been used for cleaning purposes.

Easily grown plants for well-drained soils and sunny situations. Some are allergic to lime and this should never be given deliberately to any of the species. Propagation by seed or cuttings.

S. officinalis. Bouncing Bet, Soapwort. Europe, including Britain. A plant with smooth, opposite, small-pointed leaves and panicles of several large, rosy-pink flowers. Better plants are any of the double forms, *albo-plena*, white, *roseo-plena* pink or *rubro-plena* red. All these must be watched as the roots spread under the ground.

1–3 ft. Aug.–Sept. 1½ ft. sq.

SAXIFRAGA (*Saxifragaceae*). From *saxum* (L) 'rock', *frango* 'to break'; the persistent and penetrative nature of the roots are said to break rocks.

A very large family, mostly of alpine character. The species described, however, have for many years been grown for edging purposes in gardens and become particularly valuable in shady situations. They will grow in practically any soil and may be increased by division.

S. umbrosa. London Pride, St. Patrick's Cabbage. Europe, including Britain. It is also found plentifully on mountain ranges on the west coast of Ireland.

A well-known plant, with rounded leaves, which have rough and sometimes white blotched surfaces, tapering at the base into slender stems. The flowers are pinkish-white with delicate red spots on the petals. There are a number of garden varieties including *variegata*, with white variegations on the foliage, and *variegata aurea* with yellow spots. The latter forms should be grown in full sun.

$1-1\frac{1}{2}$ *ft. May–July. 1 ft. sq.*

S. hybrida. Although most of the genus are more suited to the rock garden than the border, there are several garden hybrids of uncertain origin which may be used for frontal work. One of the best of these is 'James Bremner' (*Plate I, p. 192*), a large, white-flowered mossy Saxifrage which grows about 9 in. high and flowers in early Summer. It is very readily propagated by cuttings.

SCABIOSA (*Dipsaceae*): Scabious, Pincushion Flower. From *scabies* (L), 'itch', referring to the plant's medicinal uses.

One of the most popular garden perennials, the cut flowers being particular favourites for indoor decoration. It is difficult to understand why they have such popular appeal, for the colour range is not extensive, the blooms are scentless and not particularly long lasting, and the plant does not thrive on all types of soil. Yet, once established, the roots may be left undisturbed for years, and from a garden point of view, the long-flowering habit is a decided merit in the mixed border.

Being a natural denizen of the chalklands, Scabious is at home in calcareous soils and appreciates a little lime when grown under acid conditions. In cold, heavy clays it sometimes fails entirely, struggling along for a month or two and then disappearing. Slugs and snails too are usually prevalent on wet soils and must be kept from the plants. Grow the roots in full sun and transplant in spring only. If lime is added, use hydrated lime or ground chalk or limestone.

Propagation is effected by spring division, or cuttings can be taken with a basal heel of the old plant. These should be removed when the growths are quite small and rooted in sandy loam in a frame or greenhouse. During the growing season the plants must never become short of moisture.

S. amoena. Russia. A slender plant with small, rosy-mauve flowers.

2–3 ft. June–July. 1 ft. sq.

S. caucasica. Caucasus. This plant, which has light lavender-blue, pincushion flowers was first introduced to Britain in 1803. It is nevertheless still widely grown, although nowadays discerning gardeners prefer named varieties because of the fine colours and larger blooms.

Most of the credit for the selection and raising of the named sorts must go to J. C. House of Bristol, who over 30 years ago raised the best white form to date, ' Mrs. Isaac House '. Other good varieties are:

alba (Plate 25, p. 112), white.

Canon Andrews, rich purple.

Clive Greaves *(Plate 25, p. 112)*, rich mauve.

Constancy, powdered violet-blue.

Coronation, lilac-blue.

Floral Queen, large flowers, methyl violet.

Goldingensis, taller than the type, light blue.

Imperial Purple, 2½ to 3 inch flowers, deep lavender-mauve with frilled edges.

Miss Willmott, cream.

Moerheim Blue and Malcolm both a light navy blue.

Penhill Blue, soft blue with mauve shading.

Sally, French grey with pinkish stamens.

Silver King, silvery-white.

Souter's Violet, rich violet-blue.

Vincent, cobalt blue.

Wanda, rich blue.

1½–2 ft. June–Sept. 1½ ft. sq.

S. graminifolia. S. Europe. For the front of the border. This species has silvery, uncut leaves practically flat to the ground and pale mauve, pincushion flower heads. *9 in. July. 1 ft. sq.*

SCHIZOSTYLIS *(Iridaceae)*: Kaffir Lily. From *schizo* (Gk) ' cut ', *stylos* ' style '; the style is divided.

A fleshy rooted plant with Iris-like leaves and sprays of flowers individually shaped somewhat like a Crocus. It grows well in practically any soil, even in a boggy situation. I remember seeing it in the 1930's in the late Viscountess Byng's garden at Thorpe le Soken, growing with the rootstock submerged under 2–3 in. of water. Full sun is desirable; propagation by division in spring.

S. coccinea. Crimson Flag, Kaffir Lily. *(Plate 28, p. 128.)* S. Africa. Has bright crimson flowers, which appear late in the autumn on a short studded spike. In exposed places the roots should be protected in winter. For effective display, group 9 to 12 plants together, setting these about 9 in. apart. Var. ' Mrs. Heggarty ' is an attractive pink shade, whilst ' Viscountess Byng ' is another good pink form.

1½ ft. Oct.–Nov. 9 in. sq.

SEDUM (*Crassulaceae*): Stonecrop. From *sedo* (L) ' to sit ', referring to the manner of attachment of many species on walls, etc.

A large genus of diverse habit and requirements. The following make good border plants and may be grown in practically any soil.

S. maximum. Purple-leaved Ice Plant. Europe. A variable species with large fleshy leaves, carrot-like roots and greenish-white flowers. The species is less desirable than certain of its varieties, such as var. *atropurpureum* (*Plate 30, p. 129*), which has vivid purple stems and leaves, or var. *versicolor*, in which the leaves are variegated with silver and the stems pink. These are good plants for poor, sandy soil.

1–2 ft. Sept.–Oct. 1½ ft. sq.

S. sieboldii. Japan. A fine plant with nearly round, fleshy leaves which are blue-green in summer but turn rosy in autumn. The flowers are pink and borne in much branched, densely packed inflorescences.

1 ft. Sept.–Oct. 1 ft. sq.

S. spectabile. Japan. The most commonly grown species. A fine erect plant, with broad, glaucous leaves which are slightly toothed. The flowers are extremely showy being bunched together in large, plate-like inflorescences. They are bright pink. There are various garden forms such as var. *atropurpureum* with darker flowers; ' Brilliant ', brighter rose; *album* with white flowers. ' Carmen ', very bright carmine (Aug.–Sept.); ' Meteor ', glowing red.

1–1½ ft. Sept.–Oct. 1½ ft. sq.

SENECIO (*Compositae*): Groundsel, Ragwort. From *senex* (L) ' old man ', from the white seed down.

This genus is thought to be the largest in the vegetable Kingdom and comprises amongst others, many weedy plants which on no account should be introduced to the garden. Even the species described should be watched and divided every 2 or 3 years. They are among the most easily grown plants, flourishing in any soil and practically any situation. The silvery, variegated kinds do best in dry situations, whilst the larger leaved types are more suited to moister situations, as in heavy soil or the vicinity of the water garden. Propagation by seeds, soft cuttings, division or root cuttings. See also *Ligularia* to which this family is closely related.

S. campestris. Europe. Shaggy habit with leaves woolly beneath, the stem ones smaller and more pointed than the basal. Loose sprays of 1 to 6 yellow Daisy flowers. Var. *maritima* larger flowers.

6 in.–1 ft. June–July. 1 ft. sq.

S. cineraria. Silver Cineraria. S. Europe, naturalised in Britain. Although this plant sometimes persists in winter in very mild seasons, it is nevertheless more suited to the herbaceous border than the shrubbery and is particularly valuable by reason of the dense white woolly covering which practically covers the whole plant. This gives it a silvery appearance making it a perfect foil for brightly coloured plants like *Lobelia fulgens* and Salvias. The flowers are secondary to the foliage but of a typically Daisy shape and soft yellow.

1–2 ft. July–Sept. 1½ ft. sq.

S. cremeiflorus. Chile, Argentine. A vigorous perennial with large, almost round leaves, wavy at the edges, and terminal clusters of pale yellow flowers. *1–1½ ft. June. 2 ft. sq.*

S. doria. S. Europe. An old garden plant, flowers yellow in compact clusters; leaves smooth, oval-oblong, toothed.

4 ft. July–Sept. 2 ft. sq.

S. doronicum. Central Europe. One of the showiest members of the genus with large, bright yellow flowers and downy oval oblong leaves.

2–3 ft. Summer. 2 ft. sq.

S. faberi. W. China. Smooth, hollow, angular stems, pinnately cut leaves and flowers in compact heads 8 in. across, deep yellow.

4–5 ft. July–Sept. 3 ft. sq.

S. macrophyllus. Caucasus. Long oval leaves and terminal heads of yellow flowers. *3–4 ft. July–Sept. 3½ ft. sq.*

S. palmatus. Siberia. Free-flowering, yellow Daisy blooms, branched habit. *3–4 ft. July–Aug. 2 ft. sq.*

S. pulcher. Buenos Aires. A handsome plant which needs to be protected in exposed situations as the foliage is often damaged in bad weather. It has rosy-purple flowers 2–3 in. across, in late autumn, and long, lobed, silvery leaves. *1–2 ft. Aug.–Oct. 2 ft. sq.*

S. smithii. Falkland Islands. Discovered by Captain Cook, this has smooth, large, rather coarse leaves and close terminal panicles of small white flowers. It is perfectly hardy and does well in a moist situation. *2–4 ft. June. 2 ft. sq.*

S. tanguticus. Chinese Groundsel. China. A very handsome plant with upright spiry stems and attractive, very deeply cut leaves. The flowers are borne in pyramidal panicles. Individually these are small but the whole effect is feathery and most attractive. A good plant for the back of the border or the environs of water or woodland.

3–4 ft. Sept. 3½ ft. sq.

SIDALCEA (*Malvaceae*): Prairie Mallow, Greek Mallow. From *sida* (Gk) ' mallow ', *alcea* ' healing '; presumably because the genus shares some of the medicinal virtues of Mallow.

Graceful and hardy herbaceous perennials with a long-flowering habit. The flowers, which are borne in sprays, resemble small Hollyhocks whilst the foliage is palmately divided, similar to that of a

Buttercup. Sidalceas will grow in practically any good garden soil and are most suitable for a midway position in the border. Once established they should be left in the same position, to make strong plants and afford the maximum display. In exposed situations they are less hardy, tending to die out in very hard winters. They are good plants for cutting. Propagation by seed or division in spring or autumn. The seeds should be sown as soon as ripe, the seedlings being wintered in a cold frame and planted out in spring.

S. candida. White Prairie Mallow. (*Plate XII, p. 240.*) N.W. America. Has pretty white flowers about one inch across, loosely arranged on tall, slender stems, and basal leaves which are almost heart-shaped and divided into 5 or 7 lobes. Var. ' Rosy Gem ' has pink flowers.

$3\frac{1}{2}$ *ft. June–Aug. 2 ft. sq.*

S. malvaeflora, Prairie Mallow, Checkerbloom. California. Has deep rosy-purple flowers and is of good habit with stout erect growth. It has given rise to a number of varieties including:

atropurpurea, dark purple, *2 ft.*
Brilliant, rich carmine, $3\frac{1}{2}$ *ft.*
Countess, crimson rose, *3 ft.*
Crimson Beauty, soft rosy-crimson, *3 ft.*
Crimson King, soft rosy-crimson, *3 ft.*
Croftway Red, very early-flowering, clear, rich deep red, *3 ft.*
Dainty, pink with white eyes, *3 ft.*
Duchess, large deep rose, bushy habit, *3 ft.*
Elsie Heugh, satiny-pink, $3\frac{1}{2}$ *ft.*
Interlaken, intense silver-pink, *4 ft.*
Listeri, pink fringed at the edges, very free with good spikes, $3\frac{1}{2}$ *ft.*
Loveliness, shell-pink, $2\frac{1}{2}$ *ft.*
Monarch, crinkly, deep rose flowers, $3\frac{1}{2}$ *ft.*

Mr. Lindbergh, light Peony purple, *3 ft.*
Mrs. Galloway, clear pink, *3 ft.*
Nimmerdor, rosy-crimson, *3 ft.*
Pompadour, double scarlet, $2\frac{1}{2}$ *ft.*
Prince, warm rosy red, compact, *3 ft.*
Progress, very large pink, *3 ft.*
Rev. Page Roberts, light rosy-pink, *3 ft.*
Rose Queen (*Plate 21, p. 96*), rosy-pink, $2\frac{1}{2}$ *ft.*
Scarlet Beauty, deep rose-pink, $2\frac{1}{2}$ *ft.*
Sussex Beauty, clear soft satiny-pink, $3\frac{1}{2}$ *ft.*
Sussex Queen (*Plate 34, p. 145*), a very good form with satin-pink flowers, $3\frac{1}{2}$ *ft.*
Wensleydale, light rosy-red, *4 ft.*
William Smith, warm salmon-pink, *3 ft.*

Height variable. July–Aug. 2 ft. sq.

S. spicata. W.N. America. Straight stems with good spikes of purplish flowers.

1–3 ft. June–Aug. 1 ft. sq.

SILPHIUM (*Compositae*): Compass Plant, Resinweed. Old Greek name used by Hippocrates for a plant which produced resin.

A genus of tall perennials with resinous sap, all from N. America. The species are yellow, somewhat like Sunflowers, many with a strong turpentine odour. Planted in bold groups they make vivid splashes of colour in autumn at the back of the border, and have the merit of thriving and flowering in the worst of clay soils. Propagation by division or seed.

S. albiflorum. Texas. Has creamy-white flowers 4 in. across, and oval, leathery, much divided leaves. The whole plant is rough and prickly. *2–4 ft. July–Aug. 2 ft. sq.*

S. laciniatum. Compass Plant, Polar Plant, Pilotweed. United States. A vigorous plant with fine yellow flowers on drooping heads, which always face the east. In the young stage the leaves always turn to the north and south, a characteristic which has earned the plant its name of Compass Plant. *3–5 ft. July–Aug. 2 ft. sq.*

S. perfoliatum. Cup Plant. *(Plate 30, p. 129.)* Eastern N. America. Broad yellowish leaves and terminal heads of yellow flowers. *4–6 ft. July. 2 ft. sq.*

S. terebinthinaceum. Prairie Dock. Canada. Large, heart-shaped, much toothed leaves and numerous terminal sprays of yellow flowers. It has a strong turpentine odour. *4–8 ft. July–Sept. 3 ft. sq.*

SISYRINCHIUM (*Iridaceae*): Satin Flower, Blue-eyed Grass. From *sis* (Gk) ' pig ', *rynchos* ' snout '; swine will dig and devour the roots.
Although most species are more suited to the rock garden than the garden border, *S. striatum* from Chile is worth noting for a front row position. In general appearance it resembles a bearded Iris, the foliage being very similar. The flowers, however, are borne on long, slender stems, closely packed together for almost half their length. They are pale yellowish-white. The plant has a tendency to die out suddenly after several years in the garden, possibly due to exhaustion of the soil. It is happiest in a well-drained, sunny situation and easily propagated from seed. *2½ ft. May–July. 2 ft. sq.*

SMILACINA (*Liliaceae*): False Spikenard, False Solomon's Seal. Name derived from Smilax.
Graceful, but hardly spectacular plants for the shady border. They need rich, moist soil which will not dry out during the summer months, the same conditions in fact as suit Lily of the Valley, Ferns and Primulas.

S. racemosa. False Spikenard. *(Plate XIII, p. 240.)* N. America. Fine white-flowered species suitable for the mixed flower border or shady area. The leaves are slender, somewhat like an elongated Lily of the Valley leaf, with the small white blooms displayed on terminal branching sprays. *2–3 ft. May–June. 1½ ft. sq.*

S. stellata. Star-flowered Lily of the Valley. N. America. Needs similar treatment to *S. racemosa*; it is smaller in habit. Flowers white.
1–2 ft. May–June. 1½ ft. sq.

SOLANUM (*Solanaceae*). Kansas. From *solamen* (L) ' solace ', some of the species are narcotic.

Most members of this family are either tender or represented by climbing shrubs. However, the species *S. torreyi*, Torrey's Nightshade (*Plate 26, p. 113*), is so handsome, with its violet blue flowers, that I have given it space in this volume. In Enfield it is perfectly hardy and has remained in a south-facing position for nearly 20 years. It increases by running underground roots which go down a long way into the ground and are sometimes difficult to discover. Spring is the best time for transplanting. The plant has greyish, much-divided leaves covered with tiny prickles, along the midribs and stems, whilst the wide-open blooms are large and violet-purple, not unlike large potato flowers.
1½–2 ft. July–Sept. 1 ft. sq.

SOLIDAGO (*Compositae*): Golden Rod, Aaron's Rod. From *solido* (L) ' to unite ', from the plant's reputed healing qualities.

For many years Golden Rods were coarse garden plants which received scant attention from connoisseurs of border perennials. But for over 20 years the late H. Walkden worked on the family feeling that there was much room for improvement in the genus and after many years of hybridising and selection, found that slow but steady progress was being made.

The variety ' Leraft ', a good yellow form, 2½ ft. tall, with medium yellow flowers, was the first he considered worthy of a garden place, but later varieties showed very diverse habit—from those having arching sprays, to upright, Spiraea-like spikes and also flat-headed types. The individual flowers also bear no resemblance to the original inconspicuous blossoms, and vary to-day, from Mimosa-like buttons to Daisy-like flowers which nearly approach small Asters. In colour they range from deep yellow to almost white.

These garden sorts are the best kinds for the gardener and will thrive well in any ordinary garden soil in a sunny situation. They make good cut flowers and are propagated by division in spring.

S. caesia. Wreath Golden Rod. Eastern N. America. A free-flowering species with small clustered heads of flowers all the way up the stems, in the axils of the leaves. Yellow. *2–3 ft. Aug.–Oct. 1 ft. sq.*

S. hybrida. This name comprises all the hybrid Golden Rods of garden origin. They should be planted 2–3 ft. apart.

Ballardii, bright golden-yellow, sprays much branched.
2 ft. Aug.–Oct.
Golden Gate, light yellowish-green foliage and shapely, slightly

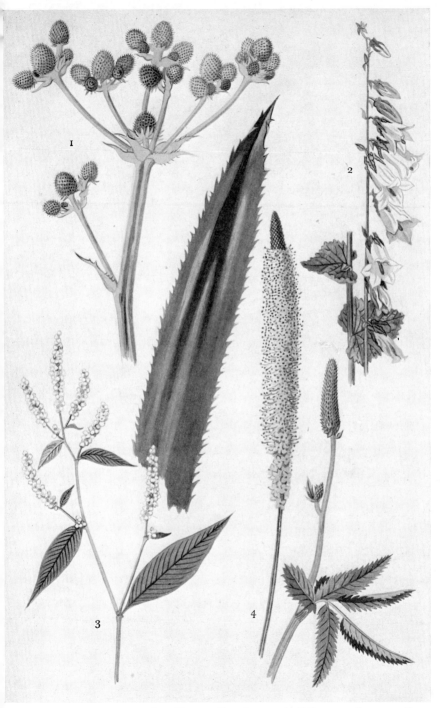

Plate XI: 1. SWORD-LEAVED SEA HOLLY, *Eryngium pandanifolium.* 2. SPURRED BELL-FLOWER, *Campanula alliariifolia.* 3. HIMALAYAN KNOTWEED, *Polygonum campanulatum.* 4. AMERICAN BURNET, *Sanguisorba canadensis*

Plate XII: 1. DROPWORT, *Filipendula hexapetala.* 2. WHITE BEACH SPEEDWELL, *Veronica longifolia albiflora.* 3. CREEPING TOADFLAX, *Linaria repens alba.* 4. WHITE PRAIRIE MALLOW, *Sidalcea candida.* 5. GOAT'S BEARD, *Aruncus sylvester*

Plate XIII: 1. FALSE SPIKENARD, *Smilacina racemosa.* 2. INDIAN POKE, *Veratrum viride.*
3. BRONZE-LEAF, *Rodgersia podophylla*

Plate XIV: 1. Japanese Anemone, *Anemone hupehensis elegans*. 2. White Japanese Anemone, *Anemone* x *hybrida* 'Whirlwind'. 3. Clematis, *Clematis heracleifolia* 'Edward Prichard'. 4. Blue Wood Aster, *Aster cordifolius* 'Photograph'. 5. Michaelmas Daisy, *Aster novi-belgii* 'Mount Everest'

arched flower spikes in a soft shade of yellow. *2½ ft. Sept.*
Goldenmosa, round, fluffy blossoms closely resembling Mimosa.
Medium habit with yellowish-green foliage.

2½–3 ft. Latter part of August.

Golden Plume, useful for the front of the border. Bright yellow.

2½ ft. Sept.

Golden Wings, branching sprays of deep yellow flowers.

5–6 ft. Aug.–Sept.

Goldstrahl (syn. ' Peter Pan '), bright canary-yellow, erect.

3 ft. Sept.

Leda, sunshine-yellow, very erect habit and spikes. *3½ ft. July–Aug.*
Lemore, soft primrose, the flowers carried in wide branching heads.

2½ ft. Sept.

Leraft, flat sprays of bright golden flowers, compact.

2½ ft. Aug.–Sept.

Lesale, Daisy-like flowers of a medium shade of yellow. Arranged
on stiff, erect, branching stems. Makes a good cut flower.

2½–3 ft. End of August.

S. missouriensis. N. America. Smooth stemmed with graceful short spikes
of yellow flowers. *2–4 ft. July–Sept. 2 ft. sq.*

S. petiolaris. Eastern N. America. A handsome, late-blooming species
with slightly downy stems, narrow, toothed elliptic leaves and large,
ragged, yellow flower heads. *3–5 ft. Sept.–Oct. 2 ft. sq.*

S. uliginosa. Swamp Golden Rod. Eastern N. America. Narrow branched
stems of small yellow flowers and smooth, oval oblong leaves. Graceful
in habit, late flowering. *2–4 ft. Aug.–Oct. 2 ft. sq.*

S. virgaurea. Europe, including Britain. A very variable species with
smooth stems and flowers borne in flat, plate-like heads. Sometimes
these run up to a conical shape. Garden varieties include var. *nana*
which grows less than a foot high and is suitable for the front of the
border. *1–4 ft. July–Oct. 1½ ft. sq.*

× SOLIDASTER (*Compositae*). A name combining the parent genera
Aster and Solidago.

An intergeneric hybrid group derived from crossing the two
genera mentioned. The plants need similar growing conditions to
Aster or Solidago and flower at the same time. They succeed in any
fertile soil, in sun or light shade and are propagated by division.

× *S. luteus.* Makes a good garden plant and has been grown in borders
since its introduction from France at the beginning of the century.
It has narrow Aster-like leaves and numerous bright yellow flowers
which fade to a lighter shade. *2½ ft. Sept.–Oct. 2½ ft. sq.*

STACHYS (*Labiatae*): Wound-wort. From *stachys* (Gk) ' spike '.

Plants of the Sage family, with spikes of red or purple flowers and attractive foliage. They grow well even in very poor soil, in sun or light shade and can be propagated by division.

S. lanata. Woolly Betony. (*Plate VIII, p. 224.*) Caucasus. A silvery-leaved plant of plush-like texture often used for edging purposes. It also makes a good front of the border plant, particularly for separating over brightly coloured neighbours. *S. lanata* thrives in any soil, and later in the summer carries spikes of crimson flowers which are almost hidden by grey woolly stems and bracts. Because of the velvety texture of the foliage the plant is also known as Lamb's Ear or Lamb's Tongue. It does best in well-drained soil of rather poor texture. Propagation by division.   *1–1½ ft. July–Aug. 1 ft. sq.*

S. macrantha (syn. *S. grandiflora*): Big Betony. (*Plate 24, p. 112.*) Caucasus. Has round, elongated, rather hairy leaves and whorls of violet flowers, each of which may be an inch in length. Var. *rosea* has rose blooms and *violacea* rich violet.   *1–2 ft. May. 1 ft. sq.*

STENANTHIUM (*Liliaceae*): From *stenos* (Gk) ' narrow ' and *anthos* ' flower '; referring to the shape of the blooms.

S. robustum. Featherfleece. (*Plate XVI, p. 257.*) United States. A beautiful but rather difficult plant which needs a warm sheltered situation and light, rich, yet moist soil. It has very stout leafy stems and dense panicles of greenish-white flowers. The foliage is long and strap-like. Propagation by division or from seed.   *3–5 ft. July. 1½ ft. sq.*

STOKESIA (*Compositae*): Stokes's Aster. Named for Dr. J. Stokes, a 19th-century English botanist.

A genus of a single species, namely, *S. laevis* (syn. *S. cyanea*) (*Plate 26, p. 113*) from N. America. This is an autumn blooming perennial with large, blue flowers very like the common annual China Aster (*Callistephus*). These are very handsome, in character for some weeks and make good cut flowers. Stokesia grows in sunny or light shady situations in any good well-drained soil. It is a variable species and the flowers in some of the better forms may be 3 in. or more across. They are usually blue or mauve, with white central base appendages. Named garden varieties include var. *rosea* with pink blooms; *alba* white; *superba* rich mauve-purple.   *1–1½ ft. Aug.–Oct. 1½ ft. sq.*

STYLOPHORUM (*Papaveraceae*): Celandine Poppy. From *stylos* (Gk) ' style,' *phero* ' to bear '; the styles are supported by the seed capsules.

S. diphyllum. Eastern N. America. A hardy, Poppy-like plant suitable for the mixed border, with large, bright yellow blossoms on black haired stems. The leaves are handsomely cut. It thrives best in light shade in ordinary soil. Propagation by division, or seed sown outside in April.   *1 ft.   April-May   1 ft. sq.*

SYMPHYTUM (*Boraginaceae*): Comfrey. From *symphio* (Gk) ' to unite ', from its supposed healing powers.

Coarse perennials only suitable for naturalising in sunny places in the wild garden, although some of the varietal forms are quite spectacular. However, they should never be sited where they can over-run more delicate plants, as the growth is invasive. They flower throughout most of the summer. Propagated by seed or division.

S. officinale. Europe, including Britain. A well-known plant with egg-shaped or lanceolate leaves which are very rough to the touch, and drooping, forked clusters of white, purple, pinkish or yellow flowers. The best variety for garden purposes is var. *argenteum* with handsome white variegated leaves and purplish flowers, but var. *coccineum* with crimson blooms is another good plant.   *2-4 ft. June-Sept. 2 ft. sq.*

S. peregrinum. E. Caucasus, naturalised in Britain. A plant for sun or shade, with leafy, much-branched stems and terminal trusses of single, fine blue, drooping bell-shaped flowers.   *3-4 ft. All summer. 2 ft. sq.*

TANACETUM (*Compositae*): Tansy. Name of doubtful derivation.

A genus which is chiefly represented by *T. vulgare*, the common Tansy, native to Europe, including Britain.

In the garden Tanacetums are invasive plants although not unattractive. The flowers borne in stiff bunches at the tops of the stems are like round, golden buttons. They resemble in fact Daisies with the outer petals removed. The leaves are rich green and hand-somely cut into fern-like segments. To keep them in bounds pieces of slate should be thrust down sideways into the soil. The roots run just below the surface and are thus kept in check. The plants grow in any open situation and practically any soil. Propagation by division. The best variety for the garden is *T. vulare* var. *crispum* which has curled, ornamental foliage.   *2-3 ft. Aug.-Sept. 2 ft. sq.*

THALICTRUM (*Ranunculaceae*): Meadow Rue. From *thaliktron* (Gk), a name used by Dioscorides for a plant with divided leaves, possibly of this family.

Attractive perennials which deserve to be more widely known and grown. The leaves are beautifully cut, some like fine Maidenhair Ferns, whilst the inflorescences are composed of myriads of tiny flowers, which give them a delicate cobwebby effect. The taller sorts make good back of the border subjects and create a splendid foil for larger flowering plants. They will grow in any soil providing it is not too hard, and in sun or light shade. Propagation by seed, or division in spring just as the plants start to grow.

T. aquilegiifolium. Columbine Meadow Rue. (*Plate 10, p. 49.*) Europe, N. America. An attractive, ornamental plant with spreading panicles of flowers in a soft purple shade and pinnately divided leaves. Var. *album*, White Meadow Rue (*Plate II, p. 193*), has white flowers. Var. 'Bee's Purple' has purple-rose flowers on 3 ft. stems (May–June), and 'Dwarf Purple', purple fluffy blooms 2½ ft. tall.

2–3 ft. May–July. 2 ft. sq.

T. chelidonii. Central and E. Himalaya. A beautiful plant with handsome much-divided leaves and cobwebby sprays of large mauve flowers. These have drooping, yellow stamens. It sometimes carried bulbils in the axils of the leaves. *1½–3 ft. July–Aug. 1 ft. sq.*

T. delavayi. W. China. Is of weaker constitution than *T. dipterocarpum*, but very similar, and needs a fertile, deeply dug soil. It has large flowers of a rosy-violet colour. *2–3 ft. July–Aug. 2 ft. sq.*

T. diffusiflorum. S.E. Tibet. A lovely but difficult plant with sprays of delicate, mauve, drooping flowers and very small leaflets on the divided foliage. *3–8 ft. July–Aug. 3 ft. sq.*

T. dipterocarpum. W. China. Has beautiful compound leaves and branching panicles of rosy-mauve flowers with conspicuous yellow stamens. Normally growing about 2 ft. high, it frequently reaches 4–5 ft. under favourable conditions. In the lush, rich soil of the late Lord Aberconway's garden at Bodnant I have seen flower spikes 8–10 ft. in height—an amazingly beautiful sight and possibly unique.

The best method of growing the plant is to mulch annually with well-rotted manure or compost and refrain from cultivating too near and too frequently round the crowns. The young growths rise very close to the old plant and a careless thrust with a fork or hoe will easily damage them. There is a double form known as 'Hewitt's Double' or Hewitt's Meadow Rue (*Plate 12, p. 64*). The flowers of this are completely round and of a rich mauve shade. They spangle the intricately branched flower sprays like polka dots. The roots should not be placed too near together or the inflorescences sometimes become hopelessly entangled. This variety must be propagated from offsets. Var. *album* has white flowers, Aug.–Sept.

2–5 ft. June–Aug. 1½ ft. sq.

T. flavum: Yellow Meadow Rue. Europe, including Britain. A distinctive and graceful plant with grey-green, finely cut leaves and feathery heads of soft yellow flowers. *2–3 ft. July–Aug. 1½ ft. sq.*

T. minus (syn. *T. adiantifolium*). Europe, including Britain. A simple plant forming compact tufts of small, glaucous, Maidenhair-like leaves. The flowers are mauve but not conspicuous. It makes a good edging plant and does well in light shade.

1½–2 ft. July. 1 ft. sq.

T. reniforme. E. Himalaya. Has mauve flowers with drooping stamens and compound leaves with leaflets as long as they are broad.

1½–3 ft. July–Aug. 1 ft. sq.

T. speciosissimum (syn. *T. glaucum*) (*Plate 8, p. 48*): Dusty Meadow Rue. S.W. Europe, N.W. Africa. A handsome border perennial with beautiful glaucous foliage which is pinnately cut and divided. The flowers are pale yellow and borne on large pyramidal panicles. Var. ' Illuminator ' is an improved form with lemon-yellow blossoms.

2–5 ft. July–Aug. 2½ ft. sq.

THERMOPSIS (*Leguminosae*). From *thermos* (Gk) ' lupin ', *opsis* ' like '.

Attractive and yet uncommon perennials, with long terminal spikes of bright yellow Lupin-like flowers. The plants are perfectly hardy and do well in light, rich soil. Some of the species spread freely at the root and may be increased by division, whilst others can be propagated from seed.

T. caroliniana. E. United States. A good late-flowering kind for the back of the border with erect racemes of Sweetpea-like blossoms. Propagation by seed.   *3 ft. July–Aug. 2 ft. sq.*

T. montana. Western N. America. Of graceful habit, with bright yellow flowers on erect spikes and divided leaves. Propagation by seed.

1–2 ft. June–July. 2 ft. sq.

TIARELLA (*Saxifragaceae*): Foam Flower. From *tiara* (L) ' diadem '; referring to the shape of the seed vessels.

Woodland plants suitable for any shady border. They need a moist vegetable soil and have attractive, heart-shaped, ground-hugging leaves rather like Heuchera, and crimson spikes of foamy white flowers. Propagation by seed or division. See also Heucherella.

T. cordifolia. Eastern N. America (*Plate V, p. 208*). Starry, creamy-white flowers; buds delicately tinged with pink. The young leaves are green, spotted and veined with deep red, but they become uniformly reddish-bronze in autumn. Var. *purpurea* has bronze-purple leaves and pale pink flowers.   *6–12 in. April–June. 1 ft. sq.*

T. wherryi. United States. Introduced by Clarence Elliott in 1939, this is an attractive plant which favours a cool, vegetable soil and the dappled light found beneath the fringe of trees. The feathery spikes of creamy flowers are most attractive in early spring, whilst the simple leaves are somewhat hairy and roughly heart-shaped.

12–15 in. May–June. 1 ft. sq.

TOLMIEA (*Saxifragaceae*). Named after Dr. W. Fraser Tolmie, 19th-century surgeon to the Hudson Bay Company.

A plant for the shady border, chiefly remarkable for its viviparous leaves. These are practically round, of a light shade of green and from mid-summer onwards produce young plants on that area where the leaf joins the leaf stalk. These may be taken off and rooted in the ground. The flowers appear in spring and are not unlike those of Heuchera. They are green and chocolate. The plant is not unattractive as a house plant and is frequently used for this purpose. It is, however, perfectly hardy and will grow in any well-drained soil.

T. menziesii: Pick-a-Back Plant, Youth on Age. This is the only species and comes from N.W. America. *1½–2 ft. April–May. 1 ft. sq.*

TRADESCANTIA (*Commelinaceae*): Spiderwort, Moses in the Bulrushes, Devil in the Pulpit. Named after John Tradescant, gardener to King Charles I.

A large family of perennials, many not hardy. Most of the border varieties, however, are dependable and will grow in sun or shade, in all soil types. They are readily propagated by seeds, cuttings or division.

T. virginiana. Spiderwort. N. America. This species and its garden forms are the most suitable for the herbaceous border. They have narrow, smooth, grassy leaves and quantities of three petalled, white, mauve, blue or deep red flowers. These have very hairy filaments. Good varieties are ' J. C. Weguelin ', very large azure-blue; ' Merlin ', lavender-blue; ' Iris Prichard ', white-tinged with violet; ' Innocence ' (*Plate XVI, p. 257*), pure white; ' Blue Stone' (*Plate 6, p. 33*), deep blue, ' Osprey ', one of the best with large white flowers, and *alba* ' Birch Var.', large pure white. *2 ft. June–Sept. 1½ ft. sq.*

TRICYRTIS (*Liliaceae*): Toad Lily. From *treis* (Gk) ' three ', *kyrtos* ' convex '; referring to the pouch-like effect created by the three outer petals.

Interesting Asiatic plants with fibrous roots, and, broad, alternate, smooth, stem clasping leaves and racemes of usually purplish-white, medium-sized, bell-shaped flowers. These are generally heavily spotted with purple. It is a very striking genus, and thrives best in a light shaded position. Grow in fairly moist peaty loam and leaf-mould and protect with a covering of leaves in very severe weather. Propagation by seed or offsets.

T. hirta. Japan. A handsome plant with leafy stems, the leaves oval-oblong, with heart-shaped base, slightly hairy and dark green. In the axils where these join the stems bunches of large, open bell-shaped, white and purple spotted flowers are borne. The plant comes to bloom fairly late in the season; it will tolerate sun as long as it has a cool, rich soil. Var. *nigra* has darker flowers which appear about three weeks before the type. Other garden forms from this species are *grandiflorus*, white flowers spotted with purple and *variegata* with finely marked and striated foliage. *1–3 ft. June–July. 1 ft. sq.*

T. macropoda. Speckled Toad Lily. China, Japan. Has a smooth stem flushed with rosy-bronze and a few oval oblong leaves. The flowers are erect, fairly large, greenish-yellow spotted with purple inside. A good plant for a cool, shady position.

1½–2½ ft. May–June. 1 ft. sq.

TRILLIUM (*Liliaceae*): Wood Lily, Wake Robin, Trinity Flower. From *trilix* (Gk) ' triple ', the leaves and parts of the flower are in threes.

An attractive genus of shade-loving perennials for woodland borders or beds beneath trees. They can, however, be grown in full sun providing the situation is constantly moist. All require a soil containing peat or leaf-mould and must never dry out during the growing season. Transplanting is best carried out when the foliage dies down in early summer but they increase rather slowly after such a move. It is also possible to propagate from seed but it takes 5 or 6 years before the seedlings develop into flowering plants. The chief characteristic of this genus is that almost all parts of the plant grow in threes—there are three petals, three sepals, three leaf segments, etc. It is possible to both force and retard Trilliums so as to get out of season flowers. In 1938 in co-operation with Mr. W. Ormiston Roy, a specialist in refrigeration plant from Montreal, Canada, Amos Perry, produced over 1000 plants of *T. grandiflorum* in full flower for the Southport Show. As this occurred at the end of August the blooms were thus retarded three months beyond their normal term.

T. cernuum. Eastern N. America. This species has medium-sized, nodding flowers which are white or pink, and slender stems with bean-shaped leaves.　　*8–12 in. May–June. 1 ft. sq.*

T. erectum: Birth Root. Eastern N. America. A species characterised by fairly large, nearly erect, purple, three-petalled flowers which have an unattractive scent. It needs to be grown in bold groups to make any effect. There is a white-flowered form var. *album* and a yellowish-white one, var. *ochroleucum.*　　*1 ft. May. 1 ft. sq.*

T. grandiflorum. (Plate V, *p. 208.*) Eastern N. America. The best species, with white flowers of good size with very long anthers. These often change to pink with age and are followed by berries which are red at first and eventually black. The foliage is handsome and resembles a giant Clover leaf. There are several varietal forms including var. flowers. *roseum*, with pink　　*1–1½ ft. April–May. 1 ft. sq.*

T. sessile. N. America. Has a short, stout rhizome, a strong stem and purple or sometimes greenish-yellow flowers, which are sweetly scented. These sit very tightly on the leaf without a separate stalk. The fragrance is somewhat like that of a Magnolia.

6–12 in. March–April. 9 in.

TROLLIUS (*Ranunculaceae*): Globe Flower. From *Trollblume* (German) 'Globeflower'.

Handsome, early-flowering perennials of erect habit with round, yellow or gold Buttercup-like heads of flowers. They may be grown in borders or by streams, or naturalised in a moist meadow, creating delightful effects. In the mixed border groups of 9 or a dozen plants should be set together for maximum effects. Propagation by division in early autumn or from seed sown as soon as ripe.

T. altaicus. Siberia. Yellow or pale orange flowers with narrow petals and Buttercup-like leaves.   *1–2 ft. June. 1 ft. sq.*

T. anemonifolius. W. China. Has rounded leaves cut almost to the base into three-rounded, toothed lobes. The flat golden flowers have very narrow petals.   *1½ ft. June–July. 1 ft. sq.*

T. asiaticus. Siberia, China, Japan. A very hardy plant which differs from our European Globe Flowers, chiefly because the leaves are very finely divided and the blooms less rounded. Flowers dark yellow. Var. *aurantiacus* is a good orange variety and var. *fortunei* has rich yellow flowers and bright orange-red anthers.

      1–1½ ft. May–June. 1 ft. sq.

T. chinensis. N. China. This plant, with golden flowers and smooth, stout stems is the parent with *T. europaeus* of many garden varieties. It is also a sturdy good plant in its own right.

      1 ft. May–June. 1 ft. sq.

T. europaeus. Europe, including Britain. An extremely variable plant which differs when raised from seed, both in foliage shape and the colour of the flowers. Usually it is pale lemon. Varietal forms that have been named include *albidus*, creamy-yellow; *giganteus*, 6 in. taller than the type, and *nanus*, a dwarf form.

      1–2 ft. May–June. 1 ft. sq.

Among the best of the garden forms raised from this species are:
> Bee's Orange, large, orange-gold, *2 ft.*
> Canary Bird, large pale yellow, *2 ft.*
> Commander in Chief, fine deep orange, must be grown in deeply-dug, well-prepared soil, *2½ ft.*
> Earliest of All, butter-yellow, *2 ft.*
> Empire Day, early, large rich orange-yellow, *2 ft.*
> Fire Globe, deep orange, *2 ft.*
> First Lancers, fiery orange, *2½ ft.*
> Goldquelle, globular, large, rich orange, *2 ft.*
> Lemon Queen, very pale yellow, *2 ft.*
> Orange Princess, orange-gold, *2½ ft.*
> Prichard's Giant, medium yellow, *2½ ft.*
> Princess Juliana, clear yellow, *2½ ft.*
> Salamander, fiery orange, *2½ ft.*

T. ledebourii. (*Plate 8, p. 48.*) Siberia, China. A handsome species with deep orange, cup-shaped flowers and brilliant orange stamens. It flowers rather later than the other species. Var. ' Golden Queen ' is orange-yellow with prominent stamens.   *2–3 ft. June. 1 ft. sq.*

T. yunnanensis. China. A smooth perennial with flat, single Buttercup-like flowers and broad, Anemone-like leaves.   *2 ft. May. 1 ft. sq.*

UVULARIA (*Liliaceae*): Bellwort. From *uva* (L) ' bunch of grapes '; referring to the fruit.

Graceful perennials closely related to Solomon's Seal and Tricyrtis. The plants produce numerous slender stems with clusters of long yellow flowers drooping gracefully from their tips. They do well in moist peaty soil and are admirably suited to the shady border. Propagation by division.

U. grandiflora. Merry Bells (*Plate 4, p. 32*). N. America. A dainty and useful woodland type. The stem is slender, forked above its centre, usually with one or two leaves below the fork. The flowers are pale yellow and droop from the tips of the stems.

6–18 in. May–June. 6 in. sq.

VERATRUM (*Liliaceae*): False Hellebore. From *vere* (L) ' truly ', *ater* ' black '; the roots are very dark.

Interesting plants of fine foliage form, the species having large pleated leaves which clasp the stem, and dense terminal spikes of yellowish-white or greenish flowers. Veratrums do best in moist, light shaded situations and are mid to front of the border plants. Propagation by division.

V. album. White Hellebore. Europe, N. Africa. Makes a fine handsome plant with yellowish-white flowers in dense terminal panicles. The stems are rather downy and the leaves a rich green. Var. *major* is an improved form with larger, whiter flowers.   *3–4 ft. July. 1½ ft. sq.*

V. californicum. W. United States. Branched and tapering spikes of greenish, bell shaped flowers which are white with a greenish base. These are succeeded by egg-shaped, membranous seed vessels. The stem is stout and rather leafy.   *3–5 ft. June–Aug. 1½ ft. sq.*

V. viride. Indian Poke. (*Plate XIII, p. 240.*) N. America. A handsome plant for those who like unusual coloration for it is one of the very few green-flowered plants. The blooms are large and the general habit extremely graceful.   *2–5 ft. July. 1½ ft. sq.*

VERBASCUM (*Scrophulariaceae*): Mullein. From *barber* (L) ' beard ', possibly alluding to the shaggy foliage of some of the species.

Old-fashioned plants mostly of biennial duration, but a few

perennial enough to be used in the border. Some of the species are very ornamental with beautiful white woolly foliage which feels and looks like silver-grey plush. They are not particular as to soil as long as this is well drained and are perfectly happy on chalky soils. Propagation by cuttings for the hybrids, and seed for the others.

V. blattaria. Moth Mullein. Europe including Britain. A tall, stately biennial with greyish-green leaves and spikes of yellow, rarely white flowers. The stamens are purplish. Var. *grandiflorum* is larger in all its parts.   *2–4 ft. Summer. 4 ft. sq.*

V. bombyciferum (syn. V. ' Broussa '). Asia Minor. A beautiful biennial which is a ' must ' for the summer border. The whole plant, stem, foliage and inflorescence is densely clothed with felted silver hairs, through which the golden flowers gleam. Var. ' Silver Spire ' is a varietal form.   *4–6 ft. June–July. 2 ft. sq.*

V. chaixii: Nettle-leaved Mullein. S. and Central Europe. White heavily felted leaves and branching sprays of yellow flowers with purple stamens. In var. *album* the blooms are white.

    3 ft. June–Aug. 2 ft. sq.

V. hybridum. The following garden varieties make good plants for the herbaceous border and associate well with Astilbes, Phlox and Delphiniums. They should be planted in groups of 3, 5 or 7, about 3 ft. apart. All bloom June–July.

    C. L. Adams, deep yellow, silvery foliage, *5–6 ft.*
    Cotswold Beauty, pale bronze, *3–4 ft.*
    Cotswold Gem, soft amber with purple centre, *3–4 ft.*
    Cotswold Queen, apricot-buff, *3–4 ft.*
    Gainsborough, pale sulphur-yellow, *4 ft.*
    Harkness Hybrid, large deep yellow, *5 ft.*
    Pink Domino, attractive rose-pink, *4 ft.*
    Lilac Domino, mauve, *4 ft.*
    Miss Willmott (*Plate IV, p. 208*), white, *5 ft.*

V. nigrum: Dark Mullein. Europe, including Britain. Bold spikes of small yellow flowers with purplish filaments. The leaves are green, oblong or often heart-shaped, slightly downy beneath. Var. *album* has white and purple flowers.   *2–3 ft. June–Oct. 2 ft. sq.*

V. olympicum. Bithynia. A handsome plant with bright golden flowers with whitish anthers. These are borne on branching candelabra-like sprays. The grey felted leaves are arranged in a large rosette round the plant.   *5–6 ft. June–Sept. 3 ft.*

V. phlomoides. Woolly Mullein. Caucasus. A handsome woolly leaved plant with tall spikes of yellow flowers on a white woolly stem.

    4 ft. June–Sept. 2 ft. sq.

V. phoeniceum. A medium-sized species which forms a rosette of radical leaves, from which rise slightly branched racemes of violet, pink, rose or purple flowers. This is probably the parent of many of our garden forms. See *V. hybridum.* It seeds freely and must be kept in bounds.

2–4 ft. May–Sept. 1–2 ft. sq.

V. thapsiforme. (*Plate 8, p. 48.*) Europe. Makes handsome clusters of large yellow flowers and has oblong lanceolate leaves. The whole plant is densely covered with yellow hair.

2–5 ft. June–Aug. 2 ft. sq.

V. thapsus. Aaron's Rod, Hag's Taper. Europe, Asia. A woolly-leaved species with a straight stem packed with soft yellow flowers. The whole plant is densely hairy. *2–3 ft. June–Aug. 2 ft. sq.*

VERBENA (*Verbenaceae*). Name derived from the Celtic *ferfain.*

An attractive family of several shrubs, a number of prostrate creeping plants and numerous half-hardy perennials useful for bedding purposes. The best of these are listed below and should be grown in rich, well-drained soil in a sunny situation. They may be propagated from seed sown under glass early in the year or from cuttings taken either in spring or about August and September, and wintered in frames.

V. bonariensis. (*Plate 17, p. 80.*) Brazil. This tall, rather slender perennial makes an effective display if grown in a mass, or else threaded through a group of compact, lower-growing herbaceous plants like Nepeta, or certain of the dwarf Rudbeckias. It has square stems, which are borne very erect and carry both at their tops and in the leaf axils small clustered heads of rich lavender-violet flowers. It sometimes flowers and seeds so freely that the parent plant dies out, a circumstance which can be prevented by cutting away the spent heads.

3–5 ft. July–Sept. 2 ft. sq.

V. corymbosa. Southern S. America. A handsome perennial which forms a compact, dark green, leafy plant carrying dense terminal bunches made up of innumerable small funnel-shaped, fragrant, Heliotrope-blue flowers. It does best in moist soil and is hardy in all but very exposed situations. *3 ft. July–Sept. 2 ft. sq.*

V. hastata. Canada, United States. Stiffly erect spikes of violet flowers which are carried in the leaf axils and at the ends of the stems. Var. *alba* is white. *3–5 ft. July–Sept. 2 ft. sq.*

VERNONIA (*Compositae*): Iron-weed. Named after William Vernon, a 17th-century North American traveller and botanist.

Coarse perennials suitable for the wild garden or the vicinity of a stream or pond. In the mixed border they should be associated with plants like Sunflowers, Heleniums and Michaelmas Daisies since all flower at about the same time. They will grow in practically any soil and may be readily increased by division, or seeds.

V. crinita. N. America. A vigorous erect plant with leafy stems which terminate in large flat heads of purplish Thistle-like flowers. Var. *alba* is white.   *6 ft. July–Sept. 3 ft. sq.*

VERONICA (*Scrophulariaceae*): Speedwell. Probably named after St. Veronica.

A large and variable family, the herbaceous species needing good garden soil and full sunshine. They have a very long-flowering period. Propagated by division in early autumn (August) or spring.

GARDEN FORMS. The following garden forms of Veronica (mostly from *V. spicata*) are suitable for the summer herbaceous border. They need a planting area of 1½ sq. ft.

Blue Peter, deep blue in compact trusses, leafy and branched stems,
    long serrated leaves.   *1½ ft. June–Aug.*
Blue Spire, deep violet-blue, erect.   *1½ ft. June–Aug.*
Barcarolle, deep rose-pink.   *1 ft. June–Aug.*
Erica, pale orchid-purple.   *1 ft. June–Aug.*
Minuet, grey-green foliage, pink flowers   *1 ft. June–Aug.*
Romily Purple (*Plate 17, p. 80*), dark blue-
    violet, upright.   *1½–2 ft. June–Aug.*
True Blue, pure blue.   *1½ ft. June.*
Well's Variety, bright blue, evergreen foliage.   *1½ ft. June.*
Wendy, clear blue, with silvery foliage.   *1½ ft. June.*

V. incana. Russia. A beautiful silvery-grey plant with oblong, slightly toothed leaves and terminal spikes of soft blue flowers. Var. *glauca* and var. *argentea* are even more silvery in all their parts with deeper blue flowers. Var. *rosea* has pink flowers.   *1–2 ft. July. 1½ ft. sq.*

V. longifolia. Beach Speedwell. Central Europe, N. Asia. Has opposite leaves, or three arranged in a whorl, and lilac-blue flowers tightly packed on long spires. There are several garden forms such as *albiflora*, (*Plate XII, p. 240*), white; *rosea*, pink; *subsessilis*, purple blue. The latter is very branched and a great improvement on the type.
        2–4 ft. July–Sept. 2 ft. sq.

V. spicata. Spiked Speedwell. Europe, including Britain. A valuable plant suitable for the rock garden or front of the border, with narrow oblong leaves and bright blue flowers in dense spikes. Var. *alba* is white; var. *rosea* bluish-pink; and ' Pavane ', strawberry rose, 2 ft.
        2 ft. July–Sept. 1½ ft. sq.

V. teucrium. Central Europe. Dark green, narrow leaves on long, slender stems and slender spires of lavender-blue flowers. The following garden varieties may also be obtained. ' Trehane ', 8 in. with golden-yellow leaves; ' Royal Blue ', gentian-blue flowers and ' Shirley Blue ', sky-blue.   *1–2½ ft. July–Aug. 1½ ft. sq.*

VIOLA (*Violaceae*). Name used by Virgil and Pliny.

A large and well-known family which includes Violas, Pansies and Violets.

Violas are particularly useful for frontal work in the border and grow readily in most soils. They do especially well in light shade. Removal of the spent flower heads encourages continuity of blooming. Propagation by cuttings.

cornuta. Pyrenees. Good varieties from this species include:

Amethyst, pale amethyst-violet.
Ardwell Gem, yellow.
Bullion, lemon-yellow.
Daldowny Yellow, good yellow and very free.
Germania, plum-purple with a yellow blotch.
John Wallmark, very large, violet.
Memoria, violet-purple with conspicuous yellow eye.
Mia Karsten, rosy-lilac.
Pickering Blue, Wedgewood blue.
Primrose, deep blue-violet.
purpurea (George Wermig), small lilac-blue, very free.
Traum, reddish-purple with yellow eye.
Velvet Beauty, deep to black-violet with very small yellow eye.
White Lady, white with gold eye.

4–12 in. All summer. 1 ft. sq.

V. gracilis. Balkans. A dainty species with fine delicate flowers of deep violet. Var. *major* and 'Lord Nelson' are deeper in colour.

4–6 in. June–Sept. 1 ft. sq.

V. labradorica. N. United States, Canada, Greenland. A decorative plant on account of the dark purplish-green foliage. The flowers are lilac. Seedlings are apt to become a nuisance. *4–6 in. All summer. 9 in. sq.*

ZAUSCHNERIA (*Onagraceae*): Californian Fuchsia, Humming Bird's Trumpet. Named in honour of Johann Baptist Zauschner, an 18th-century German botanist.

A genus of four dwarf perennials, mostly sub-shrubby, which do well in well-drained, warm situations at the front of the border. They are chiefly valuable on account of their late-flowering habit and the brilliance of the long, tubular, scarlet flowers. Propagation by division in spring or seed sown under glass in March.

Z. californica. California. Of branching habit, the stems crowded with small, oval, greyish, hairy leaves, with bright scarlet flowers in loose spikes at the ends of the branches. *1 ft. Sept.–Oct. 1½ ft. sq.*

Z. cana (*Plate 28, p. 128*). California. More slender, with rather narrow, ash-grey leaves and very brilliant sprays of Fuchsia-like flowers. It is quite hardy and makes a good autumn perennial.

1 ft. Sept.–Oct. 1½ ft. sq.

CHAPTER VII

PLANTS FOR SPECIAL PLACES AND PURPOSES

THE following lists are intended to serve as guide for those with special soils or conditions. Where the generic name (e.g. Aster) only is mentioned, it means that all the species included in the appropriate section in the book may be considered, but when full names are given, e.g. (*Aster amellus*) only the species indicated are concerned.

PLANTS FOR LIGHT OR PARTIAL SHADE

Those marked with an * will do in particularly overcast surroundings.

Actaea
Aconitum
Adenophora
Ajuga
Anemone sylvestris, hupehensis
Aquilegia
Bergenia
Brunnera macrophylla
Campanula—most species
* „ *latiloba*
Cimicifuga
Claytonia
Clintonia
*Convallaria
*Corydalis
Dentaria
Dicentra
Digitalis
Dodecatheon
Doronicum
Eomecon
*Epimedium
Gentiana asclepiadea
*Helleborus

*Hemerocallis
Hosta
Iris foetidissima
Jeffersonia
Kirengeshoma
Lamium orvala
Lithospermum purpureo-caeruleum
Lysimachia clethroides
Meconopsis
Mertensia
Omphalodes cappadocica
Orobus
Podophyllum
*Polygonatum
Primula vulgaris
Pulmonaria
Rodgersia
Saxifraga umbrosa
Thalictrum aquilegiifolium
* *Tiarella cordifolia*
*Tolmiea
Tricyrtis
Trillium
Uvularia

Plants for Moist or at least Damp Places

Those marked with an * are particularly intolerant of dryness during the growing season.

Aconitum
Ajuga
Aruncus
Astilbe
Astrantia
Bergenia
Campanula alliariifolia, lactiflora, latifolia, rapunculoides, trachelium
*Cardamine
Chamaenerion
Cimicifuga
Claytonia
Clintonia
Dentaria
*Eomecon
Eupatorium
*Filipendula
Hemerocallis
Hosta
Iris forrestii, sibirica, wilsonii
*Lobelia
Lysimachia

Lythrum
*Meconopsis betonicifolia, napaulensis, regia
*Mimulus
Omphalodes
Polygonatum
Polygonum alpinum, amplexicaule, bistorta, campanulatum
*Primula alpicola, beesiana, bulleyana, burmanica, cockburniana, denticulata, florindae, helodoxa, japonica poissonii, pulverulenta, sikkimensis
Pulmonaria
Ranunculus
*Rheum
Rodgersia
Salvia uliginosa
Senecio
Thalictrum aquilegiifolium, flavum
Trillium
Trollius
Veratrum

Plants with Ornamental Fruits

Actaea
Iris foetidissima
Paeonia mlokosewitschi, wittmanniana
Physalis

Phytolacca
Podophyllum
Polygonatum
Smilacina
Veratrum

Bee Plants

Acanthus
Aconitum
Adenophora
Adonis
Althaea rosea
Anemone
Anthemis
Aquilegia
Aruncus

Asclepias
Aster
Borago laxiflora
Buphthalmum salicifolium
Cardamine
Centaurea
Cephalaria
Clematis

Coreopsis
Crambe
Delphinium
Dictamnus
Digitalis
Doronicum
Echinops
Epimedium
Erigeron

Eryngium
Filipendula
Gaillardia
Galega
Helenium
Helianthus
Heliopsis
Inula
Isatis
Kentranthus
Kniphofia
Lamium
Lathyrus
Ligularia

Limonium
Linaria
Linum
Lythrum
Macleaya
Malva
Mertensia
Monarda
Morina
Nepeta
Oenothera
Paeonia
Papaver orientale
Penstemon

Phlomis
Polemonium
Potentilla
Pulmonaria
Salvia
Scabiosa
Sedum
Sidalcea
Solidago
Stachys
Thalictrum
Thermopsis
Trollius
Verbascum

PERENNIALS MAKING GOOD SPECIMEN PLANTS AND SUITABLE FOR INDIVIDUAL PLANTING

Althaea rosea
Anchusa italica and vars.
Artemisia lactiflora
Aruncus sylvester
Centaurea macrocephala
Crambe cordifolia var. *grandiflora*
Delphinium elatum
Echinops
Eremurus
Eupatorium purpureum
Euphorbia wulfenii
Filipendula
Gentiana lutea
Kirengeshoma

Kniphofia, all large growing forms
Lavatera olbia
Macleaya
Malva setosa
Paeonia
Polygonum campanulatum, cuspidatum
Rheum
Rodgersia
Rudbeckia nitida
Senecio
Silphium
Tanacetum
Veratrum
Verbascum

PLANTS WITH SILVER FOLIAGE
Those marked with an * particularly pronounced.

Achillea taygetea
Alyssum saxatile
*Anaphalis triplinervis
Anthemis cupaniana, tinctoria
Antirrhinum asarina
Artemisia *gnaphalodes, ludoviciana,
  *nutans, *stelleriana
Centaurea babylonica, clementei
  depressa,*gymnocarpa,pulcherrima
Dianthus
Dracocephalum sibiricum
Echinops ritro, *tournefortii

Gypsophila
Iris germanica, pallida var.
  argentea
Nepeta faassenii (*mussinii*)
Perovskia
Phalaris arundinacea var. *picta*
Phlomis
Romneya
*Senecio cineraria
  Solanum torreyi
*Stachys lanata
  Veronica incana var. *argentea*

Plate XV: 1. WHITE MUGWORT, *Artemisia lactiflora.* 2. SWAMP MILKWEED, *Asclepias incarnata alba.* 3. WHITE OBEDIENT PLANT, *Physostegia virginiana alba.* 4. AMERICAN BUG BANE, *Cimicifuga americana.* 5. SNAKE HEAD, *Chelone glabra alba*

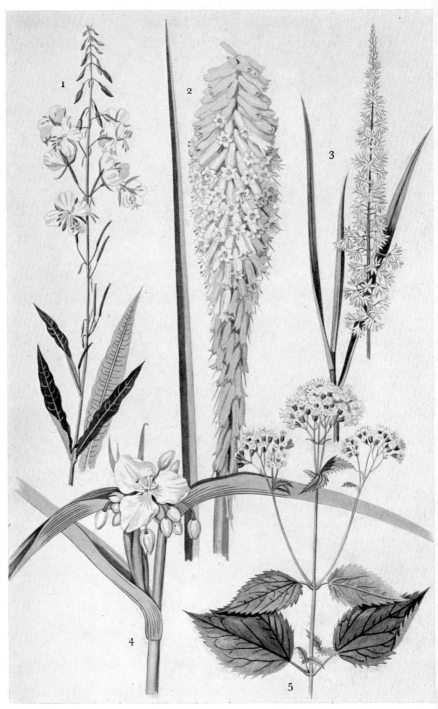

Plate XVI: 1. WHITE ROSEBAY, *Chamaenerion angustifolium album.* 2. WHITE TORCH LILY, *Kniphofia hybrida* 'Maid of Orleans'. 3. FEATHERFLEECE, *Stenanthium robustum.* 4. SPIDER-WORT, *Tradescantia virginiana* 'Innocence'. 5. WHITE SNAKEROOT, *Eupatorium ageratoides*

PLANTS FOR DRYING AND WINTER BOUQUETS

Acanthus
Achillea filipendulina and varieties
Anaphalis
Armeria pseudoarmeria (seed heads)
Astilbe (seed heads)
Delphinium
Echinops
Eryngium

Gypsophila
Heliopsis
Iris foetidissima
Limonium
Papaver orientale (seed heads)
Physalis
Pulsatilla (seed heads)

INVASIVE PLANTS

Strong-growing or seed-happy perennials which must be kept in check.

Achillea ptarmica
Aster novi-belgii
Campanula rapunculoides, trachelium
Centaurea montana
Chamaenerion angustifolium
Corydalis lutea
Digitalis purpurea
Geranium
Helianthus
Hieraceum

Lamium orvala
Lithospermum purpureo-coeruleum
Lysimachia
Macleaya
Monarda
Physalis
Saxifrage
Sedum
Thermopsis

PERENNIALS WHICH WILL GROW IN CHALKY SOILS

Acanthus mollis
Achillea ptarmica and vars.
Adenophora
Adonis
Agrostemna
Alyssum
Anthemis
Anthericum
Armeria
Aquilegia
Asphodeline lutea
Aster novi-belgii
Bergenia
Boltonia asteroides
Campanula
Cheiranthus

Corydalis lutea
Crambe
Dianthus
Dictamnus
Doronicum
Echinops
Eremurus
Erigeron
Eryngium
Euphorbia wulfenii
Gaillardia
Gaura
Geum
Gypsophila
Helenium
Helleborus orientalis

Hemerocallis
Incarvillea
Inula ensifolia
Iris germanica
Kentranthus
Kniphofia
Limonium
Linum narbonense
Lychnis chalcedonica
Macleaya cordata
Malva
Oenothera
Ostrowskia
Oxalis lasiandra

Paeonia officinalis (if kept moist at roots)
Papaver orientale
Pulsatilla
Romneya
Rudbeckia
Salvia azurea, × *superba, patens, uliginosa*
Scabiosa
Sidalcea
Tradescantia
Verbascum
Veronica
Zauschneria

PLANTS RESISTANT TO DROUGHT

Acanthus
Achillea ptarmica
Adonis vernalis
Alyssum
Anthemis
Anthericum
Antirrhinum asarina

Armeria
Aquilegia
Asphodelus
Boltonia
Codonopsis ovata
Corydalis lutea
Gaillardia

Geranium
Incarvillea
Kniphofia
Lychnis
Macleaya cordata
Veronica
Zauschneria

PLANTS WITH ORNAMENTAL FOLIAGE

Acanthus
Ajuga reptans
Anemone vitifolia
Aruncus sylvester
Astilbe
Barbarea vulgaris var. *variegata*
Bergenia
Cephalaria
Crambe
Echinops
Epimedium
Eryngium
Euphorbia wulfenii
Ferula
Foeniculum
Gazania

Helleborus corsicus, foetidus, × *nigricors*
Hosta
Inula helenium, magnifica, orientalis
Kirengeshoma
Kniphofia caulescens, foliosa, northiae
Lamium maculatum
Ligularia clivorum, japonica, tussilaginea aureo maculata
Lobelia fulgens
Macleaya
Morina longifolia
Peltiphyllum
Phormium
Rheum
Rodgersia

Plants Suitable for Edging Purposes

Artemisia stelleriana
Aster (Dwarf hybrids)
Bergenia
Campanula poscharskyana
Corydalis
Dianthus
Dicentra eximia

Epimedium
Heuchera sanguinea
Hosta
Nepeta × *faassenii*
Primula auricula, juliae, vulgaris
Saxifraga umbrosa
Stachys lanata

The Best Herbaceous Plants for Cutting

Achillea filipendulina ' Gold Plate'
　,,　*millefolium* ' Cerise Queen'
　,,　*ptarmica* ' Perry's White '
　,,　*ptarmica* ' The Pearl '
Aconitum
Alstroemeria
Anthemis ' E. C. Buxton '
　,,　　' Grallagh Gold '
Anthericum
Armeria
Artemisia lactiflora
Aster
Astilbe
Campanula latifolia var. *macrantha*
　,,　　*persicifolia*
Centaurea montana
Cephalaria alpina
Chrysanthemum
Cimicifuga
Clematis recta
Convallaria majalis ' Fortin's Giant '
Coreopsis grandiflora and vars.
Delphinium
Dianthus
Dicentra spectabilis
Doronicum
Echinops
Erigeron
Eryngium
Gaillardia
Geum ' Mrs. Bradshaw '
Gypsophila paniculata and vars.
Helenium

Helianthus
Heliopsis
Helleborus niger
Hemerocallis
Hesperis
Heuchera sanguinea and vars.
Hosta
Iris germanica, sibirica
Kniphofia
Liatris
Limonium
Lupinus
Lychnis chalcedonica
Lysimachia clethroides
Lythrum
Paeonia
Papaver
Pentstemon
Phlox × *arendsii, paniculata*
Physalis
Primula auricula, denticulata,
　sieboldii
Pyrethrum
Rudbeckia
Salvia azurea, × *superba, uliginosa*
Scabiosa
Sedum spectabile
Solidago
Thalictrum dipterocarpum ' Hewitt's
　Double '
Thermopsis
Trollius
Veronica longifolia and vars.

Perennials Untidy after Flowering

Aconitum
Anchusa
Asphodelus
Asphodeline
Centaurea macrocephala
Codonopsis
Crambe
Delphinium
Echinops
Eryngium
Gaillardia
Gypsophila

Lupinus
Lychnis chalcedonica, × *haageana*
Papaver orientale
Polygonatum
Pulmonaria
Rheum
Salvia
Saponaria officinalis
Thalictrum
Veratrum
Verbascum

Outstanding Herbaceous Plants for forcing

Aquilegia (most species and
    varieties)
Astilbe
Bergenia
Convallaria
Delphinium elatum, belladonna and
    grandiflorum hybrids
Dicentra spectabilis
Dodecatheon
Doronicum
Epimedium
Euphorbia epithymoides

Filipendula
Geum ' Mrs. Bradshaw '
Helleborus niger
Hosta
Iris germanica and *pumila* hybrids
Polygonatum multiflorum
Primula beesiana, denticulata,
    sieboldii,
Smilacina racemosa
Trillium
Thalictrum
Trollius

Plants with Fragrant Flowers or Foliage

Those marked with an * are rather strong and may not appeal to all
gardeners.

*Achillea
Anthemis
Anthericum liliago
Antirrhinum asarina
Artemisia lactiflora
Aruncus sylvester
Asclepias
Calamintha
Cheiranthus

Chrysanthemum
Clematis recta
Convallaria
Crambe
Dianthus
Dictamnus albus
Filipendula
Hemerocallis varieties
Hesperis

Iris germanica
*Kentranthus ruber
Malva moschata
Melittis
Monarda
Morina longifolia
*Nepeta
Oenothera
Paeonia
Patrinia

Perovskia
Phlox
Polygonum campanulatum
Primula
Romneya coulteri
*Salvia × *superba*
Saponaria officinalis
Thalictrum flavum
Verbena

Rabbit Proof Plants

Over a period of years we have found the following genera without interest for these vermin, which, in spite of other depredations, always seem to ignore them.

Asters
Bergenia
Echinops
Epimedium
Eryngium
Geranium
Helianthus
Iris

Kniphofia
Nepeta × *faassenii*
Papaver
Polygonum
Potentilla nepalensis 'Miss Willmott'
Romneya coulteri
Rudbeckia
Stachys lanata

Herbaceous Plants for Seaside Planting
All are tolerant of sea spray.

Armeria
Artemisia
Corydalis
Echinops
Eryngium
Geranium
Lavatera olbia rosea

Limonium
Lythrum
Nepeta
Papaver orientalis
Phlomis
Primulas juliae and vars.

Plants for Warm Dry, Sunny Situations

Achillea
Agastache
Alstroemeria
Alyssum
Anaphalis

Anthemis
Anthericum
Antirrhinum
Artemisia
Asclepias tuberosa

Asphodeline
Asphodelus
Astragalus
Buphthalmum salicifolium
Callirhoe papaver
Catananche
Centaurea
Cephalaria alpina
Dictamnus
Eryngium alpinum, planum
Euphorbia epithymoides
Filipendula hexapetala
Gaura
Geranium
Gypsophila paniculata and vars.
Heliopsis
Inula
Iris chamaeiris, germanica, pumila
Isatis

Kentranthus
Limonium
Linum
Lupinus
Nepeta faassenii
Oenothera
Phlomis
Polemonium
Polygonum alpinum
Saponaria officinalis
Sedum sieboldii, spectabile
Solidago virgaurea
Tanacetum
Thalictrum minus
Verbascum
Verbena
Veronica spicata
Zauschneria

PLANTS FOR TOWN GARDENS

Achillea
Ajuga
Alyssum
Anemone hupehensis
Anthemis
Aquilegia
Armeria
Aster
Astilbe
Bergenia
Campanula
Chrysanthemum
    maximum
Convallaria
Dianthus

Dicentra eximia
Dictamnus
Doronicum
Echinops
Erigeron
Eryngium
Geum
Gypsophila
Heuchera
Helleborus niger
Hemerocallis
Hesperis
Iris germanica, sibirica
Kentranthus
Kniphofia

Limonium
Linum
Lupinus
Mimulus
Paeonia
Papaver
Pentstemon
Phalaris
Primula juliae
Salvia patens
Saxifraga umbrosa
Solidago
Thalictrum
Tradescantia
Veronica

TALL PERENNIALS (4½ FT. AND OVER)

Achillea filipendulina
Aconitum lycoctonum, volubile
Althaea rosea
Asters (some novi-belgii vars.)
Campanula lactiflora, latifolia,
    pyramidalis

Centaurea babylonica
Cephalaria
Crambe
Delphinium elatum varieties
Echinops horridus, sphaerocephalus

Eremurus
Eryngium agavifolium, pandanifolium
Eupatorium purpureum
Ferula
Filipendula rubra, camtschatica
Foeniculum
Lavatera olbia
Macleaya

Phormium
Rudbeckia nitida, laciniata
Salvia uliginosa
Thalictrum speciosissimum,
Verbascum hybrids
Verbena bonariensis
Vernonia crinita

PLANTS NEEDING WINTER PROTECTION

Mostly a light covering of leaves or twigs. Those with an * need wintering away from frost.

*Agapanthus
Agastache
Alstroemeria
*Anchusa caespitosa
Antirrhinum glutinosum
Callirhoe
Carlina
*Celmisia
Celsia
Codonopsis
*Dimorphotheca
Eomecon
Eremurus
*Gazania
Geranium wallichianum
Helianthus sparsifolius ' The Monarch '
Kniphofia × *erecta* and most garden forms
Libertia
Linum flavum
Lobelia cardinalis
*   ,,   *fulgens, tupa**

Lychnis × *haageana*
Malvastrum
Mimulus cardinalis, cupreus
Morina
Myosotidum (well protected *outside*)
Oenothera speciosa rosea
Ostrowskia (well protected *outside*)
Oxalis lasiandra
'Pentstemon
Perovskia
Phormium
Phygelius
Primula sieboldii
Romneya
Roscoea (well protected outside or lifted)
Salvia uliginosa, azurea, farinacea
Salvia patens
Senecio cineraria
Verbena bonariensis, corymbosa
Veronica incana argentea

25 GOOD EARLY FLOWERING BORDER PLANTS

Aquilegia caerulea
Aruncus sylvester
Baptisia australis
Bergenia cordifolia
Brunnera macrophylla
Campanula glomerata

Dicentra eximia ' Bountiful '
Dicentra spectabilis
Doronicum plantagineum ' Harpur Crewe'
Epimedium pinnatum
Eremurus robustus

Euphorbia epithymoides
Geum chiloense ' Mrs. Bradshaw '
Heuchera
Iris chamaeiris
Paeonia—almost any variety
Papaver orientale ' Mrs. Perry '
Primula ' Polyanthus '
Pulmonaria

Pulsatilla vulgaris
Pyrethrum ' Eileen May Robinson '
Ranunculus aconitifolius flore pleno
Smilacina racemosa
Tiarella wherryi
Trollius—any modern variety

25 GOOD MID-SEASON BORDER PLANTS

Aconitum carmichaelii
Anthemis tinctoria ' Grallagh Gold '
Armeria pseudoarmeria ' Bee's Ruby '
Campanula lactiflora 'Loddon Anna '
Catananche caerulea major
Centaurea macrocephala
Chrysanthemum maximum ' Esther Read '
Coreopsis verticillata ' Golden Shower '
Delphinium—any of the modern varieties
Erigeron hybridus ' Mrs. H. F. Beale '
Gypsophila paniculata ' Bristol Fairy '
Helenium pumilum magnificum
Iris germanica ' St. Agnes '

Iris sibirica ' Marcus '
Lavatera olbia
Linum narbonense ' Peto's Variety '
Lupinus—any of the modern varieties
Nepeta faassenii
Oenothera missourensis
Oenothera speciosa
Potentilla atrosanguinea ' Gibson's Scarlet '
Salvia × *superba*
Thalictrum dipterocarpum ' Hewitt's Double '
Tradescantia virginiana ' Blue Stone '
Verbascum hybridum ' Pink Domino '

25 GOOD LATE BORDER PLANTS

Anemone × *hybrida* ' Queen Charlotte '
Artemisia lactiflora
Aster amellus ' King George '
Aster cordifolius ' Silver Spray '
Aster novi-belgii ' Red Sunset '
Chrysanthemum rubellum ' Duchess of Edinburgh '
Cimicifuga racemosa var. *simplex*
Echinacea purpurea ' The King '
Echinops ritro ' Taplow Blue '
Eryngium oliverianum ' Violetta '
Eupatorium purpureum
Heliopsis scabra patula

Kniphofia uvaria ' Maid of Orleans '
Liatris pycnostachya
Limonium × *olivarianum* ' Violetta '
Lobelia fulgens
Pentstemon—any modern variety
Phlox paniculata 'Sir John Falstaff '
Physostegia virginiana ' Vivid '
Polygonum reynoutria
Rudbeckia nitida ' Herbstsonne '
Rudbeckia speciosa
Sedum spectabile ' Brilliant '
Solidago hybrida ' Goldenmosa '
Stokesia laevis

Plants for a Pink, Rose, Red and Crimson Border

See Chapter VI for species or varieties of genera mentioned.

Achillea millefolium
vars.
Alstroemeria
Althaea
Anemone
Armeria
Aster
Astilbe
Bergenia
Centaurea
Chamaenerion
Chelone
Chrysanthemum
Dianthus
Dicentra
Digitalis
Dodecatheon
Echinacea
Eremurus
Erodium
Filipendula

Geranium
Geum
Gypsophila
Helleborus orientalis
Heuchera
Incarvillea
Iris
Kentranthus
Kniphofia
Lamium
Lavatera
Liatris
Lobelia
Lupinus
Lychnis
Lythrum
Malva
Mimulus
Monarda
Morina
Oxalis lasiandra

Paeonia
Papaver
Peltiphyllum
Pentstemon
Phlox
Phygelius
Physalis (fruit)
Physostegia
Phytolacca
Podophyllum
Polygonum
Potentilla
Primula
Sanguisorba
Saponaria
Saxifraga
Schizostylis
Sedum
Sidalcea
Stachys
Zauschneria

Plants for a Blue, Mauve and Violet Border

See Chapter VI for species or varieties of genera mentioned.

Aconitum
Adenophora
Agapanthus
Ajuga
Amsonia
Anchusa
Aquilegia
Aster
Baptisia
Borago
Brunnera
Campanula
Catananche
Centaurea
Cichorium
Clematis

Codonopsis
Commelina
Delphinium
Dracocephalum
Echinops
Erigeron
Eryngium
Eupatorium
Galega
Gentiana
Geranium
Hesperis
Hosta
Iris
Lactuca
Limonium

Linaria
Lindelofia
Linum
Lithospermum
Lobelia
Lupinus
Meconopsis
Mertensia
Myosotidium
Nepeta
Omphalodes
Ostrowskia magnifica
Pentstemon
Perovskia
Phlomis
Phlox

Platycodon	Salvia	Tradescantia
Polemonium	Scabiosa	Verbena
Primula	Solanum	Vernonia
Pulmonaria	Stokesia	Veronica
Roscoea	Thalictrum	

PLANTS FOR A YELLOW, BRONZE AND ORANGE BORDER
See Chapter VI for species or varieties of genera mentioned.

Achillea	Epimedium	Mimulus
Aconitum lycoctonum	Eremurus	Oenothera
Adonis	Euphorbia	Orobus
Alstroemeria	Gaillardia	*Paeonia mlokosewitschi*
Althaea	Gazania	Phlomis
Alyssum	Geum	Potentilla
Anthemis	Helenium	Primula
Arnebia	Helianthus	Ranunculus
Asclepias	Heliopsis	Roscoea
Asphodeline	Hemerocallis	Rudbeckia
Aster linosyris	Hieracium	Senecio
Astragalus	Inula	Silphium
Barbarea	Iris	Solidago
Buphthalmum	Isatis	Stylophorum
Centaurea	Kirengeshoma	Tanacetum
Cephalaria	Kniphofia	Thalictrum
Cheiranthus	Ligularia	Thermopsis
Chrysanthemum	Linum	Trollius
Coreopsis	Lupinus	Uvularia
Corydalis	Lysimachia	Verbascum
Digitalis	Macleaya	

PLANTS FOR A WHITE, CREAM AND GREEN BORDER
See Chapter VI for species or varieties of genera mentioned.

Achillea	Astrantia	Delphinium
Althaea	Boykinia	Dianthus
Anaphalis	Campanula	Dicentra
Anemone	Catananche	Erigeron
Anthemis	Celmisia	Eupatorium
Anthericum	Centaurea	Euphorbia
Artemisia	Chelone	Ferula
Aruncus	Chrysanthemum	Filipendula
Asphodelus	Cimicifuga	Galega
Aster	Convallaria	Gaura
Astilbe	Crambe	Gentiana

Geranium
Gypsophila
Helleborus
Heuchera
Hosta
Iris
Kentranthus
Kniphofia
Libertia
Lupinus
Lychnis
Lysimachia
Meconopsis

Oenothera
Paeonia
Papaver
Peltiphyllum
Phalaris
Phormium
Phlox
Polemonium
Polygonum
Polygonatum
Primula
Ranunculus
Rodgersia

Romneya
Salvia
Saponaria
Scabiosa
Sidalcea
Sisyrinchium striatum
Smilacina
Stenanthium
Thalictrum
Tiarella
Tradescantia
Trillium
Veratrum

PLANTS FOR THE WATERSIDE

Aconitum
Agastache
Ajuga
Anemone rivularis, virginana
Anemonopsis
Artemisia lactiflora
Aruncus
Astilbe
Astrantia
Boykinia
Brunnera
Bulphthalmum
Carlina
Chelone
Chrysanthemum uliginosum
Cimicifuga
Claytonia
Clintonia
Dicentra eximia, formosa
Epimedium
Eupatorium
Ferula
Filipendula
Gentiana asclepiadea. pneumonanthe
Geum rivale
Hemerocallis
Hosta
Inula helenium
*Iris kaempferi, delavayi, forrestii, ochro-
  leuca, sibirica, wilsonii*
Kirengeshoma

Ligularia
Lobelia cardinalis, fulgens, syphilitica
Lysimachia
Lythrum
*Meconopsis betonicifolia, integrifolia,
  napaulensis, regia*
Mertensia
Mimulus
Monarda
Peltiphyllum
Phormium
Physostegia
Podophyllum
*Polygonum alpinum, bistorta, campanu-
  latum*
*Primula alpicola, anisodora, aurantiaca,
  beesiana, bulleyana, cockburniana,
  denticulata, helodoxa, japonica, pois-
  sonii, pulverulenta, rosea, sikkimensis*
Ranunculus aconitifolius, acris
Rheum
Rodgersia
Salvia uliginosa
Sanguisorba
Senecio doria, smithii, tanguticus
Sidalcea
Stylophorum
Symphytum
Thalictrum flavum, speciosissimum
Trollius
Vernonia

HARDY BULBS FOR EXTENDING THE SEASON OF FLOWERING IN MIXED BORDERS

EARLY SPRING

Anemone blanda, coronaria
Chionodoxa
Corydalis
Crocus
Cyclamen
Eranthis
Erythronium
Fritillaria
Galanthus
Hyacinthus
Leucojum
Muscari
Narcissus cyclamineus
Scilla verna
Tulipa biflora, kaufmanniana

SUMMER

Allium narcissiflorum
Amaryllis belladonna
Camassia leichtlinii
Eucomis
Galtonia
Gladiolus
Ixia
Lilium
Nomocharis
Oxalis
Pancratium
Sparaxis
Tigridia
Watsonia

SPRING

Allium neapolitanum, nigrum, triquetrum
Anemone × fulgens, etc.
Brodiaea
Camassia
Fritillaria
Hyacinthus
Iris
Leucojum
Narcissus
Tulipa

LATE FLOWERING

Colchicum
Crocus
Cyclamen
Galanthus cilicicus
Iris unguicularis
Leucojum autumnale
Scilla autumnalis
Sternbergia lutea

ORNAMENTAL GRASSES FOR MIXED AND GREEN BORDERS

ANNUAL

Agrostis nebulosa
  ,,   pulchella
Aira
Anthoxanthum gracile
Avena sterilis
Briza maxima

Bromus briziformis
Chloris elegans
Coix lachryma-jobi
  ,, *aurea zebrina*
Eleusine
Eragrostis abessinica

Eragrostis interrupta
Hordeum jubatum
Lagurus ovatus
Lamarckia aurea
Zea varieties

PERENNIAL

Andropogon	Deschampsia	Melica	Poa
Arundinaria	Elymus	Miscanthus	Stipa
Arundo	Erianthus	Molinia	Trichloris
Asperella	Festuca	Panicum	Tricholaena
Chloris	Gynerium	Pennisetum	Uniola
Cortaderia	Hierochloe	Phalaris	
Dactylis	Holcus	Phyllostachys	

ROCK GARDEN PLANTS WHICH MAY BE USEFUL AT THE FRONT OF THE BORDER

Achillea	Helianthemum	Prunella
Alyssum	Iberis	*Saponaria ocymoides*
Arabis	Linaria	Saxifraga
Armeria caespitosa	Lithospermum	*Scabiosa graminifolia*
Aubrieta	Nierembergia	Scutellaria
Bellis	Oenothera	Sedum
Campanula	Omphalodes	Sempervivum
Carduncellus	Onosma	Silene
Cerastium	Ourisia	Sisyrinchium
Dianthus	*Phlox subulata*	Thymus
Genista tinctoria plena	Phyteuma	Tunica
Geranium	Potentilla	Vancouveria
Globularia	*Pterocephalus parnassi*	Veronica
Gypsophila	Pulmonaria	Viola

ANNUALS AND BIENNIALS

Annuals and biennials, or plants so treated for extending the season in the mixed herbaceous border. Many of these have annual *and* perennial species, but the former will be especially useful the first year for filling gaps and thin places. * May be sown where they are to flower.

*Adonis	*Campanula	*Delphinium
Ageratum	Celosia	Dianthus
Alonsoa	*Centaurea	*Dimorphotheca
*Alyssum	Cheiranthus	*Echium
Amaranthus	*Clarkia	*Emilia
*Anchusa	*Claytonia	*Erysimum
Antirrhinum	*Collinsia	*Eschscholtzia
Bellis	*Convolvulus	*Euphorbia
*Borago	Coreopsis	Gaillardia
Brachycome	*Cynoglossum	*Gilia
*Calendula	Dahlia (Coltness varieties)	

*Godetia
*Gypsophila
*Helianthus
*Iberis
Impatiens
*Lavatera
*Limnanthes
*Linaria
*Linum
Lobelia
*Lupinus

*Malope
Matricaria
*Matthiola
Mesembryanthemum
Nemesia
*Nemophila
Nierembergia
*Nigella
Omphalodes
*Papaver
Petunia

*Phacelia
Phlox drummondii
*Reseda
*Rudbeckia
Tagetes
*Tropaeoleum
Ursenia
Viola
*Viscaria
Zinnia

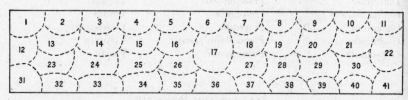

SHADY BORDER: (1) 5 *Campanula latifolia alba;* (2) 3 *Eupatorium purpureum;* (3) 3 *Aconitum* ' Barkers Var.'; (4) 5 *Thalictrum aquilegiifolium;* (5) 5 *Cimicifuga racemosa simplex;* (6) 7 *Campanula lactiflora;* (7) 5 *Cimicifuga racemosa;* (8) 3 *Thalictrum flavum;* (9) 3 *Aconitum carmichaelii wilsoni;* (10) 5 *Eupatorium cannabinum plenum;* (11) 5 *Campanula latifolia alba;* (12) 5 *Bupthalmum salicifolium;* (13) 5 *Veratrum album;* 3 (14) *Actaea spicata;* (15) 5 *Doronicum* ' Harpur Crewe '; (16) 3 *Anemone* ' Queen Charlotte '; (17) 5 *Dicentra spectabilis;* (18) 3 *Anemone* ' Honorine Jobert'; (19) 3 *Doronicum* ' Miss Mason '; (20) 5 *Polygonatum multiflorum;* (21) 5 *Veratrum album;* (22) 7 *Geranium grandiflorum;* (23) 5 *Helleborus orientalis;* (24) 3 *Orobus aurantiacus;* (25) 5 *Filipendula hexapatala grandiflora plena;* (26) 5 *Ranunculus aconitifolius flore pleno;* (27) 5 *Podophyllum peltatum;* (28) 5 *Astrantia carniolica;* (29) 5 *Digitalis grandiflora;* (30) 5 *Helleborus orientalis;* (31) 5 *Dicentra formosa;* (32) 3 *Brunnera macrophylla;* (33) 5 *Gentiana asclepiadea alba;* (34) 3 *Hosta ventricosa;* (35) 5 *Epimedium;* (36) 5 *Hosta glauca;* (37) 5 *Epimedium grandiflorum;* (38) 3 *Hosta undulata;* (39) 5 *Gentiana asclepiadea;* (40) 5 *Mertensia virginica;* (41) 5 *Dicentra eximia alba.*

DOUBLE-SIDED BORDER, ALL SEASONS, 40 × 8 Ft: (1) 6 *Gypsophila nana alba;* (2) 5 *Geum* ' Princess Juliana '; (3) 5 *Aster* ' Queen of Sheba '; (4) 7 *Delphinium grandiflorum;* (5) 7 *Heuchera atrosanguinea;* (6) 6 *Potentilla* ' Miss Willmott'; (7) 7 *Coreopsis verticillata* ' Golden Shower '; (8) 5 *Polygonum affine;* (9) 6 *Campanula glomerata;* (10) 6 *Dicentra formosa;* (11) 5 *Aster* ' Snow Sprite '; (12) 5 *Geum* ' Lady Stratheden '; (13) 6 *Gypsophila* ' Rosy Veil '; (14) 6 *Linum* ' Peto's Var.'; (15) 7 *Iris* ' Lady Mohr '; (16) 6 *Sidalcea* ' Crimson Beauty '; (17) 6 *Erigeron* ' Merstham Glory '; (18) 6 *Pyrethrum (Chrysanthemum)* ' La France '; (19) 6 *Phlox* ' Blue Boy '; (20) 7 *Sidalcea* ' Sussex Beauty '; (21) 5 *Phlox* ' Dresden China '; (22) 6 *Pyrethrum (Chrysanthemum)* ' A.M.Kelway '; (23) 6 *Erigeron* ' Wupperthal '; (24) 6 *Sidalcea* ' Rose Queen '; (25) 6 *Iris* ' Great Lakes '; (26) 7 *Delphinium belladonna* ' Wendy '; (27) 6 *Solidago caesia;* (28) 6 *Iris sibirica* ' Marcus ': (29) 7 *Aquilegia* ' Snow Queen '; (30) 6 *Tradescantia* ' Blue Stone '; (31) 6 *Papaver* ' Orange King '; (32) 7 *Catananche caerulea major;* (33) 5 *Papaver* ' Salmon Glow '; (34) 6 *Tradescantia* ' J. C. Weguelin '; (35) 5 *Aquilegia* ' Crimson Star '; (36) 5 *Scabiosa* ' Clive Greaves '; (37) 6 *Solidago* ' Golden Gate '; (38) 6 *Gypsophila* ' Rosy Veil '; (39) 4 *Aster* ' Lady in Blue '; (40) 5 *Potentilla* ' Gibsons Scarlet '; (41) 7 *Veronica incana;* (42) 6 *Heuchera* ' Pluie de Feu '; (43) 6 *Veronica incana;* (44) 5 *Oenothera fruticosa youngii;* (45) 5 *Stachys lanata;* (46) 5 *Armeria* ' Bee's Ruby '; (47) 5 *Brunnera macrophylla;* (48) 4 *Dianthus* ' Sam Barlow '; (49) 5 *Aster* ' Pink Lace '; (50) 6 *Gypsophila nana alba.*

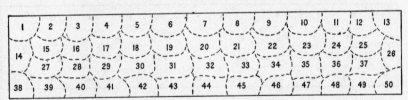

BLUE, PINK AND SILVER, 40 × 8 Ft: (1) 3 *Lavatera olbia rosea;* (2) 3 *Althaea* double *rosea;* (3) 3 *Anchusa* ' Opal '; (4) 5 *Delphinium* ' Welsh Boy '; (5) 3 *Aster* ' Harringtons Pink '; (6) 5 *Aconitum* ' Barkers Var.'; (7) 3 *Delphinium* ' Lady Eleanor '; (8) 5 *Echinops horridus;* (9) 3 *Aster* ' Barrs Pink '; (10) 5 *Delphinium* ' Blue Gown'; (11) 3 *Anchusa* ' Morning Glory'; (12) 3 *Althaea* ' Double Pink '; (13) 3 *Lavatera olbia rosea;* (14) 5 *Echinops ritro;* (15) 3 *Aster* ' Marie Ballard '; (16) 5 *Papaver* ' Queen Alexandra '; (17) 5 *Phlox* ' Pink Gown '; (18) 3 *Lupinus* ' Blue Jacket '; (19) *Chrysanthemum (Pyrethrum)* ' Princess Mary '; (20) 5 *Sidalcea* ' Sussex Beauty '; (21) 5 *Chrysanthemum (Pyrethrum)* ' La France '; (22) 3 *Lupinus* ' Apple Blossom '; (23) 3 *Phlox* ' Daily Sketch '; (24) 3 *Papaver* ' Salmon Glow '; (25) 5 *Dicentra spectabilis;* (26) 3 *Echinops;* (27) 5 *Artemisia stelleriana;* (28) 3 *Aster amellus* ' Lady Hindlip '; (29) 3 *Phalaris arundinacea picta;* (30) 5 *Hemerocallis* ' fulva rosea '; (31) 3 *Erigeron* ' Merstham Glory '; (32) 5 *Catananche caerulea major;* (33) 3 *Erigeron* ' Quakeress '; (34) 5 *Hemerocallis* ' Pink Lady '; (35) 3 *Phalaris arundinacea picta;* (36) 3 *Aster amellus* ' Mrs. Ralph Woods '; (37) 5 *Artemisia ludoviciana;* (38) 3 *Anaphalis triplinervis;* (39) 3 *Campanula carpatica;* (40) 3 *Gypsophila* ' Rosy Veil '; (41) 3 *Armeria gigantea;* (42) 3 *Dianthus* ' Inchmery '; (43) 3 *Delphinium* ' Wendy '; (44) 5 *Veronica longifolia;* (45) 3 *Delphinium* ' Blue Bees '; (46) 3 *Brunnera macrophylla;* (47) 3 *Stachys lanata;* (48) 3 *Polemonium coeruleum;* (49) 3 *Armeria gigantea;* (50) 3 *Nepeta mussini.*

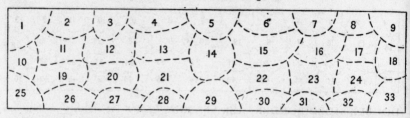

WHITE, YELLOW & ORANGE, 30 × 7½ Ft: (1) 3 *Solidago* 'Golden Wings'; (2) 3 *Althaea* 'Queen of Sheba'; (3) 3 *Aster* 'Silver Spray'; (4) 5 *Kniphofia* 'Star of Baden'; (5) 5 *Heliopsis scabra patula;* (6) 5 *Campanula lactiflora alba;* (7) 3 *Artemisia lactiflora;* (8) 3 *Aruncus* sylvester; (9) 3 *Rudbeckia nitida;* (10) 3 *Achillea* 'Perry's White'; (11) 5 *Hemerocallis* 'Hyperion'; (12) 3 *Anthemis* 'Grallagh Gold'; (13) 5 Peony 'The Bride'; (14) 5 *Scabiosa* 'Miss Willmott'; (15) 5 *Centaurea macrocephala;* (16) 3 *Anthemis* 'Beauty of Grallagh'; (17) 5 *Hemerocallis* 'Sandstone'; (18) 5 *Tradescantia* 'Innocence'; (19) 5 *Oenothera fruticosa 'youngii';* (20) 3 *Doronicum* 'Miss Mason'; (21) 3 *Solidago caesia;* (22) 5 *Phlox* 'Cecil Hanbury'; (23) 5 *Papaver* 'Orange King'; (24) 3 *Veronica spicata alba;* (25) 3 *Doronicum austriacum;* (26) 3 *Alyssum* 'Dudley Neville'; (27) 3 *Aquilegia* 'Snow Queen'; (28) 3 *Geum* 'Orangeman'; (29) 7 *Coreopsis* 'Golden Shower'; (30) 3 *Geum* 'Dolly North'; (31) 3 *Gypsophila nana alba;* (32) 3 *Alyssum saxatile plenum;* (33) 5 *Rudbeckia speciosa.*

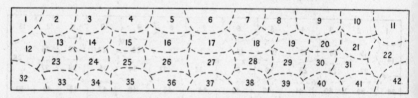

TWO-SIDED PERMANENT BORDER, 40 × 8 Ft: (1) 5 *Salvia* × *superba;* (2) 5 *Dictamnus albus;* (3) 5 *Hosta ventricosa;* (4) 7 *Incarvillea delavayi;* (5) 5 *Platycodon grandiflorus mariesii;* (6) 9 *Aquilegia* 'Crimson Star'; (7) 5 *Asclepias tuberosa;* (8) 5 *Incarvillea compacta;* (9) 5 *Hosta decorata;* (10) 5 *Dictamnus albus purpureus;* (11) 5 *Salvia* × *superba;* (12) 7 *Hemerocallis* 'Klondyke'; (13) 5 *Liatris pycnostachya;* (14) 5 Peony 'Victoria'; (15) 7 *Sanguisorba obtusa;* (16) 7 *Cimicifuga simplex;* (17) 7 Peony 'Duchess of Portland'; (18) 5 *Cimicifuga racemosa;* (19) 7 *Sanguisorba canadensis;* (20) 5 Peony *alba grandiflora;* (21) 5 *Liatris pycnostachya;* (22) 5 *Eryngium alpinum;* (23) 5 *Aruncus* sylvester; (24) 5 *Papaver* 'Mrs. Perry'; (25) 5 *Acanthus caroli-alexandri;* (26) 7 *Dicentra spectabilis;* (27) 5 *Acanthus perringii;* (28) 5 Papaver 'Perry's White'; (29) 5 *Aruncus sylvester knieffi;* (30) 5 *Eryngium spinalba;* (31) 7 *Hemerocallis fulva rosea;* (32) 5 *Gypsophila* 'Rosy Veil'; (33) 5 *Liatris spicata;* (34) 5 *Aquilegia* 'Snow Queen'; (35) 5 *Hosta fortunei;* (36) 7 *Anthericum liliastrum;* (37) 5 *Oenothera missouriensis;* (38) 5 *Platycodon grandiflorus mariesii albus;* (39) 5 *Hosta undulata;* (40) 5 *Euphorbia epithymoides;* (41) 7 *Gentiana asclepiadea;* (42) 5 *Gypsophila nana alba.*

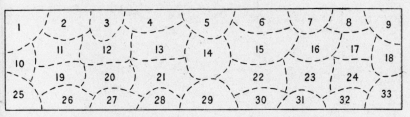

FOR A TOWN GARDEN, ALL SEASONS, 30 × 7½ Ft: (1) 3 *Aster* ' Col. F.
R. Durham '; (2) 3 *Achillea* 'Gold Plate'; (3) 3 *Echinops horridus;* (4) 5 *Campanula*
' Highcliffe Variety '; (5) 3 *Kniphofia* ' Mount Etna '; (6) 5 *Campanula latifolia* ' Brant-
wood'; (7) 3 *Echinops sphaerocephalus;* (8) 3 *Thalictrum flavum;* (9) 3 *Aster* 'Harringtons
Pink'; (10) 3 *Dictamnus albus;* (11) 3 *Paeonia* 'Pink Delight'; (12) 5 *Iris sibirica* 'Emperor';
(13) 5 *Hemerocallis* ' G. P. Raffill '; (14) 3 *Gypsophila* ' Bristol Fairy '; (15) 5 *Hemerocallis*
' Paul Boissier '; (16) 5 *Iris sibirica* ' Heavenly Blue '; (17) 8 *Paeonia* 'Victoria'; (18) 3
Dictamnus albus purpureus; (19) 5 *Armeria* 'Bees Ruby'; (20) 3 *Campanula latiloba;* (21) 3
Kniphofia 'Gold Else'; (22) 5 *Aquilegia* 'Snow Queen'; (23) 5 *Aquilegia caerulea;* (24) 3
Kniphofia ' July Glow'; (25) 3 *Campanula latiloba alba;* (26) 3 *Dianthus* 'Earl of Essex';
(27) 3 *Gypsophila* ' Rosy Veil '; (28) 3 *Heuchera* ' Pluie de Feu'; (29) 5 *Linum* 'Six Hills'
variety; (30) 3 *Heuchera* 'Apple Blossom'; (31) 2 *Gypsophila nana alba;* (32) 3 *Dianthus*
'White Ladies'; (33) 5 *Dicentra eximia.*

GLOSSARY

Annual	A plant which completes its life cycle from seed to seed in twelve months.
Asexual reproduction	Reproduction from budding or splitting within an individual; that is without male and female organs.
Bark	The outer tissues of the wood or cambium.
Biennial	A plant which requires two years to complete its life cycle, producing leaf and root growth the first year and flowers and fruit the second.
Boss	A protuberance.
Bract	Modified leaves, usually between the calyx and the normal leaves.
Calyx	Name given to the collection of sepals which protect the petals of many flowers. They are usually green.
Cambium	A layer of tissue (usually green) between the wood and the bast, i.e. the fibrous tissues which serve for mechanical support.
Campanulate	Bell-shaped.
Candelabra	Arranged in tiers or whorls up the stem.
Colloid	Substance of a gelatinous nature surrounding clay particles.
Corymb	A flat topped or convex cluster of flowers.
Embryo	The rudimentary or baby plant formed within a seed.
Fall	The lower or hanging petals of an iris.
Farina	Starchy or flour-like material.
Filament	The stalk of an anther.
Flocculation	Coagulation or dotting together, as of clay particles.
Floret	A small flower, one of a cluster.
Hybrid	A mongrel plant derived from the pollen of one species on the stigma of another.
Internode	Space or portion of stem between two nodes or joints.
Involucre	A ring of bracts surrounding several flowers, e.g. Astrantia.

Keel	Petals joined to form a ridge like the keel of a boat, e.g. Lupins, Sweet Peas.
Meristematic	Cell division, tissue ready to divide and grow.
Monocarpic	A plant which dies after flowering.
Mutation	A name given to sudden changes derived in seedlings, a tendency to revert.
Node	A joint on a stem.
Offset	A lateral or side shoot used for propagating.
Ovary	The part of the flower which contains the ovules.
Ovules	Young immature seed in the ovary, before fertilisation.
Palmate	Lobed or divided (usually leaves) like the fingers and palm of a hand.
Perennial	Plant living for several years, i.e. not dying after flowering.
Perianth	The Floral parts of a flower, calyx, corolla or both.
Pinnate	Leaflets arranged feather-like, each side of the mid-rib of a leaf.
Pistil	The female organ of the flower, consisting when complete of stigma, style and ovary.
Plume	A feathery arrangement of flowers or seeds.
Pollen	Dust-like substance in the stamens, which fertilises the female part (stigma) of the flower.
Protoplasm	The viscous, colourless substance in the cells surrounding the nucleus.
Raceme	A cluster of flowers.
Radical	Arising from the root.
Ray floret	Outer flower, strap-shaped of a composite, e.g. outer flowers of a daisy.
Rhizome	Swollen rootstock growing horizontally on or under the ground.
Rogue	A plant not true to type.
Scape	A leafless flower stem arising from the ground, as in tulip.
Scion	Young shoot used in grafting, the part put on to the stock.
Serrated	Edged with teeth-like cuts, e.g. a leaf.
Species	The type plant or unit in classification which breeds true from seed.
Spike	Flowers arranged on a common elongated axis, as an ear of Corn.

Sport	A plant or seedling which shows variation.
Stamen	Male organ of a flower, consisting of filament (stalk), anther and pollen.
Standard	The upright petals of a leguminous flower, e.g. Sweet Pea.
Stigma	That part of a plant which receives the pollen.
Strain	A race of plants which is reliable for breeding, although the individuals vary.
Striation	Marked with fine longitudinal, parallel lines or ridges.
Style	The attenuated or stalk-like part between the ovary and stigma.
Transpiration	Passing off of surplus water, in the form of vapour through the leaf pores.
Tripartite	Divided into 3 parts, e.g. Bean-leaf.
Umbel	Head of stalked flowers arising from a central axis like the ribs of an umbrella and forming a flat, plate-like head.
Variety	A form or hybrid, a departure from and not a species.
Vascular	Relating to or furnished with vessels to carry food, water, etc.
Whorl	The arrangement of leaves or parts of the flower in a circle round an axis.

BIBLIOGRAPHY

ANLEY, Gwendolyn. 1946. *Irises, Their Cultivation and Selection.* London. Collingridge.

BAILEY, L. H. 1924 and 1949. *Manual of Cultivated Plants.* New York. The Macmillan Company.

BAILEY, L. H. 1900, 1914, 1937. *The Standard Cyclopedia of Horticulture.* New York. The Macmillan Company.

BAKER, J. G. 1892. *Handbook of the Irideae.* London. George Bell.

BATSON, H. M. 1903. *A Concise Handbook of Garden Flowers.* London. Methuen.

BISHOP, Frank. 1949. *The Delphinium.* London. William Collins.

BLOOM, Alan. 1957. *Hardy Perennials.* London. Faber & Faber.

BOWLES, E. A. 1914. *My Garden in Spring, My Garden in Summer.* 1915. *My Garden in Autumn and Winter.* London. T. C. & E. C. Jack.

BRISCOE, T. W. 1932. *Hardy Border Plants.* London. Collingridge.

CAVE, N. Leslie. 1950. *The Iris.* London. Faber & Faber.

CORLISS, Phillip G. 1951. *Hemerocallis.* Privately Printed. San Francisco.

CORSAR, Kenneth C. 1948. *Primulas in the Garden.* London. Lindsay Drummond.

Dictionary of Gardening. 1951. London. Royal Horticultural Society.

DILLISTONE, George. 1926. *Dykes on Irises.* Tunbridge Wells. Iris Society.

DYKES, W. R. 1924. *A Handbook of Garden Irises.* London. Martin Hopkinson.

FITZHERBERT, S. W. *The Book of the Wild Garden.* London. John Lane, The Bodley Head.

GIFFARD-WOOLLEY, R. V. 1926. *Herbaceous Borders for Amateurs.* London. Country Life.

HALSHAM, John. 1912. *Everyman's Book of Garden Flowers.* London. Hodder & Stoughton.

HAY, Roy, and MERCER, Frank, Editors. 1952. *Hardy Plants.* Gardens and Gardening, Vol. 3. London. The Studio.

HAY, Thomas. 1938. *Plants for the Connoisseur.* London. Putnam.

HELLYER, A. G. 1955. *Herbaceous Borders Picture Book No. 5.* London. Collingridge.

JEKYLL, Gertrude. *Colour Schemes for the Flower Garden.* London. Country Life.

JENKINS, E. H. 1914, Second Edition. *The Hardy Flower Book.* London. Country Life.

JONES, E. R. 1952. *The Flower Garden.* Harmondsworth, Middlesex, Penguin Books.

JONES, Herbert. 1914. *Altar Flowers and How to Grow Them.* London. R. & T. Washbourne.

KEW. 1902. Second Edition. *Herbaceous Plants.* Royal Botanic Garden Handlist of Herbaceous Plants, etc. London. H.M.S.O.

KIRK, Lt.-Col. J. W. 1927. *A British Garden Flora.* London. Edward Arnold.

LAUMONNIER, Eugene. 1955. *Les Jardins de plantes vivaces, etc.* Third edition. Paris. La Maison Rustique.

LOUDON, Mrs. 1849. *The Ladies' Flower Garden of Ornamental Perennials.* (Fine illustrations.) London. William S. Orr & Co.

LYNCH, R. Irwin. 1904. *The Book of the Iris.* London. John Lane, The Bodley Head.

MACSELF, A. J. 1948, Revised Edition. *Hardy Perennials.* London. Eyre & Spottiswoode.

MACSELF, A. J. *Hardy Perennials.* London. Collingridge.

MAKINS, F. K. 1957. *Herbaceous Garden Flora.* London. Dent.

MANSFIELD, T. C. 1944. *The Border in Colour.* London. William Collins.

MARTINEAU, Lady A. 1934. *Herbaceous Garden.* London. Williams and Norgate.

PERRY, Frances. 1948. *The Herbaceous Border.* London. Collingridge.

PHILLIPS, G. A. 1934. *Aristocrats of the Flower Border.* London. Country Life.

PHILLIPS, G. A. 1933. *Delphiniums.* London. Thornton Butterworth.

RANSOM, E. R. 1946. *Michaelmas Daisies and Other Garden Asters.* London. Gifford.

ROBERTS, Harry. *The Book of Old Fashioned Flowers.* London. John Lane, The Bodley Head.

ROBINSON, William. Last Edition. 1956. *The English Flower Garden.* London. John Murray.

SANDERS, T. W. 1928. *Popular Hardy Perennials.* London. Collingridge.

SMYTH, Walter. 1901. *Hardy Border Flowers the Year Round.* Belfast. Wm. Mullan & Son.

SPENDER, R. E., and PESEL, L. F. 1937. *Iris Culture for Amateurs.* London. Country Life.

STERN, F. C. 1946. *A Study of the Genus Paeonia.* London. The Royal Horticultural Society.

STEVENS, G. A. *Garden Flowers in Colour.* New York. The Macmillan Company.

STOUT, A. B. 1934. *Daylilies.* New York. The Macmillan Company.

SUDELL, Richard, and PERRY, Frances. 1938. *Herbaceous Borders and the Waterside.* London. The English Universities Press.

SUTHERLAND, William. 1871. *Handbook of Hardy Herbaceous and Alpine Flowers.* London. Wm. Blackwood & Sons.

SYMONS, Jeune, B. H. B. 1953. *Phlox.* London. William Collins.

SYNGE, Patrick M. 1953. *A Diversity of Plants.* London. Geoffrey Bles.

TAYLOR, George. 1934. *The Genus Meconopsis.* London. New Flora & Silva.

THOMAS, H. H. 1928. *Herbaceous Border Flowers.* London. Cassell.

WEATHERS, John. 1913. *Beautiful Garden Flowers.* London. Simpkin, Marshall, Hamilton, Kent.

WOOD, John. 1884. *Hardy Perennials and Old Fashioned Garden Flowers.* London. L. Upcott Gill.

WRIGHT, Horace and Walter. 1909. *Beautiful Flowers and How to Grow Them.* London. T. C. & E. C. Jack.

WRIGHT, Walter P. 1911. *Popular Garden Flowers.* London. Grant Richards.

WRIGHT, Walter P. 1912. *Hardy Perennials and Herbaceous Borders.* London. Headley Bros.

INDEX
of English or Common Names

Aaron's Rod, *Solidago and Verbascum thapsus*

Aconite Saxifrage, *Boykinia aconitifolia*

African Lily, *Agapanthus africanus*

Alumroot, *Heuchera*

Alpine Knotweed, *Polygonum alpinum*

Alpine Savory, *Calamintha*

American Bugbane, *Cimicifuga americana*

American Burnet, *Sanguisorba canadensis*

American Columbine, *Aquilegia canadensis*

American Cowslip, *Dodecatheon*

American Mandrake, *Podophyllum peltatum*

Armenian Cranesbill, *Geranium psilostemon*

Asphodel, *Asphodeline and Asphodelus*

Auricula, *Primula auricula*

Avens, *Geum*

Azure Monkshood, *Aconitum carmichaelii*

Azure Sage, *Salvia azurea*

Baby's Breath, *Gypsophila paniculata*

Balloon Flower, *Platycodon*

Baneberry, *Actaea*

Barrenwort, *Epimedium pinnatum*

Bastard Balm, *Melittis*

Bachelor's Buttons, *Ranunculus acris*

Beach Speedwell, *Veronica longifolia*

Beard Tongue, *Pentstemon*

Bearded Pentstemon, *Pentstemon barbatus*

Bear's Breeches, *Acanthus*

Bear's Tail Mullein, *Celsia*

Bee Balm, *Monarda*

Bee Larkspur, *Delphinium elatum*

Beeweed, *Aster cordifolius*

Bellflower, *Adenophora, Campanula, Ostrowskia, Platycodon*

Bellwort, *Codonopsis and Uvularia*

Bergamot, *Monarda*

Bethlehem Sage, *Pulmonaria saccharata*

Big Betony, *Stachys macrantha*

Birth Root, *Trillium erectum*

Bishop's Hat, *Epimedium*

Bittercress, *Cardamine*

Bitter Vetch, *Lathyrus montanus*

Black Bitter Vetch, *Lathyrus niger*

Black-eyed Susan, *Rudbeckia speciosa*

Black Hellebore, *Helleborus niger*

Black Pea, *Lathyrus niger*

Black Snake-root, *Cimicifuga racemosa*

Bladder Cherry, *Physalis alkekengii*

Blanket Flower, *Gaillardia*

Bleeding Heart, *Dicentra spectabilis*

Bloody Cranesbill, *Geranium sanguineum*

Blue Cardinal Flower, *Lobelia syphilitica*

Blue-eyed Grass, *Sisyrinchium*

Blue Eyed Mary, *Omphalodes verna*

Blue Indigo, *Baptisia*

Blue Lettuce, *Lactuca*

Blue Meadow Cranesbill, *Geranium pratense*

Blue Pentstemon, *Pentstemon glaber*

Blue Plantain Lily, *Hosta ventricosa*

Blue Spiderwort, *Commelina*

Blue Wood Aster, *Aster cordifolius*

Blunt Plantain Lily, *Hosta decorata* var. *decorata*

Bog Sage, *Salvia uliginosa*

Bony-tip Fleabane, *Erigeron mucronatus*

Borage, *Borago*